WITHDRAWN

Spiritual, Blues, and Jazz People
in African American Fiction

Spiritual, Blues, *and* Jazz People *in* African American Fiction

Living in Paradox

A. Yemisi Jimoh

THE UNIVERSITY OF TENNESSEE PRESS / KNOXVILLE

Copyright © 2002 by The University of Tennessee Press / Knoxville.
All Rights Reserved. Manufactured in the United States of America.
First Edition.

This book is printed on acid-free paper.

Library of Congress Cataloging-in-Publication Data

Jimoh, A. Yemisi
Spiritual, blues, and jazz people in African American fiction:
living in paradox / A. Yemisi Jimoh.—1st ed.
    p. cm.
Includes bibliographical references and index.

ISBN 1-57233-172-0 (cl.: alk. paper)

  1. American fiction—African American authors—History and criticism.
  2. African American musicians in literature.
  3. Musical fiction—History and criticism.
  4. Spirituals (Songs) in literature.
  5. African Americans in literature.
  6. Jazz musicians in literature.
  7. Blues (Music) in literature.
  8. Music and literature.
  9. Music in literature.
 10. Jazz in literature.
   I. Title.
PS374.N4 J56 2002
813.009'896073—dc21   2001004286

CONTENTS

ACKNOWLEDGMENTS
vii

INTRODUCTION
We'll Understand It Better By and By
1

one
MUDDY WATERS
Music in African American Fiction
22

two
STORMY BLUES
From the Folk into Literary Form
41

three
THESE (BLACKNESS OF BLACKNESS) BLUES
91

four
DIZZY ATMOSPHERE
155

five
JAZZ ME BLUES
Reading Music in James Baldwin's "Sonny's Blues"
202

CONCLUSION
Toward a Stopping Place
216

APPENDIX
Allusions and References to Musicians
and Music in the Narratives
219

NOTES
223

WORKS CITED AND CONSULTED
245

A SELECTED LIST OF BIOGRAPHIES AND AUTOBIOGRAPHIES OF MUSICIANS
263

INDEX
267

ACKNOWLEDGMENTS

A project such as this always benefits from the oceans of information that only can be found in a librarian who will show you where to look and even, at times, help you look for some small, obscure detail that only means something to the person who requests it. Alberta Bailey and Stephen Perry at the University of Arkansas Mullins Library in Fayetteville were just such resources for me. Without the mini-sessions on computerized research to which Stephen introduced me or the detailed assistance locating difficult-to-find journal articles that Alberta provided, this would not be the book that it is. A project such as this also inevitably leads any concerned researcher to reckon with her gaps in knowledge. African American music is such an incalculable taproot supporting numerous stems that working the ground around this music would take more lifetimes than are my portion, but what I do know has been greatly assisted by Donna Wiggins of the Department of Music at the University of Arkansas, Fayetteville, by the Center for Black Music Research website, by Kenneth Wilcots, with whom I shared numerous discussions about Jazz music and whose admirable facility for identifying—with the slightest bit of information—Jazz music and musicians still surprises me, and by my mother, who is my repository for African American music, especially Spiritual-Gospel. What I have failed to learn has nothing whatsoever to do with any of them.

During the summer of 1999 I attended a National Endowment for the Humanities' Summer Institute on the Civil Rights Movement. This institute was located in the W. E. B. Du Bois Institute for Afro-American Research at Harvard University. That summer of intensely focused research, investigation, and interrogation of issues related to civil rights sharpened and deepened my perspective on the historical intersections that gather in African American music and literature. My friend Tunde Ogunleye provided me with several years of engaging discussions on Yoruba culture and generous help with the Yoruba language—Modupe. Another name that I must mention is that of Joyce Harrison of the University of Tennessee Press; her deep well of patience suffered through my shifting visions for this book. And to my family, especially my children, words are never sufficient. Finally, Lawrence Hogue at the University of Houston has been a rock of support, having read virtually every version of the manuscript for this book; there can be no true reward for bearing such a burden.

If my memory could produce for me a list of everyone who contributed to this book over the last fifteen years, from its inception as an idea to its final publication, I know that I would have a great deal of debt assigned to my name. If I failed to mention you, please know that I appreciate all that you may have added to what I have come to know about African American music and literature. To all, I simply say thank you for assisting me in bringing this book to completion.

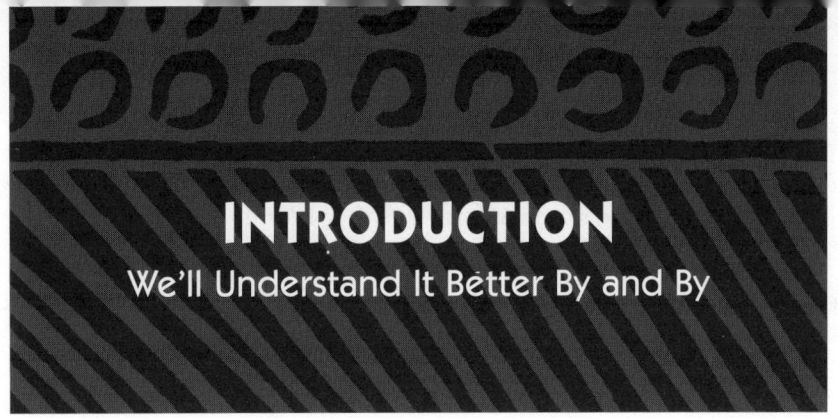

INTRODUCTION
We'll Understand It Better By and By

Contexts

From ancient times music and storytelling have been closely tied among the peoples of oral cultures worldwide. In oral cultures, quite frequently, a person comes to understand her life and the world in which she lives through the tales of the bards, troubadours, jongleurs, and fili, among others. Historically, among many African oral cultures, the ancient tradition of singing the lives of the people was given a special and valued designation. The Swahili mneni, the asunrara of Nigeria's Yoruba, and, after colonization, the griots in a number of francophone West African nations, all sang the lives of their people.

Among black people in the United States, the Old World tradition of singing the lives of a people was continued by the late-nineteenth-century African American minstrels and vaudevillians, college groups such as the Fisk Jubilee Singers, and the early-twentieth-century blueswomen and jazzmen.[1] The foundation of the music they sang and the experiences that the music records come from the field hollers, shouts, plantation songs, or Spirituals that spread throughout the South before the Civil War. The music of enslaved black people—based in the traditional musics of Africa and on the African's cultural contacts and experiences in the New World—is one of the intertextual sites of artistic expression in the texts of many African American writers.

Professional blackface minstrelsy begins in the United States in 1843 with the first organized white minstrel performance. Minstrelsy plays a part in entertainment in the United States from the early part of the nineteenth century, but it flourishes throughout the northern United States and in Europe from 1850 through 1870. Until late into the nineteenth century, black entertainers play an extraordinarily minute role in minstrelsy. But after the Civil War black musicians retrieve their music and dance from the caricature and exploitation imposed on them by blackface minstrelsy.[2] In the late nineteenth century Charles Chesnutt transforms minstrelsy into an ironic reversal in literature, which I will discuss later, and which I believe Louis Armstrong captures in many of his musical performances.

Minstrelsy does find its way into African American fiction in the twentieth century. The works of Paul Laurence Dunbar, Wallace Thurman, and Nella Larsen contain passages depicting minstrel-like behavior, a minstrel presence that is usually embarrassing or humiliating for these writers' central characters. Ralph Ellison, however, puts minstrelsy to a different use, bringing Chesnutt's and Armstrong's minstrel reversal into African American literature through his portrayal of Armstrong as well as the grandfather in *Invisible Man*. All of these writers' literary uses of minstrelsy are indicators of the connective social, historical, political, and cultural influences that shape a set of aesthetic ideas that have moved into African American art and literature, especially if one considers the philosophical, epic, and narrative qualities that scholars, writers, and social critics have found in Blues and Jazz and in this music's minstrel and plantation forebears.[3]

History and context, then, explain the variations as well as the consanguinity between the ways black people and white people have expressed themselves in art in the United States. The contrasts are illustrated in the different ways these two groups have experienced life together. Formerly enslaved Africans and their descendants locate themselves in a social-political history of exclusion. After the Civil War the already established exclusion of black people is refashioned so that the previous social policy of white dominance remains in place even as slavery is abolished. Post-emancipation and absent the social policies and practices that sanction the ownership of African Americans by European Americans, black people still find that new laws are enacted that will delineate differences that human captivity established through lived reality.[4] Thus, many of the collective (enslaved and segregated) social and historical experiences of African Americans have contours and shapes that differ from, while also adding to, the European experiences that dominate the cultural ideas within the United States.

There is a difference in the experience of being a descendant of early free settlers or early indentured servants, whose contrast with the dominant culture is not as stark as that of the descendant of Africans, whose historical position within the culture is situated on a tenuous site of specious color-based laws and social policies; there also is a difference in being the descendant of later immigrants in the United States, especially if the possibility exists for becoming "white."[5] Most—but not all—African Americans have ancestors who were enslaved in this country; and nearly all African Americans are descendants of nations that were destabilized by the loss of large segments of their populations—through internal as well as external avarice—to human captivity in the New World. And even when not enslaved, black people such as the free men and women of color in the United States as well as black people living segregated from the full bounty of the United States frequently found their lives severely demarcated by law and by common practice in this country.[6]

For many African American artists, then, a history of aesthetic ideas has been situated within the contexts of a struggle for freedom from chattel slavery and from its reformulation under segregation, numerous unwilling separations (from an ancestral home, from family, from the resident culture, etc.), forced communalism, and other formative experiences in the New World. Black people do share with white people in the United States the inheritance of Western literary traditions based in ancient Greco-Roman culture, which was part of a cross-cultural environment that stands outside the black-white simplicity of color designations.[7] Clearly, African American artists' culture-shaping contact with native peoples, immigrant groups, and the popular culture of the nation influences their artistic expression. Yet the added contours of racial discourses in the United States have shaped early Spiritual-Gospel, Blues, and Jazz aesthetic and philosophical ideas in ways that differ from the European-based popular and classical music that—until the last three decades of this century—held a central place in the dominant culture of the United States. Although there has never been a total aesthetic estrangement between African American and European American cultural texts in the United States, distinct differences in their musical aesthetic have always existed and continue to this day. In this book, I investigate many of the African American intracultural issues that inform a more broadly intertextual use of music in the making of character and theme in fiction by black writers in the United States. I present these music-into-fiction concepts, delineated below, in order to expand the way we read the traditional literary elements of theme and character in African American fictional texts, as conventional close readings of theme and character in fiction are often silent on the historical-sociopolitical discourses that increase our understanding of African American narratives.

Music into Narrative

Frederick Douglass's 1845 *Narrative of the Life of Frederick Douglass: An American Slave, Written by Himself* is perhaps the earliest published text by a black writer that discusses plantation songs.[8] In this prose account of the dehumanizing effects of slavery on the enslaver and the enslaved, Douglass prefigures an important cultural space for African American songs and verbal expressions as a site of doubleness, which is a form of oppressive psychological fragmentation that W. E. B. Du Bois will articulate as double-consciousness in his 1903 treatise *The Souls of Black Folk*. This doubleness informs a person's consciousness through the awareness that self-perceptions are shaped by both one's own ideas of self and by powerful external ideas that not only differ from the person's own consciousness of self but also contradict that self-consciousness in, at times, degrading and dehumanizing ways.

According to Douglass, the songs "to many would seem jargon, but . . . nevertheless were full of meaning to [the enslaved people] themselves." Douglass describes the Spirituals he heard as deeply meaningful and as expressing "the highest joy and the deepest sadness" as well as the "prayer and complaint" of the captive people. His observations also indicate that the songs were often improvised and profoundly paradoxical: "The thought that came up, came out—if not in the word, in the sound . . . ; [t]hey would sometimes sing the most pathetic sentiment in the most rapturous tone" (31). Douglass's passage about his experiences with these songs illustrates some of the aesthetic qualities of African American music that have shaped an aesthetic found in fiction by many African American writers: the value of improvisation, which allows reshaping of set forms; the ability to represent in art the idea of paradox as a condition of life; song as a means of recording one's life experiences; and fragmentation and doubleness as artistic techniques. These issues Douglass raises have persisted in African American music from the Spirituals to Blues and Jazz as well as other musical styles associated with African Americans. In literary texts, I find that Douglass's observations about music have moved from autobiographical memory and observation into literary metaphors that comment on life.

Improvisation in music and the term "Jazz" are nearly convertible.[9] In the 1920s, early Jazz musicians such as Kid Ory, King Oliver, and Louis Armstrong—on his Hot Five and Hot Seven recordings—perform in combos that operate from a musical ground that emphasizes collective improvisation. This style of improvisation allows each musician to comment simultaneously on the musical fragment that serves as a jumping-off point. As Jazz expands into the dominant culture during the 1930s in the United States, the locus of musical innovation in Jazz remains in each musician's collective improvisational abilities. Solo improvisation, though, shapes the Jazz sounds of swing and big band styles, which bring Jazz to a national audience. Swing and big band's most innovative adherents include Fletcher Henderson; William "Count" Basie, with Lester Young on tenor saxophone; Benny Goodman, who had the wisdom as well as the courage to hire Teddy Wilson in 1935 and then Lionel Hampton in 1936; and, quintessentially, Edward Kennedy "Duke" Ellington, who, frequently in collaboration with Billy Strayhorn, composed Jazz pieces that elegantly poise aspects of classical musical composition and inimitable solo Jazz improvisations.

Jazz's bebop moment in the 1940s and 1950s, which includes musicians Thelonious Monk, Erroll Garner, Max Roach, Dizzy Gillespie, Charlie Parker, and, later, Miles Davis, returns collective improvisation to this music; the concept of Jazz, then, becomes synonymous with spontaneous innovation and extemporaneous musical comment, as collective improvisation interrogates swing's practice of solo improvisation. Later, in John Coltrane's free-form Jazz and Ornette Coleman's experiment with free Jazz—which sets the musician's improvisations free from the melodies and harmonies established by a jumping-off piece—

improvisation, especially collective improvisation, moves into a new musical space.

In addition to his comments on improvisation, Douglass's observations on the contradictions that mark the promises of freedom and democratic governance in the United States can be most succinctly described as paradoxical when viewed within the context of the lived experiences of enslaved, and segregated, black people.[10] Enslaved black people in "a land whose freedom is to us a mockery and whose liberty is a lie" (Du Bois 151) form a special caste that is exempted from the rights and privileges established in the Bill of Rights. And, while the United States' Constitution stands in the honored position of the oldest written constitution still in effect, we recognize that during the drafting of the Constitution the status of enslaved people becomes a contentious topic; this document establishes a special category that erases native peoples and attempts to dehumanize people of African descent. The Constitution relegates native peoples to the status of outsiders and enslaved Africans to the status of property. The Civil War does not change much in terms of the status of black people; the end of legal slavery and the beginning of segregation only reinforces the status of black people living in paradox as both free and not free in the New Canaan.

The way in which the Spirituals articulate this lived reality is consistent with Douglass's statement that music presents the life—or, in other words, the joys, prayers, and complaints—of black people. Perhaps one of the earliest expressions in the United States of historical discontinuity, alienation, loss, despair, recognition of the incongruity inherent in life, and rejection of societal mythologies and ersatz histories (all fundamental components of modernism) is embodied in the Spirituals of the enslaved Africans. The alienated cry found in lines such as "Nobody knows the trouble I've seen" and "I'm a rollin, I'm a rollin / I'm a rollin through an unfriendly world" along with the sense of discontinuity and loss in "Sometimes I feel like a motherless child / a long, long way from home" collects in song the social energies that mark the feelings associated with modernity's movement out of an agrarian economy into an alienated, industrial machine economy; paradoxically, though, these songs are located in the enslaved social construct and lived reality of human capital and assembly-line machine in flesh that is written on the dark bodies of enslaved black people.

An implicit articulation of experiences of alienation and fragmentation among enslaved black people also is located in W. E. B. Du Bois's discussion of the "sorrow songs," music that serves as a site where double-consciousness is interrogated. That this expression of modern fragmentation is connected to the Spirituals suggests that enslaved black people "in the cotton field had already been confronting and evolving esthetic solutions for the problems of assembly-line regimentation, depersonalization, and collectivization" (Murray, *Omni* 63). This social reality situates the Spirituals within modernity, the larger intellectual and social context that has shaped the United States.

In 1903, just over half a century after Douglass writes the music of African Americans into literature, W. E. B. Du Bois's *Souls of Black Folk* is published. In this multigenre text, Du Bois both enacts some of the aesthetic qualities anticipated in Douglass's description of plantation songs and includes his own study of these songs and their postbellum counterparts. He also includes an analysis of one of the ways self-consciousness is shaped in formerly enslaved black people. Du Bois's analysis of the way identity is shaped in African Americans results in his appellation "double-consciousness," a type of fragmentation that he describes as "yield[ing] . . . [black people] no true self-consciousness" because there always is a sense of "two-ness": "two souls, two thoughts, two unreconciled strivings; two warring ideals in one dark body, whose dogged strength alone keeps it from being torn asunder" (8–9). It is Du Bois's concept of "dogged strength," both intellectual and psychological, that, in fact, informs the expressive technique and way of experiencing the world that Douglass observes in the music of enslaved Africans who were aware that they were expressing double ideas through words that conceal their perspectives on their lives; these perspectives are in stark contrast to the views of their enslavers, yet captive black people took care to make it appear that their views were consistent with those of their enslavers.

Many African captives were aware that the dominant and apparently prevailing social discourse about them was contrary to their own constructions of self, yet the power of the dominant discourse put into question their self-perceptions, causing, for some, a struggle with developing an idea of self devoid of inferiority. For others, such as the makers of the Spirituals, there was a constant awareness that the dominant society's perception of African Americans was erroneous; thus, enslaved black people developed ways of living in this contradiction. These views on life are illustrated in the philosophy of the Spirituals.

Double-consciousness may not be as prevalent today as it was in earlier African American history, but its psychological and philosophical strategies for living in fragmentation have proved useful for many varieties of societal alienation experienced by African Americans. And, more recently, the insights of double-consciousness—a socially imposed split in one's psyche, as articulated by Du Bois—have come to inform the ideas of feminist thinkers as well as poststructuralist theories. Du Bois employs double-consciousness himself in the structure of *The Souls of Black Folk* when he contrasts the words of Europeans and European Americans such as George Byron, Elizabeth Barrett Browning, Alfred Tennyson, John Greenleaf Whittier, James Russell Lowell, and others who are within Western tradition—with which many black people have had a tenuous relationship—and bars of music from the anonymous "sorrow songs." Du Bois, for instance, opens section 2 with a poem by James Russell Lowell. In this poem Lowell comments on the role God has in bringing about impending freedom and shows that life is a mixture of "Truth" and "Wrong." The centrality of Lowell's voice within Western culture—former Harvard professor, first editor of the *Atlantic Monthly*, editor of the *North American Review*, and ambassador to Spain and Britain—affirms Lowell's and his poem's privileged social position within the culture of the United States.

Du Bois juxtaposes a marginalized and anonymous Spiritual, "My Lord, What a Mourning! When the Stars Begin to Fall," and Lowell's poem. The words and composer of the Spiritual are not reproduced; thus Du Bois illustrates the unarticulated voice and invisible social position of its maker(s) within his or her culture, yet he inserts this black voice into a fracturing cultural space located in an early-twentieth-century moment of burgeoning modernity with its social fragmentation and personal alienation. This cultural space that later is located in Blues operates in a homological relation to modernism, and Jazz will have a similar relation to postmodernism. Blues as a metaphor in African American fiction, however, is not literary modernism; and similarly, Jazz in fiction is not postmodernism. While there are conterminous aspects between music as a metaphor in African American fiction and literary modernism and postmodernism, black writers as well as other marginalized writers have constructed new shapes for these intellectual concepts.[11]

Du Bois's positioning of a text from the dominant culture and one from African American culture discloses the similar ideas that both convey, especially when the title of the Spiritual is known. His juxtapositioning of the texts also demonstrates their social positioning—a privileged text and a marginal text; this strategy suggests that both are vying for primacy as viable expressions of change. Du Bois's pattern of representing a privileged text and then a marginal text reveals the dominant values that establish a social policy that permits Lowell to speak and to define social change for black people, yet black people have no public voice of their own. Their voices are represented through the most abstract form of expression—music; so their self-definitions and ideas for change are barely articulated in the social discourse. Du Bois reveals the tension of double-consciousness because both the poem and the Spiritual occupy the same space and vie for the same position: the voice to define and to articulate change. Lowell's poem represents a dominant and external definition for change in the condition of black people. And the Spiritual—through subtle signifying nuances—speaks to the paradox of being enslaved people in a land that was established on and engages in a discourse of freedom. Yet emancipation at the end of the Civil War along with postwar Reconstruction does not alter significantly the lived reality of black people in the United States. The paradoxical qualities of African American life are continued even after emancipation.[12]

Du Bois also enacts in literature aspects suggested by Douglass's descriptions of the plantation songs when he organizes *The Souls* as an improvisation on traditional written genres; Du Bois's study breaks the boundaries of genre yet produces a rich and satisfying text. Also in these essays, studies, story, and analyses of black life, one finds prototypes of experiences from the lives of black people as well as examples that illustrate the way paradox has become a part of how life has been written into much of the artistic expression by black people in the United States during most of the twentieth century.

Sections 6 and 7 of *The Souls* as well as the essay in chapter 9, "Of the Sons of Master and Man," depict the paradox of being both part of and not part of the United States, or of being absent while present. This lived contradiction is repeated in African American literature, most notably in Ralph Ellison's metaphor of invisibility.[13] In the story "Of the Coming of John," Du Bois illustrates the contradiction of being seen and not seen as well as that of being absent while present. He illustrates the contradiction of being absent while present through his depiction of the parallel, yet disparate, lives of the two Johns from Altamaha, Georgia. John Jones, despite his education, "must remain subordinate, and can never expect to be the equal of white men." Thus his selfhood is absent and he is barred from full participation in the society where he is a paradoxically invisible presence. Through Du Bois's portrayal of Judge

Henderson, father of the other John, this writer also conveys the racialized and specious idea that suggests John Jones's subordinate position in society is established by "nature" (175). As a result of such ideas, John Jones's intelligence, pain, and anger, as well as his other basic human qualities, are never seen; that is, John Jones's socially defined body is the only thing the dominant society of Altamaha perceives, making him an invisible presence that is seen in his physicality—for his use value—yet unseen in his humanity.

Certainly Du Bois's musical bars—in addition to exhibiting the fragmentation of double-consciousness when contrasted with the words with which they are paired—also convey paradox when one views the Spirituals as a form of art that employs a method of saying and not saying. A seemingly empty space between words and meanings in the Spirituals (Douglass's distinction between jargon and meaning) allows multiple meanings for what is said, yet also allows a space for what is not said—yet said—to be filled with unspoken, and at times unspeakable, ideas that often are not apparent in cursory examinations of this gap. Without, for instance, the words that illustrate ideas or experiences from the Spirituals, Du Bois's anonymous and untitled bars of music have the semblance of meaninglessness in relation to literature and intellectual ideas, especially when the musical bars from the Spirituals are juxtaposed with the words (ideas) of the poets he quotes and names. Yet all this apparent emptiness is actually a space for what is not permitted in speech. This gap in meaning stands as a method of saying and not saying that can "provide a way of contemplating chaos and civilization . . . [as well as provide] a mechanism for testing the problems and blessings of freedom" (Morrison, *Playing* 7).

Through the double meanings of songs such as "Steal Away," which is placed in chapter 10, and "Swing Low, Sweet Chariot," which follows Tennyson's poem in chapter 12, Du Bois illuminates the chaotic potential of selective freedom, a potential that is demonstrated through the words in songs that suggest acquiescence while calling for covert action. His inscribing of paradox is deepened if we discern the conundrum of being absent while present in his juxtaposition of bars from sorrow songs by enslaved people—whose texts were relegated to the margin of tradition—next to texts of writers who have a place in or near the center of the dominant nineteenth-century Western tradition.

Du Bois's organizational structure of *The Souls* calls for a parallel place for black people within Western tradition (in which he was clearly well versed). He also opens a space for a formal place for music as a vital trope in African American literature. His juxtaposition of centric and ex-centric (Hutcheon 57–73) texts demonstrates, early in the twentieth century, the inside-outside paradox of marginalization. People who are in bondage and on the outside of the social center feel less of the weight of the dominant cultural ideas about rules, including artistic rules. As long as music and literature by African Americans during the nineteenth century and the first half of the twentieth century do not overtly traverse the established racial discourse, they are able to express ideas that, in fact, are marginalized yet speak to intracultural concerns, including freedom and resistance. As the intertextuality between Douglass's and Du Bois's texts suggests, these two writers' observations about music and black life offer music as a viable location for African American aesthetic ideas. Music, then, is expanded and made an important means through which political-social-historical-cultural ideas are expressed by African American artists, including writers.

Douglass's and Du Bois's texts offer possibilities for the use of music as a metaphor in African American literary expression. Douglass reads the musical, social, and historical texts of the events in his society and writes them into his *Narrative;* and, through the influences of memory and history, Du Bois inserts Douglass into *The Souls* by extending and rewriting the experiences and history in Douglass's text. This dialogism or intertextual process of absorption and reshaping also is part of black musical practice. Douglass's *Narrative* need not be situated as an acknowledged source or origin in order to function as an intertext in Du Bois's *Souls*. Intertextuality obtains through implicit as well as explicit traces (Worton and Still 22) in texts. This musical practice entails reading the texts of events in contemporary society, reading the texts of other music and the texts[14] of history, and then rewriting them in contemporary song. There are life stories in African American music that present double meanings, freedom trains, the multifaced trickster hero, indomitability of spirit, and a personal and personified spirit God. These aspects of black music begin to find a place in literature through poems such as Paul Laurence Dunbar's "When Malindy Sings," which gestures toward later developments in the literary uses of music among African American writers.

Within twenty years of the publication of Du Bois's *Souls of Black Folk,* black music is influencing the form of and meaning in African American poetry. Langston Hughes's title poem in his *Weary Blues* along with poems such as "Jazzonia," most of his poems in *Fine Clothes to the*

Jew, and numerous other later poems, including "Trumpet Player" and the long poem *Ask Your Mama: Twelve Moods for Jazz*, are situated explicitly within a Blues-Jazz site of social-cultural-historical energies. Joining Hughes as an early writer who uses music in African American poetry is Sterling Brown with "Ma Rainey," "Memphis Blues," "Strong Men," and other poems that draw on the resources of Blues and Jazz music.

Within two generations of the publication of *The Souls*, scholars and writers of twentieth-century African American fiction are situating this literature within the historical-social-political and aesthetic energies of Blues and Jazz music and demonstrating the intracultural influences of the music on the literature.[15] African American writers, in the titles of their narratives, frequently make direct references to as well as allude to Spirituals, Blues, and Jazz. A brief tour through the titles of African American short stories and novels illustrates the significance of music to many black writers in the United States. In this study Wallace Thurman's novel *The Blacker the Berry . . . : A Novel of Negro Life*, Albert Murray's *Train Whistle Guitar*, John Edgar Wideman's *Sent for You Yesterday*, and James Baldwin's "Sonny's Blues" (along with numerous other titles by Baldwin)[16] make such allusions or references.

One, however, can easily note other similarly allusive/referential titles among African American writers: Sherley Anne Williams's "Tell Martha Not to Moan," Langston Hughes's "Blues I'm Playing," Richard Wright's "Bright and Morning Star," Sylvester Leaks's "Blues Begins," and Clarence Major's "Scat," along with contemporary novel titles, including Toni Morrison's *Jazz*, Bebe Moore Campbell's *Your Blues Ain't Like Mine*, and mass-market novelists E. Lynn Harris's *If This World Were Mine* and Valerie Wilson Wesley's *Ain't Nobody's Business If I Do*. Additionally, a similar allusiveness/referentiality to musicians, song titles, and lines from Spirituals, Blues, and Jazz informs Toni Cade Bambara's "Medley," which includes numerous allusions and references to Blues and Jazz music and musicians.[17]

Musicians or singers as important characters and settings in musical venues also are frequently located in African American fictional narratives. Rudolph Fisher's "Common Meter" takes place in a Jazz venue—the Arcadia Club. And in this study Paul Laurence Dunbar's novel *The Sport of the Gods*, Thurman's *Blacker the Berry*, Nella Larsen's *Quicksand*, Albert Murray's *Train Whistle Guitar*, John Edgar Wideman's *Sent for You Yesterday*, and Ann Petry's novel *The Street*, have important scenes situated in a black musical performance venue. Moreover, among the numerous singers and musicians in African American fiction are Ann Petry's drummer Kid Jones in "Solo on Drums," Langston Hughes's Blues guitarist Jimboy and Blues singer Harrietta in *Not Without Laughter*; Gayl Jones's Blues singer Ursa in *Corregidora*, Al Young's supposed sax man, Chicken Hawk, in "Chicken Hawk's Dream," Bebe Moore Campbell's hors de combat Jazz singer Lindy (Malindy) Walker in *Singing in the Comeback Choir*; and Clarence Major's dipsomanic Manfred Banks in *Dirty Bird Blues* as well as the musician characters in the novels in this study. These fictional narratives point to music as a salient feature in twentieth-century African American prose.

Further, between the 1845 publication of Douglass's *Narrative*, which includes his observations on the music of black people, and the 1903 publication of Du Bois's studies on black life and music in *The Souls of Black Folk*, there are African American writers who use the resources of music and vernacular material in their poetry and fiction. Charles Chesnutt is one such writer whose texts inscribe the language and musical rhythms of black people in the United States. "The Goophered Grapevine" is Chesnutt's first published story, appearing in 1887 in the *Atlantic Monthly*. When editor Thomas Bailey Aldrich published Chesnutt's story, he, along with the readers of this influential magazine, likely was not aware of the writer's African ancestry.[18]

Chesnutt's "Goophered Grapevine," however, marks a use of music in literature that is rare among black writers. Through his unique employment of irony, Chesnutt enacts minstrelsy. In *Modernism and the Harlem Renaissance*, Houston Baker, who also discusses Chesnutt's use of minstrelsy in fiction, says that minstrelsy in African American literature is "mastery of form"—a mocking minstrel perfection of white literary models that at the same time creates space for a black voice (15–81). Chesnutt's use of music is not the focus of this book, as it is not an expression of Spiritual-Gospel, Blues, or Jazz, and, moreover, Chesnutt's story was published in the nineteenth century and is thus outside the scope of this study. Yet I still find that his narrative technique is worth a brief discussion, as aspects of minstrelsy are present in the novels of Dunbar, Thurman, Larsen, and Ellison that I read later in this study.

"The Goophered Grapevine" is a double enactment of literary minstrelsy. Chesnutt, the black man, takes on the mask of whiteness in the form of a writer who presents a story about southern life in the *Atlantic*. In 1887 the failures of Reconstruction are clearly apparent to black people and have been for a full ten years. Chesnutt, the unreconstructed black man, becomes the man of letters (which at the time was presumed to be a white man). He then mocks tradition with a perfected and exact replica of the white writer presenting a slice of southern life from the perspective of the triumphant North. Unlike blackface minstrelsy, which was a deliberate, degenerate aberration, Chesnutt's minstrel irony mocks through this writer's perfection of form and the clever—not idiotic—wit displayed by Chesnutt's character Julius; thus minstrelsy is exemplified in Chesnutt's publishing of his story as well as in the art of his story. Chesnutt's minstrel irony, then, is shown in the depth and complexity of his artistry, including his characterization of Julius and in his perfection of the local color genre in fiction, which in its plantation school variety typically includes stories about plantation life by white writers. Yet Chesnutt's most complex mockery in "The Goophered Grapevine" is found in his perfection and reversal of the form of minstrelsy.

Chesnutt, as the black man in white face, depicts the white straight man of minstrelsy, Mr. Interlocutor, in his character who is the vintner from Ohio. He also depicts the black character of the minstrel theater in his characterization of Julius, who in the tradition of minstrelsy would probably be called Mr. Vines, as the custom of minstrelsy was to give the blackface character a name derived from an object with which he is associated, thus through metonymy reducing him to the status of a thing. Chesnutt, however, gives the black character a name and leaves the white character nameless.[19] Instead of demeaning the intelligence of the black character and making his behavior the source of ridicule, Chesnutt imbues Julius with a sense of irony and other forms of indirection that result in a wry intelligence that illuminates the vintner's smug attitude and illustrates the white character's ignorance before the sophistication of Julius's verbal play.

So as Chesnutt's grape grower and his former enslaved captive are subtly and subversively reversed intellectually while reenacting through literature the song and dance of the minstrel show, Chesnutt simultaneously acts out his own mockery as the black writer of the putative plantation tradition story. Chesnutt goes on to triple the minstrel irony through his presentation of dialect. For readers of the *Atlantic*, Julius's dialect is blackface minstrelsy, a corked-up white man representing the language of the plantation for the entertainment of whites. Chesnutt was, in fact, a corked-up black man, in the tradition of Bert Williams,[20] representing the language of minstrelsy for the entertainment of whites while mocking them in art and in life.

One of the earliest attempts in fiction to filter through the issues of dialect, minstrelsy, and close transcriptions of folk matter and to present the ideas that are embedded in the music, lives, and philosophy of African Americans is found in Jean Toomer's *Cane*, a lyrical multigenre text in which the music of black people is written into twentieth-century American literature. Toomer maintains that *Cane*, which was published in 1923 at the height of the Harlem Renaissance, is a "song of an end" to a "folk spirit" that was beautiful. Certainly Toomer perceives that black folk culture in the United States is dying as the modernism of an urban, machine culture changes the expressive lives of African Americans from a deep and complex resonance of emotions found in the paradox of the Spirituals to a deep yet fragmented, many-layered, complex Jazz expressive attitude that confronted the contradictions of African American life with a musical boldness that slavery had limited but not eliminated.[21]

In *Cane*, Toomer clearly does not present a voice that speaks from within the "peasant life" he depicts. The novel's narrator engages in a ritual journey into the South, but this journey does not reveal to him that he is the "bone of the bone" nor the "flesh of the flesh" of the people he observes. Stepto refers to this Du Boisian type of southern journey as an immersion ritual (*Behind the Veil* 164–67). Toomer's narrator fails in his immersion ritual; he is unlike Du Bois, who asserts his position as one with the people "within the veil" (4).

The distance that Toomer places between the narrator, the people in this text, and their musicality problematizes Toomer's intracultural uses of music in his multigenre text. The narrative stance in *Cane* is that of a fascinated outsider who is "perceptive" and sensitive to the life, horror, and pain expressed in the language and music of the black people who move along the Dixie Pike. This narrator also at times is titillated and repulsed by the Jazz environment of Washington, D.C., and Chicago. Toomer's poems and stories seem more in the tradition of the plantation school variety of local color—without Chesnutt's ironic subversiveness—than within a Blues or Jazz tradition in African American fiction.[22] In *Cane* the folk spirit to which Toomer refers is alienated from the narrative voice that presents this spirit. There are moments when a feeling of loss is illustrated, yet that loss can be read as the personal loss of the impact of this folk spirit on the narrator as well as the loss of this spirit within society.[23]

Toomer takes great care presenting the details of the environment that he depicts. His descriptions of the variety of colors among black people are sensitive and varied: "yellow flower," "creamy brown," "white looking," "color of oak leaves," "black skinned," "flush ginger" (10, 14, 20, 28, 50, 58). And his poem "Cotton Song" expresses some of the philosophy in the Spirituals as well as recalls the resistant spirit of these songs, which is illustrated through the poet's reworking of a line from the Spirituals into his formal rhymed quatrains: "We ain't agwine t wait until th Judgment Day" (9). Yet despite these folk elements, the persona in Toomer's "Cotton Song" seems to stand outside the experiences of those who sing the Spirituals. In "Cotton Song," Toomer establishes familiarity by his use of the word "brother," a common term of inclusion. But in this poem Toomer's poetic persona clearly has entered into the community of those who sing the Spirituals and attempts to establish a relationship with them. Also missing in "Cotton Song" is the internalized knowledge that one need not wait for Judgment Day. This idea is crucial to the philosophical perspective expressed in most Spirituals and Blues. In "Cotton Song," however, the persona seems to bring this basic Spiritual and Blues knowledge to the others in the poem.

There are additional instances of such distancing in *Cane*. The narrator in "Carma," for instance, says, "The sun . . . shoots primitive rockets into her mangrove-gloomed, yellow flower face." To view something as primitive the observer must be distanced from it. Whether one reads primitive as first and foundational or as less socially evolved yet mysteriously attractive, there is distance and difference in this image; and Toomer's sharp contrast between "primitive" and "rocket" reinforces the image of Carma as less developed than the narrator who has the words to describe her thusly. And, as in "Kabnis," the "sad strong song" is "far away" (10). Also in *Cane*, the Jazz music of the North, even though it is dangerous for the "white and whitewashed wood of Washington," is associated with "nigger life" and "nigger alleys" that would make God "duck his head in shame" (50, 39).

There are, however, a few instances in Toomer's text when the narrator seems to identify with his subjects. One of those instances is in "Bona and Paul." Toomer's most evocative depiction of black southern life, however, is in "Kabnis," yet even in this story the main character, Ralph Kabnis, is separated a priori from the "white South [that] weighs down upon him" (100), and by disposition Kabnis is alienated from the other black people in the story.

Still, "Kabnis" is Toomer's most sympathetic portrayal of the Georgia folk. In this short story he uses vernacular language to illustrate each character's social status. There remains, though, distance and alienation in Kabnis as the Sunday church music is separated from him and the other men who hear it from their small cabin (88–91). Toomer's separation of Kabnis from his environment also is depicted through this central character's alienation from the beauty of the blackness he encounters in the South. Kabnis expresses this when he says, "Dear Jesus, do not chain me to myself and set these hills and valleys, heaving with folk songs, so close to me that I cannot reach them. There is radiant beauty in the night that touches me and . . . tortures me" (83). Again, at Halsey's workshop, where Kabnis is more closely associated with the daily life in this Georgia town, his feelings of not belonging are illustrated when we are told that he is "awkward and ludicrous, like a schoolboy in his big brother's new overalls" (98). These and numerous other examples in *Cane* demonstrate that Toomer uses folk materials, including African American music, in ways that suggest their otherness. Rather than presenting folk materials as emerging from the daily lives of the folk, he most often presents these materials through the eyes of an outside observer.

James Weldon Johnson, conversely, tries to rid vernacular speech of the limitations—of strangeness and of weak artistic ingenuity—that have been imposed on the folk expression of "Aframericans." These limitations were not "due to any defect of the dialect as dialect, but to the mould of conventions in which Negro dialect in the United States has been set, [and] to the fixing effects of its long association with the Negro only as a happy-go-lucky or forlorn figure." In *God's Trombones: Seven Negro Sermons in Verse* (1927) Johnson begins the transformation of folk material into literary art, a process that, within Western tradition, is demonstrated in Chaucer, Shakespeare, James Joyce, Wilhelm Richard Wagner, and, for Johnson, John Millington Synge (7–8).

In 1926 Langston Hughes titled his first collection of poems *The Weary Blues*. His title and the style he employs in his poems demonstrate a conscious association between African American Blues and Jazz and African American literature. Hughes's title recalls either Robert Nathaniel Dett's composition "Don't Be Weary, Traveler" (Southern, *The Music* 274) or a recording of "Weary Blues," by either Clarence Williams, Johnny Dodds, the New Orleans Rhythm Kings with Jelly Roll Morton, or Louis Armstrong, all of whom recorded or performed this tune in the early 1920s. Armstrong's recording (which is upbeat and energetic, making the tune an ironic reversal of its title) is the most likely choice. In 1930 at the decline of the Harlem Renaissance, Langston Hughes published his first[24] novel, *Not Without Laughter*. In this novel, Hughes—as was the case in novels by Harlem Renaissance writers Claude McKay, Rudolph Fisher, and Wallace Thurman—makes music prominent. Sandy, Hughes's main character, has a father and aunt who are Blues musicians. Jimboy is a less-than-successful Blues guitarist, while his sister-in-law Harrietta Williams triumphs over life's difficulties and becomes "Princess of the Blues." Harrietta exemplifies a Blues singularity that is informed by the group philosophy—elaborating on a basic form—as she encourages Sandy to continue his education with her financial support. She recognizes that Sandy's education promises to expose him to fewer hardships than those experienced by his father, and she hopes education will bring Sandy a less troubled path to success than she has had. Hughes's Blues-based novel and the story it presents could easily substitute for Albert Murray's *Train Whistle Guitar* in chapter 4 of this book.

African American writers from Dunbar and Chesnutt—ending the nineteenth century and opening the twentieth century—to Harlem Renaissance writers, as well as Willard Motley, a purportedly "raceless" writer in the 1940s and 1950s who uses Duke Ellington's "Mood Indigo" to suggest Blues-like conditions in the lives of his white characters in *Let No Man Write My Epitaph* (1958), and numerous musically allusive contemporary writers, such as Bebe Moore Campbell and Clarence Major, have negotiated the terrain of a music-into-fiction discourse. Blues is the prevalent musical aesthetic philosophy that informs African American fictional characters and themes. In the texts that I will read and in African American literature in general, Jazz is and has been less frequently textualized in fiction. Increasingly, this is changing. Spiritual-Gospel philosophy, however, finds a consistent place in African American literature.

In the first chapter of this study, I delineate the characteristics of a music-into-literature discourse that I find in a number of African American literary texts. For the purposes of this study, literary uses of music point to an intersection of Spiritual-Gospel, Blues, and Jazz located within the historical, social, political, and cultural environment in which African American life and music have combined. In the ten literary texts that I read in the following chapters, I find that music has a plethora of expressions of its intertextual relation to character and theme. I begin each chapter by situating the literary texts within a broad social, historical, political, and cultural context. By highlighting historical and cultural moments that lack currency in scholarly as well as general discussions of history and culture in the United States, I attempt to refocus, expand, and redefine discussions of African American literary and musical culture. I do not purport to be comprehensive in my use of historical and cultural markers; they are, I admit, summary and provocative gestures toward my readings of the fictional texts that are situated in the same historical moment and share connective social energies that are similarly marginalized in the dominant discourse. These energies, however, are crucial to the intracultural discourse of music as a metaphor that moves into African American literature.

Early-twentieth-century novels such as Dunbar's *Sport of the Gods*, Larsen's *Quicksand*, and Thurman's *Blacker the Berry* demonstrate the subtle influence of music on theme and character in African American fiction. In Dunbar's novel, the emerging influence of Blues and Jazz—and its increasing association with northern, urban cities such as Dunbar's New York—in African American cultural life is rejected, while an idealized southern Spiritual-Gospel life in Alabama is supported.[25] Larsen, by contrast, presents a female critique of southern Spiritual-Gospel life and its restrictions on the construction of her protagonist's, Helga Crane's, identity, yet this biracial character also is unable to situate herself comfortably among the middle-class, northern and urban Blues People[26] she encounters because she is repulsed by their affected posture of race-consciousness. Helga also rejects the exotic primitivism that she endures when she visits her relatives in Denmark. She is a Blues character who cannot find a Blues space that allows her the racial as well as the gender freedom she desires.

As Daphne Duval Harrison states in relation to female Blues singers, one also can say in relation to Larsen's Helga: they lived in "a world that did not protect the sanctity of black womanhood as espoused in the bourgeois ideology" (64). Yet sometimes black women are enmeshed within the power of that ideology, as was the case for Zora Neale Hurston's Janie in *Their Eyes Were Watching God*. Wallace Thurman's female protagonist, as with Larsen's, is on a quest for identity. For Emma Lou Morgan in *The Blacker the Berry*, this quest is situated within the problematic African American class and color issues that propel Thurman's main character from one Blues environment to another in search of people whose color and class she finds acceptable. Emma Lou's problem, unlike Helga's, is not that she doesn't locate the "right sort of people"; her problem is that when she finds them, they reject her. Thurman's protagonist struggles not with external

Blues-making aspects of racial rejection but with the doubling of these Blues experiences within an intracultural problematic of color distinctions.

Hurston, Petry, and Ellison portray important Blues and Jazz characters prominently in their novels. Hurston in *Their Eyes Were Watching God* depicts Tea Cake as a traveling bluesman, and her main character Janie lives a Blues life. Janie, however, begins to rework the Blues environment of Eatonville, Florida, in order to reposition women within a Blues philosophy that is losing its efficacy as the town models itself on the values of the dominant society. Hurston's Janie in *Their Eyes Were Watching God* is an early example in literature of a particularly female positioning within Blues philosophy. What is important, though, is that both Larsen's Helga Crane in *Quicksand* and Hurston's Janie recognize the "lie the image of the lady represents" (Christian 236–37). Lutie Johnson, Petry's main character in *The Street*, recognizes the problematic nature of gender and race too late. She is a single parent who lives in an urban Blues environment; she aspires to move away from this environment because she is familiar with and believes in the dominant discourse that promotes the idea that hard work merits success. Lutie believes her talent as a Blues singer may be one way to gain success through hard work. Petry demonstrates the duplicity in the dominant discourse that erects invisible barriers and pitfalls and that creates Blues People such as Lutie. Ellison's *Invisible Man* is filled with folk, Blues, and Jazz elements that use African American experiences as a starting point for interrogating issues of modernity and identity.

Contemporary fiction by black writers includes characters and themes that have been made by writers who view music as an aspect of their aesthetic and their literary strategies. Toni Morrison explores issues of gender and friendship in her characterization of Nel Wright Greene as a Blues character and of Sula Peace as a Jazz character in her novel *Sula*, which is set in the Blues neighborhood referred to as the Bottom of Medallion, Ohio. Morrison's characters convey to readers the beauty of understanding the interconnectedness of Blues and Jazz, the music that comes to represent the connection between the friends, Nel and Sula, in the novel. Albert Murray and John Edgar Wideman illustrate the development of youthful protagonists. For Murray's Scooter in *Train Whistle Guitar*, Blues aesthetics and philosophy in his Gasoline Point, Alabama, neighborhood allow him to encounter the harsh realities of life within his environment and prepare him for maturity and success in the larger world. Gasoline Point is filled with bluesmen, with whom he can interact, and with Blues records as well as a Spiritual-Gospel environment in Scooter's home—making Gasoline Point a location that surrounds Scooter with love and protection. Finally, Wideman's musical novel *Sent for You Yesterday* interrogates the notion of historical continuity and uses music as an intertextual locus from which his youthful narrator Doot constructs a position for himself within the changing Blues community of Homewood, Pennsylvania. I end this study of music and African American characters and themes with an essay on James Baldwin's "Sonny's Blues," a classic short story that provides access to conveniently well-constructed examples of a Blues theme as well as Spiritual-Gospel, Blues, and Jazz characters.

The premise of this book is that if music is as influential in the lives and artistic expressions of African Americans as some scholars and cultural analysts suggest, one would expect that it would have an impact on the fiction of black people in the United States, just as it has on the poetry. Noted cultural critics and writers Ralph Ellison and James Baldwin have commented on the literary uses of music in fiction; they view music as a metaphor that collects lived experiences among black people. Baldwin, in fact, calls for critical articulation—such as the undertaking in this study—of this tradition of song in story ("Many Thousands" 597–98).[27]

Baldwin's charge has been taken up by scholars including Henry Louis Gates Jr. in *The Signifying Monkey*, Houston Baker in *Blues, Ideology, and Afro-American Literature*, and Hazel Carby in "It Jus Be's Dat Way Sometime." The work of these scholars, among others, informs this study and challenges me to expand the discourse on music in African American fiction. My positioning of this scholarly discourse—as in the literary texts that I read—involves formal revision as an act of expansion "rather than ritual slaying" (Gates, *Signifying* xxviii).

While my premise is that music figures importantly in the fiction of many African American writers, music is not all that there is in African American fiction, and it is not always in these texts.

one

MUDDY WATERS
Music in African American Fiction

The Music:
History, Culture, Connective
Social Narratives

As enslaved people, Africans in the New World used Spirituals[1] as a means of communication as well as a reservoir in which to collect their life stories and life philosophies. Through song, enslaved black people convey messages, sound warnings, express emotions, and ask fundamental questions about their position in the universe. Christianity, as it is professed from the dominant society, plays a complex role in the Spirituals, as enslaved Africans' uses of Scripture in the Spirituals take on unique applications by revising the biblical themes and ideas that are filtered through the dominant society's lens of white supremacy. In the Spirituals, stories of African American life are told while a refashioned spirituality is forged in contradistinction to the Christianity that permeates the dominant culture.

Within the context of these historical conditions we cannot rightly limit the Spirituals to a narrowly religious focus,[2] as Spirituals address every aspect of enslaved life. This means that they depict the tyranny, hypocrisy, and desire for freedom, which are pervasive concerns for enslaved Africans. The most persistent theme in the Spirituals centers on a life philosophy based in freedom. Thus, the traditional concepts of secular and religious music are not applied neatly in the case of antebellum Spirituals by black people; this is the case even after the era of slavery, a time when some black people begin to be attentive to clear differences between the idea of the secular and the religious. Christianity, then, becomes a safe yet powerfully resonant means through which enslaved Africans tell their stories in music. One can reasonably assert that the use of music in the "free"—unrestricted by the oppression of slavery—literature of African Americans results from the prominent role that music has had in collecting the narratives of the lives of enslaved Africans.[3]

An important practice employed by the makers of the Spirituals is their combining of innovative and unique melodies with existing material, reworking both for their own musical needs. This practice develops into the lifeblood of African American musical custom, particularly in Spiritual-Gospel and Jazz—and more recently in rap. For the Blues musician, popular phrases from a song or from the social environment travel from song to song, creating varying versions of rambling tunes, shaking peaches tunes, freight train tunes, jelly tunes, and so on. We can view these phrases in Blues as "traveling phrases." In the Spirituals, choruses from favorite camp-meeting songs and hymns eventually develop into "a body of 'wandering verses'" (Southern, *The Music* 86), which are used in any song that lends itself to the ideas expressed in these set pieces. Variation from other musical texts as well as from religious texts—which often are given double meanings that address daily life, not just religion—is important for the makers of the Spirituals.[4]

Blues illustrates the post-enslaved cultural expression of a people negotiating the modern world on terms that purport to be different from those encountered while enslaved, yet the terms are not substantially different. Spirituals were born in slavery, and while there have been a negligible number of new Spirituals since shortly after the Emancipation Proclamation, this music is the earlier context from which Blues draws its philosophical concerns and musical practices. While the Spirituals tell the stories of enslaved Africans' movement from slavery to freedom, Blues tells the stories of a second inefficacious promise. The initial failed promise of the United States as a nation of opportunity and freedom is doubled as the post–Civil War national discourse gestures toward ubiquitous freedom and then immediately reneges, revealing the freedom and opportunity manqué in which black people are relegated.

Blues, as is the case with the earlier Spirituals, collects in its words and in its sounds a sense of disconnection from a larger world. Blues also reveals, though, a sense of connection to a philosophy, a way of negotiating the world, that does not concede existential power to the world from which it is alienated. Postwar experiences during the early part of the twentieth century reinforce the familiar social discourse that had always been in place for black people in the United States; the difference is that in the twentieth century the old social policy is altered by increased mobility among black people, who are no longer enslaved. The failures of Reconstruction, which were clear by 1877, coupled with early twentieth-century postwar disappointments among black people, especially black veterans, move African Americans northward as well as into urban areas both south and north. Along with black people come the stories of black lives—formerly enslaved, many times uprooted as well as separated from the fruits of the nation—and the Blues music that carries these stories.

This post-Reconstruction era is a time when Blues and Jazz revive the rhythms of the Spirituals that have fallen into disfavor as a number of Reconstruction era African American churches turn to anthem and meter music in worship services. Outside the black church those earlier musical ideas and life philosophies are continued in the Blues. Coexisting with the post-Reconstruction Blues are the jazzy rhythms of ragtime, a form of syncopated piano music that precedes Jazz performances in ensembles and bands and is most notably associated with Scott Joplin, and the more strongly Blues-based boogie-woogie piano playing of Clarence "Pinetop" Smith, Charlie "Cow-Cow" Davenport, and Albert Ammons. Eventually Blues will reshape popular culture in the United States, as it expands into Jazz, rhythm and blues, rock and roll, and soul.[5]

Not only popular culture but also Western culture's classical music by black as well as white composers reflects the impact of Blues and Jazz. The early part of the twentieth century was a period of musical experimentation by black composers such as William Grant Still, Will Marion Cook, Clarence Cameron White, Robert Nathaniel Dett, and Harry T. Burleigh, who was a student of Antonín Dvořák (whose *New World Symphony* finds comment in Nella Larsen's and Ralph Ellison's novels in this study) when the Bohemian-born composer was head of the National Conservatory from 1892 to 1895. Later, Burleigh's "Ethiopia Saluting Colors" influences composer Margaret T. Bonds to set Langston Hughes's "The Negro Speaks of Rivers" to music.[6] These composers combine Western classical musical theory[7] with musical themes and motifs from the Spirituals and the Blues. Along with Blues and Jazz, gospel also emerges in the early decades of the twentieth century and differs from the Spirituals in its focus on orthodox religious concerns. This is the time when gospel becomes the religious music of black people in the United States. Among African Americans, the twentieth century brings northern migration, more widespread exposure to the religious music and ideas of the dominant society, and a more distinct dividing line between religious and secular music.

By the 1930s, music based in an earlier folk idiom regains its efficacy among African Americans. True to their traditionally fluid qualities, Spiritual-Gospel and Blues have expanded into an immense Jazz polyrhythm of African American life. Spirituals, Blues, and Jazz have distinct qualities that do not lend themselves to stark delineation. Yet, clearly, Blues, gospel, and Jazz locate their ancestral home in the Spirituals. Despite their common factors, some distinctions among Blues, Spiritual-Gospel, and Jazz must be established so that their application as metaphors in literature is made effective.

Two pivotal points of distinction among Blues, Jazz, and Spiritual-Gospel are the approaches to individual and group expression that are suggested in each type of music and the philosophical and/or religious ideas that are exemplified in these three types of music. Black people in the United States, because of the unique characteristics of slavery in the New World, have a history of forced communalism and necessary collectivity. For enslaved Africans, this forced communalism in the New World is not based in traditional familial or clan associations; and African Americans' efforts toward working together in a variety of ways (fields, invisible church, underground railroad, the making of the Spirituals) are all collective efforts based primarily in necessity. Without the typically shared cultural markers—language, daily customs, spiritual ideas, and so on—enslaved Africans in the New World found alternative ways to forge communal bonds and collective alliances. These bonds and alliances are negotiated within a context of similar objectives toward freedom despite any differences that may exist among the members of the group as well as within the context of their recognition of parallels and variances between their lives in Africa and their New World experiences.

The oppressive conditions of slavery, and similar attempts in later years to shatter the spirit of black people, create a body of shared experiences that have shaped the construction of an aesthetic and life philosophy located in the music of African Americans. Versions of these ideas of communalism and collectivity, or in Ralph Ellison's terms a "pre-individual" state of existence, have continued to shape philosophical and ideological discourses as well as musical and artistic texts by African Americans. In literary texts that portray a unified group that is situated in a Spiritual-Gospel philosophy, antebellum communal qualities such as a unified sense of purpose tend to present themselves.

The Spirituals, then, are a collaborative effort of the individual and the forged communal-group, without an emphasis—as in Blues—on a personal voice. One's personal voice is postulated as a given in the Spirituals, but it is brought into consonance with other voices in the collaborative effort toward freedom. Later, however, emancipation, mass northern migration, and urbanization transform the collaborative aspects in as well as the lack of distinction between secular and religious in African American music. The collaborative production of the antebellum Spirituals, however, does not mean that the individual is subsumed in the group. The idea of a totalized and monolithic moral-ethical or ideological center runs contrary to the life philosophy that influences enslaved black people in the New World.

With the advent of industrialization and emancipation, communal existence from Spiritual-Gospel life is reshaped into Blues communities. In contrast to the Spirituals, Blues emphasizes a more singular form of expression than the expression found in the communal Spirituals. The concept of a Blues community reflects the fracturing of a unified purpose that is found in the Spirituals. Lived reality in a Blues life locates African Americans in a shared condition of socially imposed limitations that restrict the movement of black bodies, which are no longer owned by individual enslavers but now are controlled by laws and social policies that are complicit with white supremacy. This condition of relative freedom allows black people to establish alliances in which a person's discretion about her or his lived reality, instead of necessary collectivity, is the basis on which connections with others are made.

These Blues communities, however, are still situated in a social policy of forced communalism. Blues communities are sites that collect the experiences of people whose lives are shaped by a racialized dominant discourse that excludes them. As a result of having been enslaved and under post-emancipation segregation, black people forge life strategies that inform a group philosophy on ways to live in the paradox of being black in the United States—the paradox of being Blues People. In Blues communities, these life strategies, situated within the group, inform one's singular response to life's dilemmas.[8]

A piquant point of interest concerning a sense of individual and community as it is expressed in some of the music and literature of black people is that singers of the Spirituals and later the Blues often use the first-person singular pronoun "I" as a collective pronoun. Although this usage is illustrative of the collaborative production of Spirituals, it does not discharge personal responsibility. When "I" is used in Spirituals and Blues as a collective pronoun, the term turns on its head the English royal use of the first person plural, "we," which is, in fact, exclusive to the individual speaker as authority center. This interesting usage of "I" is demonstrated in Spiritual and Blues songs such as "Nobody Knows the Trouble I've Seen," "I'm A-Rollin'," "I'm Going Up to Heaven Anyhow," "I Thank God I'm Free at Last," "I'm Going Back to My Used to Be," "I've Been Mistreated and I Don't Like it," and "I Be's Troubled." In many of the Blues, Spirituals, and Spiritual-based music, the "I" is perhaps inclusive of the speaker but has a more disperse application, so that it only refers to those listeners who find that the issues raised in the song fit, or can be made to fit their own sentiments, experiences, or philosophy.[9]

This study is based in the idea that black people in the United States have shared the conditions of living in the tyranny of de facto and de jure oppression, yet at the same time they have lived individual lives. I view the Spirituals as a site that draws to it both collective and individual experiences that are expressed in music that calls for physical freedom along with an implied recognition of existential freedom.[10] Alain Locke, in his essay "The New Negro," provides a succinct statement on the issue that seems to unify black life in the United States, and in so doing he opens up a place for my analysis, in this study, of the role of the individual in the Spirituals. "The chief bond . . . [among blacks]," Locke notes, "has been that of a common condition rather than a common consciousness; a problem in common rather than a life in common" (7). It is in this idea that the present study posits music as a metaphor in African American literature, beginning with the Spirituals.

As a result of the complex of issues that created the Spirituals, black people in the United States have produced a musical context from which exploitation, suffering, tyranny, mistreatment, oppression, disappointment, pain, adversity, and other dispiriting experiences can be examined and quelled. In many Spirituals there is still a sense of the value of life, the impetus toward survival, the resolve to triumph, love of self, resistance to oppression, and at times there is even playfulness. For Spirituals, then, there is a philosophical context that asserts the prominence of freedom as a quality of the human condition and that acknowledges the realities of a social policy that restricts freedom. The central passion of the Spirituals, then, is freedom—earthly freedom.

Implicit in this philosophical viewpoint from the Spirituals is the idea of a constructed way of living in the world, a collaborative project, shaped by its practitioners, collectively and individually, in response to their lives, and subject to change. Spirituals, then, illustrate a life philosophy, and later Blues incorporates the philosophical ideas in the Spirituals while adding an emphasis on self-reflexivity. If the dominant idea in the Spirituals is that they illustrate, through music, a communal response to lived experiences with a call for ubiquitous freedom and justice, then this idea is expanded in Blues so that group-informed yet self-reflexive, personal solutions in the face of continued disappointment, pain, and oppression are the dominant ideas.

Similar to Blues, Jazz emphasizes multiple, unique personal expressions—innovative personal style; but in contrast to Blues, Jazz moves away from singular expression firmly situated within and largely informed by group experiences. Jazz philosophy emphasizes one's connections to numerous fragments of experience in the social and cultural environment, without making permanent and wholesale connections to a particular location—such as Blues life—from which experience occurs. Yet Jazz still retains fragmented ties to Spirituals and Blues. It continues to express ideas of freedom and justice that shape the Spirituals and that influence a personal approach to complex problems expressed in Blues music. At the same time, Jazz expands and reshapes its predecessors, resounding the Spiritual singers' and Blues performers' expressions of modernist fragmentation found in life lived in the estrangement of double-consciousness as well as life lived in the many possibilities of the paradoxical experience of being a black person in the land of the free.

Jazz philosophy also posits an awareness of the instability of categories, including musical ones, and elucidates an aesthetic that results in a final product that emphasizes simultaneous expressions of multiple approaches to a single musical idea. It is the simultaneity of expression and the free subjectivity—improvisation—in Jazz that most clearly distinguish the philosophical, historical, and cultural contours of its musical aesthetic.

Moreover, unlike European-based classical music in which the composer is emphasized and the artistry of the music resides in production of the artifact and later in a musician's exact reproduction of it, the artistry of Jazz resides in the artist's use of the artifact as a vehicle for multitudinous improvisations and for elaborating or expanding the implications suggested by the artifact. The performer of Jazz is simultaneously the composer of the improvisations that define the collaborative musical project termed Jazz. Jazz musicians work from arranged pieces of music that are basic frameworks for multifarious changes and alterations. A jumping-off piece may be a new composition by a Jazz composer; it also may be a fragment from another musical text. Improvisation in the music of black people in the United States refocuses and expands the musician's role as artist and destabilizes the aesthetics of a musical text so that variance, not exact replication, is emphasized.

Jazz also revises Blues aesthetics in music, which emphasizes a group-informed yet singular human voice. In Jazz *many* singular voices are brought together to comment musically on a particular idea. Jazz expands from the singular human voice, typically found in Blues, and employs the musical instruments to elaborate on the guiding idea. For many Jazz musicians, the human voice is one among the many other musical instruments that comment, in their own innovative way, on the musical idea that shapes a particular performance. Jazz musicians, in fact, oftentimes attempt to replicate, on their instruments, many of the unique musical shadings from Blues and Jazz singing voices.

Jazz is innovative, multifaceted, oblique and direct, deep and shallow. It expands, includes, reshapes, and elaborates. It makes no claims on the permanence of its form, on its purity, or on its originality. Jazz musicians recognize that there are many approaches to a constantly "changing same."[11] Jazz philosophy embodies the idea that there is a space for one to go beyond the margin into the unknown in order to change the rules within the existing structure, to present the "unpresentable," to say the unsanctioned. In this space, "contemplating chaos" (Morrison, *Playing* 7) becomes possible and living in it is necessary for triumph or survival. Through music, Jazz creates a space for this survival or triumph, even when these concepts seem impossible.

Jazz, in contrast to both Spirituals and Blues, is from but is not anchored in a group. In Jazz, one's innovative personal style results from a conglomeration of fragments from experience; there is not just one body of shared knowledge that informs Jazz. Hence, Jazz evinces personal voices that are not situated as a singular expression within one group discourse, such as Blues, that informs it. Jazz enacts collective improvisation—many distinct, personal voices gathering to respond simultaneously to an idea.

Jazz finds its most powerful social impetus in the migration of African Americans following both wars at the first half of the twentieth century. These experiences of migration expose masses of black people to new varieties of life, and African American war experiences as well as postwar violence against black veterans open new ground for resistance to the racialized social policy of an emerging world democratic power. Jazz suggests a sense of urgency, and its refusal to remain situated in a fixed position allows it to collect African Americans' lived experiences, which include early-twentieth-century moves against social and political injustice.

All three musical approaches have moved into fiction by a number of African American writers. This musical influence in African American literature makes it possible for us to locate in African American fiction elements from the informing discourses that have shaped African American music. The ten literary texts that I will read as situated within a literary-musical discourse (a discourse that informs numerous African American narratives throughout most of the twentieth century) illustrate the operations of music in literature within time and demonstrate the prevalence of differing varieties of this discourse over time.

Music as a metaphor in African American literature, but in fiction in particular, is a distinct cultural practice. I investigate this practice in narrative texts by African American writers and explain how the material conditions that construct a generalized historical-social-political as well as cultural discourse shaping the lived experiences of African American people have moved into fictional texts through a process of intertextuality; I do not, of course, reconstitute all of the historical-sociopolitical or cultural contexts. One clearly is hard-pressed to find such a reconstitution in any one text. This also is not a study of sources and influences in the traditional sense of such literary endeavors. I interrogate the textuality of an African American music-into-literature discourse as a textuality of dissemination. This means then that I approach the concepts of text and textuality in their broad poststructuralist sense as intersecting sign systems that are freed from fixity.[12] In this study, the literary text is situated as one intersection from which we depart in order to traverse a broad terrain.

Music, then, as a metaphor in African American fiction, enacts intertextuality in time and over time, an intertextual process articulated by Julia Kristeva in the French edition of *La Révolution du langage poétique*.[13] Among other scholars who articulate approaches to intertextuality, there is on the one hand—from a Barthesan diachronic sense of textual influence—the view that literature is made as each new text replicates and expands acknowledged as well as unrecognized influences from predecessor texts: "any text is an intertext; other texts are present in it, at varying levels, in more or less recognisable forms: the texts of the previous and surrounding culture" (Barthes 39). On the other hand, literary texts within synchronic intertextuality as posited by Louis Montrose, Stephen Greenblatt, and Mikhail Bakhtin are shaped by and shape the social energies of their times. Intertextuality operates in these texts through their participation in shared codes—which are located in the cultural, political, and social discourses—that are articulated and simultaneously transformed within the contemporary moment of the literary text, enacting a process of rupture and continuity.[14]

I also situate this approach to reading music in literature within Michel Foucault's concept of discursive formations as a means by which to interrogate the movement of music-into-literature. Spirituals, Blues, and Jazz, along with their operation out of specific social, cultural, and historical formations, have discrete expressive configurations in African American fiction. These expressive configurations inform what Foucault terms "discursive formations." Discursive formations or discourses are knowledge bases for which the rules—both explicit and implicit—that construct their formation also inform the agency of individuals who operate within the discourses. A discourse, then, operates as a meeting place of social, political, historical, and cultural forces that have consolidated into a knowledge base. I interrogate Spiritual-Gospel, Blues, and Jazz as texts—or the intersection of multiple discourses—that operate together as well as separately and distinctly in African American culture as a "body of rules." This ability of Spiritual-Gospel, Blues, and Jazz to exist together and to form rules within a social, historical, and political construct makes it possible for these three types of music to operate in a number of sites within the culture, including music as the site of a plenitudinous metaphor that opens readers up to issues of aesthetics and philosophy in African American fiction (Foucault 27–39).

Spiritual-Gospel, Blues, and Jazz suggest an aesthetic that recognizes beauty where it is least acknowledged in Western culture. This aesthetic often is situated in the muck and mire of society's margins: slave quarters, jook joints, speakeasies, shotgun houses, black bottoms, urban communities, and even the sublime beauty located in justified anger found in art. In this music, one also finds a philosophical position—a discussion with one's self and with society—concerning the way in which a person negotiates the world in which she is situated.

A discourse, such as music, consists in a body of rules—always subject to transformation and change—that are shaped by and within a particular social construct. Texts, including literature, are entities that are impacted by the various discourses (body of rules) with which they interact and on which they also have some influence. Spirituals bring to fiction a discourse consisting in a communal cry of the human spirit in bondage, expressed through a fluid form that recontextualizes the Bible, Isaac Watts's and Charles (brother of Methodist founder John) Wesley's hymns, and any other social element that the makers of the Spirituals found viable for their purposes. In Blues we do not find a static form. The typical three-line stanza, in the United States, seems particularly linked to Blues and may operate as an African residual,[15] yet it is strikingly expressed ideas that represent the dominant aesthetic practice in Blues. Through its shifting basic shape and through absorbing and reshaping other musical texts, as well as social and cultural intertexts, Blues evinces in fiction group-informed yet open-ended singular approaches to human problems.[16]

Jazz, as an extension and elaboration of earlier African American musical expression, enacts its inter-texts with Spirituals and Blues, while breaking all boundaries that limit expression, even in African American fiction. In Jazz, one finds broad intertextual connections, ranging from the musical influences mentioned above to classical music and nursery rhymes.[17]

African American music has been consistently situated in a decentered position in relation to the dominant discourse. From an African American intracultural perspective, however, free subjectivity is complicated—in both music and fiction—by political and social realities in the United States, which paradoxically have implicitly imposed an impetus toward cohesiveness on black people in the land of the free and individual. In Jazz as well as in Jazz as a metaphor in fiction, musicians such as Charlie "Bird" Parker, John Birks "Dizzy" Gillespie, Thelonious Sphere Monk, Miles Dewey Davis III, Ornette Coleman, John Coltrane, along with Jazz characters such as Wallace Thurman's Alva, Zora Neale Hurston's Tea Cake, John Edgar Wideman's Albert

Wilkes, and Ralph Ellison's Rinehart enact a double pulling away from the limitations imposed by the dominant culture as well as those imposed by African American culture.

An Approach to Reading Texts

The following descriptions of a discourse of music in the fiction of ten African American writers from the first eight decades of the twentieth century will illustrate the distinct operations of music as a metaphor that collects as a body of rules or discursive formations shaping character and theme in this literature. Within the context of this study, music as a metaphor in African American fiction forms a music-literary discursive formation, a body of rules. These literary uses of music, however, do not directly replicate the musical practices of Spirituals, Blues, and Jazz. In fiction, African American writers who construct Spiritual-Gospel themes and characters, in contrast to their antebellum musical predecessors, are informed by an early-twentieth-century African American idea of religion and rely on the revealed will of God for solutions. Similar, though, to its enslaved musical counterparts, literary Spiritual-Gospel is shaped by repetition and may resist the strictly linear as well as the simply rational.

Blues in African American fiction recalls an antebellum Spiritual idea that uses the internal resources of one's individual will—some of which may be spiritual—to find solutions. In Blues music as a metaphor in fiction, the religious doctrines that the twentieth-century brings into Spiritual-Gospel music do not necessarily affect one's Blues solutions; such solutions can be found without resort to institutionalized religion. Additionally, Blues literary texts most often have an open-ended, often linear, narrative within which the ground of a basic Blues pattern is shaped and reshaped by singular responses.

Spiritual-Gospel communal philosophy and Blues community philosophies are situated in group connections that inform the ground of their music-into-fiction discourses. Both types of music, then, as expressed in the themes and characters of musically informed African American fiction are similar, with one conspicuous distinction: in a text that represents Spiritual-Gospel philosophy, earthly survival is a transitory state that results in heavenly triumph. Fictional texts or characters that are informed primarily by Spiritual-Gospel philosophy instantiate earthly survival as a transitory state and heavenly triumph as a victory. Spiritual-Gospel characters and themes do not emphasize human agency, and these texts also indicate that all fortuitous events occur through the will of God.

Blues characters and themes do not operate in this way; for Blues characters or themes with Blues—which both mark a clear distinction from characters and themes in Spiritual-Gospel Text—one's internal resources (emotional strength, spiritual belief, intellect, wit, and so on) are not bracketed. These resources are required to traverse the new terrain of modernity and its newly shaped twentieth-century processes for delimiting black people. The basis for Blues resources and singular solutions, though, are still informed by group ideas. There is, however, an important similarity between Spiritual-Gospel and Blues music as metaphors in fiction. Through a writer's development of theme or delineation of character, both Spiritual-Gospel and Blues philosophies affirm hope or triumph. It is the writer's locus of authority from which the triumph is produced that distinguishes these two musical expressions in fiction: a singular Blues person or an omnipotent spiritual power.

Blues music speaks to the travails of the moment, to "trouble in mind," and to singular existential moves against becoming mired in the chaos of the moment, an attitude easily located in the songs of Gertrude "Ma" Rainey (Gertrude Pridgett) and Bessie Smith. Both women, in their music, respond to Blues life with strength and tough-minded resolve. Ma Rainey's "Yonder Come the Blues" and "Counting the Blues" convey this Blues resilience, as do Bessie Smith's "Reckless Blues" and "Young Woman's Blues" and Alberta Hunter's "Down Hearted Blues" (also recorded by Bessie Smith) and "I've Got a Mind to Ramble." Central to Blues as a metaphor in fiction is the writer's representation of the ability of the human spirit to go beyond the difficulties and disappointments in life as well as to engage in pragmatic spiritual triumph on earth. Literary Blues is a response to a persistent environment of estrangement, alienation, change, uncertainty, urbanization, and fragmentation, without resort to debilitating despair or perpetual lamentation. Within this context, literary Blues is an artistic mechanism for depicting how an understanding of the group informs a person's strategies for moving through the fire of chaos into triumph. Fictional characters and themes are read as literary Blues when they clearly have a type of hope—supported by the group—that Langston Hughes describes as "I'm-gonna-be-happy-anyhow-in-spite-of-this-world" ("Jazz" 492–93).

Past disappointments and current personal struggles are significant in shaping texts that depict a Blues-informed philosophy; these Blues texts illustrate how disappointment becomes a triumph of the will in a fully lived Blues life. A Blues philosophy in literature, then, exemplifies group-informed triumphs of the human spirit, as demonstrated through singular strength of will, which is apparent in most of the Blues characters in this study. Sometimes, however, Blues triumphs are limited to mere survival. Blues characters that triumph in survival or by surviving do so at great expense. Such survival, though, is its own victory, as is the case for Nella Larsen's Helga Crane.

Finally, neither Blues in fiction nor Spiritual-Gospel in fiction traverses new realms. Exploration is the domain of Jazz. Jazz retains the ideas, except heavenly triumph, in Blues and Spiritual-Gospel expressions. The back beat or rhythmic basis in Jazz locates its intertextuality in gospel and Blues, both of which are influenced by Spirituals. Jazz as a metaphor in fiction includes Blues and gospel polyphony—melody or personal expression—that is syncopated with other distinct melodies or voices. Jazz also includes polyrhythms—contrasting rhythms or personal expressions voiced concurrently. In this way Jazz philosophy is simultaneously an expression of shared experiences and group solutions from the Spirituals, a singular expression of personal solutions to group conditions found in the Blues, and multivocal Jazz expressions that carry fragments of shared ideas which serve as catalysts for multifarious expressions of innovative personal style. Jazz, then, expands into polyrhythmic sounds that resonate from a Blues/Spiritual fragment/chord into a simultaneous expression of distinct, not harmonized, voices, such as we hear in the music of Charlie Parker, including tunes such as "Yardbird Suite," "Ornithology," "Cool Blues," and "The Hymn," as well as in the Dizzy Gillespie tunes "Bebop" and "Night in Tunisia," among others.

In fiction these multivocal expressions reveal a space for infinite options, radical change, resistance, and revolution. Jazz is a contrapuntal expression of innovative personal style that moves away from but does not totally escape the underlying rhythms and melodies of the group. Jazz breaks the linear narrative form that is suggested by Blues. Instead, Jazz uses the stories told in the music of the Blues or fragments of those stories in a multiple-voiced discursive retelling of Blues experiences. The multivocal space created by a Jazz aesthetics and philosophy is most often marginalized in African American fiction. These marginalized elements represent resistance that often is implied, yet frequently not stated overtly, in the Blues. There are, then, literary Jazz characters and themes in African American fiction, but they often are placed at the edges of African American fiction and made disjunct or not fully narrativized in the way that a Blues philosophy is most often represented.

A writer's marginalization of a Jazz space enacts in literature one of the paradoxes embedded in the music of black people in the United States. Literary Jazz may be presented in a way that illustrates nonconforming movement within a chaotic and often hostile society, while literary Blues will likely point to a desire for a position within the existing power structure. With literary Blues, societal restrictions on one's desires result in writers emphasizing the injustice of this position of exclusion from that to which they or their characters desire access while marginalizing rebellion, radical resistance, and revolutionary change as responses to an unjust society. These marginalized elements challenge the elasticity of the literature, testing how far it will expand before it no longer holds resistant members as they move away from the margin. Finally, literary Jazz is situated in the concept of unique expressions of personal style contrasted with as well as coexistent with the collectivity implied in Spiritual-Gospel and Blues music.

In literary Jazz, writers depict character and theme as representations of a confident, yet not necessarily consistent (except consistently changing), personality within a social context that may not support such confidence and multiplicity. Jazz philosophy is situated in a fragmented connection to group ideas and thus is not totally disconnected from tradition; yet, at the same time, literary Jazz emphasizes innovation that branches from the small core of tradition that remains. The paradoxes and contradictions that make up African American life combine in the music of Jazz and in African American fiction. These paradoxes include nebulous color distinctions, Jim Crow laws as unfree freedom from enslavement, as well as an undemocratic existence in a purportedly democratic society. African American musical expression reveals that the lives of black people in the New Canaan have been lives lived in paradox, an idea that is corroborated in Jazz aesthetics and philosophy. Jazz, then, is an innovative perspective on traditional ideas and at the same time it is a deeply personal response to life. Neither the past, the present, nor the new are summarily rejected.

In many African American fictional texts, Blues, Spiritual-Gospel, and Jazz are synthesizing terms from music that collect the polysemous qualities of life deeply felt and broadly experienced. Music is the most abstract artistic means through which life is expressed. There is no limit on the literary themes and characters that writers have and can present through music as a metaphor within this African American music-literature discourse. In addition to responding to the historical-socio-political discourses that shape the music, African American writers fill their narratives with Blues People, or literary characters who have internalized the philosophical concepts and ideas that are situated in Blues and shape Blues communities. Narratives by writers such as Zora Neale Hurston, John Edgar Wideman, and Albert Murray, as illustrated in this study, also employ Spiritual-Gospel, Blues, and Jazz musical strategies, such as worrying the line and riffing—important musical strategies that have moved into African American fiction.

Worrying the line in literature is a type of slant repetition;[18] it is not mere repetition but repetition with some alteration of the phrase, an alteration that will impress on the reader's mind the importance of the idea being conveyed. Albert Murray's style in *Train Whistle Guitar* illustrates, to great effect, fictional uses of worrying the line. If readers are unclear about the importance of Blues to Murray's novel, his passages that recapitulate the numerous "blue" elements in his main character's life creatively worry skeptics into belief. When writers such as Murray worry the line in fiction, they suggest the vernacular uses of repetition as emphasis and as a mnemonic device, techniques that influence the styles of Blues and Jazz musicians.

Jazz riffs are another kind of repetition. By their uses of riffs in fiction, writers repeat or resonate an idea throughout their narratives by strategically situating in their text a Spiritual-Gospel, Blues, or Jazz tune, a nonmusical word or phrase, or an enigmatic character.[19] Riffing, unlike worrying the line, is a subtle echoing effect that is used within a text to resound and often reformulate an important concept or key idea found within the narrative or located in a resonant external text. Such riffs are a type of repetition not only because they recur in the literary text but also because of their allusive qualities when they are references to extratextual predecessors. Readers' knowledge of extratextual references or attention to intratextual predecessors enriches their reading of the narrative. The connection between the narrative ideas and a riff is not always immediately apparent to readers. This is the case for Ralph

Ellison's use of the grandfather as a riff in his novel *Invisible Man*. By the conclusion of his novel, Ellison, in fact, leaves open a number of interpretative possibilities for his grandfather character.

Another type of riff occurs when a writer momentarily introduces into a literary text, through the speech of a character, a brief, subtle musical fragment. With this type of riffing, the writer does not necessarily repeat the musical fragment throughout the text and does not call attention to the fact that the fragment is from a musical source. This riff also is allusive; it resounds a musical text in order to emphasize/repeat in the narrative a specific idea that is collected in the musical tune. Zora Neale Hurston in *Their Eyes Were Watching God* and John Edgar Wideman in *Sent for You Yesterday* place musical phrases in their characters' mouths. The riffs, in these fictional texts, as in lived experiences, serve as parables or cultural wisdom. For the purposes of clarity, this second type of riff is termed a "verbal riff."

In the music of black people in the United States we find the same human, social, aesthetic, and political concerns that also are in African American narrative. In Blues, Jazz, and Spiritual-Gospel aesthetics among African Americans, music is a palimpsest that uses techniques such as pastiche (satirically and for expansion of an idea), montage, and mélange separately and at once with pleasing results; this music has been turned toward its literary uses by African American writers. Both the music and the fiction resist fixation, and both value the insights of the incongruent voices (flatted thirds and sevenths/blue notes and flatted fifths/bebop sounds).

The chapters that follow will demonstrate that music is a distinct influence in a number of African American fictional texts not only as presented through the titles of stories and novels and through quotations from songs but also in the shaping of thematic content and characterization. These uses of music are both deliberate on the part of many writers as well as intertextual in the sense that we may refer to as cultural historicism, by which I mean my positioning of a literary text within a particularly selective discursive moment in its history, while reading through the contemporary moment that shapes my own understanding of traces from the past. This concept is articulated most effectively by Louis Montrose in "Texts and Histories," his prologue to *The Purpose of Playing*. In that essay Montrose raises the question of reading literary texts as a "dialogue between *poetics* and *politics* of culture" (16). He further observes that our contemporary position concerning history and literature is most effectively defined as an interpretive process that accounts for the "historicity of texts and the textuality of history," by which Montrose means that literature is situated in a particular "historical specificity" and that history can never be recuperated in any sense that demonstrates "a full and authentic past." More important, though, Montrose states that the historical traces that survive do not do so simply by chance, and that historical-cultural survivals "must be presumed to be at least partially consequent upon complex and subtle social processes of selective preservation and effacement" (5–6), an approach that seems to me to describe the process by which African American music has persisted as a consistent force in African American as well as American culture and thus become an intertextual influence in African American fiction.

At the intersection of literature and music, I locate an intertextual relationship between social-historical experiences and the formation of cultural ideas. Numerous versions of this position, in relation to Blues and Jazz as well as other African American artistic products, are taken up by Albert Murray, Richard Wright, Amiri Baraka, and others. What this means in terms of music as a metaphor that refers to the life we find in African American fiction is that we must view the music—as it finds it way into fiction—as part of a historical moment that is involved in the connective social energies of the times.[20] This does not mean that the music and the fiction fail to speak outside their times, only that we expand our knowledge of the music, the fiction, and the times by viewing them in conjunction with one another. History and context, then, are important to a thorough understanding of the shaping influences of any art.

The following readings of a music-literary discourse in fiction are situated within a similar historical context as the one that Stephen Greenblatt and Louis Montrose define in their studies that discuss the convergence of poetics and politics. In the preceding discussion, I have described a music-literary discursive formation that I will use in the rest of this study to read nine novels and James Baldwin's short story "Sonny's Blues." These literary texts are illustrative of the synchronic as well as the diachronic intertextual uses of music as a metaphor in fiction. I take as my premise the concept that Blues and Jazz collect ideas that make this music metaphorical sites for human emotion and experience as they are found in many African American narratives. My readings of these texts will illustrate instances of a music-literary discourse in African American fiction during the first eight decades of the twentieth century.

I do not present these readings as final or definitive ways to engage this subject nor these literary texts. Yet I hope that others will find that this approach to music in African American fiction can produce rich readings of a music-literary discourse in these and other narrative texts by African American writers.

two

STORMY BLUES
From the Folk into Literary Form

The opening of the twentieth century is a crossroads at which old folk forms and dominant literate forms meet in African American literature. This is an era of reawakened northward migration of African American people, an issue that arises in both Paul Laurence Dunbar's novel *The Sport of the Gods* and Nella Larsen's *Quicksand*. Farah Jasmine Griffin, in fact, refers to Dunbar's novel as the first migration novel in African American fiction (25). Griffin locates migration narratives in literary, musical, and visual media, all of which she views as sites that collect the migration experiences in African American culture. This also is an era when urban migration reveals the insufficiencies of Booker T. Washington's plans for positioning black people within a form of rural industrial education. By the second decade of the twentieth century, black people are becoming more urban, and a burgeoning northern machine economy is displacing a preindustrial rural agrarian economy.[1] In Harlem, during the early decades of the twentieth century, for instance, black residents begin to move into homes that were built in 1891 for wealthy white residents.

These homes are located on West 138th and 139th between Seventh and Eighth Streets; in the 1920s, Harlem residents refer to this block of homes as Strivers Row because of the proximity of these homes to their even wealthier neighbors in the Sugar Hill area.

New Negro era writer Wallace Thurman's book *The Blacker the Berry . . . : A Novel of Negro Life*, to a lesser degree than the novels in this study by Dunbar and Thurman's fellow New Negro writer Larsen, involves northward migration in search of greater opportunity. Dunbar and Larsen, in contrast to Thurman, explicitly engage issues of white supremacy, including internalized forms of it by black people, and social domination as key issues motivating their characters' migration. This northward migration and its increased opportunity for upward mobility, both educationally and economically, during the Harlem/New Negro Renaissance, found its most telling demonstration at A'Lelia Walker's literary salon at her mansion located at 108 West 136th, established in 1928, and referred to as the Dark Tower, a name she took from Countee Cullen's poem and his literary column in *Opportunity* magazine. The walls of the salon were painted with the words from "The Dark Tower" and Langston Hughes's poem "The Weary Blues."

From 1910 to 1920 the number of black people migrating into Chicago from the South reaches fifty thousand, making the early decades of this century a social, historical, and cultural nexus (Griffin 49).[2] The reasons for African American northern migration are multiple, yet most often black migrants to the North seek economic opportunities as well as escape from southern oppression such as lynching. In African American literature, though, lynching serves as a metaphor that evokes unimaginable horrors. This metaphor continues to function as an important vehicle by which African American writers move their characters north ward while also critiquing the racialized social policies of the United States. While lynching is not a motivating factor for the migration of Larsen's and Thurman's female characters, in broader applications of the term, a courtroom lynching of Berry Hamilton is the reason for the migration of Hamilton's wife and children in Dunbar's novel.[3]

Ida B. Wells-Barnett's Anti-Lynching League documents the early part of this century as a period when black people in the United States have good cause to fear the violence of white people against them.[4] Barnett's longtime activist challenges to lynching, through her Anti-Lynching League and her Negro Fellowship League, give momentum to the increased anti-lynching activity in 1919 of the biracially organized

National Association for the Advancement of Colored People (NAACP). Walter White, assistant secretary of the NAACP, becomes this organization's principal investigator of lynching. In 1919, the NAACP establishes a significant defense fund to challenge lynching. This fund includes a substantial donation from the wealthy businesswoman Madame C. J. Walker (Sarah Breedlove), the mother of A'Lelia Walker.[5] The historian Rayford Logan reports that during the first decade of the twentieth century there is an increase of slightly more than 10 percent over the previous decade in the percentage of lynchings in the formerly Confederate South as well as in Missouri and in the soon-to-be new state of Oklahoma. During this ten-year period 91.1 percent of all lynchings occurred in the above states and 11.4 percent of those lynched were white people (348). The work of Barnett, the Tuskegee Institute, and others record at least 754 lynchings of black people in the first decade of the twentieth century. The formerly enslaved and the descendants of formerly enslaved people—as did enslaved black people—seek refuge in imperfect northern cities, which are increasingly becoming modernist, industrial, urban centers.

African American responses to lynchings and to a social policy of northern as well as southern white supremacy in the first and second decades of the twentieth century include (a) organized protests; (b) politicized religious organizations such as Noble Drew Ali's (Timothy Drew) Moorish Science Temple; Elder Micheaux's Church of God movement; the African Orthodox Church, founded by George Alexander McGuire; and the Ahmadiyya branch of orthodox Islam;[6] (c) self-help organizations such as Marcus Garvey's Universal Negro Improvement Association (UNIA); (d) civil rights organizations, most notably the NAACP, which is formed in 1909 after Du Bois's Niagara movement—established in 1905—joins forces with a biracial coalition; and (e) spontaneous resistance such as the Red (bloody) Summer of 1919.[7]

In 1919 violence erupts in a number of (mostly northern) cities and towns across the country, as African Americans respond to violent attacks on veterans and other black people who insist that the United States stay true to its professed discourse of freedom and democracy. In Chicago, among the worst of that summer's melees, several days of violence occur after a black youth is killed when he crosses into the section of the beach reserved for white swimmers at Lake Michigan. In this year, Claude McKay publishes his poem "If We Must Die" in the *Liberator*. McKay's poem captures the sentiments of many black people regarding the events of the summer of 1919. Fewer than two years later, in 1921, the all-black community of Greenwood in Tulsa, Oklahoma, is ravaged by white vigilante mobs; in 1923 the black town of Rosewood, Florida, is similarly despoiled. Against the odds, the black residents in both communities, unsuccessfully, attempt to protect their livelihood and property against these attacks.

In the political realm, by 1922 black sharecroppers in Elaine, Arkansas—the town where Richard Wright's Uncle was found murdered five years earlier—form a union. This action results in deaths, torture by vigilantes, and arrests of the black sharecroppers who were deemed "Black Revolutionaries." Those sharecroppers who live to face the kangaroo court are condemned to death, until Ida B. Wells-Barnett publishes her pamphlet *The Arkansas Race Riot*. This pamphlet brings a rash of negative publicity, and the remaining men eventually are freed after the Supreme Court rules that their trials were unjust (Decosta-Willis 193).

By the third decade of this century the effects of the Depression deepen African Americans' attention to their marginal position within the economic, social, political, and cultural discourse of the dominant society. Increasingly, lynching is taken into the courtrooms instead of the backwoods. Throughout the 1930s, black people continue to resist racialized social policies, just as they had in the previous two decades. Spontaneous outbreaks, similar to the ones in 1919, also continue in the 1930s. In 1935, for instance, black people demonstrate their frustration through melees such as the Harlem rebellion, which follows the beating of Lino Rivera by a white store clerk.

Also, in this era of a national economic downturn, African Americans continue to establish organizations that are firmly situated in a conservative and bourgeois ideology yet are fervently positioned in a discourse that rejects white supremacy. In northern cities such as Detroit, black groups including the Nation of Islam, which was established in Detroit in 1930 (later in the decade locating its headquarters in Chicago), and the Beth B'nai Abraham Synagogue, which was organized by Wentworth Arthur Matthews and Arnold Josiah Ford in Harlem in 1924 but in 1930 was reorganized as the Commandment Keepers of the Living God (also referred to as the Black Jews), make religion the site of a Garvey-like discourse of nationalism among its followers.

In the political and social arena, there is a secular parallel to early politicized religious organizations in black groups, such as the labor-based National Negro Congress (NNC), which positions itself as a more radical organization than the liberal NAACP. The NNC's southern youth division is established in 1937, as the South is seen as the most blatant transgressor on the rights of back people, who comprise a large number of the laborers in the region. Following formation of the youth division, some of the division's members organize the radical Southern Negro Youth Congress (SNYC)[8] in Richmond, Virginia, to fight white supremacy throughout the South, an important move that inaugurates organized resistance by black, southern youth. In the 1930s membership in this labor-influenced organization includes Birmingham, Alabama's Sallye Davis, the mother of Angela Davis. Also during this time, black club women—the members of the National Council of Negro Women (1935) and Jack and Jill (1938), for example—establish the ground for an era of organized political and social resistance among the slightly expanding numbers of black women who are more comfortably situated than the mass of black women.

In Alabama, the 1931 Scottsboro case of the nine youths and young men who were falsely arrested, then wrongly convicted and sentenced to death on spurious charges of raping two white women becomes emblematic of the new social policy of containment for African American people, particularly males. This case finds the NAACP unprepared to respond to the widespread outrage this injustice generates. After years of persistent agitation within the organization by prominent attorney Charles Houston, the NAACP becomes responsive to mass-based activist issues.[9] In 1933 the NAACP begins to use the courts to change educational policies that segregate schools; their first case is against the University of North Carolina. Yet the danger to the NAACP and others who pursue similar cases is illustrated by the Supreme Court's 1938 ruling in favor of the plaintiff in *Gaines v. Canada*, a ruling that orders states to provide equal professional school and graduate education for black students in their home states (W. Martin 25, 117–18). The plaintiff in this case, a Missouri native named Lloyd Gaines, disappears after the favorable ruling and is never heard from again.

President Franklin D. Roosevelt's New Deal and his Black Cabinet during his first administration help usher in the shift in black voters from the Republican to the Democratic Party and contribute to Roosevelt's success in winning a second term. These black votes are primarily those of African Americans in the North, as the voting rights of black people in the South are severely abridged by poll taxes and literacy tests; and when those restrictions are ineffective deterrents, established social policies and other forms of white supremacy in the South prove effective measures against the suffrage of black people.

In the arts, early-twentieth-century painters such as Archibald Motley, elder brother of 1940s writer Willard Motley, depict urban life and convey a range of experiences from the mundane *Woman Peeling Apples* to jazzy dance hall scenes in his paintings titled *Syncopation, Saturday Night, Stomp*, and *Blues*. Motley also paints imaginative scenes of Africa in *Waganda Charm Maker* and *Kikuyu God of Fire*. Aaron Douglas arrives in New York in 1925. His artistic rendering, in black-and-white sketches, of James Weldon Johnson's *God's Trombones* (1925) demonstrates his characteristically angular style. His drawings also are included in Alain Locke's anthology *The New Negro*, which also is published in 1925.

Sculptors such as Meta Vaux Warrick Fuller and Augusta Savage gain national prominence for their works in the early decades of this century. Augusta Savage's well-known sculpture *The Harp* is based on James Weldon Johnson's composition "Lift Every Voice and Sing," written in 1900 to commemorate Abraham Lincoln's birthday.[10] The World's Fair committee commissions a sculpture by Savage for the 1939 New York World's Fair. Also during the 1930s, under the tutelage of Charles Seifert, a respected self-taught scholar in African art, painters such as Robert Savon Pious and Earl R. Sweeting make new versions of biblical images that depict Egyptians as well as the Madonna and child as black people. In 1931, Katherine Dunham's Negro Dance Group is organized in Chicago. And throughout the 1920s and 1930s photographer James Van Der Zee—whose pictures of Marcus Garvey's UNIA events provide an excellent historical record—documents this era in Harlem.

Many artists and writers, including Charles Alston, Jacob Lawrence, Ralph Ellison and Zora Neale Hurston, Willard Motley, and Richard Wright, work in President Roosevelt's WPA (Works Progress Administration, or, after 1939, Work Projects Administration) Federal Writers, Theater, and Arts Projects. In Wright's collection of short stories, *Uncle Tom's Children*, published in 1938, he employs Spirituals as well as the black sermonic tradition throughout, yet Wright's rejection of Jazz situates him within the aesthetic narrative of Paul Laurence Dunbar, a narrative that rejects the transformation of Spirituals as they move into the modern world.[11]

Alston's 1935 WPA mural still is a landmark at the Harlem Hospital. Alston, with the support of the WPA, also teaches beyond-capacity art classes at the 135th Street library in Harlem in the 1930s. As a result of the demand for the classes offered through this program, Alston establishes another class site at 306 West 141st Street. During discussions in Alston's apartment above this second studio—referred to as 306—and after hearing Charles Seifert lecture at the 135th Street library, Jacob Lawrence is encouraged to paint his forty-one-piece *Toussaint L'Ouverture* series, completed in 1938. In the late 1930s, Alston's close friend and later his artistic collaborator Hale Woodruff completes his *Amistad* mural at Talladega College in Alabama.

Recordings of black music and musicians begins early in the twentieth century. In 1901 Bert Williams and George Walker record with the Victor Talking Machine Company; this year also marks the beginning of a series of Fisk Jubilee Quartet recordings, which the company produces until 1917. The year 1917 also marks James Reese Europe's recording of W. C. Handy's "Memphis Blues." Reese is the first musician to record Handy's tune, which now is a Jazz standard.[12] The year 1912 is a propitious one for the Blues, as three justifiably labeled Blues titles find their way into print: "Baby Seals Blues," "Dallas," and "Memphis Blues." Wilbur Sweatman's 1903 recording of Scott Joplin's "Maple Leaf Rag" is the first recording by a dance band, and in the early 1920s Sweatman records Blues tunes on the Pathé record label; these recordings include W. C. Handy's Blues tune "Joe Turner."[13]

In 1920, Mamie Smith and her Jazz Hounds, with Coleman "Bean" Hawkins on tenor sax, record Perry Bradford's song "Crazy Blues" on the Okeh label; this is the first recording of Blues-Jazz and the beginning of the phenomenon termed "race records"—the proliferation of white-owned record labels featuring tunes by black musicians. Within several months of the debut of Perry's "Crazy Blues" on the Okeh label, Harry Pace—following the end of his business relationship with W. C. Handy—establishes the Black Swan recording label, named after nineteenth-century black concert singer Elizabeth Taylor Greenfield, popularly deemed the Black Swan. Pace, in 1921, begins pressing records by black musicians, and in an ironic play on the racial hierarchy of the day and a precursor to the ironies of the club and cabaret scene of the burgeoning Harlem Renaissance, Black Swan markets its recordings as "The Only Genuine Colored Record—Others Are Only Passing for Colored." On the Black Swan label, Pace records Alberta Hunter, Trixie Smith, Ethel Waters, his employee Fletcher Henderson's[14] Novelty Orchestra, and others, yet Pace refuses to record Bessie Smith because he considers her style too rough-edged (Lewis 174). Black Swan's success in the Blues and Jazz market is marked by Pace's profitable recording of Ethel Waters singing "Down Home Blues" and "Oh, Daddy" in 1921.

Six years after the earliest so-called classic Blues recording by Mamie Smith and three years after Bessie Smith's successful recording of Alberta Hunter's "Down Hearted Blues," this music surpasses so-called country Blues in record sales. Sylvester Weaver records the first down-home/country guitar Blues song in 1923; yet down-home Blues music does not gain appreciable record sales until Papa Charlie Jackson's 1924 recording of "Lawdy, Lawdy Blues" (Southern, *The Music* 365–72). If Bessie Smith, Clara Smith, Mamie Smith, Trixie Smith (none of the Smith blueswomen are related), Ma Rainey, Ida Cox, Victoria Spivey, and Sippie Wallace (Beulah Thomas) are signal examples of the classic Blues in the 1920s, then "Memphis Minnie" (Lizzie Douglas), John Lee "Sonny Boy" Williamson, Blind Lemon Jefferson, Charley Patton, William Lee Conley "Big Bill" Broonzy, Tampa Red (Hudson Whittaker/ Woodbridge), "Georgia" Tom Dorsey (also known as Barrelhouse Tom), and Robert Johnson illustrate in their music the lingering musical flavor that is associated with the country Blues of Alabama, Arkansas, Georgia, Louisiana, Mississippi, South Carolina, Tennessee, Texas, and other southern locales. In the 1930s, a number of down-home Blues musicians update their music as they find that recording careers as well as live performances depend on their cultivation of a marketable sound. Many of these musicians freely fashion themselves in the salable mantle of the times, as their predominantly black audiences become more urban than rural and want a polished sound that resonates home. In the early decades of the twentieth century, technologies such as radio and recording help disperse Blues music, including down-home Blues, faster than itinerant Blues musicians had moved it in the past.

Memphis Minnie is one of the few women in the down-home Blues group of musicians and singers. She begins her recording career in 1929 with the song "Bumble Bee," and she makes her mark as an accomplished Blues guitarist and Blues songwriter with songs such as her "Weary Woman Blues." She keeps her music firmly grounded in its rural, southern roots while appealing to an audience that is in a state of transformation from being rural to becoming urban. Other down-home Blues musicians include Big Bill Broonzy, who begins recording music in 1926, and Tampa Red, who records in 1928 and on his second record joins Georgia Tom Dorsey to record the risqué Blues song "It's Tight

Like That." By 1930, Dorsey, as a result of the influence of Charles Albert Tindley, turns to a new type of religious music that he refers to as gospel, and in 1932 he publishes his now widely known gospel song "Take My Hand Precious Lord."

From its early shaping in the nineteenth century out of folk, Spiritual, and work songs, Blues has had numerous performers whose talent ranges from middling to superb. These performers are frequently found in local neighborhoods playing guitar or harp (harmonica) on their porches or at community social events, as Albert Murray illustrates in his novel *Train Whistle Guitar*. These down-home Blues musicians, along with the relatively few who are recorded, the numerous itinerant bluesmen, or those performers who are part of the 1930s territory bands, challenge the language of origins, the tedious hyperbole, and the titillating use of salacious biographical details found in many discussions of excellent down-home Blues musicians such as Robert Johnson, whose contribution to recorded down-home Blues music is *among* the best available.[15] Johnson's recordings are particularly valuable for their preservation of early examples of arhoolies, most poignantly on "Kindhearted Woman Blues" and "Me and the Devil Blues," and for his complicated guitar technique on songs such as "Stop Breaking Down";[16] other Blues musicians, it seems to me, also have a similarly complicated technique—Big Bill Broonzy and Memphis Minnie, for instance.

From 1900 to 1939, this dispersement—mentioned above—of Blues among southern, rural, black people provides a strong basis for discussions of the Blues as an intracultural force, especially within the context of early-twentieth-century technologies such as radio and recording.

Blues continues to have a socio-political turn, even as its popularization through a proliferation of recordings of Blues songs about disappointed love—often disguises this fact. In 1928 and 1929, Blind Lemon Jefferson records "Broke and Hungry" and "Penitentiary Blues." Leroy Carr's "Prison Bound Blues"[17] also is on the market in 1928. The 1931 Scottsboro case prompts folk and Blues singer Huddie Ledbetter, "Leadbelly," to write and record the song "Scottsboro Boys"; Leadbelly also writes biting social commentary in songs such as "Bourgeois Blues."

Jazz gains an early national audience through the new technology of radio, a venue that finds Thomas Wright "Fats" Waller entertaining listeners as early as 1923, and in the late 1920s Duke Ellington's band broadcasts on CBS Radio from the Cotton Club, bringing Ellington national prominence. Count Basie's band broadcasts live in 1936 from the Cherry Blossom, a Kansas City, Missouri, club. Jazz's recording history also is located in the early decades of the twentieth century. Edward "Kid" Ory's Sunshine Orchestra records the first instrumental Jazz record in 1922 in Los Angeles. Joseph "King" Oliver migrates in 1918 from New Orleans' Jazz-filled Storyville to Chicago, joining Bill Johnson's New Orleans Original Band[18] and the developing Jazz scene in this rapidly growing industrial center.

After working with Johnson, Oliver forms his own Creole Jazz Band in 1920. In 1922, Oliver encourages Louis Armstrong, who will ultimately become the musical improviser who draws a national and international audience to Jazz, to join him in Chicago. And in 1927, Oliver, whose dedication to Blues-influenced Jazz music probably causes him to reject an offer to play at the Cotton Club, is known as the musician who gave a lucrative Cotton Club engagement to an eager young musician from Washington, D.C.—Duke Ellington. One of the best known jazzmen is Louis Armstrong ("Satchel Mouth"/"Satchmo"), who records with a number of different bands before he makes his first recordings with his own bands, the Hot Five and the Hot Seven, in 1925. Duke Ellington records "Creole Rhapsody" in 1931 and Fats Waller records "Ain't Misbehavin'" in 1932. In 1934, Ella Fitzgerald, who was born in Virginia but reared in New York, emerges as an early Jazz musician whose singing illustrates an often overlooked Jazz instrument—vocals. Fitzgerald joins drummer Chick Webb's band for a five-year period in which the band finds great success performing and recording. Following Webb's death in 1939, Fitzgerald directs the band until the early 1940s. By the end of the third decade of the twentieth century, in 1939, Billie Holiday records Lewis Allan's song "Strange Fruit," which underscores the horrors of lynching.

Technological modernity enters African American musical life through radio and the mechanical reproduction of music on records, as well as the production of films marketed for an African American audience—race films. Between 1910 and 1950 more than five hundred race films are produced. Early race films, in contrast to early race records, are produced by black-owned companies such as Noble Johnson's Lincoln Motion Picture Company, which produced its first film in 1916. The most prolific African American producer of race films during these early decades is Oscar Micheaux, whose debut film is an adaptation of his own novel *The Homesteader*. This 1918 film is the first feature-length race movie. Paul

Robeson's film debut occurs in Micheaux's 1925 production *Body and Soul*. And in 1923 Micheaux adapts for film Charles Chesnutt's novel *The House Behind the Cedars*. Micheaux also produces a response to D. W. Griffith's racist film *Birth of a Nation* (1915), which is based on a trilogy— *The Leopard's Spots* (1902), a response to Harriet Beecher Stowe's *Uncle Tom's Cabin*, *The Clansmen* (1905), and *The Traitor* (1907)—by Thomas Dixon Jr., a white minister. Griffith's film causes outspoken responses from African Americans, including protests by black club women, who have been rejecting various permutations of the best-selling book *The Clansmen*—including live traveling shows and parades in its honor—since its publication in 1905. Micheaux's film response to *Birth of a Nation*, titled *Within Our Gates*, is released in 1920 and is heavily censored in a number of cities because of fears that it will reignite the racial anger that resulted from Griffith's film. Micheaux's film is not the only production that seeks to revise Griffith's celluloid image of black people. In 1918 the Birth of a Race Photoplay Corporation releases the film *Birth of a Race* to audiences at the Blackstone Theater in Chicago.

Most early-twentieth-century race films, however, are designed to uplift the image of African Americans or to model appropriate morals for recently emancipated black people and their first generation free children in the United States. It is very likely that uplift and morals are the motivating factors that lead the black-owned company Reol Productions to make a film version of Dunbar's novel *The Sport of the Gods*. The 1921 film adaptation was very likely Reol's first production.

In 1929 RCA's Gramercy studios attempts to tap into the African American film market with the film short *St. Louis Blues*. W. C. Handy contributes to the script, and Bessie Smith is cast as Bessie, the female lead role. This film, unfortunately, is rife with racialized stereotypes and sexist ideology, including the violent and financially dependent black man, Jimmy Mordecai, and the victimized black woman who is mesmerized by this stereotypically dangerous black man. The film prompts boycotts by black people who are offended by its racist images. After 1929 race films decline as the economy sinks into an economic depression.

For film scholar Donald Bogle, the film *Imitation of Life* (1934), based on the novel published the previous year by Fannie Hurst, for whom Zora Neale Hurston worked as a secretary in the 1920s, is the "first important 'black film' of the 1930s" (57). This film stars the black actresses Louise Beavers, who plays Delilah, and Freddi Washington, who plays the daughter Peola. Although the film's basic content reinscribes the existing social policy, Peola, the rebellious biracial daughter, not only denies her mother in order to position herself within the dominant society but also defies in fact and in consciousness delimiting racial categories. She is, according to Bogle, a subversive character, a "New Negro demanding a real New Deal" (60). Also in the 1930s, Hollywood beckons and Harlem Renaissance writer Wallace Thurman responds with two screenplays in the "social problem"[19] mode of the day. In 1934 Thurman's first screenplay is released as *Tomorrow's Children*, a film that addresses the question of forced sterilization. The following year, Thurman is the screenwriter for the film *High School Girl*, which investigates the issue of teenaged pregnancy.

In 1927 white performer Al Jolson's burnt-cork rendition of "Mammy" in the *Jazz Singer* brings minstrelsy to film and introduces the talking motion picture. In the 1930s Jazz musicians take swing music onto the big screen. Duke Ellington's band appears in the Amos and Andy movie *Check and Double Check* in 1930. And Fats Waller, whose trickster disposition on stride piano recalls Louis Armstrong's stagecraft,[20] appears in the films *Hooray for Love* (1935) and *King of Burlesque* (1936).

Live musical entertainment continues to have an important place early in the twentieth century, even though films are a new medium in which music also will be situated. In New York, the club and cabaret scene at venues such as Ed Small's Paradise and Harlem's Savoy Ballroom continue the migration and expansion of African American music. Early in this century, the proprietor of Small's Paradise, a black-owned club, seeks a white audience and usually entertains an even mix of white and black customers. The white-owned Savoy opens its doors in 1926. Among the opening night bands at the Savoy is the Rainbow Orchestra, led by Fletcher Henderson. Henderson's Jazz is orchestrated and smooth, a style that is ruthlessly imitated instead of improvised on by Paul Whiteman; this sort of imitation may explain the 1940s and 1950s bebop impetus toward making music that is complicated and difficult to imitate. Different from Small's and the Savoy is Harlem's Cotton Club, which is well known for the topnotch black musicians who play to white audiences there. Illustrating the paradoxical conjoining of race with the founding concepts of the United States, the Cotton Club, early on, does not admit black customers.[21] But in African American neighborhoods and homes in the South as well as in the North, live performances of Blues and bluesy

Jazz—especially piano—permeate house parties, jook joints, and rent parties, where Ma Rainey, Georgia Tom Dorsey, Big Bill Broonzy, or Robert Johnson might be found wailing the Blues or where Fats Waller, James P. Johnson, or Willie "The Lion" Smith might be found striding along the ivories.

The early decades of this century are a time when the Depression and war years result in black people expanding and dispersing African American culture, especially music, into midwestern and northern cities such as St. Louis and Kansas City, Missouri, Philadelphia, Chicago, and New York. Similar to the rural-to-urban movement in the South, which produced Basin Street in New Orleans and Beal Street in Memphis, this northern and western migration of people and culture results in well-known musical districts such as 125th Street or Lenox Avenue in Harlem, Central Avenue in Los Angeles, and Maxwell Street in Chicago, where Chicago Blues reportedly was developed. Papa Charlie Jackson's 1925 recording of "Maxwell Street Blues" documents some aspects of Blues life in the 1920s in Chicago. The migration of southern Blues People results in African Americans encountering a multidimensional, fast, industrial, urbanity that transforms into a new sound, the New Orleans Jazz and the Memphis Blues, as well as the down-home Blues, which move, along with black people, out of rural southern towns.

These decades also find black people in New York stomping at the Savoy and lindy hopping at the Apollo (Count Basie's Orchestra opens at the Apollo in 1937 with vocalists Jimmy Rushing and, from Baltimore, an enthralling female singer named Eleanor Fagan, whom Lester Young dubs Lady Day; most people know her as Billie Holiday); doing the black bottom at the Sunset Cafe, the Pekin Inn, the Vendome, and the Regal in Chicago; swinging at the Howard Theater in Washington, D.C.; jitterbugging at the Royal Theater in Baltimore; shimmying at the Club Alabam (formerly the black-owned Apex nightclub) in Los Angeles; doing the Charleston at the Paradise in Detroit; and jamming all night long at the Cherry Blossom in Kansas City, where in 1933 Lester Young and Coleman Hawkins engage in their well-known, and perhaps apocryphal, saxophone competition. Also in 1933, "Mad Mab" Charlie Barnet brings the first white band to the Apollo Theater and finds success among Harlem's discerning dance hall crowd.

Early in this century, as the 1930s close, African American music's intertextuality finds its earliest overt expression in two different Carnegie

Hall performances. The first such performance is the premier of composer and stride pianist James P. Johnson's rhapsody for symphonic orchestra and piano, *Yamekraw*, in 1928; he is joined by stride pianist Fats Waller, composer and arranger William Grant Still, and Blues composer and conductor W. C. Handy. Johnson's *Yamekraw* includes music based in Spirituals and Blues. The other performance is John Hammond's famous 1938 and 1939 From Spirituals to Swing concerts, which include performances by Joe Turner, Sonny Terry, Charlie Christian, Jimmy Rushing (Mr. Five-by-Five), Big Bill Broonzy,[22] Count Basie, Lester Young, James P. Johnson, Sidney Bechet, and a number of white Jazz musicians. The Golden Gate Quartet, Sister Rosetta Tharpe, among others, perform Spiritual-Gospel music at Hammond's concert.

Also in 1938, boxer Joe Louis wins his second bout—after losing in 1936—against Max Schmeling. This feat raises Louis to hero status among many black people, who see him as a representative of the potential for change in the status of racial relations in the United States, as Louis, through his victory over Nazi Germany's Schmeling, becomes an international symbol for democratic values.

The New Negro Renaissance, of which Larsen and Thurman were participants, spans the second decade of the twentieth century. As an important site of artistic production, the Harlem Renaissance is a crucial locus of intertextuality in African American cultural production. Yet the meeting of folk forms and dominant literate forms is expressed in a myriad of ways in the texts of twentieth-century black writers before, during, and, as will be demonstrated in later chapters, beyond the era of marked artistic production that is regularly referred to as the Harlem Renaissance.

In Paul Laurence Dunbar's novel *The Sport of the Gods*, Nella Larsen's *Quicksand*, and Wallace Thurman's *Blacker the Berry*, music moves into literature in three distinct ways. Dunbar critiques Blues life, and at the end of *The Sport of the Gods* he commends a Spiritual-Gospel–like life for the Hamiltons, whose solutions to spirit-crushing incidents in their lives come through the machinations of a greater power. Dunbar then provides a rare example of a Spiritual-Gospel theme in a novel that is not explicitly religious.

Larsen, in contrast to Dunbar, depicts a propitious Blues character in Helga Crane, who finds that she ultimately has no personal or financial resources that will help her satisfactorily conquer the quicksand of gender limitations after she marries and has children. Larsen's biographer, Thadious Davis, explains that Larsen's own life illustrates the difficulties involved in a woman of color's desire for position and power; such aspirations result in Larsen's recognition of "the hypocrisies of the elite, the false promises of the American dream, and the female's ultimate breakdown" (6).[23] These same qualities are present in Larsen's autobiographically influenced protagonist Helga Crane. Thus, Larsen in her novel *Quicksand* critiques gender limitations and portrays how a woman's access to a self-empowering Blues life is circumscribed by gender-related restrictions. Such limitations are especially apparent when we recognize that Larsen does not situate Helga Crane within a discourse of womanist Blues that is located in the music of Alberta Hunter, Bessie Smith, and Ma Rainey; accordingly, her Blues victory is limited to a Blues triumph in survival. Similar limitations are in place when we discuss women and the issue of migration, another social phenomenon that is important in Blues studies. Hazel Carby points out that blueswomen "occupied a privileged space" in terms of mobility; for many women, migration "often meant being left behind" ("It Jus Be's" 751).

In Thurman's novel *The Blacker the Berry*, his main character, Emma Lou Morgan, develops a Blues approach to life after rejecting an oppressive ideology of intracultural color prejudice among black people who revere light skin color and revile dark skin color. The quizzical turns that a racialized discourse makes—among people whose power already is delimited by such discourses—become the focus of Thurman's novel, in which he limns a Blues theme.

Larsen, Thurman, and Dunbar all make reference to black music in their novels. Dunbar uses ragtime and Blues-Jazz music as a counterstatement, a negative example. Larsen and Thurman, however, situate the music that they employ in their novels within the context of African American aesthetics, and they present the music as a social entity that comments on African American life. Dunbar, Larsen, and Thurman situate their novels within the Blues-making contexts of social, economic, and legal distinctions—based in a specious concept of race—that have shaped the lives and cultural products of black people in the United States. Without specific references to Blues aesthetics or philosophy, these writers depict characters and thematic concerns that evince a number of the informing ideas in literary Blues. These three writers' metaphorical uses of music to present character and theme are subtle and resonant, yet all three writers, at some point, situate one of their characters within a musical discourse that calls attention to conflicts of race, culture, and social policy in early-twentieth-century African American life.

Paul Laurence Dunbar: *The Sport of the Gods*

Paul Laurence Dunbar's novel *The Sport of the Gods* (1902) is his last of four novels, and it is the only one in which he focuses on black life. In this novel Dunbar uses eighteenth- and nineteenth-century literary contrivances such as the obligatory faint by a delicate character, melodramatic dialogue tags, and language such as "old chap," and "shan't," which seem anachronistic in a novel set in a small southern town and in New York early in the twentieth century (62, 155, 201). Dunbar's characters, for the most part, are types that represent moral ideas of good and bad. With the exception of Joe Hamilton, Dunbar does not develop his other characters psychologically and emotionally. And Joe, the only character Dunbar allows to learn from his experiences, is degraded by his knowledge. He loses all control, becomes a murderer, and is imprisoned. These occasional lapses demonstrate Dunbar's weaknesses as a novelist, but they do not destroy the value of his novel as a particular literary response to post–Civil War and post-Reconstruction life in the United States and as a text that demonstrates the movement of music into the presentation of literary characters in African American fiction.

In the following reading of literary Blues in Dunbar's *Sport of the Gods* I situate Dunbar's novel in an intertextual music discourse that contrasts Houston Baker's vernacular theory. Baker's position is that Dunbar's novel "gestures toward . . . [the position of] a blues book most excellent" (*Blues* 115). In Baker's vernacular theory, he does not address the historical situatedness of the discursive formations that inform the approach I present in this book. Blues, for Baker, appears to be a transcendent African American cultural marker that results from the historical reality of slavery. In the reading of *The Sport of the Gods* that follows, this novel's historical, social, political, and literary texts intersect both synchronically and diachronically.

After twenty years of trustworthy devotion as servants to the Oakleys and a privileged life among fellow black people, Fannie and Berry Hamilton's lives are disrupted by Mr. Oakley's false charges of theft against Berry. Even after the Oakleys discover their error, they do not rectify the situation by having Berry released from prison, nor do they immediately return the Hamilton family to the cottage behind the Oakleys' mansion, where the Hamiltons lived before Berry's imprisonment. Through his depiction of Mr. Oakley and other members of the southern town where the Hamiltons live, Dunbar delineates the bigoted thought processes of the people who will charge and convict Berry Hamilton based on circumstantial evidence. Berry Hamilton's imprisonment comments on the increasingly prevalent use of the prison system to contain black men. Berry's innocence comments on this in a way that his son's imprisonment later in the novel cannot, even though Mrs. Hamilton views her imprisoned son as society's sacrifice. Dunbar, however, juxtaposes Berry Hamilton's unjust confinement against his son Joe's confinement for a murder that results from Joe's dissipated life-style, which Dunbar associates with the North and with African American secular music.

In the title of his novel, with its allusion to Shakespeare's *King Lear*, Dunbar summarizes the attitudes that contribute to Berry Hamilton's conviction. Within the context of the novel, however, Dunbar's title connotes a number of meanings. It refers to the legally enforced, godlike control that allows a social policy of white supremacy in the United States to retain power over black lives after emancipation. This novel is set during the era of Jim Crow laws and social policies that, after Reconstruction, reestablish an unequal status for black people in the United States. Dunbar presents examples of people from the dominant society who situate themselves as gods and manipulate the lives of others without much consideration for the human consequences that result from their godlike behavior. These self-appointed gods are supported by societal mores and customs as well as by the legal system. The Hamiltons have very little individual recourse against this power, so they must find ways to live in these spirit-shattering conditions without losing themselves. But Dunbar also portrays the Hamiltons as a type of demigod among fellow black people. They have no power or control over the lives of other black people, yet their behavior and possessions—nice cottage home, consistent work, comfortable "things handed down from 'the house'"—exalt them above others, at least in the minds of the Hamiltons (3).

Another meaning associated with Dunbar's title is its reference to the God of organized religion. Dunbar indicates that God's "plan" for the lives of people on earth is so impervious that, until they experience His fortuitous intervention, this "plan" appears to be part of a cruel game by a disinterested higher being. The workings of such a plan are in operation in the lives of the Hamiltons, whom Dunbar depicts as benefiting by such intervention, as it saves them from the corrupt North, affirms the efficacy of their faith, and returns them to Dunbar's sentimentally portrayed South; thus, Dunbar vindicates the Hamiltons through divine intervention, and in the end contrasts their virtuousness with the cancerous corruption of Maurice Oakley, whose mad shrieks remind the Hamiltons of the price of evil. Dunbar depicts the depth of societal corruption through his characterization of Maurice Oakley as the false-god-in-flesh who embodies the racial attitudes of the South during the early twentieth century. In terms of literary predecessors, Oakley is clearly Dunbar's version of Nathaniel Hawthorne's Dimmesdale in *The Scarlet Letter*. The suffering that results from Oakley's letter (hidden in his breast pocket) from his brother, which would vindicate Berry Hamilton, is similar to Dimmesdale's hidden sin. Dunbar makes Oakley representative of societal corruption, as does Hawthorne with Dimmesdale.

In *The Sport of the Gods* Dunbar associates Fannie and Berry Hamilton with the religious sense of the meaning in his title, thereby connecting them to a Spiritual-Gospel life. This is not the case for the Hamiltons' children, who move to New York with their mother as a means of escaping their unjust infamy in the small southern town where they were reared. In the urban North, Kit and Joe Hamilton are in an increasing state of degeneration as a result of their ragtime (an early form of Jazz-Blues piano music that later is transformed into boogie-woogie and stride piano) lives. In this way Dunbar, then, critiques the Blues life of the North. He depicts the urbanization of the Hamiltons as a degenerative move away from tradition. The family becomes increasingly fragmented until, eventually, they are totally estranged. Kit Hamilton, who is barely a shadow in the novel, finally becomes a stage singer; and her future is foreshadowed in the used-up but Blues-fortified Hattie Sterling, whom Kit's brother Joe kills. Joe, who is immersed in Blues life and tries to live that life, is convicted and imprisoned for Hattie's murder.

The family's corruption begins soon after they arrive in New York. Dunbar portrays the beginning of their corruption when he demonstrates Fannie Hamilton's conflicting feelings during a theater performance by black musicians. While Kit and Joe are enthralled, "Mrs. Hamilton was divided between shame at the clothes of some of the women and delight with the music" (103). Later in the evening Mrs. Hamilton's response softens even more: "At first she was surprised at the enthusiasm over just such dancing as she could see any day from the loafers on the street corners down home, and then, like a good, sensible, humble woman, she came around to the idea that it was she who had always been wrong in putting too low a value on really worthy things. So she laughed and applauded with the rest, all the while trying to quiet something that was tugging at her away down in her heart" (106).

Eric Lott characterizes Dunbar's as well as Thurman's fictional uses of the cabaret scene in New York as examples of "some version of racial false consciousness," a view of minstrelsy that Lott[24] complicates and critiques in his book *Love and Theft: Blackface Minstrelsy and the American Working Class* (35). Fannie Hamilton's resistance to the women's sexualized dress and the commercialized packaging of everyday street dancing turns eventually into acceptance. Mrs. Hamilton's acceptance of these urban Blues experiences demonstrates, in Dunbar's terms, her move away from her own Spiritual-Gospel tendencies. Before long, Fannie recognizes that in New York her life is increasingly alienated because "she drifted farther away from her children and husband [who is imprisoned in the South] and all the traditions of her life" (131). For Fannie's son, Joe, however, tradition is not important; it is traditions such as those that his mother supports that have allowed his father to be and to remain imprisoned unjustly. New York, then, becomes a place where he might reshape the pattern that has been set for his life by social policy.

Joe Hamilton and his father Berry are very similar, yet there is one important difference between the two: faith. Under the stress of racialized and personal struggles, Dunbar's Berry and Joe Hamilton both have thoughts of revenge and murder. Clearly, then, Joe actually is not too unlike his father Berry. Dunbar, however, leaves Joe to find solutions through his own resources, which are few and underdeveloped. But Berry is saved by the resources of divine fate, since his moments of anger and revenge are short in comparison to his lifetime of quiet, devoted, and patient behavior, and since, for Dunbar in this novel, Berry's southern social environment does not bring him to the point of scarring his soul through criminal activity and moral weakness.

Joe also lives in an oppressive society, but his life before Berry is imprisoned is one of relative ease. The first sign of disruption in Joe's life occurs when his family is ostracized in the small southern town of his birth, a situation which foments thoughts of anger and revenge: "Of all the family, Joe was the only one who burned with fierce indignation. He knew that his father was innocent, and his very helplessness made a fever in his soul; . . . when he saw his mother's tears and his sister's shame something rose within him that had it been given play might have made a man of him, but, being crushed, died and rotted, and in the compost it made all of the evil of his nature flourish" (60). Later Joe voices his feelings of revenge when he says, "I'd like to cut the heart out of a few of em" (75). His mother discourages this type of thinking, as she realizes the futility and danger in it. Later she also will reject his New York City–based Blues lifestyle because she doesn't recognize the potential of Blues philosophy as a basis for community support against society's oppressive conditions.

The only model for survival that Dunbar's elder Hamiltons offer Joe is one of silence, work, and patience. Joe rejects this model, yet his lifestyle of relative privilege in the South leaves him unable to respond effectively to the struggles into which he is thrust when his life does not replicate his parents' in its positive aspects and only repeats his father's life when Joe is eventually imprisoned. Dunbar also does not provide Joe with enough depth to perceive the viable options available to him in New York. Joe, then, is left without any internal resources for survival; he does not understand how to use Blues philosophy to transform himself in order to navigate through adversity; and he apparently lacks a reserve of virtuous behavior that would warrant divine deliverance. He, consequently, becomes thoroughly corrupt through his association with Dunbar's other Blues characters at the Banner Club.

Dunbar uses the term "ragtime" to define the music that he associates with Joe—who frequents the Banner Club; the life ideas of the people in the Banner Club are consistent with a literary Blues philosophy. This novel was published in 1902, so Dunbar's references to ragtime do not make distinctions among Blues, Jazz, and ragtime, as—increasingly— will be the case within the next twenty years. Often such distinctions are difficult even today.

In Dunbar's Banner Club, the Blues character Sadness Williams attempts to deepen Joe's Blues "education" by pointing out that the people in the club have lived through life's injustices, disappointments, and their own foolish peccadilloes, yet no one thinks any less of them for their success; or, in other words, in the Banner Club they are not criticized for triumphing through or surviving their dispiriting conditions. Sadness further explains to Joe that this group is so numerous that there is no need for them to be dependent on others in order to establish their worth; their position in life gives them so many companions that they find themselves together whether they desire it or not. Sadness's education of Joe teaches him that these Blues People have not chosen this difficult life for themselves; they have learned, though, to negotiate their lives beyond the boundaries imposed on them by social limitations.

Dunbar's tone in this passage suggests heavy irony tinged with complex seriousness;[25] he also associates a type of Blues philosophical irony to Sadness Williams when this character tells Joe that he does not avoid the grief that life has brought him. Since the time when his father was hanged "with a very good rope and by the best citizens of Texas," Sadness has been "ungratefully sad." According to Dunbar's Blues philosopher, only the very low in life or the very high in life avoid sadness. Sadness himself, in fact, has "aspired to the depths" but he just cannot manage it (146–47), illustrating—even within the context of Dunbar's critique—Williams's psychological resilience. Such Blues philosophy guides also are found in Wallace Thurman's Uncle Joe in *The Blacker the Berry*, Zora Neale Hurston's Tea Cake in *Their Eyes Were Watching God*, and Ralph Ellison's Peter Wheatstraw in *Invisible Man*.

From Sadness's perspective, "[i]t's only the independent who depend on others" (149). Through the Blues philosophy of Sadness, Dunbar restates and revises Nietzsche's ideas about the master-slave relationship (170–72). Sadness's Blues philosophy conveys the idea that without those from whom the independent can differentiate themselves, their separateness has no meaning. In this passage, Dunbar's Sadness Williams delineates Blues philosophy only to have the narrator undercut this approach to life by characterizing its practitioners as a growing mass that lives "like the leech, upon the blood of others" and as people whose "loyalty one to another makes them a great hulking fashionably uniformed fraternity of indolence" (150). While Dunbar's narrator does not acknowledge society's part in imposing this mass mentality on the lives of the Blues People in the Banner Club, Dunbar still positions Sadness's Blues philosophy as a means toward opening Joe's eyes to the reality of the life they are living, even though it is a life the novel—as the narrator indicates—will finally reject and critique for its limitations. With a clearer understanding of Blues life, Sadness hopes that if Joe remains among Blues People, he will do so as a fully conscious participant; if not, he will be destroyed by his inability to adapt, unless he returns to the set pattern for his life that his parents taught him to live—a life that, for Joe, has a similarly destructive potential.

Through Sadness Williams's discussion with Joe, Dunbar establishes that as a fully conscious Blues character, Joe needs to find within himself a singular response to the conditions in which he and numerous other Blues People are living; he must fortify his internal resources instead of finding his only strength to survive in others such as Hattie Sterling. Instead of recognizing these Blues philosophical ideas, Dunbar's Joe Hamilton "feels wonderfully 'in it.'" He perceives the similarity between himself and the others in the Banner Club, but he does not recognize the crucial difference between them and him. They are part of a group, yet these Blues People use the group knowledge about their situation to establish their own singular responses to adversity. This is what Joe misses in Sadness Williams's discourse and what Dunbar's narrator fails to acknowledge. Joe, then, lives through the group, rather than developing his own singular responses for addressing obstacles. Joe's partial knowledge of Blues life "gave him a false bravery" based in his connection to the group at the Banner Club. Sadness recognizes this and tells Joe that the education that he gives Joe has been a fool's bet (149). Within minutes, Joe is thinking his pre-Blues-education ideas again. Dunbar's narrator observes, "Somehow old teachings and old traditions have an annoying way of coming back upon us in the critical moments of life, although one has long ago recognized how much truer and better some newer ways of thinking are" (152).

Dunbar never allows Joe to grasp Sadness's lessons in Blues philosophy. Joe cannot perceive of any options that will move him away from the disappointment he feels about his life. He is unable to see that the limitations he experiences restrict his body, but not his mind. Dunbar's Blues philosopher Sadness, however, illustrates his knowledge of the range and limit of a twentieth-century New York Blues life when he says that "dancing in ragtime is the dialect poetry" (203). This comment resonates with Dunbar's own struggles with establishing himself as a poet instead of just a dialect poet, a position to which William Dean Howells and the dominant society's discourse of racialized literature consigned him. In musical terms, ragtime—piano music—is indeed transformed by the emergence of Jazz bands. As is the case with dialect poetry, ragtime is a transitory middle term between the old and the new as well as a combination of African American and European American musical styles. Through his portrayal of Sadness Williams, Dunbar demonstrates that resourceful Blues characters transform their difficulties through their strength of will, even though there are limits placed on them. For Blues People, such as Sadness, dissipation and death are tragedy and defeat; Blues is not tragic. It is victorious, triumphant, unconquered, and self-empowering, even when conditions suggest otherwise. Dunbar, clearly, does not make this the case for Joe.

When Hattie Sterling—a Blues character whose name accurately describes her firmness and persistent strength—breaks off her relationship with Joe, Dunbar depicts Joe's Blues life as creating hopelessness and despair instead of survival or triumph. After five years of living with Joe's intermittent periods of self-sustenance and periodic retreats to the lowest depths of society, Dunbar's Hattie ends their relationship, singing, "You'll have to find another baby now" (200). With this song Dunbar firmly situates Hattie within a Blues philosophy. Through her song she expresses her singular ideas about the disappointments she has experienced in her relationship with Joe.

Here again Baker and I disagree on the Blues aspects of Dunbar's novel. Baker analyzes Dunbar's name for this blueswoman as ironic. For Baker, Hattie Sterling is "anything but 'Sterling,'" especially in terms of possessing traditional qualities that are associated with her role as a woman (128). This is, in fact, true. Yet in certain quarters of the paradoxical Blues world, this truth also is all right. This music-into-literature discourse is situated within the context of Blues as a critique of the dominant discourse not only in terms of the way this discourse constructs race but also in terms of its construction of gender and of social values. Dunbar in *The Sport of the Gods* does not commend the people in the Banner Club to us, but he does portray the club as a site of social and cultural critique. Hattie Sterling is a blueswoman along the lines of Bessie Smith and Ma Rainey. Hattie revises gender roles that limit her. This blueswoman engages in a relationship with a younger man, and she rejects him when he, along with his reckless irresponsibility, no longer suits her. Hattie Sterling, in other words, does not define herself within the context of her life with Joe. Hattie's actions are consistent with Angela Davis's description of blueswomen in her book *Blues Legacies*, which addresses the issue of blueswomen and Blues life as vehicles of social critique. I read Hattie Sterling within the Blues context of social and cultural critique. Without Hattie as his anchor, Joe—not Hattie—loses all his bearings and becomes the "Frankenstein" for which chapter 14 is named. In a fit of self-pity, Joe kills Hattie, while blaming her for his failure. Dunbar again critiques Blues life by describing Joe as "one whose soul is dead, and perhaps it was; for all the little soul of him had been wrapped up in the body of this one woman, and the stroke that took her life had killed him too" (210). Again, this, of course, is Joe's failing, not Hattie's.

Dunbar persistently critiques Blues life in *The Sport of the Gods*. At the end of the novel, for instance, Dunbar's Spiritual-Gospel character Fannie Hamilton views her son as a "martyr" (215). To Fannie, Joe is a Christ figure who is made to suffer unjustly, as society does not allow his potential to flourish. She believes Joe is denied a virtuous life because he is limited within the society of his birth. Thus, through Fannie Hamilton, Dunbar suggests that Joe's imprisonment comments on the ills of his society more than it exemplifies that Joe fails to grasp the broader implications of Blues life, which Dunbar's Fannie Hamilton rejects. It is true, however, that Joe fails to understand the variety of options available in the philosophy of Blues life that Sadness explains to him, yet Dunbar makes Joe fail in his Blues life and then Dunbar uses this character's failure as a catalyst that allows him to present the Spiritual-Gospel life of the Hamiltons as an unfortunate but more viable choice than the Blues approach to life that Joe tries to make.

Dunbar is consistent in his theme, which is that the Hamiltons are naïve and delicate southerners who are unable to survive the "hard necessities" of northern city life: "[T]he South has its faults—no one condones them—and its disadvantages, but . . . even what they suffered from there [the South] was better than what awaited them in the great alleys of New York" (213). In this novel Dunbar sentimentally praises the moral sanctity of southern life, and at the same time he questions the conditions that limit the full participation of black people in the United States, especially the post-emancipation South. Blues moved from the South during the era of northern migration among formerly captive black people. Dunbar's assessment that southern oppression was the lesser of two evils distorts the realities of Blues life in the South as well as the North. The only options for his main characters are patience in the South or destruction and dissipation in the North.

Dunbar depicts his black characters in this novel as extremes or types, yet in order to demonstrate the varieties of racial bigotry, Dunbar presents areas of gray among his white characters—who are also stock types. Skaggsy, for instance, is a white character—from the North— whose news story results in Berry Hamilton's release. Among Dunbar's white southerners, though, he portrays distinct types of racial bigotry, each type of bigotry provides a character with a specific kind of racialized view. Horace Talbot, whom, on the one hand, Dunbar ironically points out is "noted for his kindliness towards people of colour," believes that Berry took the money "with the same innocence of purpose with which one of our servants a few years ago would have appropriated a stray ham." On the other hand, there is Beachfield Davis, who asserts, "All niggers are alike and there's no use trying to do anything with them." And Colonel Saunders, slightly contrasting with his fellow white southerners, considers the idea that Berry may be innocent (52–57). Saunders, however, does not want Berry released when, later, he is in fact proven innocent. He even becomes angry with the white northerner who brought "shame upon a Southern name" by writing a truthful story that vindicates Berry (239).

The novel's ending is troubling. At the same time that Dunbar writes the eventual implosion of racial bigotry into his text through Maurice Oakley's "shrieks of madness," which the Hamiltons hear from their "little cottage . . . across the yard" (where they have been restored to their previous servile condition), he also notes that the inferior position the Hamiltons resume in the South is "not a happy life, but it was all that was left to them and they took it up without complaint . . . ," waiting for their oppressive circumstances to be changed by a more powerful "Will." Dunbar shows that this same "Will" ends the Oakleys' control over the lives of the Hamiltons, but it does not change the society in which they live. And, consequently, the Hamiltons remain in a position of inferiority. Thus Dunbar (again echoing Hawthorne) suggests, through his portrayal of the Hamiltons, that moral fortitude and faith in God are sufficient solutions for addressing barriers in life. This view exemplifies the Spiritual-Gospel theme that shapes the novel. As a result, Dunbar does not provide Fannie and Berry Hamilton with any personal resources for changing their own lives; their lives at the end of the novel remain entangled in the sport of an invisible power, or a "Will infinitely stronger than their own" (255). In this way, Dunbar makes the elder Hamiltons into Spiritual-Gospel characters whose options are quiet acceptance of a God's inscrutable game of life or debilitating corruption if they attempt to reshape their traditional responses.

Dunbar's writing style in this novel is highly ironic, as he uses irony to deflect firm meanings in many passages. Through his use of a deeply ironic questioning—attained through the silence of what is not said and through suggestion—at the end of *The Sport of the Gods*, he says the unsayable. That is, through inference, Dunbar asks these questions: What manner of God could remain silent as, in the words of a later poet, Countee Cullen, "Tortured Tantalus / Is baited by the fickle fruit . . ."? How could God—in the words of Cullen again—doom "Sisyphus / To struggle up a never ending stair" (1305). Fannie and Berry Hamilton are the spiritual victors against the sport of the false, self-appointed gods. That victory results from Dunbar's deus ex machina, which employs a "Will infinitely stronger" (255) than the Oakleys' and the system of racial tyranny that supports them. Yet that same God retains the system of oppression under which the Hamiltons live. Why is this the case? Dunbar silently asks this question, and the ending of the novel leaves the answer to that question open. The silence that follows creates a space for a number of troubling questions that Dunbar dares to ask, without, of course, asking.

Nella Larsen: *Quicksand*

In New Negro Renaissance writer Nella Larsen's 1928 novel *Quicksand*, the main character, Helga Crane, is depicted as possessing the personal fortitude to conquer the obstacles of alienation, loss, estrangement, and rootlessness that she encounters throughout the novel. Helga, because of her African ancestry, is alienated from the mainstream of life in the country of her birth. She has lost both parents; her mother dies when Helga is fifteen, and her father leaves his wife and child when Helga is young. She also is estranged from her Uncle Peter because he fears social reprisals if others know that his sister had a child with a black man. Throughout the novel Helga's rootlessness takes her from the South back to her northern birthplace in Chicago, then to New York, and to Denmark, her mother's birthplace, and finally—as is the case with Dunbar's Fannie and Berry Hamilton in *The Sport of the Gods*—back to the South, attempting to find a place where she feels a sense of belonging.

In *Quicksand* Larsen takes readers through Helga Crane's psychological landscape. Helga has moments of impulsiveness that occasionally shake "the bulwarks of . . . [her] self restraint" (5) as well as the power of her strong will (10). In Helga Crane, Larsen has created a rich complexity of contradictions, shaped by Blues philosophy and Helga's singular solutions. Larsen's other characters also are metaphorical; they, for the most part, illustrate ideas and attitudes that Helga critiques and rejects. And in the names of the other characters in this novel, Larsen delineates additional ideas and attitudes that Helga rejects. Helga's fiancé at Naxos, James Vayle, for instance, is, for Helga, the embodiment of self-satisfied acceptance of the veil that blocks opportunity by blurring the vision of black people like those in Naxos. Deborah McDowell's argument that Naxos is an anagram for Saxon deepens the connection that Larsen makes between James Vayle and W. E. B. Du Bois's concept of the veil as a barrier that disallows any recognition of African American gifts to the broader culture. James Vayle eventually becomes principal at Naxos, a school that Helga decides cuts "all to a pattern, the white man's pattern" (4).

Helga Crane rejects the mind-set that is prevalent in Naxos when she finds that her youthful desire to help others is thwarted in Naxos, "giving place to a deep hatred for the trivial hypocrisies and careless cruelties which were, unintentionally perhaps, a part of the Naxos policy of uplift" (5). Helga, in fact, sympathizes with the students who are degraded and humiliated by staff and faculty at Naxos, who do violence to their students' psyches by embedding inferiority in them. Miss MacGooden, whose purported good is ironically detrimental, greets the girls in the morning by inculcating them with the idea that an important part of their education is to attain the school's version of the best Anglo-Saxon deportment. She says to the students, "Well! Even if every last one of you did come from homes where you weren't taught manners, you might at least try to pretend that you're capable of learning some here, now that you have the opportunity." Miss MacGooden follows these statements with, "*[P]lease* at least try to act like ladies and not like savages from the backwoods" (11–12). This harangue on manners and cultivation results from nothing more than a slammed shower door.[26] Experiences such as this make Helga recognize in James Vayle the "shame, lies, hypocrisy, cruelty, servility, and snobbishness" at Naxos. Larsen later reminds readers of all that Naxos is when James and Helga meet again years later in New York. Helga discovers that Vayle "hadn't . . . changed at all" (100). Larsen's critique is focused on the "policy of racial uplift and of black intellectual leadership." As Hazel Carby observes, in this novel the "black bourgeoisie . . . [is] attacked on many levels: for its hypocrisy, for its articulation of the race 'problem,' and for its moral and aesthetic code" (*Reconstructing* 170–71, 173).

Instead of being made over into the Naxos woman with the status and power that marriage to James Vayle could accomplish for her, Helga rejects the precut pattern of life in Naxos and finds her own singular response. She "could neither conform, nor be happy in her unconformity" (7). Helga revolts. Her resistance is indirectly a response to the shared societal oppression to which she and the other black people in Naxos are subjected. But more directly, Helga revolts against the responses, which she finds among black people, to the racialized social policy in the United States.

Helga Crane comes close to being a Jazz character who recognizes that there are many options from which one can choose to address struggles in life. Yet this is not the case with Larsen's characterization of her protagonist. Although Helga is a Blues character who is not quelled, her victory is limited. As with Blues characters, Helga's basic traits are consistent. Larsen shapes and reshapes Helga's basic responses to situations that may become impediments to Helga's finding a place where she belongs, but she does not break the basic form within which Helga has been drawn. She depicts Helga's consistent search for a place of stability, comfort, and acceptance—a group connection. When these conditions are not forthcoming, Helga resists these limits and moves to another place that she believes may offer her those conditions in the measure she desires. Larsen's consistency in representing these qualities in Helga demonstrates Helga's Blues characteristics. Throughout the novel Helga does not abandon her Blues idea that she must become an individual piece in a larger pattern. And, although the possibility is there, she never becomes an innovative Jazz character among many other similarly improvisational personalities. (Contrast these Blues and Jazz concepts with the Naxos concept that everyone must be cut from the same pattern, must reproduce the artifact.) Helga's first move—in her search for a place where she can belong comfortably—is from Naxos to Chicago, where she meets Jeanette Hayes-Rore.

In the characters of Jeanette Hayes-Rore and Anne Grey, Larsen again uses names as metaphors that illustrate Helga's perspective on her environment and on other characters in the novel. Mrs. Hayes-Rore is a "prominent 'race' woman" (37) in Chicago who employs Helga as a temporary traveling companion who will edit and organize her speeches. Larsen depicts Helga's employer as an interesting yet foggy-minded (Hayes/hazzy) and shortsighted lecturer who emphatically (Rore/roar) delivers her "patchwork of others' speeches and opinions" (38). Since

Helga is not successful in her job search in Chicago and is rejected by her Uncle Peter, she agrees to travel with Mrs. Hayes-Rore to New York, hoping to find a permanent position there.

In Chicago, Helga is "horribly lonely," as she recognizes that "in all the climbing massed city no one cared one whit about her" (34). Unlike her employer's "oratorical voice [that] boomed above the city's roar" (40), Helga discovers that her singular voice in the city is a cry into an immense, paradoxically plenitudinous, void where many others singularly create their own lives. They are not unchanging patterns, as are the people in Naxos, where one's life mould is set in advance. In Helga's recognition of the structure of city life, there is the Blues philosophical concept that she must use her own resources to survive. Helga, then, is not crushed by the uncertainty that confronts her in Chicago. She faces it with personal resolve. She seeks options, for instance, that do not include her Uncle Peter after he refuses to see her when she visits his home in Chicago. And she persists in her job search, even though her prospects are few. Helga's brief stay in Chicago and her employment with Mrs. Hayes-Rore are a period of blurred personal vision, yet Helga survives the calamitous conditions of this city. Through Larsen's depiction of Mrs. Hayes-Rore and of Chicago—the city for which she is a metaphor—she illustrates Helga's environment as well as her attitude toward the approach to race issues taken by her employer. For Helga there is in her employer a roar of words without clarity of vision. And, as for her environment, Helga's concerns about her ability to survive in Chicago cause her to live in a haze of uncertainty in the urban roar of the city.

Larsen describes Helga's first comfortable link to a group once her central character arrives in New York. Her life is more stable in Harlem, where she lives with Mrs. Hayes-Rore's niece Anne Grey and begins working for an insurance company. For a while, Helga has the feeling "of having come home . . . ; she considered that she had . . . 'found herself'" (43–44). Thus, Helga believes that her desire to be her own unique self while being connected to a larger group is achieved in New York with Anne Grey. Larsen makes Helga a determined Blues character by demonstrating how this character's "unchildlike childhood among hostile white folks in Chicago, and her uncomfortable sojourn among snobbish black folks in Naxos" have strengthened her so that for a time she lives happily in the "continuously gorgeous panorama of Harlem" yet retains her singular voice. Before long, however, Helga finds that her experiences in Harlem lead her to examine herself as closely as she has examined others. Soon Harlem loses its luster, and she falls into a malaise when she recognizes "it was of herself that she was afraid." All of this time Helga had seen the flaws in her outside environment but had failed to examine her own internal landscape beyond the level required to manage survival. Her malaise causes a "sensation of estrangement and isolation" toward the Harlem that she had previously found so welcoming, and to which she had established group ties. But now Helga begins to "dislike her friends" and becomes "annoyed" with the people she had previously found so beautiful on Harlem streets (45–48).

Helga's increasing sense of disconnection from her Harlem lifestyle becomes apparent in the cabaret club that she attends with Anne Grey. When Helga enters the all-black Harlem club, the "blare of jazz split her ears." This boisterous Jazz aesthetic seduces Helga until she considers how this Jazz space is just a momentary retreat into a sensual obliteration of self: "Helga was oblivious of the reek of flesh, smoke, and alcohol, oblivious of the oblivion of other gyrating pairs, oblivious of the color, the noise. . . . She was drugged, lifted, sustained, by the extraordinary music." Yet, for Helga, this cabaret is a space that constructs a meretricious freedom in which "this oppressed race of hers" briefly engages. Helga's response is not immediate; it is deliberate and puissant. Her comments about the Jazz life she finds in the cabaret almost align her—though speaking of a different extension of the cultural spectrum—with Miss MacGooden's disparaging remarks to the girls at Naxos. Even though Helga at times seems on the verge of engaging Jazz philosophy, Larsen's cabaret scene makes clear that Helga finds this life wanting (58–62).[27]

Even in Harlem there is something missing for Helga. Her aspirations overreach the closed racial ranks and confused ideology she finds there. She believes there must be a place where she can connect with others on a level that goes beyond race, since her experiences with racial unity seem so tenuous. Larsen places Helga among the best situated black people in Harlem. What Helga finds among these people is a self-assured facade of black uplift serving as a veneer covering a deeply rooted love of all that these people profess to disdain. Larsen depicts this attitude most clearly in Anne Grey. While Anne proclaims "the undiluted good of all things Negro," her professions of love are weakened by her actions. The music, dance, and speech of black people are offensive to her, and her lifestyle fully emulates that of the supposedly "despised people of the white race" (48–49). For Helga, Anne's attitude represents confusion, someone with a gray consciousness who is unable to establish her own feelings about both black and white people. Larsen, then, establishes that making a connection with people is not simply about color. For Helga, "Something broader, deeper, . . . made folk kin" (55). And, as Margaret Perry[28] explains, Helga has a strong passion "to repudiate the ethic of the bourgeoisie" that she finds among Harlem's well-positioned black people (74).

Helga's Blues singularity—that is, her own peculiar response to disappointment and adversity—is firmly rooted in a group connection, but Helga comes close to being uprooted and situated in Jazz when she sails to her mother's Danish homeland. For Helga, Denmark will disconnect her from the debilitating love-hate relationship that the black people she has met have with themselves. That is, Helga comes close to using the fragments of her life to create her own personal responses to the barriers she finds in the United States. But she remains a Blues character because she is still searching for a foundation of similarity, even in Denmark, to which she can be a part. Helga cannot work from the fragments (black, white, North, South, United States, Denmark) of her life and create herself as a unique Jazz personality among many other fragmented personalities.

Helga does not want to abandon or deny her African ancestry, but neither does she want the facts of her heritage to consume every aspect of her life. She most strongly rejects the conflicted way that black people in the United States rejected their own selfhood. Helga believes, "What they wanted, asked for, begged for, was to be like their white overlords. They were ashamed to be Negroes, but not ashamed to be something else." In Copenhagen, Helga finds an attitude of "[t]o each his own milieu" (74–75). Thus, among the Danes, she hopes to find "that blessed sense of belonging to herself alone and not to a race" (64).

Yet Larsen demonstrates that Helga's color does matter in Copenhagen. Its significance is based in Helga's European kinspeople's exoticized belief that her color gives her a vibrancy and liveliness that they lack; they perceive of Helga's color as an invigorating quality from which they can draw vibrancy and liveliness vicariously, through their contact with her. She realizes that "all along . . . [the Danes] had divined its presence, had known that in her was something, some characteristic different from any that they themselves possessed. . . . And they hadn't despised it. No they had admired it, rated it as a precious thing to be enhanced, preserved" (83).

In the Danish environment, where there are relaxed racial attitudes, Helga is able to stand outside the chaos of racial conflict and examine her own racial duality. Larsen uses music to conjoin Helga's dual heritages. At a performance of Antonín Dvořák's symphony *From the New World*, Helga found that the "wailing undertones of 'Swing Low Sweet Chariot' were too poignantly familiar." Now she knows what "lurked formless and undesignated these many weeks in the back of her troubled mind. Incompleteness. 'I'm homesick, not for America, but for Negroes.'" Dvořák's symphony is a metaphor for Helga's life in Denmark. For Helga, the overwhelming Europeaness of the symphony is enlivened by its "undertones," which resonate with the music that Dvořák heard in the African American Spirituals of the United States. The firm and formal crispness of Dvořák's earlier compositions is altered in *From the New World*, in which he uses Spiritual-like slides to move into succeeding notes as well as gliding stretches through a particular note. In this way Dvořák appropriates African American Spirituals to modify the formal trills and glissandos that are more representative of European classical music. This African effect on European music parallels Helga's effect on the people of Copenhagen. She invigorates the "formal calm" and "pale serious faces" of her mother's native environment in the same way that the Spirituals enrich European classical music (92).

Larsen, however, makes an essentialist connection between Helga and Dvořák's musical "undertones." These undertones help Helga understand her father and make her feel "irresistible ties of race, now that they dragged at her own heart" (92). Larsen uses the "undertones" in Dvořák's symphony to connect Helga to some of the deeper complexities of black life in the United States. But she suggests that race, not experience, makes Helga respond as she does to the undertones in Dvořák's New World symphony. As Helga begins to listen more carefully to the aesthetic in Spirituals, she establishes a connection with the narratives that are collected in these songs; she finds there stories that tell how the makers of Spirituals have devised strategies to retain an unsubdued spirit despite their suffering and hardships. After Larsen connects Helga to the deeper ideas in Spirituals, Helga begins to feel that she does not want to live completely separated from African Americans,[29] and she may, at this point, unconsciously and erroneously decide that a Spiritual-Gospel philosophy is what will sustain her.

While listening to Dvořák's symphony, Helga finalizes her decision to return to the United States, yet it is her invitation to Dr. Anderson and Anne Grey's wedding that "added somehow, to her discontent" in Denmark (81). By placing Helga in the situation of attending the wedding of her friend and the man that Helga desires, Larsen adds gender and sexual tensions to the racial issues in the novel and increases the complexity of Helga Crane and her Blues life. Larsen retains Helga's concern with being able to move freely within a foundation with which she is comfortable. Helga, then, wants to be connected to a group, but she does not want that to be a group connected by oppression and a social policy of inequality, both of which inform African American group experience and Blues philosophy. Similar to Helga's ideas about race, she also wants an intimate relationship that does not limit her singular voice. This approach to intimate relationships situates Helga firmly within womanist Blues ideas. She rejects the dominant social policy that subordinates women in the social discourse; for Helga, unfortunately, class and religious concerns intervene. Among the more fortunately situated black people in Harlem, there is a tendency toward replicating the dominant social discourse in most areas except race. This repels Helga. In a misguided attempt to find a cultural foundation and an intimate relationship, however, Helga accepts another discourse she has previously rejected: unexamined religion.

After illustrating Helga's more fully developed understanding of her racial complexities, Larsen places her in a position to examine her repressed sexual desires. Helga desires Anderson but cannot admit that she does. Throughout the novel she seems seduced by thoughts of him. There are times when "involuntarily, which was somehow frequently, her mind turned on" Anderson and his ideas about social change (45–46). Yet Helga always finds a reason to overrule her feelings. Early in the novel Anderson tries to convince Helga that she should not resign her position at Naxos, but Helga feels a desire to commit to Anderson and not to her work. Helga "was silent, feeling a mystifying yearning which sang and throbbed in her. She felt again that urge for service, not now for her people, but for this man who was talking so earnestly of his work, his plans, his hopes."

Anderson's influence on Helga is broken when he suggests that her social position could improve since her poverty is compensated for by her "tendencies inherited from good stock," or, in other words, inherited from her white ancestry (20–21). Helga seems to miss his meaning, but her anger still is aroused at what she believes are references to superficial class distinctions. She responds to his statements by maligning the moral character of her parents in an attempt to reject the Naxos ideology of class and caste reigning over merit. Both Anderson and Helga leave Naxos, separately, and end up in Harlem. When they meet again, Helga feels "a strange ill-defined emotion, a vague yearning rising within her" (50).

Thus, Larsen creates parallels in Helga's personality that result in similar consequences when this character searches for a place to belong and when she attempts to establish a relationship with a man. Helga finds all of her potential mates deficient just as all of the places where she lives are not completely satisfactory. James Vayle was too limited and limiting. Axel Olsen, the Danish artist who proposes marriage to Helga, is rejected because she believes that as "excited and pleased as he was with her, her origin a little repelled him" (84). She recognizes in his proposal the suggestion of their marriage as the fulfillment of a certain primitivist desire. So Helga tells Olsen, "[I]f we were married, you might come to be ashamed of me, to hate me, to hate all dark people. My mother did that" (88). Only Robert Anderson, the black man whose family name is common in Denmark, shares the refined manner and American experience that Helga Crane apparently seeks.[30] When in Denmark, Helga compares Anderson and Axel Olsen. After Helga rejects Olsen's marriage proposal, she observes that his demeanor is precisely appropriate because "no other man . . . of her acquaintance could have managed it so well—except, perhaps Robert Anderson" (88–89).

Upon Helga's return to Harlem, Larsen demonstrates that Helga must investigate her feelings about Anderson. Her earlier impulsive actions toward him have dissuaded any deep interaction between them and blocked Helga from investigating the "long-hidden, half-understood desire" she has for him. That desire is awakened after Robert Anderson kisses Helga. This kiss produces in her an "ecstasy which had flooded her" and makes her decide to remain in the United States and explore "to the end that unfamiliar path into which she had strayed," even though Anderson is married and inaccessible. Previously, Helga has been unable to remain in a situation long enough to work through her own solutions. She always has moved on to the next city, trying to find a place where she might belong; she also has ignored and repressed any deep emotional or sexual feelings toward men. Cheryl Wall notes that Helga has been "taught well to repress any sexual feelings [so] she denies them" (100). When Helga finally acknowledges her sexual feelings, her response is irrational and seemingly desperate. At the critical point, when Helga must recognize that she has to make other choices because Anderson is not available, she decides that self-analysis is "too hard" (105–10). In place of self-examination and personal solutions, Larsen turns Helga—a character who earlier had rejected rigidity, oppressive authority, and religion—to Spiritual-Gospel (34). For Helga, the "persistence of some unconquerable faith beyond time and reality" and the old Spiritual songs that are a faint memory from what seems "hundreds of years" ago become a fearful source of comfort and group connection in her present state of mental discomfort (111–13).

Larsen uses Spiritual-Gospel music as a metaphor to depict the "dim vision" within Helga that connects her to black people in the United States. Spiritual-Gospel music and the church service into which Helga stumbles become her connection to "rites of a remote obscure origin" that begin to "resound in . . . [Helga's] own heart." Through her marriage to Reverend Pleasant Green and her relocation to Alabama, Helga symbolically marries into the Spiritual-Gospel life of the very "rites" that are foreign to her experience but to which she somehow feels connected. Larsen does not establish, however, whether Helga is "lost—or saved" as a result of her impulsive marriage to Pleasant Green (113). For Larsen's earlier Helga Crane, there certainly is a loss. She loses her freedom to be connected to the fullness that she associates with life in Harlem. She also loses the freedom to escape to Denmark, where there is not intense focus on race. And she loses the childless freedom that her refusal to marry had given her, that is, the freedom to avoid adding "any more unwanted tortured Negroes to America" (103).

If Helga has been saved by her marriage to Pleasant Green, perhaps—within the context of the novel—she has been saved from rejecting those experiences that connect her to black people. Even though throughout the novel Larsen depicts Helga as a character who makes an argument for freedom from *restrictive* social narratives, she "wasn't, after all, a rebel from society, Negro society. It did mean something to her. She had no wish to stand alone" (107). Thus Larsen clearly does not make Helga a Jazz character, because Larsen portrays Helga's constant desire for a connection that allows room for singular expression. Helga is, therefore, a Blues character who, against her true personal disposition, tries to live the Spiritual-Gospel life when she marries Reverend Green.

Larsen describes Helga's husband as a "rattish yellow man," a description in stark and ironic contrast to his name—Pleasant. Rats most often are associated with unpleasant, unclean, and dangerous situations, and his yellow coloring contrasts the images of life, freshness, and beauty suggested by the preacher's family name, Green. Through this contrast between the minister's name, which metaphorically represents Helga's newfound idealized concept of religion, and his physical description, Larsen illustrates the confused understanding that Helga has about the life that she has chosen by marrying Pleasant Green. Helga has the mistaken notion that religion will give her an idyllic life of calm and beauty. This is far from the reality for Helga. Instead, her "anesthetic satisfaction" allows her to be "done with soul searching" (118–21). This means that Helga's Spiritual-Gospel life absolves her from taking responsibility for making herself.[31] And eventually Helga is relieved "to be able to put the entire responsibility on someone else": God (126).

Helga's life with Pleasant Green is a potentially tragic situation that is conquered through Larsen's returning Helga to Blues philosophical principles. Helga is not a tragic figure because Larsen depicts her as a character possessing a number of traits that humanize rather than idealize her, so she is not made exemplary above others: she is impulsive, she lacks persistence, and she is motivated by self-interest. Larsen also does not depict Helga as a character who is overly determined by external forces. Helga recognizes that within certain limitations, she makes her own life. Hence, Larsen returns Helga to ideas about life that actually complement her disposition as a Blues character and that explain Helga's choices at the end of the novel. Helga is neither tragic nor the Spiritual-Gospel person she tries, unsuccessfully, to become. In the essay "Richard Wright's Blues," Ralph Ellison states that Blues "at once express both the agony of life and the possibility of conquering it through sheer spirit. They fall short of tragedy only in that they provide no solution, offer no scapegoat but the self" (94).

When Helga's life becomes "an unbearable reality" under the pressure of bearing her fourth "little dab of amber humanity," she contemplates her "artificial faith" and the condition in which she finds herself. In this moment Helga accepts her own culpability in creating this "quagmire in which she had engulfed herself." She has permanently tied herself to "this hypocritical land"; she has brought children into a life of perpetual racial striving and into the deferring of happiness and recompense to the "kingdom come" (127–33). This condition Helga despises. Yet her resolve to leave Pleasant Green is modified by her consideration for her children. Helga, then, rejects her false connection to a Spiritual-Gospel life and employs her Blues philosophy to help her survive in the Spiritual-Gospel environment she encounters in Alabama.

Although Helga is not completely destroyed by her situation,[32] her resigned acceptance complicates her Blues hope and triumph when it is combined with the quicksand of gender roles. Unlike her father, she cannot allow circumstances to push her away from her children. As Helga acknowledges that her marriage and the resulting children are "all her own doing," she also realizes that she cannot accept death, which was her mother's way out after marriage and the birth of her daughter Helga enmesh her in the quagmire of race in the United States (134). Larsen presents in Helga a female Blues characteristic that Hazel Carby refers to as "an empowered presence" ("It Jus Be's" 747); this empowered presence, which is a type of resilience against a multiplicity of difficulties, is circumscribed, nonetheless, by the limited mobility of women who have children and thus do not share in the gendered Blues tradition of the traveling bluesman.

In Daphne Duval Harrison's study of blueswomen, *Black Pearls: Blues Queens of the 1920s*, she reproduces Clara Smith's version of "Freight Train Blues"; this Blues tune accurately illustrates a gendered response to Blues mobility as Smith asserts that women retreat to their rooms and hide when they get the Blues while men hop freight trains (90). Angela Davis further points out the "absence of the mother figure in the blues," especially those sung by blueswomen. Davis attributes this absence to the lifestyle of blueswomen, who "found the mainstream cult of motherhood irrelevant to the realities of the female Blues singers' lives." An actual blueswoman in the 1920s is an "independent woman free of the domestic orthodoxy of the prevailing representatives of womanhood" (13). Davis further presents blueswomen as examples of the possibilities in life that women who listen to the Blues could attain. In her study of Blues singers, Davis also makes the point that mobility is a privilege that blueswomen enjoy, but the masses of black women in the 1920s and 1930s do not (71–72).

Both Harrison and Davis discuss Blues as a means through which the freer blueswomen present advice to other women. Davis explains that performers such as Ma Rainey, Ida Cox, and Alberta Hunter, with songs such as "Traveling Blues," "Wild Women Don't Wear the Blues," and "I've Got a Mind to Ramble," give other women vicarious access to mobility and open the possibility for a rambling blueswoman philosophy (Harrison 110; Davis 42–65). Yet the freedom of a blueswoman's life still vexes the question of motherhood. Larsen's Helga Crane is an example of that reality. For Ann Ducille, literary scholars who position Helga

Crane outside a Blues discourse bring a limited perspective to the Blues and to the stories of African American life that collect in the Blues.[33] Helga, Ducille argues, is an example of "bourgeois blues." This character also sings the Blues; "[i]t is just that no one has listened" (432).

In the general sense of the term, we can discuss Helga as tragic, but as a Blues character she overreaches tragedy by prevailing in situations that are designed to shatter the human spirit. For Blues characters there are no final solutions that fit every case. Blues People, who are situated in the wisdom of the group, find answers within themselves, and they make themselves the final place of accountability for their choices. Larsen establishes that Helga does this regarding her marriage. She chooses to abandon herself for her children, something that her parents did not do for her. Thus, Larsen ends *Quicksand* on the idea that Helga finds the social narrative that shapes her gender role as a mother and a wife insurmountable only because she chooses to consider her children's lives. As Thadious Davis explains, Helga, as well as Larsen's protagonist in her novel *Passing*, "disappear from their active lives into passive enactments of their own worst nightmares" (17). As a Blues character, then, Helga makes the singular choice to mother her children instead of to live solely for herself. This choice imperils Helga's freedom, but perhaps she can give to her children the familial love that she did not get as well as develop in them the self love that they need to survive the impediments that she is sure they will meet in life. Helga's connection to the lives of her children stays her impulsiveness and influences her decision to continue in the role she plays as wife of Reverend Mr. Pleasant Green.

Wallace Thurman: *The Blacker the Berry . . . : A Novel of Negro Life*

Wallace Thurman's novel *The Blacker the Berry . . . : A Novel of Negro Life* (1929), published in the waning years of the Harlem Renaissance, is a Blues-theme novel for which readers gain their first understanding of its Blues influences from its title. Thurman takes his title from a traveling phrase in W. C. Handy's "St. Louis Blues." Handy, of course, borrowed this phrase from African American vernacular culture outside of the Blues. In Thurman's novel his main character, Emma Lou Morgan, must come to conscious recognition of a Blues philosophy in order to live a self-directed life, a life of "acceptance of herself by herself" (227). This is a crucial Blues philosophical concept. Blues characters situate themselves within the group wisdom, but solutions come from within the self; hence, successful Blues characters reject the notion of devaluing the self from which these solutions develop. Thurman's main character, Emma Lou, journeys through life aimlessly until she recognizes that she controls her own life; Emma Lou continues to misdirect her life until she learns to like herself. She believes that her struggle is with intraracial prejudice, against darker skin, among black people, but Thurman demonstrates that "[s]he had ever been eager to shift the entire blame on others when no doubt she herself was the major criminal" (226). This idea riffs throughout Thurman's novel and forms one of its important themes.

Emma Lou, whose skin in very dark, is socialized into a family of white-, yellow-, and brown-hued African Americans. Thurman says, "She had been born in a semi-white world totally surrounded by an all-white one." The only sensible message that Emma Lou receives as she grows up is from her Uncle Joe, who "never seemed to regret, to bemoan, or to ridicule her blackness of skin" (6–8). He tells her that "[s]alvation depended upon the individual" (19). From her Uncle, Emma Lou is given the core of Blues knowledge that she needs to make her life her own despite social and intraracial difficulties. Emma Lou's Uncle Joe performs the same Blues philosopher function in this novel as Sadness Williams does in Dunbar's *Sport of the Gods*, as Tea Cake does in Hurston's *Their Eyes Were Watching God*, and as Peter Wheatstraw does in Ellison's *Invisible Man*. Since Uncle Joe's voice is a lone voice among many opposing, yet harmonized, voices in her family and community, she leaves home deeply affected by the negative narrative about blackness that dominated her life in Boise, Idaho. Emma Lou's mother and grandmother, for instance, are leading proponents of the "[w]hiter and whiter, every generation" motto (22). So, while Emma Lou professes to believe her Uncle Joe, she has deeply internalized the color consciousness of her other family members and their friends so that her own behavior against herself seems appropriate to her. Emma Lou, then, goes into the world also professing an ideology of color consciousness and social caste.

Thurman illustrates the pervasiveness of color consciousness among black people by moving Emma Lou to different geographical locations only to have her encounter different varieties of intraracial prejudice. Black people in small-town U.S.A., Boise, Idaho, practice the same intraracial color exclusion as those in Los Angeles and those on the cosmopolitan East Coast in Harlem. The only region of the nation that Emma Lou does not experience is the South, but her ideas about that region are clear. The South represents all that is dull, unimproved, and backward. Thurman demonstrates Emma Lou's negative attitude toward the South when she rejects the friends of Grace Giles, another dark-skinned student at the University of Southern California, who is rejected by the socially prominent, light-skinned students. The classist Emma Lou finds Grace's friends a "dull, commonplace lot for the most part people from Georgia, Grace's former home, untutored people who didn't really matter" (45). Thurman's protagonist holds the same negative attitudes about black people that those in the "blue vein, circle" and "whiter and whiter every generation" set in Boise hold: "Emma Lou borrowed a word from her grandmother and classified them as 'fuddlers,' because they seemed to fuddle everything" (11–12).

Emma Lou is unable to reject the small group of economically and socially privileged yet color conscious black people in Los Angeles. She is unable to find her own place apart from them, and she is unable to befriend Grace Giles and other black people whom Emma Lou believes are socially inferior. Emma Lou has a prejudicial, classist attitude. Yet among the people she labels the "right sort of people," dark skin is unacceptable in a female unless she brings numerous other assets that might purportedly "compensate" for her dark skin. Still, Emma Lou refuses to rethink her classist attitude, so she rejects anyone who does not meet her social standards (46–48). While Thurman's novel critiques the notion of color-consciousness as a whole, his choice of a female protagonist is crucial. Until very recently in the United States, the pervasive racialized discourses on beauty and skin color, while affecting males, fell more heavily on females. This discourse of race and beauty takes on a variety of odd shapes within the intracultural environment of African Americans; a number of variations on this discourse are presented in Thurman's novel.

In *The Blacker the Berry* Thurman deepens the complexity of Emma Lou and complicates her predicament because he depicts her as a character who not only suffers under external as well as internalized color consciousness but also is socialized among the light-skinned and more privileged black people in her town. That socialization results in her internalization of their classist ideas as well as their racial ideas. Emma Lou's own attitudes about her social entitlement complicate her problems with intraracial prejudice. She refuses to associate with black people whom she deems below her socially, yet she continues to seek acceptance among the "right sort of people," who are the very people who reject her because of her dark skin and whose light skin and intracultural privilege elevate them racially as well as socially. Emma Lou, consequently, is in a paradox shaped by discourses of race anchored to class within the social policy of the United States and among black people. These racial ironies will be illustrated more fully below as I discuss Emma Lou's ventures into Harlem's cultural life.

Emma Lou's desire for a group connection is indicative of a Blues character, but she is unable to find such a connection because the group with which she desires a connection rejects her. Thus, she is an alienated character within her group as well as from the dominant culture. She searches for a connection that at least will alleviate her intracultural alienation. Because Emma Lou despises her own color, those with whom she might find a place are rejected summarily by her because she believes that black people who are less well placed socially represent the truth of the dominant society's many mythologies of black people. And the people whose acceptance Emma Lou covets represent to her the exceptions to the dominant mythology. Yet the basis for their being excepted from the scorn heaped on the masses of black people is skin color. And Emma Lou does not pass that test, nor does she recognize that many other decent, intelligent, hard-working people like herself are among the dark masses that also are rejected by the light-skinned, privileged class of black people. Thurman leaves Emma Lou separated from a group connection, even though she is deficient in the internal resources required to live a life that lacks this connection. In order for Emma Lou to become Thurman's fully developed Blues character, who stands among other members of a group yet finds singular solutions to disappointments in life, she must move beyond the superficial ideas that consume her life and must make an existential examination of herself in order to locate the many Blues options available to her.

Thurman shows in this novel how intraracial color consciousness becomes an obstacle to Emma Lou's developing a Blues philosophy that can rework stumbling blocks and make them building blocks of the spirit. Because of her intraracial color consciousness, Emma Lou is unable to analyze the world clearly since she does not know herself, except as she is defined by those who reject her. As a consequence of this confusion, Emma Lou concocts numerous strategies designed to gain her entrance into the right society of people. All of her strategies illustrate how she is weakened by the ideas she has internalized about dark skin and how she is precluded from forming a healthy identity as a result of her attitudes.

In Harlem, Emma Lou finds a wider variety of attitudes about color than she found at home in Idaho; these attitudes, however, do include the intraracial exclusion of dark-skinned people that is found among those she considers the "right sort of people." She, consequently, experiences intraracial color discrimination while in Harlem. Because Emma Lou is dark-skinned, she is not offered a job in a real estate office owned by two black men. Yet this does not change her behavior. Emma Lou seems to believe that she will be an exception. Because she has internalized the hatred of dark skin that is prevalent among many of the people in Thurman's 1920s United States, she has turned against herself and others who are dark. She is complicit in some of her own suffering, as she makes comments as well as behaves in ways that show how much she has accepted the very social policies that limit her.

An example of Emma Lou's complicity in intraracial color discrimination occurs after she finds she is unable to obtain "congenial work." As a result, she begins working for a white actress, Arline Strange, who is playing a biracial character in an "alleged melodrama of Negro life in Harlem." When Emma Lou's employer takes an unexpected leave for two weeks, Thurman's protagonist refuses to work as a maid for the understudy, who is "a real mulatto" (98–100). Instead, she takes a two-week vacation. The ironic narrator comments on this situation and illustrates Emma Lou's attitude: "Imagine her being maid for a *Negro* woman! It was unthinkable" (119).

Thurman portrays Emma Lou in a number of situations that depict her complicity in her color-conscious morass. Her attitude toward John, a prospective suitor, most clearly illustrates this aspect of her character. She rejects a serious relationship with John because his skin is dark, he is a southerner, and he is a porter. John, however, is a true friend to Emma Lou. He helps her find a room and teaches her how to use the subway and other public transportation. He also walks comfortably with Emma Lou in public after an evening at the theater. Yet, for Emma Lou, John "was too pudgy and dark, too obviously an ex-cotton-picker from Georgia" (89–90). She could not be "satisfied with the company of such unintelligent servitors" as John and his friends (106). Despite John's kindness, Emma Lou decides that "she wanted something more than just the mere physical relationship with someone whose body and coloring were distasteful to her." The purportedly "pleasingly colored" men whom Emma Lou desires are unmindful of her and do not come near (120–22).

Instances such as these deepen Emma Lou's angst about her dark skin. And because Thurman has Emma accept the intraracial discourse of separation that oppresses her, he also has her employ the rules of that discourse against herself. During Emma Lou's vacation from her job as a maid for Arline Strange, she experiments with ways to lighten her skin and resolves to find the man she has danced with at Small's, a black-owned Harlem Blues and Jazz cabaret that, along with other clubs at the time, prided itself on attracting white audiences. Historian David Levering Lewis reports that Ed Small's Paradise "sought white clients enthusiastically and sometimes even Fawningly." At venues such as the well-known Cotton Club, where Duke Ellington gets his important break in music, black people are not allowed in the club except as employees. Ironically, the Harlem site for the Cotton Club (before it was relocated to Fifty-second Street) once housed the Club Deluxe, which was owned by the boxer Jack Johnson (Lewis 209). These sorts of racial contradictions in the dominant social discourse found a home among African American people as well.

Thurman's section on Small's serves two functions. First, it advances Thurman's critique of the artificial environment and the exploitative practices in Small's. He depicts this exploitation through the behavior of the Blues singers who must perform their music with the exoticized nuances that the audience has inscribed on it. One of the Blues singers, for example, suggestively hints at "just a promise of an obscene hip movement" as she accepts money from someone in the audience; and the other singer is depicted "rolling her eyes, shaking her hips" and accepting money from a white patron of the club. Then both of them end their performance by raising their dresses (104–5). Thurman's description of the Blues singers indicates that they employ these exoticized nuances because without such antics the audience to which Small's catered would be disappointed. For Small's white audience, Blues music is an excursion into mysterious and forbidden territory where they, momentarily, can remove their chains of social propriety and vicariously experience what they perceive as primitive wild abandon.

Thurman continues his critique of the environment at Small's by having the narrator describe the performance of the Blues singers as "melodramatic and absurd"; and, furthermore, Thurman's narrator opines, the cabaret scene "seemed staged; they were in a theater, only the proscenium arch had been obliterated. At last the audience and actors were as one" (104–5). The audience is acting as though they are experiencing a segment of what they believe is black life, and the performers are acting as though they are exposing the audience to evening social life among black people. All the while, a strict racial discourse is enacted. Within the context of the cabaret, especially Small's, everyone can act as though racial roles have been abandoned.

Despite Thurman's critique of Small's, his second function in this section of *The Blacker the Berry* is to depict how Emma Lou's experience in the cabaret moves beyond the exploitation and artifice imposed on the music. Thurman uses her experience in Small's to connect her to a Blues aesthetic from which she is alienated. Because Emma Lou has dark skin, she is constantly pushed toward Blues People because she is not accepted among people with light skin; she is forced to make contact with the people and the experiences that she has been socialized to reject. In Small's, however, Emma Lou finds that there is something in Blues music—the music of those Georgia cotton pickers (90) and purported "fuddlers" (45), which she associates with her dark-skinned college friend Grace Giles and her Harlem friend John—that "mesmerized" her and "stirred and tingled" her on the inside. Emma Lou's reaction to the Blues singers is an unsettling pleasure for her, and she is not interested in making her own connection to the philosophy in Blues or further participating in Blues aesthetic after she leaves Small's (104–5). In fact, Emma Lou attributes her feelings to having had her first drink. Thurman's presentation of Emma Lou's response to the music suggests that she has an essentialized racial response to the music, as does Larsen's Helga Crane when she hears strains of "Swing Low, Sweet Chariot" while listening to Dvořák's *New World Symphony*. Thurman, however, undercuts the notion of a connection with his presentation of Emma Lou's assessment of the situation as alcohol-induced. Emma Lou then attributes her most memorable moment in the cabaret to her dance with Alva.

Alva is the man of Emma Lou's fantasies. He has the physical characteristics and social appearance to which Emma Lou is attracted. But he is too much of a free spirit to consider a long-term bond with her. Thurman describes Alva as the product of an American biracial mother and a Filipino father (97). "He was her ideal. He looked like a college person. He dressed well. His skin was such a warm and different color, and she had been tantalized by the mysterious slant and deepness of his oriental-like eyes" (121). Thurman's descriptions of the characteristics that attract Emma Lou to Alva illustrate that she views him in terms that are as exoticized as those the white audiences in Small's take toward the Blues singers. Both the whites in the club and Emma Lou deceive themselves.

Alva is very unlike Emma Lou's surface impression of him. Through Alva—a Jazz character—Emma Lou moves more deeply into a Blues environment, which she has been taking pains to escape. Alva moves comfortably from the club scene to the rent-party environment. He lives in the moment with little concern for the stability of any narrative that he happens into. Alva is not repulsed by black skin, and he rejects the light-skin privilege that circumscribes Emma Lou's life. Alva, in fact, likes dark women (110, 138), but he occasionally weakens under the pressure of his friends' "[p]ertinacious bandinage" regarding his preference (130). More important to Alva than Emma Lou's skin color is her convenience as an additional source of income. Thus, he reads the texts inscribed in Emma Lou's favorable behavior toward him and finds ways to gain her commitment. Emma Lou, however, reads all of his responses to her in relation to her complexion.

To secure Emma Lou's confidence, Alva strategically uses his friendship with a group of prominent writers and artists to convince her that he is not ashamed to take her among his friends (138–39). Alva acts as the artists' and writers' guide at a rent party in Harlem. And he invites Emma Lou to go with him. At Alva's house, before the party, there is a discussion about the ills as well as the causes of intraracial color prejudice, a situation that serves as another opportunity for Emma Lou to evaluate the efficacy of her color conscious attitudes. Yet her response is to feel that Alva's friends are cruelly using signifying[34] indirection to comment on "something that seemed particularly tragic to her" (148).

Later at the party, Emma Lou is affected by the music she hears, just as she was moved by the music at the cabaret. Thurman's description of the music at the rent party depicts a Jazz aesthetic as the informing style at the party: "There was a moment of cacophony, then the long supple fingers [of the piano player] evolved a slow, tantalizing melody out of the deafening chaos." This music makes Emma Lou feel as though she would fly "into an emotional frenzy. . . . She had become very fluid, very elastic . . ." But she also feels very alien to this music. Thurman, further, presents this musical environment as somewhat distant to the other friends that Alva escorts to the party; they seem fascinated, but not part of the rent-party environment. Emma Lou's as well as Alva's other friends' experiences at the rent party position them in a social space outside that of the "Dark Tower" environment of uplift that is associated with the economic and intellectual luxury of A'Lelia Walker's (daughter of Madame C. J. Walker) home. This is what Emma Lou desires and is where Alva's other friends likely frequent. Alva himself is not at all bothered by the rent-party environment (150–51). Thurman's descriptions of the ambiance at the rent party are a contrast to his descriptions of Small's. Most of the people at this party, except those who attend with Alva, are native to the environment, and the musician is someone who "acted as if he were king of the occasion, ruling all from his piano stool throne" (153). His behavior at the piano evolves from his own personality and his feelings about the music he plays. The only interlopers appear to be Alva's friends, including Emma Lou.

As the evening wears on, Emma Lou's brief moment of ecstasy fades and she becomes afraid and uncomfortable. Emma Lou is particularly uncomfortable as she watches the piano player improvise. "The melody of the piece he had started to play was merely a base for more bawdy variations," and Emma Lou finds his performance maniacal (152–53). Through her response to Jazz, Thurman exemplifies Emma Lou's fear of the daring and freedom that she perceives in the music. The variety of options for change and for transformation that is suggested in the music seems powerfully frightening to Emma Lou.

Later in the novel Thurman again makes Alva the conduit through which Emma Lou gains exposure to the Blues and Jazz aesthetic she despises. He takes her to the vaudeville show at the Lafayette Theater—another actual night spot in Harlem—which serves a black clientele. There she hears Jazz and Blues as well as sees other entertainment, including a degrading "Topsy-like" comedy routine (179). Eric Lott[35] resists Thurman's use of fictionalized minstrelsy as a critique of intraracial color consciousness, especially if the minstrel images suggest that color-consciousness among black people is a discourse that is imposed on African Americans. If, however, this minstrel-like Topsy character appears on the stage of the Lafayette in an attempt to subvert the value of the Blues and Jazz performances and make them parallel to the stereotypical notions associated with Topsy, this is an unsuccessful attempt with Emma Lou, who has no esteem for this music, as she already places Topsy, Blues, and Jazz in the same category.

Topsy's lack of success in undermining the Blues and Jazz performances is likely the case for others in the audience as well, but for different reasons. Thurman's protagonist actually misreads the environment. She views the minstrel-like Topsy as a mocking caricature of dark-skinned people, while others in the audience may view the Topsy character as an obligatory aspect of the—often white-owned—traveling shows that bring them the music and musicians that they love to hear. They also may recognize in the Topsy character a subversive explosion of stereotypes, a rupture in the static commonplace, both of which are familiar to them in performances by Bert Williams as well as Louis Armstrong and, later, Cab Calloway and Dizzy Gillespie. Topsy's performance along with some of the performances of these musicians suggests that "[w]e all know I'm a vicious lie. This minstrelsy hides my value, which resides around the corner in a Blues space that we all know."

Thurman brings Emma Lou to a crossroads at the Lafayette. She initiates her relationship with Alva as an attempt to avoid the Blues life that she associates with people such as her first Harlem friend John. Yet Alva returns her to John's world, as Emma Lou and John previously had been to the Lafayette together. On this trip to the same theater with Alva, though, Emma Lou is pleased because she prefers the Lafayette over the house-rent party (177–78). Here Thurman delineates Emma Lou's position as a developing Blues character and not a Jazz character since she is more comfortable at the Lafayette Theater and at Small's than she is at the rent party, which situates free-spirited experimentation firmly within its milieu. Thurman's Jazz character Alva, however, is comfortable in both environments. Thus, through Alva, Emma Lou gains exposure to the social groups she previously had rejected, but she does not recognize how she can use the lessons of her exposure to transform her own debilitating behavior.

Emma Lou, in fact, perceives Alva's attempts to take her out with him as insensitive to her. She tells him, "First you take me out with a bunch of your supposedly high-toned friends, and sit silently by while they poke fun at me. Then you take me to a theater where you know I'll have my feelings hurt." Alva becomes frustrated with Emma Lou's unreasonable position and tells her there are numerous people with dark skin in Harlem and they do not go "around a-moanin' cause they aint half white" (183–85). This confrontation breaks the relationship between

Alva and Emma Lou, as she decides that Alva's only purpose in life is to find pleasure in every moment (207–8). Thurman does not investigate the full dimensions of his Jazz character, yet his development of Emma Lou, a Blues character, indicates that a Jazz life such as Alva's is not the way that she perceives that the "right sort of people" live.

Thurman continues to show the persistence of Emma Lou's attitudes toward color and caste, as she still refuses to recognize the strength and fortitude of the self-defined Blues and Jazz people that she encounters, even after Alva exposes her to them and she is stirred by them. Throughout the novel, Thurman moves Emma Lou closer and closer to sources from which she can learn to develop her own Blues responses, and, at the same time, he shows the strength of her earlier socialization, which will not allow her to investigate Blues aesthetics and philosophies. Thus, when Emma Lou finds that Alva is living with an "olive colored" woman named Geraldine, Thurman's protagonist decides to transform her life and reevaluate the effect Alva has had on her (138).

During a two-year hiatus from Alva, Emma Lou meets Gwendolyn Johnson and returns to school to become a teacher. She believes that she has recovered from the downward spiral in her life that had left her with diminished self-respect (196). She no longer frequents the Blues and Jazz circles to which Alva had exposed her. Gwendolyn is an educated "light-brown-skinned" (203) woman from South Carolina and is, for Emma Lou, the "right sort of people." Yet Gwendolyn's socialization as a child is significantly different from Emma Lou's. Thurman characterizes Gwendolyn as someone who understands the social pressures under which her dark-skinned friend Emma Lou lives. As a friend, Gwendolyn, consequently, understands Emma Lou's worries about her color and tries to move Emma Lou away from these debilitating ideas. Gwendolyn's mother believes that her friends and relatives who are slightly privileged because of their light skin color and who care about this are perpetuating trivialities (204).

Gwendolyn's mother also teaches her daughter to recognize the convoluted thinking that supports color consciousness. Mrs. Johnson points out, for instance, that both light and dark people with African ancestry had "to attend the same colored school . . . , to ride in the same section of the street car . . . , and were . . . both subjected to be called nigger by the poor white trash who lived in the adjacent block." As a result, Gwendolyn's mother advocates against color-consciousness among black people and "insisted that Gwendolyn must marry a dark brown man so that her children would be real Negroes." While Gwendolyn encourages her friend, Emma Lou can only think about her own desire to trade Gwendolyn's light brown skin for her dark complexion, since Gwendolyn is quite comfortable with dark skin. Emma Lou gains contact with the "right sort of people" through Gwendolyn, but these people fail to satisfy her. Her energetic and carefree life with Alva and the lively Jazz people with whom he is connected have given her experiences with which she can contrast Gwendolyn and her friends. In contrast, the world to which Gwendolyn exposes Emma Lou is narrow and has a lifelessness as well as contradictions that do not appeal to Emma Lou. When Thurman's central character finally associates with the society folk of her generation, she finds that the "right sort of people" are "quite wrong" (204–8).

Thurman, now, begins a process of transformation in Emma Lou that moves her closer to a Blues life. She begins by abandoning the concept of the "right sort of people." But she has yet to find a successful solution to her deepest conflict: she hates dark skin. Thurman, interestingly, moves Emma Lou away from class-consciousness more easily than from color-consciousness. The impact of a discourse of color is more deeply a part of Emma Lou's psyche than is the impact of class considerations, perhaps because color establishes class in both the dominant discourse as well as among early-twentieth-century black people.

Thurman demonstrates Emma Lou's need for a Blues philosophy by depicting her on a persistent quest for acceptance under a social policy that is structured against her gaining such acceptance. She must find power in her own internal resources before she can survive her negative socialization and avoid tragic or complete loss of her own self. Emma Lou continues to work within a discourse of light-skin privilege while denying how that discourse eliminates her. Thurman shows that Emma Lou needs to recognize how a more flexible Blues philosophy opens a space for group wisdom that shapes the resources of one's singular spirit and allows Blues People to move beyond, through, or around external obstacles. Since Emma Lou is not open to revising her perceptions, nor is she willing to resist the negative beliefs about herself that she has learned, she wanders from situation to situation hoping to become the one who will be excepted from the social policies that exclude her.

Thurman demonstrates how Emma Lou will benefit from recognizing the value of the discourse that influences Uncle Joe, Grace Giles, John, and the Johnsons. Until, moreover, she understands the absurdity of skin privilege, she will not have the characteristics that would bring her the life she wants and allow her to use her own internal resources to define and direct her life. Without these qualities Emma Lou is not a viable Blues character. Emma Lou's movement toward self-acceptance is long and hard, and Thurman does not bring her to this point until the end of the novel. We can, however, understand her "pyrrhic victory" as a Blues victory. Blues victories come at great costs. Who can determine the value of racialized psychological damage, social and political inequities, family destruction, deprivations of education, and economic ruin, which have been the costs of African American Blues survival and victories?

Emma Lou's victory occurs after she returns to Alva for six months. As in their prior relationship, Alva allows Emma Lou into his life so that he can benefit from her obsession with him. This time she cares for his disabled child. She decides to leave when she realizes that she must return to herself in order to understand exactly what that self is. In the final pages of *The Blacker the Berry*, Thurman makes Emma Lou a full Blues character. She now realizes that "everyone must find salvation within One's self" and that she must fight to accept herself rather than seeking acceptance from others. Now her motto is "find—not seek" (225–27). Finally, she believes that one who seeks does not have the thing for which she is searching, but one who must find something is looking for that which is her own. With this turn of events, Thurman's major Blues theme—which is that one's self-definitions and self-evaluations must be the starting point in shaping a singular identity—exemplifies his use of Blues philosophy in African American fiction.

three

THESE (BLACKNESS OF BLACKNESS) BLUES

In the 1940s and 1950s, black writers in the United States find that Blues-making events continue to inform their lived experiences. Many of these writers persist in situating their narratives within the unsettling racialized discourse of the United States and in responding to the strictures of this discourse. William Attaway in *Blood on the Forge* (1941) employs both a migration theme as well as music as he aligns migrant sharecropper Melody Moss with Jazz. This character is a guitar player whose mother changes his name to Melody so that his name would match his personality. The Moss Boys, Melody and his brothers Big Mat and Chinatown, leave Kentucky sharecropping for the mills of Pennsylvania. Other writers, such as Willard Motley, brother of Harlem Renaissance painter Archibald Motley, enter the market as so-called raceless writers in the 1940s; these writers focus on white characters in their novels. This is the case in Motley's novels *Knock on Any Door* (1947), *We Fished All Night* (1951), and *Let No Man Write My Epitaph* (1958). Yet Motley consistently employs music in these novels. Often he reinforces his setting with popular songs from the dominant social milieux as well as with Blues or Jazz tunes, such as Duke Ellington's "Mood Indigo," which he uses in *Let No Man Write My Epitaph*. These black writers, along with others, join Zora Neale Hurston, Ann Petry, and Ralph Ellison in their uses of music in African American fiction. Yet black writers in the 1940s are prompted to abandon the question of racial inequality and to write on purportedly universal topics, as the publishing houses and reviewers for prominent publications encourage them to produce what the publishing industry views as "raceless" writing.[1]

The 1940s are turbulent years in terms of race relations in the United States. Black people boycott the New York City bus system in 1941, returning after one month, when their demands for black bus drivers and mechanics are met. There are riots in North Carolina and Detroit in 1941 and 1942, respectively. Also in 1942, white students stage a walk-out in Gary, Indiana, to protest desegregation of Gary's public schools. And until President Franklin D. Roosevelt issues Executive Order 8802, which disallows discrimination in war and government industries and establishes the Fair Employment Practices Committee (FEPC), labor leader A. Philip Randolph continues to organize the first march on Washington in 1941 and ignores FDR's requests to call off the march.

The war years bring an increase in racial controversies to the country. In 1943 black people are admitted into the United States military on a quota system to control the numbers of African Americans in military service. This year there are uprisings in Mobile, Alabama; Beaumont, Texas; Los Angeles; Detroit; and Harlem. Civil unrest also occurs this year in Harlem after an altercation between a black serviceman and a police officer results in the serviceman being shot. Ralph Ellison depicts this event in the surreal riot scene at the end of *Invisible Man*, as does Ann Petry in her short novel *In Darkness and Confusion* (1947). During the war, much of the civil unrest is sparked by attacks on black servicemen by white servicemen or by white civilians. These injustices result in the call for a Double V campaign[2] among politically conscious African Americans: victory over fascism abroad and racism at home. The campaign mediates the schism that many black people feel as a result of finding themselves or their family members rallying to end tyranny and oppression abroad while continuing to experience it at home. For these reasons, Petry's character Boots Smith in her novel *The Street* actively resists military service.[3]

As black veterans in the 1940s demand their rights, there also is an increase in organized efforts to bring the United States to fulfill its promise of democratic freedoms for all. The Congress of Racial Equality (CORE) organizes its first sit-in at a Chicago restaurant in 1943, and its first freedom rides challenging segregated interstate bus travel are organized in 1947. By the end of the war, black veterans, repeating the postwar civil disruption that occurred among black veterans in 1919, demand the same political and social justice as well as freedom from tyranny that they fought for others to have, causing unrest in 1946 in a number of cities, including Philadelphia; Columbia, Tennessee; and Athens, Alabama. President Harry Truman responds by forming the Commission on Civil Rights.

By the 1950s, black people in the United States are primed for moving this country into a new era of equality, as the battles of the 1940s fatigue the nation while shaking its racial assumptions. The calm of the early fifties seems beneficent and hopeful to many black people. This moment of quiet lulls many Americans, black and white, into a false confidence in the surety of impending and rapid change in the racial policies of the United States.[4] In 1952, Tuskegee Institute, which had by then collected data on lynching for seventy-one years, finds that there are no reports of lynching for that year. Yet in 1951, white people in Cicero, Illinois, riot in response to a black family's plans to move into the town. In Chicago, there are riots and civil disruption from 1953 to 1956 in protest against black families that are scheduled to move into a public housing project in this major midwestern city. And continuing in the tradition of politicized religious organizations of previous decades, in 1953 Albert Cleage Jr. (Jaramogi Abebe Agyeman) establishes the Shrine of the Black Madonna of the Pan African Orthodox Christian Church in Detroit, Michigan. This faith-based organization, as is the case with its many predecessors, is situated in a discourse of African American spiritual, economic, personal, and collective empowerment that proactively resists a racialized social policy of exclusion and white privilege.

The momentary sense of calm and affirmation that welcomes the 1950s is veritably upset when Joseph McCarthy imagines that there are Communists proliferating throughout the United States and his House Un-American Activities Committee (HUAC) questions the loyalty and patriotism of many U.S. citizens—both black and white—including Paul Robeson, W. E. B. Du Bois, and Langston Hughes. The hopefulness for calm in race relations also departs, as the White Citizens' Council is organized in Indianola, Mississippi, in 1954. And the following year, a fourteen-year-old boy named Emmett Till is kidnapped and lynched in Money, Mississippi, for purportedly admiring a white woman. Emmett Till's murder occurs just three months after the landmark "Brown II" decision that orders the immediate desegregation of public schools. Shortly after Till's murder, a black woman in Montgomery, Alabama, named Rosa Parks refuses to play her putative role in the racial drama of the United States. Her actions spark the successful one-year-long (from 1955 to 1956) Montgomery bus boycott. The NAACP's aggressive legal strategies for civil rights gain a landmark victory in the 1954 *Brown v. Topeka Board of Education* case, which establishes the unconstitutionality of separate schools and breaks the stranglehold of fifty-eight years that the *Plessy v. Ferguson*—separate but equal—Supreme Court decision had on the social policy of this nation. At the middle of the century, these events set in motion the possibility for even more change and for more vigorous initiatives toward that change.

Films in the 1940s still include black musicians in limited as well as limiting roles, but these films also begin to raise with increased vigor the question of the United States' racialized social policies in what are termed "problem pictures."[5] In 1943 Jelly Roll Morton (Ferdinand Joseph La Menthe) and Lena Horne appear in *Stormy Weather*. Lena Horne also appears in the role of Georgia Brown in the 1942 musical *Cabin in the Sky*. Black actress Hazel Scott's debut in *Something to Shout About* brings her acclaim and leads to her appearance in a number of films during the 1940s, including *Rhapsody in Blue*, a film biography of George Gershwin. The problem of "passing" as a concern in films continues as the 1949 film *Pinky*, based on the novel *Quality* by Cid Ricketts Sumner, reprises the 1930s story line of the book-based film *Imitation of Life*. In *Pinky*, white actress Jeanne Crain—Pinky—performs the title role as the biracial grandchild child of Dicey Johnson, played by Ethel Waters. This film expands the problematical concerns found in its 1930s predecessor by depicting an interracial romance on the big screen. And Pinky, in contrast to Peola in *Imitation of Life*, decides to situate herself in the southern town where she was born; she also, before it is too late, abandons her previous thoughts of passing.

In the arts, African Americans continue the socio-cultural and political strand that influences the art of black people through very recent times in the United States. Jacob Lawrence begins the 1940s with his

Migration of the Negro series (1940–41), which brought him acclaim and escalated Lawrence's artistic career into a period of over fifty years of success. In 1957, John Biggers's painting *Jubilee: Ghana Harvest Festival* looks back to the 1920s Harlem Renaissance artistic ideas, which locate an intertexutal relation between African American and continental African cultural expression. Charles Alston's paintings during the 1950s and 1960s record his concern with social history; he terms a number of these pieces "protest paintings." One such piece, *You Never Really Meant It, Did You, Mr. Charlie?* depicts the 1957 integration of public schools in Little Rock, Arkansas. And Alston's 1955 painting titled *Walking* is inspired by the Montgomery bus boycott. This era also finds sculptor Elizabeth Catlett so discomfited by the racial and political conditions in the United States in the late 1940s and early 1950s that she moves to Mexico. As was the case for music produced during the Harlem Renaissance, in the 1940s and 1950s music continues as an inspiration for African American artists. Charles Alston's sketches of Jazz and Blues musicians, including his well-known portrait of Bessie Smith, endear him to the musicians whose art he admires. Elizabeth Catlett's bronze portrait sculpture of Louis Armstrong still stands in the New Orleans park named for this Jazz musician. Norman Lewis continues a music-into-other-arts intertext in his 1948 painting *Jazz Musicians;* this piece moves away from direct representation and renders Jazz music in free abstract form.

By the end of the 1930s the movement of white bands into the swing arena displaces a number of back musicians, as the enlivened orchestrated sound of swing no longer represents to white audiences a view of the other or a journey into the mysterious and unattainable unknown. With compositions such as William Grant Still's "Blues," white swing bands such as Artie Shaw's continue the tradition established by Harry T. Burleigh and Antonín Dvořák of combining African American music and classical music. These later compositions emphasize the music of the Blues and Spirituals rather than the classical sounds that dominated early compositions.

Swing's peak years, 1935 to 1945, find black musicians struggling to maintain a broad-based audience. The situation, ironically, is worsened in the 1940s as a result of local civil rights legislation in northern states. Booking agents, fearing lawsuits by African Americans who might attempt to attend concerts by black performers at venues that traditionally entertain white customers, simply refuse to hire black bands.[6] African American musicians encounter further difficulties during the war years as wartime rationing of gas, the youthfulness of many musicians (which qualified them for the draft), and disruptions in bus and train travel make the former 1930s one-nighters difficult if not impossible for most black musicians. In the 1930s many black musicians earned their living traveling along the East Coast and throughout the South, but this changes during the war years as factors related to the war along with racialized social policies and social upheavals, among other factors, result in their move back to small combos and infrequent travel, as well as their move from Harlem to Fifty-second Street in midtown Manhattan. Another change the war years bring is an increase in the number of women musicians and their success as performers on the national scene. The multiethnic International Sweethearts of Rhythm is one such group that plays to enthusiastic crowds throughout the 1940s.[7]

By the 1940s, among African Americans, Jazz music has moved through Louis Armstrong's Jazz age and Duke Ellington's swing era and now is preparing for Charlie Parker's and Dizzy Gillespie's bebop revolution in Jazz. As established Jazz musicians—Duke Ellington, Count Basie, Coleman Hawkins—draped in the elegant robes of swing encounter newer Jazz musicians outfitted in the hip or nonchalant as well as resistant style of bebop (not to be confused with the romanticized self-alienation of bohemian artists of the era, who set themselves up as dichotomous outsiders to established orthodoxies), the older musicians find that swing's cohering harmonic continuities and rhythmic extensions are interrogated by the contrapuntal ruptures of harmony and rhythmic dissonance found in the bebop of Parker, Gillespie, and Thelonious Monk. Still, there is no clear break between swing and bebop, as—early on—Parker, Gillespie, "Prez" Lester Young, and other proponents of the new sound play in the bands and combos of Count Basie, William Clarence "Billy" Eckstine, Earl "Fatha" Hines, Jay "Hootie" McShann, and Coleman Hawkins. From, for instance, 1942 to 1943, Hines's band includes Sarah Vaughan but also Billy Eckstine, Dizzy Gillespie, and Charlie Parker. And Mary Lou Williams swings the band for Andy Kirk throughout the 1930s as an arranger and a pianist and then investigates the new sound as a result of her contact with Thelonious Monk.

In 1943, Dizzy Gillespie and his band are playing bebop at the Onyx Club on New York City's Fifty-second Street. His band includes Oscar Pettiford on bass; George Wallingford (occasionally Thelonious Monk) on piano; Lester Young—as Gillespie is unable to locate the often enigmatic Charlie Parker—on tenor sax (until Young returns to Count Basie's band following the firing of Don Byas, who then plays tenor sax in Gillespie's band); and Max Roach on drums, as Kenny Clarke (Klook/Klook-Mop) is in the military. The band's performance is among the earliest efforts to bring the new small-combo sound to an audience. Later, Charlie Parker's quintet brings in new sounds while also returning Jazz—which had moved to a big band and orchestral sound in the 1930s—to its small-group and Blues heritage; this new sound, as did Jazz, later embraces and revises its disparaging appellation—bebop.

During the 1940s, wartime as well as the postwar migration of black and white southerners increases racial tensions in West Coast cities such as Los Angeles. Wartime labor shortages result in virtually full employment across gender lines, for people of color as well as for white people, in war industries located in the Los Angeles area. After the war, however, women along with black employees lose their jobs. By the 1940s, black migrants to Los Angeles join the Chinese, an exiguous number of Japanese, and the already existing Mexican American and other populations that locate their heritage in the Spanish speaking Americas. The presence of people of color appears to precipitate racial animus in white people, resulting in the notorious attacks on people of Spanish-speaking heritage in the Los Angeles zoot suit riots in 1943.[8]

The increase in the number of African Americans in the Los Angeles area results in the development of a vibrant nightlife along Central Avenue. The shifting cultural terrain in Los Angeles, and the resulting racial tensions, prompt Norman Granz to organize a number of jam sessions in Hollywood nightclubs; he insists that these performances will be open to black customers. In Culver City, California, at Frank Sebastian's Cotton Club, for instance, just as in the New York club with the same name, black musicians perform for white audiences. Granz's success in the Hollywood clubs prompts him to produce a Jazz concert at the Los Angeles Philharmonic Auditorium in 1944. He names these concerts Jazz at the Philharmonic (JATP). For these performances, Granz again insists that paying customers of all ethnic designations will be admitted. In 1945, trumpeter Howard McGee brings the bebop sound to Los Angeles' Central Avenue. And by 1949, when Ella Fitzgerald, Charlie Parker, and Dizzy Gillespie, along with Oscar Peterson in a surprise United States debut performance, appear together in their famous JATP performance at Carnegie Hall, Granz's concerts have become touring shows.

During the early 1940s bebop musicians are testing and formulating their new Jazz sound at a few clubs in Harlem as well as at the more recently established clubs midtown on Fifty-second Street. In 1940, though, New York's Cotton Club closes—five years after its move to Fifty-second Street; Frank Sebastian's Cotton Club in California also encounters a similar fate. And in 1943 the Savoy loses its license. In 1938 Henry Minton opened Minton's Playhouse in New York City; the club flourishes through the 1940s and becomes the site where bebop musicians gather for jam sessions that will shape the musical innovations they are investigating and where, in the late 1940s, Carmen McRae (whose teenaged composition "Dream of Life" was recorded by Billie Holiday in 1939) performs on piano and sings during intermissions. Henry Minton—an African American tenor sax player—strictly follows the legally established 4:30 A.M. curfew in his club. This practice moves many musicians to after-hours venues such as Clark Monroe's Uptown House, which thrives in the 1940s. A similarly flourishing music scene in the 1940s and 1950s is located at the Down Beat Room and the Club Alabam on Central Avenue in Los Angeles. The Club Alabam, an important venue for African American music, opens in 1931 and survives the Depression, Prohibition's (1920–33) last years, and the war years.

In 1942, the American Federation of Musicians calls a strike against recording; in 1944 this ban is lifted completely. Yet there are few indicators suggesting that the innovators of bebop are ready to record the new music in its desired small-combo format prior to their first record in 1945. By the middle of the decade, though, bebop musicians have established a repertoire of standards that include Dizzy Gillespie's "Bebop," "Blue 'n' Boogie," "A Night in Tunisia," and "Dizzy Atmosphere" as well as Thelonious Monk's tunes that he writes for the competitive environment at Minton's: "'Round Midnight," "Epistrophy," "Well You Needn't." In 1944, Charlie Parker's combo officially heralds the bebop sound in a performance at the Three Deuces Club on New York's Fifty-second Street.

Bebop is, for record producers, the new postwar race music. A few recordings of bebop pioneers preserve this music's formative years in the early 1940s. Charlie Parker's first commercial recordings are cut in 1941 while he is with the Kansas City–based swing band led by Jay McShann. Jerry Newman—a white Jazz aficionado—may have recorded the earliest example of the new bebop sound on a portable disc recorder in 1941. Drummer Kenny Clarke's and guitarist Charlie Christian's jam session performance of "Topsy" ("Swing to Bop" is the title under which the tune is recorded commercially) at Minton's also is preserved for history on Newman's recording. During 1943, while Charlie Parker, Dizzy Gillespie, and Oscar Pettiford are in the Earl Hines band, they record, in a Chicago hotel room, a bebop version of "Sweet Georgia Brown," providing perhaps another recorded sample of bebop in the making. These informal recordings provide the best source of information about pioneering bebop efforts, as the 1942 recording ban occurs in the midst of bebop's developmental stage.

Dizzy Gillespie, Bud Johnson, Max Roach, Clyde Hart, and Oscar Pettiford provide an early sample of the potential for the new bebop sound while playing in Coleman Hawkins's band. In 1944 these musicians record bebop-influenced music in Hawkins's large-band format. Bebop's most complimentary format, though, is still the small combo. Charlie Parker's first important recordings are with the four-string guitar player Lloyd "Tiny" Grimes for Savoy in 1944. These recordings demonstrate Parker's crossroads consciousness—his impulse to connect older Blues to modern Jazz. By 1945 Parker and Gillespie bring bebop to listeners in its most salient form in their Savoy recordings of "Blue 'n' Boogie," "Groovin' High," "Koko," "Now's the Time," "A Night in Tunisia," "Dizzy Atmosphere," and "Be-Bop." During the early decades of this century, musicians make records for the purpose of enticing listeners to attend live performances; at this time, recordings of music are not profitable for the musicians. By 1949 bebop's status as an art form as well as a profitable vehicle for live performances is demonstrated by Charlie Parker's opening-night performance at Morris Levy's Birdland (named in Parker's honor) in 1949.

Around 1949 race records are designated "rhythm and blues," and the first black-owned radio station, WERD, begins broadcasting from Atlanta, Georgia. Mahalia Jackson first records her gospel songs in 1943, and by 1946 Jackson's recording of Herbert Brewster's composition "Move on Up a Little Higher" sells one million copies. Jazz vocalist Sarah Vaughan, already an established talent with Earl Hines's band, wins amateur night at the Apollo in 1943, and the recordings that follow land her the title the Divine One.

Swing's symphonic sounds in the 1930s and 1940s—with releases such as Duke Ellington's Jazz suite "Black, Brown, and Beige" in 1945—along with cool Jazz's measured Europeanized sounds in the 1950s all situate Jazz in a comfortable space within the dominant culture,[9] yet

Blues is still an incontestable favorite among African American people in the 1940s and 1950s, with the electrified Blues sound gaining prominence. During the 1940s the popularity of down-home Blues musicians shrinks considerably among African Americans, as the faster rhythms of urban Blues gain influence. This new urban Blues sound includes electric instruments and raucous rhythms in both the sound of the music and the style of the vocals. It can be found in the 1940s and 1950s Blues sounds of, among others, Muddy Waters (McKinley Morganfield) on "Mannish Boy" and "Rolling Stone" (after he moved from Mississippi to Chicago in 1943 and later abandoned his acoustic guitar); Aaron Thibeaux "T-Bone" Walker on "Stormy Monday Blues" (Walker's Blues sound gained prominence after his 1939 performance at the Cotton Club in New York made his electric Blues guitar performance of "T-Bone Blues" a standing favorite); Howlin' Wolf (Chester Arthur Burnett) on "Moaning at Midnight"; Peetie Wheatstraw (William Bunch) on "The Devil's Son-in-Law" and "The High Sheriff of Hell" (until his death in 1941, Wheatstraw enjoyed immense success among black Blues fans with clever and witty songs); and Marion "Little" Walter Jacobs on "Off the Wall."

Down-home Blues musicians continue to record in the 1940s, even though the electrified Blues sound has gained prominence. In 1941 both Booker T. Washington "Bukka" White and Sonny Boy Williamson record important down-home Blues tunes that convey serious commentary on the racialized social policy of the United States. White's "Parchman Farm" refers to the neo-plantation environment of the Mississippi prison with that name, and Williamson's "My Black Name," ostensibly about the loss of love, critiques the position of "blackness" in the United States. Williamson's music serves as a transitional point in Blues. In the early 1940s he electrifies his harp while still keeping a rough down-home edge. His favored position among the electrified Blues musicians finds his tunes, such as "My Black Name," covered by John Lee Hooker as well as fellow down-home Blues musicians Lightnin' Hopkins and Big Joe Williams. At the end of the decade, in 1949, Big Bill Broonzy augments the efforts of his fellow down-home bluesmen with his politicized Blues tune "Black, Brown, White," which makes critical comment on the racial divide of the United States.

Jazz rhythms of the 1940s and 1950s, such as those found in the music of Art Blakey's Jazz Messengers, persist in the move to maintain a Blues basis and social context that will keep some form of Jazz situated within a broad-based African American cultural milieu. Among the many distinguished alumni of Blakey's Jazz Messengers is Lee Morgan, whose 1957 recording of "Sidewinder," which later becomes the title tune from Morgan's best-known album,[10] combines Jazz and Blues sounds in an accessible style. Blakey and Morgan's sound often is termed "hard bop." There is, however, even more on the music horizon. In 1956 James Brown and the Fabulous Flames release their hit record "Please, Please, Please." In Brown, African American music gets something new: soul. Brown becomes Soul Brother Number One and the Godfather of Soul, and later Aretha Franklin becomes the Queen of Soul. In terms of Spiritual-Gospel innovations, the 1950s and 1960s mark the era of the freedom songs, which are primarily part of the southern civil rights movement, a movement that finds significant numbers of black people, along with their white supporters, employing transformed versions of black church—and sometimes popular—music in protest against Jim Crow racial exclusion and tyranny in the United States.

In 1954 the first Newport Jazz Festival organizers convince the residents of Newport, Rhode Island, to allow them to bring Jazz music to the area. The residents fear the music, perceiving it as a vehicle for violence and lascivious activity in their community. In 1960, though, crowds of mostly white males storm the filled-to-capacity festival and cause it to close early. Langston Hughes and Muddy Waters compose a Blues song on the spot to memorialize the moment—"Goodbye Newport Blues." In 1959 an enterprising black man in Detroit by the name of Berry Gordy establishes Hitsville, USA—Motown Records—and expands black music in the United States with another new sound. Blues experiences, however, still dominate in African American lived culture and fiction.

The high point of the Harlem Renaissance is in the past, yet in 1950 Gwendolyn Brooks makes history as the first African American writer to win the Pulitzer Prize. Her prize-winning book of poems *Annie Allen* provides an enlightening perspective on postwar life among black people in the United States, including some of the sentiments of wartime veterans who do not live the lives they fought for others to have. Ralph Ellison in *Invisible Man*, which won the National Book Award, also portrays postwar black veterans in their disappointment and anger. In 1959 Lorraine Hansberry's play, *A Raisin in the Sun*, about a black family moving into a white neighborhood, becomes a successful non-musical Broadway hit.

Post–Harlem Renaissance production among black writers in the United States demonstrates the persistence of music in African American fiction, even though the dominant cultural emphasis of this period shifts away from placing value on the presumably invigorating potential of folk materials in literature. Zora Neale Hurston's *Their Eyes Were Watching God* is written after the height of activity during the Harlem Renaissance and is set in an indeterminate post–Civil War period, probably during the post-Reconstruction era, when a number of independent black towns such Boley, Oklahoma—the town on which Toni Morrison bases her novel *Paradise*—are established. Ann Petry's World War II era novel *The Street* examines the struggles of Lutie Johnson, a single mother, as she seeks to improve her life while encountering the difficulties that both color and gender impose on her. Ralph Ellison situates his *Invisible Man* within the contemporaneous setting of the tumultuous 1940s; this novel is published during the seemingly calm interlude that precedes the formative years of the mass-based organizing of the 1950s civil rights era. All of these novels portray, at the center of their texts, characters based in a Blues aesthetics and philosophy.

The Blues philosophy characters in these novels are situated in or have a desire to be part of a base of support with which they have similar ideas. Yet they also speak from or learn to speak from their base of support with singular voices; that is, they find solutions to spirit-crushing experiences in their lives by using singular approaches to shape the group philosophy to which they are linked. Hurston and Ellison also depict in their novels characters located in a Jazz aesthetics and philosophy. These Jazz characters exemplify distinct voices that contain fragments from a number of larger groups. Jazz characters, however, do not ground themselves in the philosophy of any particular narrative; they move at will among the discourses from which they are fragmented, thus making collective improvisation an important aspect of Jazz style. Jazz collective improvisation in fiction permits different and differing voices to occupy the same space without engaging in destructive contention. This Jazz space is a site that is occupied by the uncontained. In their novels, Hurston and Ellison investigate Jazz philosophy, even though the lifestyles of their Jazz characters are ultimately rejected and their Jazz characters are marginalized.

Hurston's Jazz character Tea Cake is killed. Janie, the main character in *Their Eyes Were Watching God*, abandons Tea Cake's Jazz life and returns to her Blues life in Eatonville. But Janie, Hurston's female Blues character, returns to Eatonville with new ideas culled from a Jazz existence on the muck[11] with Tea Cake. Ellison's Jazz character Rinehart also is marginalized. The Blues narrator in Ellison's novel considers Rinehart's approach to life and rejects it as cynical and exploitative as well as frighteningly free. Among the three writers in this section, Ellison's and Hurston's uses of Blues as shaping aspects of their art are more apparent than Petry's. Ellison combines elements of the picaresque and the Bildungsroman along with the Blues in order to make what he terms his "blues toned" narrator. Unlike Hurston and Ellison, though, Petry has no Jazz characters, but she does employ Jazz riffs throughout her novel. Petry's novel, however, is filled with Blues characters that point to a broad spectrum of Blues responses to life.

Zora Neale Hurston: *Their Eyes Were Watching God*

In her 1937 novel *Their Eyes Were Watching God*, Zora Neale Hurston brings the transforming effects of the novelist's art to the folkloric material she gathered as an ethnographer. In the essay "Spirituals and Neo-Spirituals," Hurston finds that African American music is a container of historical, cultural, and philosophical experiences. Hurston brings that knowledge to her writing as she comments on Blues in *Their Eyes Were Watching God* and other fictional texts, including *Seraph on the Suwanee* (1948), Hurston's ironic counterpoint to *Their Eyes Were Watching God*, which focuses on two white characters, Jim and Arvay Meserve. In this novel Hurston's bluesman, Joe Kelsy, serenades Jim and Arvay and teaches their son Kenny how to play Blues guitar.

As several scholars have recognized, Hurston uses Blues aesthetics and philosophy in her characterization of Janie Crawford. In *Behind the Veil*, Robert Stepto discusses Janie's experiences with Tea Cake on the muck as an immersion ritual (164–65). Houston Baker, in *Blues Ideology*, states that Janie returns from the muck as a Blues singer (59). Alice Walker, Hurston's most vocal champion, situates this writer with Billie Holiday and Bessie Smith as women who "form a sort of unholy trinity." For Walker, Hurston "belongs in the tradition of black women singers" (xvii). Lorraine Bethel concurs with Walker's recognition of a womanist aspect in Hurston's literary Blues, pointing out that "Janie's narrative . . . reflects the black female blues aesthetic" (180). Likewise, for Cheryl Wall, Janie is "a literary counterpart of the blues" and Hurston "was the one literary woman who was free to embrace Bessie Smith's art [and] who was also heir to the legacy evoked in the blues" (140).

Hurston's Eatonville is a Blues environment. In this small, newly formed town governed by black people, Hurston's characters are situated in a group philosophy that informs the communal life of the town. The residents of Eatonville, except Janie—after her husband Joe Starks dies—do not deviate far from their shared ideas. Hurston illustrates the communal group behavior of the people in Eatonville when Tony Taylor welcomes Joe and Janie to the town. The Eatonville community has set in place a certain iterable model,[12] which they expect will be enacted by Tony. This model operates as a repetition of a performance; such repetition allows each instance of the performance event to operate in its own unique way. Events or performances such as plays or even a signature operate in this way; there are certain expectations as to the general mode of presentation of the event, yet each performance—each production of a play or each time a person's signature occurs—is its own unique repetition. In Tony's welcome, however, he fails to refer to "Isaac and Rebecca at the well," even though making such a reference in a welcome speech is an Eatonville custom. As a result of this error, Lige Moss asserts that Tony is "way outa . . . [his] jurisdiction." And all of the other residents supported Lige's assertion. For them, "It was sort of pitiful for Tony not to know he couldn't make a speech without saying that" (68). In this passage, Hurston exemplifies the established pattern, the discursive formation from which the people in Eatonville operate. And Tony demonstrates his ignorance of appropriate behavior when he does not employ the right rhetorical structure in his welcome speech.

As residents in an all-black town, the relative distance—though not complete isolation—that the people of Eatonville sometimes have from the racial discourse of the dominant society allows them to function as a site of a communal (as was the case in pre–Civil War Spirituals) instead of a community philosophy, which is the typical environment of Blues People. Eatonville's communal life is informed by the racial discourse that makes the town possible, but the town's internal workings are not shaped by the racialized discourse of the United States, even though some of the dominant society's values are reshaped for life in Eatonville. This semi-autonomous condition makes the residents of Eatonville more cohesive than black people who do not have the same level of distance from the racialized discourse of the dominant group.

Another aspect of Blues life in Eatonville is the material conditions of life there for most of the residents. With the exception of Joe, people in Eatonville live in houses that resemble slave quarters (75), and some of them were reared on turpentine stills and others on a saw-mill camp (64). The life of the people in Eatonville includes hardships and demoralizing conditions. Yet Hurston, along with all of the conformity and the difficulties she exemplifies in the people of Eatonville, also depicts her characters' singularity. When her communal Blues characters encounter dispiriting situations, they—similar to their community-based counterparts—employ group-informed solutions that are particular to their own dispositions. Hurston demonstrates most clearly in Janie that Blues singularity is crucial among Blues People. She uses specific references to Spiritual-Gospel songs among the residents of Eatonville but not explicit references to Blues, thus demonstrating Eatonville's transitional position as the residents move from a communal philosophy to a Blues community philosophy. Hurston, however, does use verbal riffs from Blues songs, which she associates with her Jazz character Vergible Woods, or Tea Cake, and with Janie after she meets Tea Cake and decides to marry him.

Hurston situates Eatonville within the context of its residents' transition into a Blues philosophy not only through her illustration of their lifestyle but also through her specific references to music. She uses Spiritual-Gospel songs in ways that recall the antebellum Spiritual makers whose music was not divided into categories of secular and religious. The Spiritual-Gospel music in *Their Eyes Were Watching God* supports a Blues environment. Even though Hurston's title refers to the eyes of the survivors peering into the darkness of the storm on the muck and to the heaven-ward glance of those who have died on the muck, her novel still interrogates the life possibilities available to Blues People. Her first specific reference to music is at the lamp lighting, when Mrs. Bogle sings "Walk in the Light." This song follows a verbal riff by Joe Starks, whose speech includes the phrase "Let it shine, let it shine, let it shine," a phrase Hurston takes from the song "This Little Light of Mine" (73). Her next significant use of this music comes during Joe Starks's funeral march: Eatonville's residents sing "Safe in the Arms of Jesus" for Janie's despotic second husband (136). Hurston's use of this song helps readers place Joe in perspective, within the context of the Blues environment in Eatonville. In an independent black town such as Eatonville and among early-twentieth-century Blues People, "Safe in the Arms of Jesus" is a typical funeral song. Hurston's Eatonville residents, then, are consistent in their Blues philosophy when they sing this Spiritual-Gospel song. In this funeral passage, Hurston also makes it clear that Janie is not at all grieved by Joe's death. Janie recognizes that "life had mishandled him too," so she pities Joe (134). Hurston's use of this funeral song conveys the idea that Joe's Blues life finally leads to heavenly protection from harm and relief from suffering, even though he doesn't rely on this. Janie's sympathetic perspective on Joe's tyrannical attitude also is shared among the residents of Eatonville. They do not like his attitude, but they understand that Joe found for himself a response to societal barriers that worked for him. They understand his hardships and accept his failings.

Hurston's specific reference to Spiritual-Gospel music in connection with Tea Cake occurs when he spends Janie's money without consulting her. Tea Cake returns home singing "Ring de bells of mercy. Call de sinner man home" (180). Hurston, again, uses music to request mercy for Janie's errant partner. Tea Cake recognizes that he has hurt Janie, so he employs the Spiritual-Gospel signifying practice of double meanings when he sings this song as a plea for mercy and a call for Janie to allow him back into their home instead of as a reference to God's mercy and a call to a heavenly home. In this song Hurston includes an analysis of Tea Cake that is similar to the analysis of Joe located in the Spiritual-Gospel song that the residents of Eatonville sing at Joe's funeral. Janie reads Tea Cake's actions—just as she read Joe's—within the context of his life and of the world in which they live. So the music that Tea Cake plays and the music at Joe's funeral become the vehicle through which Hurston helps readers understand these two characters.

Tea Cake lives a fragmented Jazz life. In order to triumph over the marginalized position that the dominant society reserves for him, he moves from town to town and absorbs the fragments of experience that he gains in his travels. He lives each moment as it comes, and he makes his own rules. Consequently, his actions often may present a contrast to notions of right among the people in towns, such as Eatonville, that he passes through. The group-oriented people in these towns might define Tea Cake as a sinner in need of mercy. Although Tea Cake's actions are not excused by the people in these towns, his behavior elicits sympathy and forgiveness.

Tea Cake also is a Blues musician, playing both piano and guitar. Early in Janie and Tea Cake's courtship, he plays Blues for Janie. The music accompanies the first moments of intimacy between Janie and Tea Cake: "The sounds [of the Blues music] lulled Janie to soft slumber and she woke up with Tea Cake combing her hair" (156). In this intimate encounter, Hurston uses music to connect Janie to a Blues life, from which she is alienated because of the life she has been socialized to live. Hurston, then, depicts Janie as a young, repressed Blues character who later—as a mature woman—returns to Eatonville and establishes Blues ties. Janie's Blues life is repressed early in the novel as a result of her socialization by Nanny, her grandmother, who was formerly enslaved; Nanny taught Janie to distance herself from Blues life. Nanny rightfully believes that the best life for Janie is a life without the hardship, suffering, oppression, and pain that comprise the old woman's life. Bethel associates Nanny with "the Black religious folk tradition embodied by spirituals" and positions Janie within "the black female folk aesthetic contained in the blues" (181). Because Nanny is active in ordering the events in Janie's life and does not rely solely on the will of God or attribute her own actions to God's designs, she is not a literary Spiritual-Gospel character. When she says that God will provide a husband for Janie, Nanny is clearly working out of the knowledge that Logan Killicks already is interested in Janie, and she works to make Killicks's interest coincide with hers. Nanny is a Blues character with a spiritual basis; she wants to preach a message but never does. And it is not until Nanny recognizes that her own death is imminent that she releases Janie—who has no one else—into the hands of God. Nanny fears that Janie's earthly protection, Logan Killicks, may not be suitable after the old woman's impending death.

After Nanny is no longer enslaved, her life is still a constant struggle to remain just a few steps away from her formerly enslaved condition. Thus, her model for the best life for Janie is the life she perceives among more privileged white women. Nanny's perception of white women, however, is that the spirit-shattering conditions that make her a "cracked plate" (37) are dispelled by the "protection" (30) white women receive from white men, who provide them the leisure to sit on porches. Janie, ironically, finds that she is banished from the porch she finally obtains. Even though Joe promises Janie a porch that resembles the one in Nanny's sermon: "A pretty doll-baby lak you is made to sit on de front porch and rock and fan yo'self and eat p'taters dat other folks plant just special for you" (49). Among the black people of Eatonville, the porch is not the site of stasis suggested by Nanny's leisurely porch modeled on the examples of white women. Janie's porch in Eatonville is lively and active. Still, as Wall observes, the Starks' porch[13] does not give women as much "personal freedom and power" as the Blues does: "Free of the constraints of ladyhood, the bonds of traditional marriage, and the authority of the church, [blues]women improvised new identities for themselves" (166). Hurston will demonstrate this female Blues empowerment in Janie after she returns from the muck informed by her Blues experiences there.

To Janie's grandmother, the lives of white women "looked lak uh mighty fine thing." As an enslaved woman, Nanny could not control her life in simple ways, such as being able to sit down when she was tired (172) or living her own "dreams of whut a woman outghta be" (31). Yet Nanny's distance from the inner life of privileged white women does not allow her to see the impediments on the spirit that their lifestyle produces. Her limited viewpoint causes her to "mis-love" (138) Janie. Janie's friend Phoeby, though never enslaved, also exhibits Nanny's view on the ideal position for women. Phoeby tells Janie that she would love to have the experience of "sittin' on porches lak de white madam" for just one year. And likewise Janie's Nanny directs her granddaughter's life toward an imitation of the models of womanhood that "look lak heben" to women such as Phoeby and Nanny, who have significantly less comfortable lives. Yet Janie "nearly languished tuh death up dere" because of the alienation from other people and the idleness that Nanny's model of sitting "on de high stool" portends (172).[14]

Through Janie, Hurston demonstrates that women within the racialized discourse of a Blues environment find that they must surmount the minimizing discourse of gender and the complexities that race brings to gender. Janie's grandmother teaches her granddaughter this lesson early in the novel when she says that the "white man throw down de load and tell the nigger man tuh pick it up. He pick it up because he have to, but he don't tote it. He hand it to his womenfolks. De nigger woman is de mule uh de world so fur as Ah can see" (29). Nanny doesn't want Janie to be a mule, so she encourages her granddaughter to protect herself by marrying a man who can provide her a measure of ease. Early on Nanny says that she wants to "preach a great sermon about colored women sittin' on high," as she believes she has seen white women do, but there "wasn't no pulpit" for this formerly enslaved woman. Nanny "save[s] the text for" Janie (31–32).

Later, when Janie takes-up Nanny's text, she preaches it in the manner that Michelle Russell uses to describe the preaching of Bessie Smith. The blueswoman Bessie Smith "preached a spiritual lesson," Russell says, "but she took it from the Blues Book, chapter nine" (131).[15] Janie, then, is socialized to remain among Blues People and to make the choices that will approximate for her the lifestyle of bourgeois white women. This is what Janie does in her first two marriages. When, however, Logan Killicks, Janie's first husband, makes suggestions that indicate his willingness to use Janie as though she is a mule, Janie leaves him and marries Joe Starks. In her marriages to both Joe and Logan, Janie does not reject Nanny's solution for resisting hardships—seeking male protection—but through Janie's marriage to Joe, Hurston demonstrates how Nanny's solution fails Janie.

At Janie and Joe's first meeting, Hurston shows that Janie, reared as a Blues child, has Jazz desires. Janie wants the freedom to meet the world on her own terms, especially within the context of her desire for sexual fulfillment: "Janie pulled back a long time because he [Joe] did not represent sun-up and pollen and blooming trees, he spoke for far horizon. He spoke for change and chance. Still she [Janie] hung back. The memory of Nanny was still powerful and strong" (50). Janie's first inclination is toward sexual freedom, which Hurston metaphorically depicts as "pollen and blooming trees." Janie does not wait for what she actually wants, and until she is encouraged by Tea Cake to pursue her own desires, she is unhappy. My reading of Janie as well as Houston Baker's assessment of Janie as a literary Blues singer when she returns to Eatonville (59), along with Angela Davis's view of the blueswoman as a symbol of female sexual freedom, all situate Janie within a particularly female literary Blues philosophy. Davis observes that "the freedom to choose sexual partners was one of the most powerful distinctions between the condition of slavery and the post-emancipation status of African Americans" (131).

Joe Starks offers Janie an ideal marriage according to Nanny's standards. He exposes Janie to the possibilities available to a man who refuses to acquiesce to the barriers in his life. For Janie, though, marriage to Joe deadens her spirit. Because Janie is Joe's wife, she is not permitted to be a woman in the world, a person with complex feelings and thoughts of her own. The set pattern in life that both Nanny and Joe want for Janie is onerous. On the one hand, Hurston's protagonist is influenced by Nanny, who wants her granddaughter to have the model of female comfort that she sees among financially privileged white women; on the other hand, when Janie gets the model of female comfort that Nanny posits, she finds that her husband Joe employs a tyrannical model of power and authority with which he is familiar and under which he too lives. Joe believes "[s]omebody got to think for women and chillun and chickens and cows" (110), and that somebody is men. Joe speaks feelingly yet with trepidation as to the certainty of his position, as we find later that he recognizes Janie's potential to stand outside this bourgeois model of marriage in which he operates. Hurston demonstrates Joe's instability within the bourgeois narrative through his unjust supposition that Janie is using conjure to incapacitate him (127).

Life with Joe alienates Janie from other people. Joe does not allow Janie to socialize with the people of Eatonville. Her joys in life, as Joe views them, come through him. Joe tells Janie, ". . . Ah aimed tuh be a big voice. You oughta be glad 'cause dat makes uh big woman outa you." This view of marriage also is present in Toni Morrison's novel *Sula*. Marriage squeezes Morrison's character Nel Wright Greene into an expanded version of her husband Jude. Hurston illustrates how Joe's words affect Janie and cause her to feel disconnected and distanced from the flow of life in Eatonville: "A feeling of coldness and fear took hold of her. She felt far away from things and lonely" (74). After Joe dies, Janie begins to consider possibilities for her own philosophy about life. She is unable to live in Nanny's life narrative, in which, as Joe becomes a big voice, her voice is silenced. By the end of the novel Janie finds her voice; it is a self-reflexive and self-empowering Blues voice.

Janie's marriage to Joe Starks is a union that provides Nanny's granddaughter a "protected" life. Even though Nanny is not alive when Janie marries Joe, Janie acts out Nanny's script. Janie is miserable in Eatonville because she wants to be part of the Blues People who sit on the porch of their store and use "a side of the world for a canvas" (85). On the high stool, where Joe has separated her from others, Janie's existence is empty; there is no activity, no life. It is an existence of quietism. (169). Janie's quiet life is in direct contrast with the lives of the exuberant, active people of Eatonville. Janie yearns to join the Blues philosophers— on her porch—who boldly assert that nature is the "onliest thing God ever made" (101). She also admires the verbal seduction enacted by the Blues tricksters of Eatonville, whose love exceeds human ability: "Ah'll take uh job cleanin' out de Atlantic Ocean fuh you any time you say you so desire" (108). To Janie, this Blues world represents "crayon enlargements of life" (81) where there are profound discussions on nature and nurture as well as a playful enactment of a mundane courtship rituals. Janie's longing for these Blues aspects of life evinces her dissatisfaction with the life that Joe provides. She wants to be part of the signifying Blues world of the Starkses' porch, which operates in a fashion similar to the briarpatch in Albert Murray's *Train Whistle Guitar* and John Edgar Wideman's *Sent for You Yesterday*. The porch is a public version of the submerged briarpatch. Hurston's porch is a safe as well as "sacred space" (Hubbard 55), removed from overt influence by or concern with the racialized social policies of the United States.

This Blues world of lying and signifying that Janie longs for is explained by Henry Louis Gates, who takes Hurston's novel as the first instance of a speakerly text in African American literary tradition. A speakerly text is a literary text that pays homage to signifying, or verbal word play, in African American folk culture; or, in Gates's words, it is a literary text that employs a "rhetorical strategy designed to emulate the phonetic, grammatical, and lexical patterns of actual speech and produce the 'illusion of narration.'" Speakerly texts value the qualities found in the spoken word. In speakerly texts, "certain rhetorical structures seem to exist primarily as representations of oral narration, rather than as integral aspects of plot or character development. These verbal rituals signify the sheer play of black language, which *Their Eyes* seems to celebrate." Hurston's passages on the Starkses' porch clearly exemplify an assenting nod to the cultural value of verbal play among Hurston's Blues People. Hurston's novel, as Gates discusses it, "cleared a rhetorical space for the narrative strategies that Ralph Ellison would render so deftly in *Invisible Man*" ("Hurston and the Speakerly" 165, 178).

Janie's marriage to Tea Cake takes her off of the high stool and brings her onto the porch and beyond it to a Blues-Jazz world exemplified by the muck and her third husband Tea Cake, who is significantly younger than she is. When Janie and Tea Cake decide to marry, Hurston's main character asserts that she has "lived Grandma's way, now Ah means tuh live mine" (171). Hurston not only uses the Blues music that Tea Cake plays for Janie to bring her into the Blues world that she desires but also introduces Janie into the Blues world through Tea Cake's use of the same signifying train and ship love ritual that is used on Janie and Joe's porch by Jim and Dave as they playfully try to win Daisy's affections (107–8). To win Janie, Tea Cake asks her if she wants a battleship or a passenger train.[16] Janie seeks stability and chooses the train. "If it blow up Ah'll still be on land," she says. Tea Cake encourages Janie to be true to her own feelings instead of being true to the rules that Nanny and Joe Starks have established for her. He tells Janie, "Choose de battleship if dat's whut you really want" (153).

Hurston's portrayal of Tea Cake situates him within Jazz aesthetics and philosophy. He plays Blues guitar and piano, and he is not grounded in any particular place or tied to any authority, except his own. Tea Cake lives from place to place, and he boasts that there is no gambler better than he is (187). He takes chances by moving outside structured narratives such as Blues. Illustrating his Jazz adeptness, he moves between places such as the muck and Eatonville with little difficulty. Hurston clearly depicts Tea Cake's Jazz style through her use of Blues philosophy during the first meeting between Janie and Tea Cake. When Tea Cake tells Janie that he lives seven miles from Eatonville, she wonders how he will get home. Janie suggests a train; Tea Cake, however, says he will walk, and, through a verbal riff, he lets Janie know he is a jazzman who can completely locate himself in the bluesman's life of hopping trains. Tea Cake's response to Janie suggests a Blues traveling phrase that could be found in numerous freight train or traveling Blues tunes: "When Ah takes uh notion Ah rides anyhow—money or no money" (148). Hurston employs another verbal riff through Tea Cake when he comments on Janie's beauty; as he combs her hair, he riffs a line from Alberta Hunter's "Down Hearted Blues": "Youse got de world in uh jug[17] and make out you don't know it" (157).

Through Janie's exposure to Tea Cake's ideas about freedom and his rejection of authority, Janie begins to break the restrictive pattern in which she has lived her life. She returns to the philosophy of "de old folks" who do not try to imitate the life-style of the dominant society that rejects them. Janie changes the set pattern in her life and accepts indeterminacy. Hurston shows this change in her protagonist through the response Janie gives to Tea Cake's query about whether she would gamble: "Ah'm born but Ah ain't dead. No tellin whut Ah'm liable tuh do yet" (160). As Tea Cake's wife, Janie is willing to accept the idea that "new thoughts had tuh be thought and new words said" (173). Hurston demonstrates the Blues basis of Janie's decision to think new thoughts and Janie's closer alignment with Tea Cake's Blues life as she depicts clothing, including a blue satin wedding dress. Thus, Janie's awakening into her Blues life, which has been repressed, comes through Tea Cake, a Jazz character whose love for Janie as well as his Jazz personality allows him to create an environment that nurtures Janie's Blues life. As Cheryl Wall explains, Tea Cake is Janie's Blues philosopher or advisor or "cultural guide" (88). Sadness Williams has a similar function in Paul Laurence Dunbar's *Sport of the Gods*, as does Uncle Joe in Wallace Thurman's *Blacker the Berry* and Peter Wheatstraw in Ralph Ellison's *Invisible Man*. When, in fact, Janie's decision to marry Tea Cake is settled in her mind, Janie's best friend Phoeby is unable to alter this decision. Hurston's use of a verbal riff, which ends Pheoby and Janie's conversation about the viability of Janie's marriage to a man who is younger and less economically stable, illustrates Janie's newly awakened Blues aesthetic. Janie's words repeat a Blues tune and recurrent Blues idea as she riffs a line from "Going Away Blues": "Some of dese mornin's and it won't be long, you gointuh wake up callin' me and Ah'll be gone" (173).

Hurston's strongest Blues character in *Their Eyes Were Watching God* is Janie; Tea Cake is her most clearly drawn Jazz character. Janie remains a Blues character throughout the novel, even though she goes to the muck with Tea Cake. Life with Tea Cake provides Janie an opportunity to rewrite the narrative into which she has been socialized. Janie, however, does not abandon all of the ideas from her previous life in Eatonville to become a free floating Jazz subject with Tea Cake on the muck. She is a dynamic character who grows in knowledge as a result of her experiences with Tea Cake, but she does not completely embrace Tea Cake's Jazz life. Janie's love for Tea Cake allows her to live with him on the muck and to be a part of everything that is part of his life (186); Tea Cake's love for Janie does not really change his Jazz lifestyle, but she changes him emotionally, as she is the only woman who is capable of holding him (181); in fact, there is nothing else that can influence Tea Cake besides Janie. Her hold on him, however, is his choice.

While under the influence of Hurston's Jazz character, Vergible Woods/Tea Cake, Janie sees the world differently, but she does not completely break away from Blues life while she is married to Tea Cake. He is, though, the person who shows Janie that she must free herself and find her own singular solutions to life's difficulties, instead of accepting preset solutions. Hurston establishes that Tea Cake's life is among "hopeful humanity," people who make and use Blues "right on the spot"; this is the case during the talks on the porch on the muck. For them, "[n]ext month and next year were other times. No need to mix them up with the present" (196–97). In Tea Cake's world, people organize their lives for the moment. Hurston's Janie does not choose to live this way after Tea Cake's death, but Janie's third husband shows her that she has choices.

Through her experiences on the muck with Tea Cake, Janie realizes that the possibilities available to a woman with no limits or boundaries allow her to destabilize the hierarchies into which she has been socialized and to insert herself into a Blues life in Eatonville, the town from which she had been alienated because Joe Starks cut her off from the common people in the town. Joe denies Janie a quotidian life among the people of Eatonville because he believes that succeeding economically and gaining power are associated with attaining a bourgeois lifestyle modeled on the dominant discourse, a lifestyle that is difficult for most of Eatonville's residents to attain. After Joe's death, Hurston depicts Janie's subversion of Joe's bourgeois attitudes as well as her rejection of the dominant social values that he mimics. Janie connects herself with the Blues People of Eatonville as a woman who is free, autonomous, and who has loved and been loved by Tea Cake. In *Blues Legacies*, Angela Davis also discusses blueswomen as people who disrupt supposed stable categories, especially gender categories. Blueswomen present an image of women "free of the domestic orthodoxy of the prevailing representations of womanhood through which female subjects of the era were constructed" (13). Blues "helped construct an aesthetic community that affirmed women's capacities in domains assumed to be the prerogatives of males, . . . [including] sexuality and travel" (120).

In *Their Eyes Were Watching God* Hurston demonstrates that Blues philosophy for Janie, particularly as a married woman whose life (during her marriage to Joe) is somewhat privileged, is complicated by a socialization process that conflates her voice into her male companion's voice. Janie tells a dying Joe, "[Y]ou wasn't satisfied wid me de way Ah was. Naw! Mah own mind had tuh be squeezed and crowded out tuh make room for yours in me" (133). Hurston rejects this silencing process and returns Janie to the suffering Blues People on the muck, so that she can gain an understanding of the spirit of triumph that sustains life in people who are considered "[u]gly from ignorance and broken from being poor" (196). The dominant society in the United States, the church, and some middle-class African Americans—because they locate themselves in the dominant discourse—tend to situate Blues (especially the type on the muck) in an outsider position. This is in contrast to "the masses of black people," especially during the first eight decades of the twentieth century, who view Blues singers as their "most intimate insider"

(A. Davis 125). Janie brings this spirit of success and triumph into the developing town of Eatonville, where the dominant society's ideas about life threaten Blues philosophy.

Janie and Tea Cake's marriage breaks the bourgeois model for the female's role in society. And when Janie returns to Eatonville, she suggests that women in this town also should break the boundaries of their gender relations. Before Janie's return to Eatonville, Hurston indicates that the women there have a voice, but it is a choral voice that is lacking examination, reflection, and discipline. The women in Eatonville are not masters of the words they voice. "They made burning statements with questions, and killing tools out of laughs. It was mass cruelty. . . . Words walking without masters, walking altogether like harmony in a song" (10). The women have not used the basic Blues chords as a back beat on which they inscribe their own narrative in the foreground. Thus, Janie's experiences become an exemplar of the necessity and the possibility for a woman's singular voice.

Janie does not want to be part of Eatonville's harmonized female voices—which most often speak against themselves as they speak in support of established ideas—nor does she want her tongue excised by the paralysis of the dominant society's gender roles. When Janie gains control of her tongue, she avoids the distortions of a harmonized and a silenced voice by choosing the person to whom she will give her tongue/voice/words: "Ah don't mean to bother wid tellin' 'em nothin', Pheoby. 'Tain't worth de trouble. You can tell 'em what Ah say if you wants to. Dat's just de same as me 'cause mah tongue is in mah friend's mouf" (17).[18] Janie, then, has her own story, which is told in a voice that is apart from the group to which she is gladly associated. The words Janie gives Phoeby tell Janie's Blues story and warn against accepting a dominant discourse that seems to be heaven but actually results in spiritual hell. Phoeby is immediately influenced by Janie's story. As Janie's friend prepares to go home, she says Janie's words have made her grow ten feet just because she heard them. And, as a result, Phoeby asserts, "Ah ain't satisfied wid mahself no mo'. Ah means tuh make Sam take me fishing wid him after this" (284).[19]

Hurston's description of the black people in the courtroom at Janie's trial also resounds Hurston's conception of the way that completely harmonized voices distort and destroy. The black people—Hurston's "anonymous herd"—in the courtroom "were there with their tongues cocked and loaded, the only real weapons left to weak folks. . . . [A] tongue storm struck the Negroes like a wind among palm trees. They talked all of a sudden and all together like a choir and the top part of their bodies moved on the rhythm of it" (275–77). Such blending of voices does not allow people to "find out about livin' fuh theyselves" (285). Blended voices limit Blues People and result in an unnecessarily proscribed Blues community.

Hurston ends *Their Eyes Were Watching God* by making Janie's story of love and mutual respect a simultaneous story of Janie's return to a Blues life. She evinces a Blues rejection of the stasis implied by the dominant discourse on black life, and she brings to the women of Eatonville a blueswoman's perspective on gender. Janie now is situated within a Blues philosophy that allows people to change and that encourages their singular voices to speak of ideas and solutions that go beyond the traditional chords while remaining connected to the Blues song.

Ann Petry: *The Street*

Ann Petry, in her sizable novel *The Street* (1946), depicts a World War II era 116th Street in New York City filled with urban Blues characters. Through characters such as Min, Mrs. Hedges, and Boots Smith, Petry illustrates how seemingly interminable social and economic barriers create a survivalist environment in which her characters' responses demonstrate their paradoxical condition of oppression in a supposedly free society. Many of Petry's characters—Mrs. Hedges, Min, Boots Smith—surmount, to some extent, their conditions by living outside of the dominant society's values. Yet Lutie Johnson, Petry's main character, accepts these values and struggles against living the lifestyle that others who are on or from the street live.

Lutie, however, is still a Blues character. She is implacable as she attempts to find her own solutions to the economic, racial, and gender impediments that connect her to the people on the street. Because Lutie's singular solution to these dispiriting conditions is naïvely unreal, Petry depicts her protagonist as being on a collision course with disaster. Petry's Blues character, surprisingly, is not destroyed. Unlike some of the other characters in the novel, though, Lutie tries to live by the rules. Her singular approach to difficulty places faith in the principles espoused by the dominant society. Because of Lutie's ingenuity and thrift, Petry depicts this character—early in the novel—as someone who supposes herself akin to Benjamin Franklin. Lutie ascribes to the values of hand work and virtue as well as conformity to the established rules of society; thus, Lutie uses Franklin as her model for success (63, 72). Many of Petry's other characters, however, do not ascribe to Lutie's ideas about gaining success based on merit and hard work. In the 1940s, on 116th Street, where Lutie lives, such ideas as Lutie has are truly singular. Petry demonstrates that Lutie, unlike some on the street, does not wait on God to vindicate her suffering after she dies, and she refuses to cross moral and ethical lines that others on the street easily transgress. Hence, Petry's main character accepts, without question, the dominant society's ideas about success, whereas most others on the street do not.

Min, another Blues character, is Petry's representative of many of the women in the Blues environment on 116th Street. A domestic worker, Min is physically broken because on the street "women have to work until they become drudges . . ." (186), an idea that restates Nanny in Zora Neale Hurston's *Their Eyes Were Watching God*, when she observes that black women are the mules of the world (29). Petry shows that Min also has no willpower, and unless she strengthens herself from within and depends less on external solutions, her future seems limited to that of an itinerant wife/woman of various men on the street. Petry's Min operates within the same social narrative as Hurston's character Nanny; she seeks male protection. Min's term in each relationship, as with the other women on the street, is determined by the man with whom she lives. In fact, Mrs. Hedges says, a number of the women on the street are separated from their men (76). Petry illustrates Min's Blues qualities through this character's seemingly permanent status as a resident on the street or a similar neighborhood; thus, she is tightly bound to the life of the group. Petry also illustrates Min's Blues approach to life through her willingness to seek her own singular solutions to difficult problems instead of depending on a set response.

Min, for instance, determines that the church has no satisfactory answer that would solve the problems she has in her relationship with William Jones. Min believes that "even the preacher must know there were some things the church couldn't handle, had no resources for handling. This was one of them—a situation where prayer couldn't possibly help" (122–23). Min's solution is a root doctor, David the Prophet, a spiritual source that is not sanctioned by the dominant society. But there is a growing spirit of personal triumph in Min because this "was the first defiant gesture she had ever made. Up to now she had always accepted whatever happened to her without making any effort to avoid a situation or to change one. . . . And here she was sitting waiting to see the Prophet David—committing an open act of defiance for the first time in her life" (126–27). Later in the novel Petry develops Min even further, so that over time this character garners her own internal resources and transforms her condition instead of depending on external resources. Min begins to change when her values change. She begins to value "room to breathe in" instead of a man to pay her rent (362). This change gives Min the strength to decide that she will leave Jones, yet I wonder if she has just moved her problems to another street. Marjorie Pryse believes that Min's move does not take her to another street similar to 116th. Pryse also views Min as a possible model, for Lutie, providing her—in her visit to Prophet David—an alternative strategy for surviving the street (125–27). Petry's characterization of Min illustrates Blues philosophy as it is lived in day-to-day life on the street. Min's concerns are mundane yet important to her; her Blues solutions, though, take her successfully through daily life.

Petry's portrayal of Mrs. Hedges illustrates another instance of a Blues character whose survival depends on working outside the dominant discourse concerning values. Mrs. Hedges depends on her own intelligence and will to create a satisfactory life for herself. She experiences adversities that both strengthen and harden her, but also develop in her a Blues philosophy that is unquelled. In Mrs. Hedges, Petry presents a sympathetic portrait of a transgressive female Blues character; Petry's character is in contrast to Paul Laurence Dunbar's Hattie Sterling, a far less sympathetic transgressive female Blues character in *The Sport of the Gods* and Petry's own Mamie Powther in *The Narrows*.

During the war years, another migratory movement of black people out of the South into northern cities takes place. Military service and a broader perspective on the world following their wartime experiences encourage men to relocate. Some women make similar moves seeking a better life or seeking family members, including migrating spouses. Mrs. Hedges leaves Georgia and travels to the North seeking a better life. In New York, however, Mrs. Hedges becomes homeless. While homeless she suffers from persistent hunger, wears only thin and tattered clothing and men's shoes that she finds on the street (241–42). She even survives a fire that leaves her body terribly scarred. But it is as a business partner and the brains behind Junto—a white man who eventually owns everything on the street—that Mrs. Hedges develops economic security.

The name Junto is another allusion to Benjamin Franklin; it is the name of a club he established to engage in inquiry on questions of morality and politics (Franklin 72). Thus, Petry's character Junto requires readers to confront the issue of race, particularly the racial attitudes of individuals, and consider how it—race—contributes to the conditions on the street. Through her characterization of Junto, Petry suggests that racial impediments transcend individual attitudes and are complicated by economic concerns.[20]

When Junto meets Mrs. Hedges, he is earning his living as a junk man, and she provides Junto with a business plan that leads to his success. She also helps him develop his first piece of real estate so that he can increase his profits. Mrs. Hedges's advice does not benefit only Junto. As a result of her suggestions to Junto, she realizes increased profits (243). Now, on the street, if a person "wanted to sleep, they paid . . . [Junto]; if they wanted to drink, they paid him; if they wanted to dance, they paid him, and never even knew it" (275). Mrs. Hedges also develops an economic plan and eventually begins her own business, a house of prostitution that provides women only for black men—"men who had to find escape from their hopes and fears, even if it was just a little while. She would provide them with a means of escape in exchange for a few dollars" (250).

Petry establishes that Mrs. Hedges confronts hardships yet is not defeated. Even Junto says Mrs. Hedges's strength of will is amazing, matching only his own (245). Petry demonstrates Mrs. Hedges's Blues philosophy through this character's determination to empower herself through her own singular solutions, despite the many hardships she has experienced. Mrs. Hedges, however, also is committed to her life among the people on the street, so she maintains her connection with them and refuses to move, even when Junto provides her with the opportunity. Thus, Petry further confirms Mrs. Hedges's Blues life by illustrating her desire to maintain her connection to the Blues People on the street. And as Hilary Holladay suggests, Petry presents Mrs. Hedges as "the Street personified" (50–53).

Petry's Boots Smith is also a character who lives on the edge of the societal rules that limit his life. As a club musician, Boots lives well. His economic situation is relatively good because of his position as a piano player in Junto's Casino Club. Although Boots does not live on 116th Street, he does not escape all of the demoralization that the residents of the street experience. There is one caveat: Boots is Junto's man. Thus, Boots maintains his lifestyle by acting on behalf of Junto, the white man who owns both the apartments the people live in on the street and the social outlets they frequent. Petry elucidates Boots Smith's demoralization—despite his improved economic conditions—through her illustration of the relationship between Boots and Junto. Junto tells Boots, "I made you. If I were you, I wouldn't overlook the fact that whoever makes a man can also break him" (263–64). Boots understands what his life will be if Junto fires him. He once was a porter and lived in a neighborhood such as 116th Street; now he lives to avoid that life at all costs. Boots subordinates his own concerns to those of Junto and thus does not break away from the established pattern that society has set for his life; he just moves up a rung on the stepladder of economic uplift. Boots will not give up his success, as limited as it is, because he knows that his options are few. But he still does not break the pattern of life that the dominant society establishes for him.

Petry's portrayal of Boots Smith's experiences as a Porter—his nameless, de-individualized condition—is a precursor of Ralph Ellison's portrayal, in *Invisible Man*, of invisibility as the modern condition as well as the ironical state of the Blues of blackness in the United States. Boots has vivid memories of his life before he worked for Junto: "Porter this and Porter that. Boy. George. Nameless. He got a handful of silver at the end of each run, and a mountain of silver couldn't pay a man to stay nameless like that. No Name, black my shoes. No Name, brush me off. . . . No Name. No Name. . . . 'Here boy,' 'You boy,' 'Go boy,' 'Run boy,' 'Stop boy.' . . . 'Yes, sir.' 'No, sir.' 'Of course, sir.'" Boots, then, is paradoxically seen and not unseen; he is seen only as an object whose function is to serve others. As a person with feelings, thoughts, and ideas, however, he is invisible. Through Boots's memories of the hardships he has encountered in life, Petry illustrates his Blues determination to maintain his small measure of success. When Boots considers what he would do to avoid being a porter again, Petry demonstrates that Boots's solutions are self-interested and singular. Few people really would consider what Boots considers. He will transgress even the most fundamental of social rules if in so doing he retains his own position of relative security: "You'd sell your old grandmother if you had one, he told himself. Yes, I'd sell anything I've got without stopping to think about it twice, because I don't intend to learn how to crawl again for anybody" (264–67).

Petry depicts Boots as a character whose connection to Junto is similar to those of the people on the street. Even though Boots does not live on the street, he lives his life within the same restrictions found there. He lives under the control of Junto, only Boots is somewhat more economically privileged than the residents on 116th Street. Yet the dominant society's power relations are still in place. All of Petry's aforementioned Blues characters live their lives at the edge of the dominant discourse and the values it constructs. Their victories seem lessened by irrationality and criminality. Petry's novel, actually, shows how oppressive social policies sometimes make Blues triumphs a subversive victory, a victory of mere survival that leaves its victors—such as Mrs. Hedges—strengthened by their scars.

Lutie Johnson, however, battles against transgressing the values of the dominant discourse but fails. Yet she too remains unvanquished by the dispiriting effects of the street. Lutie is a gifted Blues singer who is trying for herself and her son Bub to make their lives different from the lives of other people on the street. Lutie, who knows that the street is "an evil father and a vicious mother" to the children who live on it, wants to give Bub a better life (407). Petry's descriptions of the frigid cold weather on the street illustrate the oppressive conditions that Lutie encounters, the cold weather metaphorically connecting the city and the street to a wintry hell through which Lutie and Bub must live.

The apartment that Lutie finally rents is located on the fifth floor, at the top of a steep staircase. Lutie's ascent up the stairs is analogous to the conditions on the street outside: "The farther up they [Lutie and the building Superintendent] went, the colder it got. And in summer she supposed it would get hotter and hotter as you went up until when you reached the top floor your breath would be cut off completely" (12). Similarly, on the street outside, the harder Lutie tries to improve her life, the more difficulty she finds. In this novel, Petry demonstrates that in the environment where Lutie lives one is likely to find "a newer and more intricate—a much-involved and perfected kind of hell" (6). Such descriptions indicate that the street represents a paralyzing, Dantesque hell for Lutie, yet at the same time the street gives her a group connection that both affirms her and foreshadows the impediments she will encounter later. As Lutie rides home on the subway, she "never felt really human until she reached Harlem. . . . These other folks feel the same way, she thought—. . . once they are freed from the contempt in the eyes of the downtown world, they instantly become individuals. Up here [in Harlem] they are no longer creatures labeled simply 'colored' and therefore all alike" (57).

Lutie is part of the Blues life on the street, but she is unable to negotiate the maze of options to which she is limited. She believes that she can live by the same rules by which people from the dominant society live, and she wants to emulate the media images that parallel the lifestyle in the homes of her rich employers, for whom she is a maid and nanny. An advertisement on a subway train reminds Lutie of her goals: "a sink whose white porcelain surface gleamed under the train lights. The faucets looked like silver. The linoleum floor of the kitchen was a crisp black-and-white pattern that pointed up the sparkle of the room. Casement windows. Red geraniums in yellow pots. It was, she thought, a miracle of a kitchen. Completely different from the kitchen of the 116th Street apartment she had moved into just two weeks ago" (28).

Petry's contrast of Lutie's real life with a fictional image suggests that this character has unreal—media-influenced—expectations about life. But she also depicts Lutie in the environment of wealthy people who have the material objects that Lutie desires. Petry shows that the image of material wealth is fictional for Lutie, but not for some others who are located in the dominant society. Petry's depiction of the Chandlers, Lutie's employers before she moves to 116th Street, establishes their material wealth along with their spiritual dearth. Mrs. Chandler is not attentive to her son, or to her husband, and Mr. Chandler is an alcoholic. For Lutie, the life-style of the Chandlers "was, she discovered slowly, a very strange world that she had entered. With an entirely different set of values. It made her feel that she was looking through a hole in a wall at some enchanted garden. She could see, she could hear, she spoke the language of the people in the garden, but she couldn't get past the wall. . . . [T]here was this wall in between which prevented them from mingling on an equal footing. The people on the other side of the wall knew less about her than she knew about them." In the Chandler home Lutie is demeaningly categorized in ways that not only limit her options in society because she is black but also mark her as promiscuous (39–42). As Cheryl Wall observes, black women, especially during the early decades of this century, live in "a society reluctant to recognize sexuality in most women, [yet] black women were burdened with an almost exclusively sexual identity" (14).

Despite this, Lutie still absorbs the mainstream values that the Chandlers profess: "the belief that anybody could be rich if he wanted to and worked hard enough and figured it out carefully enough" (43). Their values are the ones Lutie tries to employ in her own behalf as she attempts to improve her life. When this approach proves unsuccessful, she is not completely deterred. As a Blues character, Lutie reshapes her approach to change. She tries other options, even after Jim, her husband, leaves and she moves to 116th Street.

Lutie, in fact, is not completely a product of the street. Her youth, as it is constructed in the novel, is lived very likely at a time when 116th Street in New York is transforming from a lively burgeoning neighborhood of hopeful black migrants living in comfortable homes to a Depression era neighborhood of economically and racially dispossessed black people. The death of Lutie's mother is a signal of the neighborhood's transformation into the street. After her mother dies, Lutie is reared by her grandmother. Petry introduces Lutie's Granny—a character similar to Janie's Nanny in *Their Eyes Were Watching God*, but without the "mislove"—as a stabilizing force in Lutie's life and as an example of a Spiritual-Gospel philosophy that shapes Lutie's life as a child. Lutie's greatest struggle is her determination to rear Bub without destroying his spirit. Lutie realizes, however, that she survived because of Granny. Unlike Bub, Lutie was not alone and afraid at home because Granny was always there to comfort her granddaughter by singing, "Sleepin', Sleepin', Sleepin', in arms of the Lord" (404). Petry's use of Spiritual-Gospel music here situates her main character in an established base of support that gives her a feeling of security, not only with her grandmother but also with God. Lutie's home life is a nurturing and loving one when she is growing up. Even though she has very few material comforts as a child, she has a bountiful spiritual reserve in her grandmother. Petry's portrayal of Lutie's childhood directly contrasts with her portrayal of life in the Chandlers' home. Lutie, however, is unable to give Bub the same nurturing environment that she has had because her husband Jim has left her and Lutie's mother has died from the dangers that have begun to permeate the street and have transformed the comforting place where Lutie was reared. Bub, then, does not have his grandmother; and his grandfather, Grant, has succumbed to the influences of the street—since the death of his wife—and has become a conniving drunk (56). Thus, Lutie's need to work leaves Bub to the destructive parenting of the street, which in the words of Hilary

Holladay, situates Bub as a "Bigger Thomas in the making" (60). Bub also provides Petry's Blues character Lutie her most difficult challenge.

Lutie does not retain the spiritual beliefs of her grandmother, but Petry connects Lutie to the strength that Granny's Spiritual-Gospel philosophy represents when Lutie hums a song that her grandmother used to sing: "Ain't no restin' place for a sinner like me" (17). According to Pryse, Petry demonstrates the potential that Lutie's grandmother has as a wise counsel for Lutie (124). With these songs Petry recalls the Spirituals of the pre–Civil War era, which were not purely religious and often conveyed double meanings. These songs did not separate spiritual and secular concerns and often expressed both secular and spiritual ideas at once. Thus Granny's song signifies on the puritanical concept of a sinner as someone who is born in sin and is in a lifelong battle against succumbing to it. At the same time, the song conveys the idea of the sinner as the resistant, rule-breaking individual whose struggles are formidable yet whose solutions often are justified, even if they deviate from established but flawed rules of society. Granny's song suggests that the sinner's struggles are not unconquerable and must be confronted because there is no way to avoid them; in other words, there is "no restin' place." This song reminds Lutie that the hell-like conditions that she encounters on 116th Street are shared experiences among people on the street.

Petry illustrates how Lutie's Blues philosophy—shaped by her singular combination of internal drive and faith in the success narrative situated in the dominant discourse—influences her to work hard and pass the civil service examination; Lutie's progress still is very slow. She experiences a turn in her fortunes when she meets Boots Smith in Junto's Bar and Grill, where Lutie goes to relax one evening. Boots suggests to Lutie that she might make money singing, thus causing Lutie to hope that things will change for her. At Junto's Bar and Grill, Petry establishes a direct connection between Lutie and a Blues aesthetic through Lutie's response to the music. The jukebox in the bar is playing "Swing It Sister," and Lutie "hummed as she listened to it, not really aware that she was humming or why, knowing only that she felt free here where there was so much space" (146). Lutie's receptivity to the music as well as its effect on her spirit demonstrates that a Blues aesthetic suits her.

Boots Smith, however, wants to expose Lutie to another aspect of Blues life when he hears Lutie sing—in Blues tones that Petry describes as "a thin thread of sadness running through . . . [her voice] that made the song important, that made it tell a story that wasn't in the words—a story of despair, of loneliness, of frustration. It was a story that all of them [in the bar] knew by heart and had always known because they had learned it soon after they were born and would go on adding to it until the day they died" (148). Boots suggests to Lutie that singing professionally might be a way that she can add to the story in her voice by prevailing over some of the despair and frustration the music of her voice conveys.

Boots Smith's business proposition to Lutie eventually causes her to encounter the obstacle in her life that she has failed to scrutinize adequately: Junto. Throughout the novel Lutie uses the strength that she gained through her grandmother's faith, and she follows the guidelines for success that have been established by the dominant society. Lutie brings her own singular solution to her spirit-crushing conditions. But things do not change for her because she does not analyze her circumstances sufficiently. Petry's narrator points out that Lutie has naïvely "built up a fantastic structure made from the soft nebulous, cloudy stuff of dreams. There Hadn't been a solid practical brick in it, not even a foundation. She had built it up of air and vapor and moved right in. So of course it had collapsed. It had never existed anywhere but in her mind" (307–8).[21]

Junto embodies the characteristics of tyrannical oppression, ruthless power, and privilege. Mrs. Hedges, in fact, is the only person on the street for whom Junto has any serious regard. All others seem to be a means of income or are subjected to his will because of his control of most everything on the street. Petry employs a Jazz riff to establish Junto's control; she subtly riffs examples of his power throughout the novel until he looms large as a representative of tyranny and injustice. These internal echoes in the novel foreshadow Junto's many avenues of control over Lutie. Petry introduces Junto as a riff in her novel when Mrs. Hedges states that "a nice white gentleman" is interested in Lutie and can help her make a little money (84). Petry resounds Junto's control on the street when Mrs. Hedges tells William Jones, the superintendent of Junto's apartment building where Lutie lives, "Ain't no point in you lickin' your chops, dearie. . . . There's others who are interested" in Lutie (90). Petry's Jazz riff illustrates Junto's control over both Jones and Lutie when Mrs. Hedges finally tells Jones, "I just wanted to tell you for your own good, dearie, that it's Mr. Junto who's interested in Mis' Johnson" (238). Yet Junto's claims on Lutie are made without any regard for what Lutie wishes to happen.

Among Petry's other Jazz riffs that indicate that Junto is an unseen power on the street is his power over Boots Smith. Boots's upscale apartment has all of the requisite accoutrements of life off the street—cavernous ceilings, lush greenery, a doorman in uniform, and an elevator attendant—but Junto controls Boots's success. Both Boots and Junto realize that Junto's control could easily end Boots's music career from coast to coast. Boots recognizes that a number of venues for his music have begun selecting bands comprised of white performers and that wartime restrictions have decreased travel, thereby limiting road trips for all bands. He also is profoundly aware that the racialized social policy in the United States during the 1940s makes Junto almost a necessary conduit for any success that Boots attains, unless that success remains negligible. Boots is attracted to Lutie, but he decides that as Junto's "right hand man" he will subordinate his own desires and will act in behalf of his boss. Because Junto wants Lutie indebted to him (264), he organizes conditions on the street so that she will come to him for help. He refuses, for instance, to allow Boots to hire Lutie to sing at the Casino Club. Junto is well aware of the conditions on the street; he bides his time until Lutie is forced to accept help from him. But Lutie does not recognize the reality of the street in the way that most others who live there do. She does not realize that more than her air-filled dreams have been a stumbling block for her (307–8).

Throughout *The Street*, Petry re-articulates Junto's power as a riff that evinces his pervasive control of the street, yet at the same time she uses other characters to critique the exclusionary discourse, based in skin color, that supports Junto's power and privileges him with control. Mrs. Hedges and Boots both work closely with Junto, yet they separate him from the social policy that privileges him. And their malevolence toward this social policy of exclusion is what connects Lutie, Mrs. Hedges, and Boots Smith. Mrs. Hedges says Junto doesn't "ever stop to think whether folks are white or black and . . . [he does not] really care. That sort of takes . . . [Junto] out of the white folk class" (250). Similarly, as a result of Boots's relationship with the owner of most everything on the street, Petry's bluesman distinguishes his employer from the privilege that Junto uses to empower himself. Junto gains this power through a racialized discourse of privilege within the dominant society. Boots "didn't feel the same toward him as he did toward most white men. There was never anything in Junto's manner, no intonation in his voice, no expression that crept into his eyes, . . . nothing that he had ever said or done that indicated he was aware that Boots was a black man. . . . Junto was always the same, and he treated the white men who worked for him exactly the same way he treated the black ones" (263).

Petry makes it clear that on a personal level any conflict that Boots and Junto have is not based in color distinctions. It is a personal conflict based in sex and power. That a racialized discourse allows Junto to have power over Boots or shapes his sexual desire for Lutie is incidental to Petry's symbolic use of Junto as self-interested, avaricious power. Junto ruthlessly uses his power to his own advantage and for his own pleasure. Neither Boots nor Mrs. Hedges blames Junto for taking advantage of the skin-color privileges to which he has access; they, in fact, would do the same thing if their lives were not limited by a racialized dominant discourse. Both Mrs. Hedges, who "has no use for white folks" (251), and Boots, who has a deep anger toward white men (263), express rage at their own exclusion from the resources to which Junto has access. While Boots and Mrs. Hedges, then, are wise beyond Lutie's idealism, all three of them eventually confirm the color-based construct of many of the hardships they encounter in life.

Lutie finally acknowledges that some of the effectiveness of her hard-work-and-strong-values attitude is limited when Junto refuses to pay her for singing at the Casino. For Lutie, now her "bitterness and the hardness increased. In every direction, anywhere one turned, there was always the implacable figure of a white man blocking the way, so that it was impossible to escape" (315). In this passage, Petry reinforces Lutie's Blues philosophy as Lutie increases her determination to get off the street. Lutie does not disdain the people on the street with whom she is connected through their shared social and economic barriers. Instead, she disdains the dominant discourse that constructs neighborhoods such as the street; this discourse makes people small and withdrawn when they are in the world away from the street. "The same people who had made themselves small on the train, even on the platform, suddenly grew so large" as they moved toward the street (57–58). As Petry exemplifies further through her portrayal of Junto, the same racialized discourse that constructs the street also limits the power of Blues People, even on the street where they live. Petry further depicts Lutie's Blues philosophy through this character's recognition that a Blues life of hardship and degradation is a shared condition. Not only Lutie and not only people on 116th Street in New York experience the effects of the street. "Streets like the one she [Lutie] lived on were no accident. They were the North's lynch mob, . . . the method the big cities used to keep Negroes in their place" (323). The street is broader than Lutie's little world.

Petry's use of Junto as a metaphor that illustrates injustice and ruthless power helps Lutie understand more clearly why people on the street make some of their choices. Lutie "began thinking about Junto: . . . Junto hadn't wanted her paid for singing, Mrs. Hedges knew Junto. Boots Smith worked for Junto" (417). And now she, Lutie, is beginning to realize that the "creeping, silent, thing," the "formless, shapeless, . . . fluid moving mass—something disembodied that she couldn't see, could only sense," is Junto, or that which Petry limns through her portrayal of Junto—a racialized social policy that empowers Junto and impedes Lutie. Lutie, with this knowledge, despises the way Junto's power oppresses others, so her Blues strength of will allows her to use her knowledge of Junto's power to compel her to attempt to bypass him, even when she thinks she needs money to get Bub out of the children's shelter. Instead of going to Junto, Lutie goes to Boots, because she does not recognize the extent of Junto's control over life on the street, including Boots Smith's life (315).

Petry illustrates Lutie's final and strongest expression of Blues philosophy through this character's confrontation with Boots. Lutie is a time-bomb after she finds that Junto also is at Boots Smith's apartment building when she arrives to borrow money from Boots. Lutie "halfway hope[s] Boots will say something or do something that will give [her] . . . an excuse to blow up in a thousand pieces." The following comment from Boots does just that: "Let him [Junto] get his afterward. I'll have mine first." Boots Smith's spontaneous decision to act against established narratives of power and his slaps to Lutie's face cause him to become the object on which Lutie vents her pent-up rage and frustration: "The anger surging through her wasn't directed solely at him. He was there at hand. . . . He happened to be within easy range at the moment he set off the dangerous accumulation of rage" (425–29). Petry describes Lutie's disposition very carefully so that readers can understand that Lutie is striking out against the racialized discourse that limits her life, not at Boots Smith's insult and physical attack on her. Boots, unfortunately, is killed, because he is Junto's mediator. Petry makes a deft distinction between Boots the character whom Lutie kills and Boots the intermediary who increases Lutie's hardships by acting in behalf of Junto. Lutie doesn't necessarily want to kill Boots. She want to crush his sexist ideology, which authorizes him to believe that her body is Junto's playground and, by extension, within the social discourse of male authority, his. Lutie further wants to destroy the racial construct that he upholds—even against himself—as a mediator for actions that perpetuate Junto's power and privilege.

This same type of distinction is made between Junto the character who has no racist feelings and Junto the white man whose use of his social privilege oppresses others. Petry's distinctions between her characters and the larger ideas that they embody illustrate the difficulty Lutie encounters when she tries to surmount her problems. Since the source of Lutie's barriers is shapeless, silent, and illusive, she—as any Blues character would—seeks a singular option that will enable her to negotiate the small territory available to her. But peculiar to Petry's portrayal of Lutie as a Blues character is this striving young woman's inability to accurately analyze her situation until late in the novel. Lutie is closed to a number of options that may prove successful for her. Such options, though, would place her in the transgressive category of Boots Smith and Mrs. Hedges. Both of these characters are in a category that Lutie has battled throughout the novel to avoid (426); she wants to stay within the social values of the dominant discourse. Boots and Mrs. Hedges exemplify collaboration, criminality, and the lack of feeling that the street creates in people. Lutie's frustration eventually causes her to take extreme action that situates her within the outlaw trickster tradition of the Blues, a position that takes a pragmatic view on circumstances and toward solutions. The outlaw trickster subverts and undermines, often in transgressive ways, traditional value systems when such systems construct an unjust society. For Lutie, taking a life is wrong. She does not have criminal intentions, yet the situation that brought her to kill Boots and the injustice that she is likely to encounter as a result of her racialized and gendered position in society—which does not protect the sanctity of her body—allow Lutie to take Boots's money and leave town after he assaults her.

In a rage Lutie kills Boots Smith. This action, however, does not bring Lutie to suicide, endless despair, insanity, or any other tragic posture. Killing boots situates Lutie in an even more transgressive position than the one that she has been trying to avoid, yet cannot do so, throughout the novel. In this moment of rage, Lutie recognizes herself as a resident of the street; she perceives within herself the Blues philosophy of other residents on the street, which she believed she could transcend. Petry most powerfully depicts Lutie's use of Blues philosophy when Lutie removes the money in Boots Smith's wallet and leaves for Chicago (Petry's nod to Richard Wright),[22] after she quickly analyzes her situation and assesses her usefulness to Bub. Lutie finally decides that in her current situation she doesn't have enough to offer Bub. She also decides that her suffering will not crush her. Lutie's Blues philosophy informs her decision to revise the narration of her life. In the essay "Slave Codes and Liner Notes," Michele Russell explains that the Blues of Bessie Smith is situated in a philosophy that asserts "since the apocalypse was a condition of everyday life, our resurrection had to be too" (131). Petry's Blues character, Lutie Johnson, acts within this philosophy as she decides to remake her life. Lutie chooses to move on. She likely will have little choice except to live, perhaps, on another street. Petry chooses the city where Richard Wright's Bigger Thomas once lived on one of America's streets: Chicago (435).

Ralph Ellison: *Invisible Man*

Ralph Ellison permeates his landmark 1952 novel *Invisible Man* with folkloric and musical tropes and ideas. In Ellison's 1981 introduction to *Invisible Man*, he makes clear the musical basis of his protagonist when he identifies the speaking voice in this novel as "blues toned" (xiii). Houston Baker and Larry Neal both point out that Ellison emphasizes the literary aspects of his own writing as well as that of other black writers such as Richard Wright while also recognizing his debt to vernacular culture (Baker 174, 197). Neal observes that Ellison "thought enough of the concept of hidden cultural compulsives in Black American life to *translate* them into art [even though Ellison clearly] locates his cultural, philosophical, and literary sentiment in the West" (69–70). Ellison, as well as Albert Murray and James Baldwin, has commented extensively on the influence of music in African American literature. His views on this subject are collected in *Shadow and Act* and in *Going to the Territory*. In the essay "Richard Wright's Blues," Ellison provides a definition of Blues that supports his theme and characters in *Invisible Man*, yet Ellison's definition also is an eloquent statement of Blues philosophy:

"The blues is an impulse to keep the painful details and episodes of brutal experience alive in One's aching consciousness, to finger its jagged grain, and to transcend it, not by the consolation of philosophy but by squeezing from it a near-tragic, near-comic lyricism" (*Shadow* 78).

Invisible Man, the first-person narrative voice in the novel, is in turn and often at once ironic, naïve, philosophical, and satirical. As a voice from the "lower frequencies" (568), Ellison's invisible narrator also resonates pain, disappointment, degradation, implacability, determination, and indomitable resilience. Thus Ellison's dominant musical aesthetic and philosophy in *Invisible Man* is Blues. Neal perceptively refers to the novel as "one long blues solo" because Louis Armstrong's music "forms the over-all structure for the novel" (71). Yet among Ellison's plethora of musical allusions, specific references to songs, and characterizations, he also employs Spiritual-Gospel, Blues, and Jazz as metaphors to express his complex and arguably existential ideas on the myriad possibilities available through human potential. Ellison's novel is a complex text with many paths that warrant investigation, as Robert O'Meally in his rich reading of this novel observes: "No one formula . . . can explain the capacious novel" ("*Invisible Man:* Black and Blue" 78). And no one approach to music in literature will contain the fullness of Ellison's uses of music in *Invisible Man*. As Albert Murray explains, this novel is "the literary extension of the blues.[23] It was as if Ellison had taken an everyday twelve bar blues tune . . . and scored it for full orchestra" (*Omni* 167).

Over a period of approximately five years, Ellison's Invisible Man moves from a naïve young man who fails to understand the ironies in his own life into a Blues philosophical man, or Ellison's "thinker tinker" (7), who recognizes and accepts the paradoxical aspects of his life. This growth occurs as a result of Invisible Man's recognizing that within the society of his birth he is seen yet unseen; he is "an invisible man . . . because of a peculiar disposition of the eyes of those with whom [he] . . . come[s] in contact" (3). Ellison's Invisible Man observes, ". . . I was and yet I was invisible, that was the fundamental contradiction. I was and yet I was unseen" (496). Through this trope of invisibility Ellison illustrates the setting of his novel, which is the United States in the 1940s, a place and time that allow no visibility for a black adult male because a racialized social policy supports a discourse that says being black and a man—who is visible in society—is a paradoxical idea. Yet by the end of Ellison's novel, Invisible Man is a man—not because he is seen as one by others, but because he has looked around the corners of his psyche and removed the impediments that both he and society have erected. Thus, he made himself from himself; that is, he made himself from his own shaping of the experiences in his life.

Early in *Invisible Man*, Ellison illustrates that Spiritual-Gospel music once contained powerful philosophical ideas, but now it is employed in a confused and disoriented manner. In Ellison's prologue to Invisible Man, where—because "[t]he end was in the beginning" (558)—he places his final ideas about identity and selfhood, his Blues character Invisible Man enters one of the breaks in a Louis Armstrong tune and investigates it. He "not only entered the music but also descended, like Dante, into its depths. And *beneath* the swiftness of the hot tempo there was a slower tempo and a cave." In this passage, Ellison illustrates Blues' intertextual expansion of Spiritual-Gospel. He goes further and demonstrates even more poignantly the intertextual relationship between Spiritual-Gospel and Blues with his image of the old woman and the girl. Directly in and below Armstrong's Blues there is an old woman who sings Spirituals; on an even lower level is a naked girl who is being sold to a group of enslavers; and even further down there is a preacher who delivers his sermon—an explication of the "Blackness of blackness"—in the antiphonal style of African American sermonics. Ellison uses these images of pre-Blues experiences—Spirituals, captivity, invisible church—to point out how Armstrong's Blues is informed by these dispiriting experiences and the methods for surviving them (8–9). At the same time, Armstrong's up-tempo music expresses a sense of triumph or exuberance that may cause some people to miss the plenitude in the breaks or silences in the music—the pain in the laughter or in other instances the laughter in the sadness.

Ellison places a seemingly nonsensical sermon at the lowest level in Armstrong's Blues. This sermon illustrates life lived in paradox, a life lived in a material body, yet a life lived unseen. Such a life is not easy. It is "Bloody"; thus, it is difficult and filled with suffering and hardship because invisible people are subjected to being violated because so many "visible" people are blinded by their own inability to see that someone is there. But this is how life is in Ellison's novel; black is invisible. For Ellison's blackness of blackness preacher, however, if a person views skin color as the sole determinant of her or his possibilities, then "Black will git you," but if one sees around the corner of life, then "Black won't" become a deterrent to achieving one's possibilities. This knowledge, however, does not preclude black from landing a person in the "WHALE'S

BELLY." Ellison is using Herman Melville's whale and blackness metaphors to represent the deepest and most unexplored parts of the dominant psychological mind-set in the United States. There is blackness—a black voice, a black presence, a black body—that is hidden deep within the great white whale—the United States. For Ellison, then, true blackness within—the great white whale—is underground and unseen; it is the humanity of his invisible man.

The unseen blackness that Ellison's preacher elucidates manifests itself as potential freedom because, of course, all options are open when one is not seen. Thus, people who are unseen can investigate the unexplored crevices of their own minds and become empowered to "tempt . . . Old Aunt Nelly!" (10). In other words, one can transgress the established limits and behave in ways that are prohibited, such as becoming visible by revealing one's invisibility—as Ellison does in *Invisible Man*. In order to place emphasis on the impact people have when they resist oppressive prohibitions, Ellison employs extreme metaphors that depict prohibitive behavior. Thus, he equates the impact of *Invisible Man*'s eventual resistance as equivalent to tempting one's old aunt. He presents this transgressive theme again in the Trueblood passage.

In the prologue to *Invisible Man*, Ellison also contrasts the old woman who sings a Spiritual, the young female who is being sold, and the preacher in order to illustrate the idea that the deeper one goes into Blues music, the more profound the ideas in the music are. The preacher's Blues philosophy blackness of blackness sermon—which elucidates the always, already-there status of his humanity—informs the slavery scene, which in turn informs the Spiritual that the old woman sings, which finally informs Armstrong's tune. However, between the preacher's sermon and Armstrong's music, which makes "poetry out of being invisible," something is lost. The old woman "done forgot" what the freedom that she sings about really means. Freedom, according to George Kent, is the fundamental thematic concern in Ellison's novel. Kent argues that the woman and her sons define freedom as "the ability to articulate the self, and as a question that can be answered only by each individual's confrontation with the self. Louis Armstrong and his Jazz reflect both an articulated self and a mode of breaking through the ordinary categories of Western clock time" (163). Armstrong, however, is "unaware that he is invisible" (Ellison 8–11). More precisely, because Armstrong is at least twice removed from the blackness of blackness sermon, his perception that he is visible to his audience is part of his inheritance; that is, everyone forgot to tell him that he really cannot be seen. Thus, Ellison's novel questions whether Armstrong's musical critique of his audience really is being heard and whether the audience that Armstrong critiques in his song really knows what is at the bottom of his music. Yet Armstrong continues to ask the question that O'Meally recognizes as an important theme of this novel, a question expressed in the Andy Razaf and Fats Waller tune: "What Did I Do to Be So Black and Blue" (86).

Through Invisible Man's journey into Blues music, he learns that what has been lost or forgotten—freedom—must be remembered; the prohibited blackness of blackness must be examined so that the even more invisible "darkness of lightness" is seen and the interconnectedness of both is understood. Ellison establishes the danger in Invisible Man's knowing about the blackness of blackness when "a voice of trombone timbre screamed . . . 'Git out of here, you, fool! Is you ready to commit treason?'" Invisible Man has come too close to the truths in the music into which he has fallen. This is a dangerous and chaotic space, and Ellison uses the old woman to illustrate this point. This old woman imbues the advice of Job's wife with double meaning when she tells Invisible Man, "Go curse your God boy and die" (6–10). While the old woman in Ellison's novel recognizes the viability of Invisible Man's ridding himself of the god to which she refers, she, herself, is unable to do so because she both loves and hates the god she tells Invisible Man to curse.

Ellison makes clear that the god of both Invisible Man and of the old woman is the deified view of whiteness that is lodged in the psyche of black people who believe in white omnipotence. The old woman knows that this is a false god and it must be abolished, but she also realizes the difficulty and danger involved in challenging a powerful force; one of the risks is death, but another consequence also might be triumph, since a false god, even if it is a powerful force, is always vulnerable to being vanquished. In this instance Ellison indicates that the death Invisible Man will experience if he follows the old woman's advice is the death of that enslaved aspect in his psyche that is loyal to the dominant discourse that limits him.

Ellison also shows that the post-emancipation old woman has very limited ideas about freedom. Her Spiritual has lost the black that "do" (9), the black that is defined by the "lessons of [one's] . . . own life" (559), not by social policy. The old woman's ideas are well within the philosophy of an antebellum Spiritual until she considers freedom. She knows that the power in her society that limits her is not a god and that such an idea—that man-made power is omnipotent—needs to be destroyed. Yet she is unable to encounter the idea of freedom except in terms of its definition in relation to the man-made laws of society, which she helps destroy. In order to avoid the blood bath that would occur if her poorly armed yet angry sons attack their enslaver—also their father—with knives made by their own hands, the old woman gives their enslaver the poison that withers him and takes his life.[24]

Now that there are no longer laws that legally enslave the old woman, the meaning of freedom confuses her and causes a fever in her brain. She is not able to free her mind of the "mental slavery" (Marley) that shackles her to the racialized discourse of the United States. She no longer understands existential freedom, which Ellison's preacher discusses in his blackness of blackness sermon and which is contained in her Spirituals. For Ellison's "old singer of spirituals," the idea of psychological transcendence has become alienated from as well as confused with the idea of physical freedom. Thus, Invisible Man's questions about freedom make the woman reply in frustration, "Leave me 'lone, boy; my head aches!" (11).

Ellison's other uses of Spiritual-Gospel music as a metaphor also support the idea that the Spirituals once contained a life philosophy that is now fractured, fragmented, and dispersed. Invisible Man distances himself from these songs even as he finds that he feels some connection to them. At Invisible Man's college—modeled on Tuskegee Institute, which Ellison attended—it is obligatory for the students to perform Spirituals or for a "country quartet" made up of local farmers to perform when white visitors are on campus (46). For the white founders of the college who are in the audience, the Spirituals reinforce their feelings of paternal power as they are reminded of their control over the lives of the people who inherited Spirituals, which were developed in response to the control their forefathers had over the lives of the makers of the Spirituals and which, to the white founders, express the singers' satisfaction with earthly life and ultimate rewards in heaven. Ellison's Invisible Man observes how the founders were "not merely acting out the myth of their goodness, and wealth and success and power and benevolence and authority in cardboard masks, but themselves [in flesh] these virtues concretely!" (109).

On the occasions when the Spirituals are sung at the college, Invisible Man points out that the songs are "[a]n ultimatum accepted and ritualized, an allegiance recited for the peace it imparted, and for that perhaps loved. Loved as the defeated come to love the symbols of their conquerors. A gesture of acceptance of terms laid down and reluctantly approved" (109). Within this context, Ellison demonstrates how the Spirituals impart fear in the black people in the audience, who feel as though they are moving away from the era that caused them to create Spirituals. Yet an obligatory performance of these songs at the behest of the white founders of the college drains the songs of their philosophical impact, which the founders probably do not hear, and reenacts the previous power relations, which the black people, perhaps naively, believe are ending.

For the black college officials who organize the school chorus as well as the Blues quartet in which Trueblood sings, a performance of Spirituals functions as an offering of appeasement, given to ward off people such as the founders, who are associated with the hardships and degradation that caused the songs to be made at all. Invisible Man says, "[W]e were embarrassed by the earthy harmonies they sang, but since the visitors were awed we dared not laugh at the crude, high, plaintively animal sounds Jim Trueblood made as he led the quartet" (46–47). The students and officials of the college fear the idea that they, too, may have been or could become a Trueblood. Thus, they want to distance themselves from the suffering that he, Trueblood, and Spirituals represent. Jim Trueblood, whom Ellison depicts as being abysmally degraded since he impregnated his own daughter, represents how one survives the lowest type of degraded conditions, a degradation from which Trueblood is unable to absolve himself completely, even though he is asleep when it occurs. Jim Trueblood is Ellison's metaphor illustrating the condition of black people who were enslaved and later segregated and made invisible. For Ellison's formerly enslaved people, "such problems as good and evil,[25] honesty and dishonesty [are] of such shifting shapes that . . . [they] confuse one with the other, depending upon who happens to be looking through . . . [them] at the time" (559).[26]

When Trueblood awakens to find that he has degraded himself and abused his daughter in his sleep—a sleep that Ellison uses to symbolize the state of consciousness of formerly enslaved black people—the sharecropper says, ". . . I can't move 'cause I figures if I moved it would be a sin. And I figures too that if I don't move it maybe ain't no sin 'cause it happened when I was asleep." Trueblood's paradox is to find a way to "git myself out of the fix I'm in without sinnin'. . . . There I was tryin' to git away with all my might, yet having to move *without* movin'. . . . I done thought 'bout it since a heap, and when you think right hard you see that that's the way things is always been with me." Ellison employs this grotesque and complex image in order to make clear the immense horror and complexity of enslaved and segregated black life, to illustrate how the choices that enslaved and segregated black people have for changing their circumstances often induce moral dilemmas that keep them where they are—which is wretched—or pose options that are equally chaotic. One option Trueblood considers is severing his penis, but he decides that is "too much to pay to keep from sinnin'" (59). Ellison illustrates, then, that the paradoxical conditions of enslaved and segregated life create terrifying choices. Trueblood, consequently, perceives that his choices are to stay in a degrading situation or to mutilate himself in the process of leaving.[27] He thinks "'bout how I'm guilty and how I ain't guilty" (65). Through Trueblood's degradation Ellison depicts the state of enslaved and segregated consciousness that one might find among African Americans—a consciousness that is asleep; Trueblood's is a mind that is psychologically anesthetized. Ellison also shows the paradoxical life that helps shape that consciousness.

Again, as with the old woman singing Spirituals in the prologue, Ellison turns the confusion that is generated from Trueblood's transitional Spiritual-Gospel philosophy into a resonant Blues tune. Trueblood says he "*ends up* singin' the blues. I sings some blues that night ain't never been sang before, and while I'm singing them blues I make up my mind that I ain't nobody but myself. . . . [And] I'm still a man" (66). Trueblood's indomitable spirit allows him to triumph through, rather than succumb to, destruction (51). Ellison establishes that Trueblood now is a fully self-conscious Blues character who has transformed the confusion that causes some people to misdirect Spiritual-Gospel philosophy and insist on waiting for God's intervention. O'Meally refers to the language in Ellison's Trueblood passage as having achieved "a kind of blues cadence; [s]omehow the blues provide just the vehicle for coming to terms with the twisted and painful details of Trueblood's situation" (86–87). Through Trueblood, Ellison illustrates the paradoxical life that the makers of Spirituals survived, and he demonstrates that it is the same life that the students and officials at the college fear.

Invisible Man is a Blues character because he wants to retain a group connection while seeking singular solutions to complex questions about life. Ellison's passage on the old woman, however, demonstrates that his narrator/protagonist has difficulty finding solutions within a group construct because he is unable to discern the ideas that inform the group—particularly Spiritual-Gospel philosophy. After Invisible Man has frustrated the old woman to tears with his questions on freedom, one of the old woman's sons attacks Invisible Man and tells him, "[N]ext time you got questions like that, ask yourself!" (12). As black people move out of enslavement, Ellison indicates, the question of freedom is answered singularly and is not attained solely through membership in a marginal group.

Invisible Man ascends from the underground world and hears Louis Armstrong innocently asking, what he has done to be so black and blue. In Armstrong's music Invisible Man "had discovered unrecognized compulsions of . . . [his own] being—even though . . . [he] could not answer yes to their prompting." Invisible Man's inability to answer yes to the "promptings" within him indicates his fear of breaking group connections and his fear of operating from his own mind—even a mind connected to a group (13). To really respond to Armstrong's song Invisible Man must address those "unrecognized compulsions" that take him beyond the surface, thus beyond the words of the song and into the breaks and silences where Invisible Man perceives the social critique woven into the deceptively melancholy lyrics. Ellison, of course, suggests that Armstrong knows what is at the lower frequencies of his music, but Armstrong does not recognize how profoundly limited his audience's access to that knowledge is.

As a Blues character, Ellison's invisible narrator/protagonist moves beyond the confusion and frustration of the old woman who sings Spirituals. He determines—as Ellison states later—that "the true darkness lies within . . . [his] own mind" (566). Ellison, here, employs signifying practice through his double-meaning words. The darkness to which he refers is Invisible Man's construction of his own life as well as the dearth of self-knowledge that would create a void in his consciousness. Ellison also gives the word "lies" double meanings because "true darkness" both resides in Invisible Man's mind—that is, true knowledge of himself resides there—and "true darkness" fabricates ideas in Invisible Man's mind when he fears delving deeply into darkness by looking around corners.

The music with which the youthful Invisible Man identifies himself is not the obligatory Spirituals the visitors want to hear but the more reserved a cappella singing of "a thin brown girl" in whose music Invisible Man perceives a "controlled and sublimated anguish" that he, at this point in the novel, misses in Trueblood's country quartet or in the Spirituals that are sung on campus. Because Invisible Man "couldn't understand the words, but only the mood, sorrowful, vague, and ethereal" of the brown girl's song, perhaps the girl is singing an operatic aria or perhaps a cadenza from European Western tradition. Yet her voice fills the song with its own force, and the force in her voice "sought to enter her, to violate her, shaking her rhythmically" (114–15). Robert O'Meally takes another position on this passage. For him, the thin brown girl's song is a Spiritual (94). Following the logic of Ellison's novel, this does not seem to be the case. At this point in his development, Invisible Man is unable to appreciate the beauty of the Spirituals and the Blues; moreover, his inability to recognize the words in the song also points to the likelihood that the girl is singing in a language other than English.

The girl's performance brings an intense silence upon the audience. Her rendition confounds the expectations of the white founders of the school, who smile with approval at her song, which they perceive as bringing her closer to their ideal and making her more like them. Ellison reinforces this idea by having the audience of black students, staff, and faculty follow the girl's song by singing, *"Lead me, lead me to a rock that is higher than I am."* Invisible Man says the sound of this congregational hymn "contained some force more impervious than the image of the scene of which it was the living connective tissue" (115). Ellison uses this hymn to reinforce the ideas that inform the atmosphere of uplift in which the song is presented. He also reveals that in the sound of the hymn and beneath its words there is a more powerful idea that is often missed, yet this idea persists in the music through its traces, which "few really listen to" (12).

Ellison also indicates that the "force" in the girl's song contains ideas that are missed. His suggestion in this passage is that Spiritual-Gospel brings something to music—Blues, classical, and so on—that transforms it in some way. When fully understood, a Spiritual philosophy proves beneficial because it is situated in a life philosophy, not organized religion. Ellison also indicates that even when Spirituals are hidden under the "dominant theme" of Western classical music, such as in Dvořák's symphony *From the New World*, Invisible Man perceptively "kept hearing 'Swing Low, Sweet Chariot' . . . [his] mother's and grandfather's favorite spiritual" (132). Invisible Man, then, is unable to escape the cultural forms that have emerged from black life in the United States, even when he is absorbed in dominant culture. The dominant culture of the United

States is so tightly engaged by the influence of the African in this country that often it is difficult to disconnect the parts of one from the other, although there are some clear disjunctions.

Ellison's elucidation of the complexity of Spirituals as well as the ramifications involved in the obligatory performance for the visitors is resounded in Invisible Man even after Ellison's invisible narrator/protagonist leaves the South. In New York, after Invisible Man is made an official member of the Brotherhood, a drunken white member asks him to sing a Spiritual or perhaps "one of those real good ole Negro work songs" (304). Ellison uses this passage to illustrate a morass of issues that surround the performance of Spirituals by black people. The other people at this gathering are singing folk songs, from their own traditions, loudly and off key, but the drunken member's request and his declaration that he is "for the rights of the colored brother to sing!" embarrass the other Brotherhood members at the gathering, all of whom, except Invisible Man, are white. This incident makes Invisible Man consider the real meaning of brotherhood. He wonders, "Shouldn't there be some way for us to be asked to sing? Shouldn't the short man have the right to make a mistake without his motives being considered consciously or unconsciously malicious?" (307).

Through Ellison's contrast between the obligatory singing of Spirituals and the drunken request for Invisible Man to sing, Ellison exemplifies the gap that separates Invisible Man from those who represent the dominant society in this novel. Invisible Man is not a brother to the whites in the apartment at the Chthonian just because they enunciate the word; he is a brother when he is no longer a special case (292). Ellison also uses Invisible Man's encounters with the Spirituals to connect his main character to the "lower frequencies" when he is in the North. Brother Tarp, a former section gang laborer who is now a member of the Brotherhood, connects Invisible Man to traces of Spiritual-Gospel through his gift of a leg chain that he wore while on the section gang. Invisible Man does not want to accept Tarp's gift. He also doesn't know what to do with it, yet he "felt that Brother Tarp's gesture in offering it was of some deeply felt significance which . . . [Invisible Man] was compelled to respect." Tarp's gift is akin to Invisible Man's receiving his inheritance; it "at once joined him with his ancestors, marked a high point of his present, and promised a concreteness to his nebulous and chaotic future" (380).

Ellison connects Invisible Man to Tarp through the leg chain and makes clear Tarp's connection to traces in Spirituals by introducing the "throaty voice singing with a mixture of laughter and solemnity" that Invisible Man hears outside his window after he receives the chain. The words to the song that Invisible Man hears are "Don't come early in the morning . . ."; they recall a double-voiced Spiritual that contains words suggesting redemption while conveying a message of escape. Ellison uses this song to convey double meanings in *Invisible Man*, but his narrator/protagonist does not really hear the song. Invisible Man has "no time for memory, for all its images were of time passed" (381). Thus, he does not really listen to Brother Tarp's message or the message in the Spiritual outside his window. These are messages that Invisible Man does not understand, and thus he believes he would rather forget them. Yet he is unable to avoid the efficacy of the ideas ingrained in Spirituals. Fragments of these ideas recur throughout Ellison's novel.

At Tod Clifton's funeral, for instance, an old, dolorous male voice sings the traditional Spiritual "Many Thousands Gone"; he is accompanied by another man on a euphonium. Soon other mourners join in, and Invisible Man "felt a wonder at the singing mass. It was as though the song had been there all the time and he [the old man] knew it and aroused it; and I knew that I had known it too and had failed to release it out of a vague nameless shame or fear. But he had known it and aroused it." The old man and the man with the horn "had touched upon something deeper than protest or religion. . . . It was not the words for they were all the same old slave-borne words; it was as though [the old man had] changed the emotion beneath the words while yet the old longing, resigned, transcendent emotion still sounded above" (441–42). At this emotional moment, Invisible Man recognizes something of the philosophy in Spirituals, yet he does not really connect himself to the music or to this philosophy located in the music.

Ellison again introduces traces of Spiritual-Gospel philosophy when Invisible Man is dressed as the multifaced Rinehart. Ellison does not associate Rinehart's exploitative Holy Way Station with Spirituals. But he connects traces of a Spiritual-Gospel philosophy to an old woman on the street who believes Invisible Man is "Rine the runner" and wants to know what the numbers for the day are. Invisible Man associates this woman with the traditional Spiritual "Old Ship of Zion," which Thomas Dorsey arranged into gospel form. Ellison ties the old woman more closely to fragments of a Spiritual-Gospel music when she analyzes Invisible Man's shoes: "If I'd looked at your shoes I woulda known" (that Invisible Man is not Rine the runner) (480–81). Everyone has been misreading Invisible

Man because of his dark glasses and hat, but the old woman analyzes the bottom—his shoes—not just the top. She investigates the lower frequencies, where the Spirituals are located, and realizes that Invisible Man could not be Rinehart. Ellison establishes that the old woman observes the small traces that most people fail to investigate; there are other similar traces of Spiritual-Gospel that Invisible Man is unable to escape, since Ellison indicates that Invisible Man perceives of the woman as an Old Ship of Zion. Invisible Man is a Blues character, yet Ellison demonstrates this character's Spiritual-Gospel intertextual traces.[28]

Invisible Man is a Blues character who recognizes that he is alienated from the dominant society in the United States and that his access to full rights and privileges in that society is severely limited. He observes this incongruity and attempts to surmount the dispiriting impediments that he encounters. He does not attempt to take action solely in his own behalf. He perceives of himself as a leader, and through the philosophy of uplift he attempts to address the concerns of others with whom he shares experiences of loss, despair, and hardship; thus, he employs a Blues philosophy and tries to retain his connection to a larger group that he believes is a stable foundation. Ellison's Invisible Man also is naïve. He believes that there is one-right-plan for change. Ellison, consequently, reveals how this aspect of Invisible Man's youthful innocence causes him to misread the Blues responses of his grandfather, Bledsoe, the vet, and other Blues characters in *Invisible Man*. Invisible Man does not recognize the Blues shaping and reshaping, the singularity, the "changing same" (Baraka, *Black Music* 180) in the aforementioned characters.

Ellison most clearly depicts Invisible Man's static thought processes through his encounter with the Blues-singing cartman Peter Wheatstraw, who also is named Blue. (Ellison takes Wheatstraw's name from the stage name of bluesman William Bunch, who was well known for his Blues versions of High John the Conqueror legends [Garon 136]). Ellison associates Wheatstraw with Blues philosophy and the concept of blue in a number of ways: this character sings a Blues-influenced tune associated with Count Basie and Jimmy Rushing—"Boogie Woogie Blues" (O'Meally 88); Invisible Man meets Peter Wheatstraw when the sky is "morning-blue"; Wheatstraw's cart is "piled high with rolls of blue paper, [blueprints], and . . . [Invisible Man] heard him singing in a clear ringing voice. It was a blues . . ." (169). Thus Ellison signals a direct confrontation between Invisible Man and the Blues. Peter Wheatstraw is a piano player who volunteers to teach Invisible Man "some good bad habits" (173). Statements such as this make Wheatstraw appear an anomaly to Ellison's naïve Invisible Man, who is newly arrived in New York when he meets the cartman and is still optimistic about his possibilities as a leader and a student. Ellison uses Wheatstraw to prepare Invisible Man for the possibilities of change and the necessity for variety. This type of Blues education, which comes through a Blues philosopher or advisor, also is present in the novels of Thurman, Dunbar, and Hurston. Uncle Joe tries to educate Thurman's Emma Lou, Dunbar's Sadness Williams tries to impart Blues wisdom to Joe Hamilton, and Tea Cake guides Janie through her Blues awakening.

Wheatstraw is a cartman who collects blueprints; the word "blueprint" is a double-meaning metaphor that both elucidates the idea of a plan or an outline and limns Blues philosophy. Ellison signifies on the word "print," which denotes a copy (thus more than one) but still not the final project; therefore, plans are part of a kinetic process. Ellison also stretches the meaning of the word "blue" beyond the color of the paper on which the plans are written; he expands it to include a Blues philosophical process that is a constantly changing plan resulting from adversity, suffering, demoralization, disappointment, mistreatment, and other dispiriting conditions. Wheatstraw, himself, does not have just one plan for the way he lives life. He is "a piano player and a rounder, a whiskey drinker and a pavement pounder" whose different names—Peter Wheatstraw and Blue—and rhyming spiel resound childhood memories in *Invisible Man*, yet the more profound messages in those childish rhymes are lost on Ellison's narrator.

Through Invisible Man's conversation with the cartman, Ellison makes clear Wheatstraw's function as a Blues philosopher or advisor in the novel. Wheatstraw tells Invisible Man that people always change their plans. Ellison indicates Invisible Man's immature Blues qualities through the response his narrator gives to Peter Wheatstraw, which reveals that Invisible Man has not grasped some fundamental Blues ideas that one gains through childhood games. Invisible Man says, "Yes, that's right, . . . but that's a mistake. You have to stick to the plan." Wheatstraw's response to Invisible Man confirms Ellison's presentation of this character as one that is lacking a fundamental Blues understanding of his world. Wheatstraw looks "suddenly grave" and tells Invisible Man, "You kinda young daddy-o" (172).

Ellison establishes Peter Wheatstraw's efficacy as a character with insight, despite his playfulness, through Wheatstraw's description of himself as one who has deeper knowledge, according to folk belief. Wheatstraw's status as the seventh son of a seventh son, his special qualities as someone born with a caul, or his birth sac, intact, and his connection to aspects of conjure such as black-cat bones and high John the conqueror root give him four connections to knowledge that goes beyond the simple appearance of things. Invisible Man, however, is baffled by even the most basic Blues ideas that Wheatstraw tells him, so the cartman's more complex Blues tune *"She's got feet like a monkee. / Legs / Legs, Legs like a maaad / Bulldog. . ."* leaves Invisible Man perplexed. These are words that he has heard all of his life, yet he is unable to discern if this strange phrase is "about a woman or about some strange sphinxlike animal." (173). Through this seemingly lighthearted Blues song, which ostensibly is about an unattractive love interest, Ellison exemplifies a grotesque repulsion-love relationship between Blues People and the United States.

Peter Wheatstraw's singing causes Invisible Man to bypass his recent experience with Blues singing on the college campus, where he last heard a Blues tune after Bledsoe dismissed him from the school, because the cartman's music takes him further back to life memories that Invisible Man had blocked from his mind (169–70). Throughout the novel, Ellison's invisible narrator/protagonist never finds any value in folk-centered concepts such as those Wheatstraw advances, but as the cartman departs, Invisible Man "strode along, hearing the cartman's song become a lonesome broad-toned whistle . . . that flowered at the end of each phrase into a tremulous blue-toned chord." Invisible Man is struck by the beauty of the tune and the versatility of Wheatstraw, who "could whistle a three-toned chord." Invisible Man's life goal, however, has been to distance himself from the Blues People from which he comes and to establish a new construct to which he will lead people such as Peter Wheatstraw. Thus, he responds to Wheatstraw as a fascinated onlooker when he says, "They're a hell of a people!" But Invisible Man finds that Wheatstraw and his music confound him with feelings that Invisible Man associates with both pride and repugnance.[29] Through Peter Wheatstraw, Ellison's Invisible Man encounters a Blues philosophy that challenges his ideals of uplift and makes change a matter of "a little shit, grit, and mother-wit" (172–74).

Invisible Man's illusions are finally destroyed during his visit to Mr. Emerson's office—after his encounter with Wheatstraw. Before long, Ellison's protagonist/narrator is alone in New York. But he is unable to survive apart from group ties; thus, Ellison reconnects Invisible Man's group ties through Mary Rambo, a Blues character. At Mary's house, Invisible Man is suffering from the effects of his experiences in the factory hospital. By the time he arrives, even more of his innocence is lost, and he is now able to hear the various voices that resonate from a base of shared Blues experiences. Yet he has not found his own voice to add to the many songs he hears; Invisible Man, in fact, is unnerved by the diversity. He says, "If only all the contradictory voices shouting inside my head would calm down and sing a song in unison, whatever it was I wouldn't care as long as they sang without dissonance; yes, and avoided the uncertain extremes of the scale" (253). Invisible Man still is not a mature Blues character. Ellison's portrayal of Invisible Man at Mary Rambo's apartment places him in nurturing surroundings that recall the protective environment of his childhood home—of which Wheatstraw's song also reminds him. There is a lot of love accompanying the Blues struggles that occur in Mary's apartment, demonstrated, for instance, through the Blues traveling phrase she sings to soothe Invisible Man. O'Meally observes that Ellison does not have Mary sing the subsequent line of this Blues phrase that she greets Invisible Man with, but it is that line that soothes and comforts Ellison's narrator. As O'Meally notes, Ellison uses the participatory process of call and response in his presentation of this Blues traveling phrase. Mary calls the first line of the song—"If I don't think I'm sinking, look what hole I'm in"—and a knowing Blues People can make the appropriate response, which is the unmentioned second line of the Blues phrase (88–89). Invisible Man, does not acknowledge his Blues connections right away, but he eventually replies to Mary's call when, toward the end of the novel, he says that he has come to know "the hole I was in" (559).[30]

Mary creates an environment of interdependence in her apartment. She does not evict Invisible Man when he has no money to pay rent, even though she, too, has very little and is encountering hardships. Ellison parallels Invisible Man's southern, folk, and Blues experiences and his Blues life with Mary, who transplants rural Blues ideas of collective responsibility into an urban context. Ellison does not allow Invisible Man to escape his Blues ties. And through Mary, he makes Invisible Man express a sense of obligation (290) that extends to his Blues ties. Ellison affirms Mary's link to Blues and Invisible Man's ongoing growth into a more mature Blues character through this southern woman's singing of a Blues song. When Invisible Man hears Mary singing the Bessie Smith tune "Back Water Blues" in a "clear and untroubled voice, though she sang a troubled song," he is reminded of how much he owes her. So, through Ellison's metaphorical uses of Blues music as a place where ideas, emotions, and experiences from African American life collect and his use of Mary as an embodiment of Blues philosophy with strong Spiritual-Gospel influences—including Mary Rambo's allusions to Mahalia Jackson's signature gospel song by Herbert Brewster, "Move on Up a Little Higher"—he establishes Invisible Man's conflicting feelings about his dream of uplift and about his Blues background. These feelings of indebtedness prompt him to gain employment with the Brotherhood and move out of Mary's apartment. As Invisible Man leaves, he hears Mary sing a Blues tune (319), which emphasizes his continued link to the Blues philosophy from which he severs himself when he joins the Brotherhood. Ellison, though, poignantly attaches Invisible Man to this Blues philosophy through his idealistic notion of uplift.

As a member of the Brotherhood, Invisible Man loses sight of the Blues philosophy to which he was exposed earlier, but the murder of Tod Clifton allows him to see things differently and to consider his views in light of the people whom he wants to uplift. These people "speak a jived-up transitional language full of country glamour, think transi-tional thoughts, though perhaps they dream the same old ancient dream." These people are near at hand to Invisible Man all along, yet he too had not seen them because they were "outside the groove of history." Ellison's *Invisible Man* considers whether black people such as Frederick Douglass, someone who manages to get into the "groove of history," was an anomaly. Perhaps, Invisible Man speculates, someone such as himself or Frederick Douglass finds a propitious moment every hundred years or so, even though the flow of history indicates that charismatic leadership, to which Invisible Man aspires, was losing its force during the first half of the nineteenth century (130–32). Through his narrator's speculations on charismatic leadership, Ellison demonstrates a social-political reality in this novel, a reality in which an emergent Jazz philosophy is situated as a transition from Blues—which anchors people in group-informed concepts that can support a charismatic leader—to a more disperse Jazz philosophy. Ellison's invisible narrator/protagonist is somehow caught between both; he is immature in his Blues philosophy and is unable to engage Jazz philosophy and aesthetics.

Ellison inscribes modernity into Invisible Man's perceptions of "a languid [urban] blues" when his narrator/protagonist finally notices the music that surrounds him. Ellison illustrates how the modern presentation of urban Blues music on records marks a process of fragmentation that will take many forms in the people and in the music as it expands into Jazz. This urban Blues is not voiced by someone such as Mary Rambo or Peter Wheatstraw but is mediated through the modern recordings that local record shops amplify onto the street in order to draw pedestrians. Blues singers are fewer. Blues life is changing, and Invisible Man questions whether Blues philosophy goes far enough: "Was this the only true history of the times, a mood blared by trumpets, trombones, saxophones and drums, a song with turgid inadequate words?" Invisible Man's disdain for Blues music allows Ellison to comment on the prevailing misunderstanding of Blues music as sad and lacking social critique, a misunderstanding that is supported by his narrator/protagonist's indoctrination in the Brotherhood.[31] This indoctrination does not permit Invisible Man to listen to the lower frequencies in the music because he has "been asleep, dreaming" (433).

In Ellison's epilogue to *Invisible Man* his protagonist awakens from his dazed state and moves toward a deeper knowledge of Blues. He now has matured in his understanding of this music. Invisible Man accepts the idea that we are unable to escape the "chaos" that shapes the Blues and the idea that it is one's own singular voice that shapes one's life, as there is no established plan that fits every life. He now understands that in the self one finds the material for transforming the chaos that disrupts life's supposed certainties. As Invisible Man emerges from his underground hibernation, he *listens* to Armstrong's Blues music instead of just *hearing* the surface, the words of Armstrong's rendition of Jelly Roll Morton's "Buddy Bolden's Blues." He listens to the music, which is in contrast to the words to this song, words that exhort listeners to "throw the bad air out." Armstrong's jazzy Blues version juxtaposes the conflicting ideas that are located in the words to this tune and that reside in his inimitable trumpet style. When Ellison's narrator finally perceives the joke, he realizes that Armstrong "wouldn't have thrown old Bad Air out, because it would have broken up the music and the dance" (568).

Ellison establishes Invisible Man's mature Blues philosophy through this character's comments on Armstrong's playing of Morton's "Buddy Bolden's Blues." Legendary New Orleans cornet player Charles "Buddy" Bolden stands as a superb musician among musicians. His talent was uncontested among fellow musicians who heard him play. Bolden's talent, unfortunately, is not preserved on record, as he suffered psychological difficulties prior to the period of early music recordings and never recovered sufficiently to resume his musical career.[32] Ellison suggests here that Invisible Man cannot escape hardships and difficulties of life, nor can he abandon the troubles he has lived. Both will remain a part of him, become part of his own dance of life. Now that Invisible Man is anchored in Blues philosophy, he realizes that he cannot live the illusion found in monolithic and totalized thought; there must be room for a separate self (563–68).

Ellison inculcates his novel with both Spiritual-Gospel and Blues philosophy, allusions, references and characters. He depicts one Jazz character—Rinehart, whose name echoes a reference in a tune that Ellison may associate with Jimmy Rushing, whom Ellison remembers was a local musician in Oklahoma City before Rushing became nationally known as a vocalist with the Count Basie Band.[33] Ellison also utilizes a potent Jazz riff through his portrayal of Invisible Man's grandfather. In addition to the dominant Blues philosophy he employs and the Blues aesthetic environment in which he situates his characters, Ellison brings Jazz philosophy into *Invisible Man*. Through Rinehart and *I*nvisible Man's grandfather, Ellison portrays literary Jazz. Rinehart is a shifting, chameleon-like personality that develops from Invisible Man's "blues-toned" experiences. Invisible Man, however, resists the infinite options of Rinehart's innovative Jazz style, which is pressing in on Invisible Man's Blues life. Rinehart is the rine (rind), or tough, insensate protective outer layer as well as the hart (heart), or inner core, where feelings, vulnerabilities, and desires, as well as ruthlessness, cruelty, and opportunism, reside. How does one know which quality is at the heart of Rine? Thus, he is ambiguous. When Invisible Man takes on the image of Rinehart, this Jazz character articulates contradiction. Beneath the outer image of Rinehart's dark glasses and hat is Invisible Man, who wonders about the paradox of being both "rind and heart" (487).

Ellison portrays Rinehart as a character who embraces his invisibility as freedom. His heart is unseen, and this gives him access to options that a group connection might disallow. Rine is a free actor on the stage of life. He is at once a preacher, pimp, numbers runner, gambler, briber, lover. "His world was possibility and he knew it." As Tony Tanner explains, "Rinehart is not a man to be met so much as a strategy to be made aware of" (87). Rinehart, Ellison's Jazz character, is years ahead of his Blues character, Invisible Man, because Rinehart knows that the "world in which we lived was without boundaries. A vast seething, hot world of fluidity." While Ellison's Invisible Man realizes the freedom that Rinehart's Jazz personality represents, Invisible Man is unable to embrace the shifting sands of Rinehartism. To be Rinehart requires having "a smooth tongue," which Invisible Man has, but Ellison's Rinehartism also involves having a "heartless heart and be[ing] ready to do anything," a philosophy Invisible Man rejects (482–87).

Another view of Ellison's portrayal of Rinehart is given by O'Meally, who refers to Rinehart as Ellison's "blues villain" (90). While I do not see that Ellison actually situates Rinehart in a good-bad binary that would firmly define him as a villain, I recognize that Rinehartism is rejected by Ellison's narrator. This rejection, as I see it, is similar to Lutie Johnson's failed attempt to reject the Boots Smith and Mrs. Hedges types on the street in Ann Petry's novel *The Street*. Characters such as Rinehart as well those mentioned in Petry's novel are more complex than villain and hero categories can contain. In the essay "Ellison's Zoot Suit," Larry Neal makes the important point that the Blues world in *Invisible Man* "[i]s non dialectical. The novel attempts to construct its own imperatives, the central one being the shaping of a personal vision, as in the blues . . ." (70). In music, when this vision is expanded and pushed beyond its boundaries, it is the sound of John Coltrane, Pharaoh Sanders, Ornette Coleman, or Leon Thomas, a sound that is "a synthesis and rejection of Western musical theory all at the same time" (77). Neal's perceptive view of Rinehart demonstrates the complexity of this character in Ellison's novel and explains the logic of Kent's argument that Rinehart is a "symbol of possibility through imagination and masking, [which takes us] back to Western tradition" (Kent 168). Ellison's Invisible Man points out that both Rinehart and the Brotherhood feed on mass ignorance, so perhaps people are "as willing to be duped by the Brotherhood as by Rinehart" (491).

Ellison seems to suggest that there are circumstances that lead to Rinehartism, but perhaps those who employ it misdirect their efforts. Invisible Man rewrites Rinehartism. For Invisible Man the target of his Rinehartism is the Brotherhood, which he says is "forcing . . . [him] to Rinehart methods," but he still believes that the least desirable world is one in which Rhinehartism finds success; it is a world of ruthless last resort, or, in other words, a world of guerrilla warfare. But Rinehartism not only increases Invisible Man's invisibility in the dominant society, as Rhinehart, he also is invisible in Harlem. His true character is inaccessible even to other black people. Through *Invisible Man*'s views on Rinehart methods, Ellison critiques the concept of a Jazz aesthetic and philosophy that are completely fragmented, even though his character Invisible Man advances Rinehartism as a challenge to the Brotherhood's detached, scientific logic—which makes Invisible Man "[b]oth sacrificer and victim." Yet Ellison actually demonstrates that in the logic of the Brotherhood there are also the "charlatan" qualities of Rinehart (493–95). Thus Invisible Man is fighting fire with fire when he uses Rinehart methods on the Brotherhood.

Ellison illustrates his narrator's ambiguous attitude about Jazz when, on the one hand, Invisible Man asserts that he does not want Rinehart's freedom, yet, on the other hand, he recognizes that there is something empowering in Rinehart. He represents "infinite possibilities" because if a person is able to stand outside the limited construct of "reality," as Rinehart does, she or he enters chaos, or the imaginative space that allows new ways of thinking and being (562–63). Rinehart is a principle of chaotic life, which is mastered through shifting—and often exploitative images; and/or he is a principle of transformation, forged through the powers of the mind. Ellison juxtaposes the changing face of Rinehartism against Invisible Man's attempt to adhere to the emotionless dogma of the Brotherhood, which has a predetermined answer to everything, and against the masking humility that he learns from his grandfather.[34] None of these approaches to life work for Invisible Man, so he retreats underground into his own mind.

In addition to his characterization of Rinehart as a Jazz character, Ellison also employs Jazz philosophy in *Invisible Man* through his uses of this invisible narrator/protagonist's grandfather as a Jazz riff throughout the novel. Ellison introduces the grandfather on his death bed, where the old man elucidates the humble mask to his son (Invisible Man's father) and implores him to "[l]earn it to the younguns" (16). Through Invisible Man's grandfather, Ellison reinscribes and revises Paul Laurence Dunbar's poem "We Wear the Mask." In Dunbar's poem, the "grins and Lies"—Ellison's "grins" and "yesses" (16)—hide the "torn and bleeding hearts" and the "tortured souls" (*Complete Poems* 71) of those who wear the mask. Both Dunbar, through the persona in his poem, and Ellison, through his characterization of Invisible Man's grandfather, affirm the concept of invisibility, or hiding one's soul or spirit from people who want to destroy it.

Ellison's grandfather-character transforms the pain that collects behind the mask. In Ellison's novel the hidden "tears and sighs" of Dunbar's poem become—for Invisible Man's grandfather—a new weapon, replacing the one he gave up during Reconstruction (16). Invisible Man's grandfather advises that one should employ an appearance of humility to "overcome," "undermine," and bring "death and destruction" upon the injustice in one's life. Thus, Ellison adds radical resistance to Dunbar's earlier theme of patient endurance.

As a revision of Dunbar's poem, Ellison's portrayal of the advice of Invisible Man's grandfather elucidates the distortion that time wrought on masking among African Americans. So, after Invisible Man's grandfather explained the dynamics of masking, his family members dismiss his words as the mad ravings of a dying old man. As a result, Invisible Man is set on a path of patience and endurance that contorts the advice that his Blues philosophy grandfather bequeaths to him. The old man's advice represents a solution that has taken him successfully out of captivity and Reconstruction and into the middle of the twentieth century. And his singular voice commenting on shared experiences has a profound effect on Invisible Man. He internalizes his grandfather's advice more powerfully than he accepts the approaches to group difficulties that he encounters later in the Brotherhood, with Ras, or with Rinehartism. Invisible Man has to decipher and analyze his grandfather's true message for himself, since the prevailing interpretation of humble black masking corrupts the grandfather's Blues philosophy. The words of Invisible Man's grandfather as well as visions of him recur as a Jazz riff at crucial moments throughout the novel.

When, for instance, Invisible Man wins his scholarship, he believes he has escaped his grandfather's "deathbed curse." True to form, Invisible Man's grandfather erupts from Ellison's narrator/protagonist's unconscious in a dream and reveals to him the inadequacy of the world that the men at the smoker have prepared for him. Through this dream, Ellison demonstrates that the acceptable road that the prominent men from the smoker have opened for Invisible Man includes a demeaning racialized circus where he is one of the freaks and the men at the smoker are the ringmasters (32). Invisible Man's circus dream foreshadows his grandfather's wisdom about the school and the ideas it perpetuates.

Ellison, later in the novel, again riffs his invisible narrator/protagonist's grandfather through a dream when Invisible Man is at a low point in New York because none of his prospects for a job have contacted him. Invisible Man's dream joins images of his grandfather with a sense that Bledsoe and Norton were involved in Invisible Man's difficulties finding work. Invisible Man, however, is unable to formulate his feelings into concrete ideas, and Ellison does not provide the details of his dream because Invisible Man is not yet ready to remember the dream and address its message from his grandfather about Bledsoe and Norton. Consequently, the dream merely prompts thoughts that Invisible Man can dismiss as preposterous and impatient (167). Ellison uses Invisible Man's grandfather as a Jazz riff throughout most of the novel. With this use of Jazz riffing, Ellison reveals his narrator/protagonist's lack of knowledge and immaturity as well as his inability to read both African American and dominant cultural ideas.

Invisible Man's immense confusion about his grandfather's dying words also adds to his agony about his suspension from college. Ellison, after Invisible Man's suspension, resounds the grandfather and his advice through a Jazz riff. Invisible Man wonders, "How had I come to this? I had kept unswerving to the path placed before me, had tried to be exactly what I was expected to be. . . . And now to drive me wild I felt suddenly that my grandfather was hovering over me, grinning triumphantly out of the dark" (144). He hears his grandfather's words—"yes" them and "grin" them (16)—but he has no idea what they mean. As Invisible Man says, "I knew of no other way of living—except to do what powerful people say—nor other forms of success available to such as me" (144). Clearly, Invisible Man is profoundly naïve and lacks the basic skills for reading the double meanings in his grandfather's Blues philosophy.

Invisible Man eventually embraces and critiques the ideas of his grandfather's era. During, for instance, his fight with Lucius Brockway, the paint factory basement engineer, Invisible Man uses his grandfather's approach when he insults Brockway with epithets he remembers his grandfather using: "old-fashioned, slavery-time, mammy-made, handkerchief headed bastard." These insults counteract the mistaken notion that enslaved Africans were acquiescent, caviling people such as Brockway. Ellison depicts Brockway's age and toothlessness to emphasize the obsolescence of his ideas; there is no bite in the attitude that he promotes through his behavior. Ellison's Jazz riff of Invisible Man's grandfather-inspired insults and his narrator's comment that the old factory employee "should know better" cause Brockway to retreat (222). Invisible Man is now beginning to alter his views on the effect his grandfather's memory has on him. After his confrontation and reconciliation with Brockway, Invisible Man's response to his memories of his grandfather are more positive.

Ellison also uses the grandfather to exemplify Invisible Man's developing awareness of Blues philosophy, which his grandfather's presence resounds. At, for instance, a Brotherhood gathering, Invisible Man realizes that "white folks seemed always to expect you to know those things which they'd done everything they could think of to prevent you from knowing." Invisible Man is reminded, through Ellison's use of a Jazz riff, of his grandfather's solution to this dilemma: "be prepared"—which his grandfather was when the older man was required to "quote the entire constitution as a test of his fitness to vote" (307). We again encounter the grandfather on the day of Invisible Man's first Brotherhood speech. Invisible Man thinks of his grandfather right before the speech while he represses "the dissenting voice, . . . [his] grandfather part . . . the traitor self that always threatens discord" (327). After the speech, Ellison riffs the grandfather in the novel again when Invisible Man questions his own comments about becoming "more human" and then he wonders, "What had an old slave to do with humanity?" (345). Ellison also riffs the grandfather in the novel when Brother Tarp gives Invisible Man a picture of Frederick Douglass and when Invisible Man thinks he sees his grandfather looking through Brother Tarp's eyes following the narrator's receipt of an anonymous letter (374, 381).

When Invisible Man finally decides to try his grandfather's approach on the Brotherhood, he still is not sure that he understands precisely what his grandfather meant, even though Invisible Man is now ready to allow the Brotherhood to "gag on what they refuse to see." Ellison's narrator decides that the Brotherhood only required from him "one belch of affirmation . . . heard in one big optimistic chorus of yassuh, yassuh, yassuh." Invisible Man decides to "yea, yea, oui, oui, si, si, and see, see them too. . . . I'd become a supersensitive confirmer of their misconceptions." He ultimately decides that "somewhere between Rinehart and invisibility there were great potentialities" (497–99). Thus, Ellison makes clear that there are no absolute answers, yet through his portrayal of Invisible Man, he points out that "grandfather had been wrong about yessing them to death and destruction or else things had changed too much since his day" (552). Ellison establishes that Invisible Man's questions about his grandfather's advice, by the end of the novel, are less troubling to his narrator, but they are not resolved with conviction. Invisible Man is "still plagued by his deathbed advice. . . . Perhaps he hid his meaning deeper than [Invisible Man] thought, perhaps his anger threw [Invisible Man] off." Ellison's narrator is indecisive on this point, but he ventures to posit the idea that his grandfather meant "affirm the principle on which the country was built and not the men . . . who did the violence" (560–61).[35]

The grandfather and his advice form a riff that resounds a Blues philosophy throughout the novel. This Blues philosophy subverts all of the other inadequate ideas that Invisible Man encounters as he tries to triumph over his spirit-crushing conditions. His grandfather's advice is less than a plan yet more viable than its simplicity suggests. Ellison reveals its viability when Invisible Man wonders if his grandfather is capable of "thoughts about humanity," and then he realizes that his formerly enslaved grandfather had no need for phrases such as "this and this or this has made me more human. . . . Hell, he never had any doubts about his humanity—that was left to his free offspring. He accepted his humanity just as he accepted the principle. It was his . . ." (567).

Invisible Man's experiences free him so that he can emerge from his underground hibernation as someone who engages the options that life has to offer. Through Invisible Man's Blues experiences, as well as through Blues philosophy and a Jazz riff of the narrator's grandfather, Ellison elucidates for his readers the necessity for Invisible Man to recognize that he is integral to the process of making his own singular Blues identity.

four

DIZZY ATMOSPHERE

The novels of Toni Morrison, Albert Murray, and John Edgar Wideman were published after the tumultuous 1960s, a period that found many African Americans, as well as others who were in support of civil rights, actively resisting the racialized social policies of the United States. This is an era of sit-ins, wade-ins, stand-ins, pray-ins, boycotts, demonstrations against a plethora of unfair racial practices, and numerous attempts to desegregate all levels of education in the United States. In 1960, just under twenty years after the first sit-in protesting segregated public facilities in Chicago, the well-known sit-in at a lunch counter in Greensboro, North Carolina, initiates increased activity against segregation in the South. Shortly after this sit-in, the Student Non-Violent Coordinating Committee (SNCC) is established by students from Shaw University in Raleigh, North Carolina, with the guidance of Ella Baker. The nonviolent resistance of the civil rights movement is met with persistent terrorism and violence by private and public citizens holding fast to the status quo. A rash of church burnings and bombings begins in 1962 and culminates the following year in a devastatingly tragic loss of lives. Less than one month after the historic March on Washington and Martin Luther King's eloquent "I Have a Dream" speech, presented in the black sermonic tradition on August 28, 1963, the Sixteenth Street Baptist Church in Birmingham, Alabama, is bombed and four young girls—Cynthia Wesley, Addie Mae Collins, Denise McNair, and Carole Robertson—are killed. That same summer, Medgar Evers, the NAACP field secretary in Jackson, Mississippi, is murdered, and in November, the president of the United States is assassinated. By the end of the decade Malcolm X (Malik Shabazz), Martin Luther King Jr., and numerous others are killed during these war-torn as well as politically and racially charged years.

The second half of the decade marks the beginning of a new political posture of self-defense and active resistance among an emerging group of African Americans; they believe that the civil rights position of nonviolent, passive resistance is ineffective and unreasonably slow. This attitude is demonstrated in the more than two hundred instances of resistance that follow the assassination of Martin Luther King Jr. and is presaged in Malcolm X's well-known speech "The Ballot or Bullet," which he presents in 1964 at a meeting organized by the Congress of Racial Equality. The following year, frustrated residents of urban black communities begin imploding, starting with the Watts riots, which spark what are now called the "long, hot summers" of the 1960s. President Lyndon Johnson signs the Civil Rights Act in 1964 and the Voting Rights Act in 1965, but the acts' effects are not immediate.

Among 1960s civil rights groups such as SNCC there are frustrations about strategy. The resulting disagreements lead to changes that result in SNCC's alliance, in 1967, with the Black Panther Party, organized by Huey Newton and Bobby Seale in 1966. The Panthers' rallying cry is "Power to the People," which is transformed into the slogan "Black Power" after Stokley Carmichael uses the phrase at a SNCC rally in Greenwood, Mississippi.[1] There are other organizations holding a middle-ground position, such as the integrated Mississippi Freedom Democratic Party (MFDP),[2] which unseats the all-white Mississippi delegation to the 1968 Democratic National Convention in Chicago; their earlier attempt to subvert the unfair Democratic Party process in Atlantic City, New Jersey, in 1964 is not successful in unseating the Democratic Party's delegation.[3]

More than fifty years after Jack Johnson's defeat of Jim Jeffries in 1910, and almost thirty years after Joe Louis unsettles white supremacy in the global context with his defeat of Germany's boxing contender in the 1938 Olympics, and just over twenty years after the second major war of this century ends, another pugilistic athlete, Muhammad Ali (Cassius Clay), positions himself within the racial and political history of the United States when he refuses to honor the Vietnam War draft in 1967. Ali reminds the United States that its military and political policies have no efficacy for him, as no Vietnamese person has ever disparaged him because he is a black man. Ali converts to Islam in 1962 but does not announce his conversion until 1964, after his defeat of Sonny Liston; Ali also challenges his draft on religious grounds and again positions Islam in the public consciousness outside its association with the martyred Malcolm X. During the 1970s and 1980s, the tumult of the 1960s calms, yet the process of change continues.

The music that shows signs of change in the 1950s is, by the 1960s, undergoing yet another transformation. Blues and Jazz sounds expand into even broader territory, while the social content and context of the music becomes more strident than in previous years. Jazz—always open to the new—is again the site of innovation in new sounds. In 1960 vocalist Abbey Lincoln (Anna Marie Wooldridge), later Aminata Moseka, performs a vocal version of Max Roach's "Freedom Now Suite" on the drummer's album *We Insist*, featuring Lincoln, Coleman Hawkins, and the Nigerian musician Michael Olatunji. The early years of this decade of change in the United States also mark the release of Guggenheim fellow Ornette Coleman's 1960 album *Free Jazz*, which reunites—in a new way—Jazz and classical sounds. More expansion of Jazz comes in the form of John Coltrane's innovative uses of world music from Africa, India, and the Arab world; with the release of his 1964 album *A Love Supreme*, Coltrane expands Jazz and includes an even wider variety of sounds to the Blues, popular, and classical influences already in this music.

Blues also makes another transition in the 1960s. The music of B. B. King (Riley B. King), Johnny Taylor, Bobby "Blue" Bland, "Wicked" Wilson Pickett, Betty Wright, and Otis Redding continues to shape a sound that is transforming race records into rhythm and blues. This music reaches large audiences as performers such as Ike and Tina Turner (Anna Mae Bullock) go on the road in 1960 with their rhythm and blues show. This also is the year that a vocalist named Ernest Evans sings and dances his way to popularity with a Hank Ballard song (and accompanying dance) "The Twist," which he performs on Dick Clark's *American Bandstand*; he records his new song under the name Chubby Checker and makes the dance-song formula his signature mode of performance. A new combination of sounds is now influencing Blues, the music of everyday life among black people in the United States. African American music in the 1960s and 1970s is characterized by its variety of sounds: Motown, R&B, soul, Philly, West Coast. In 1961, Mary Wilson, Diana Ross, and Florence Ballard go under contract to sing on a relatively new record label—Motown. Berry Gordy, the founder of the label and the engineer of its new sound—which situated itself in the space that is left as Jazz moves away from the dance and social venues in African American culture—names this new female group the Supremes; they do not make a successful record for the company until 1964, when they record "Where Did Our Love Go." William "Smokey" Robinson gives Motown its first major nationwide hit record with the song "Shop Around," which, in 1961, skyrockets to the top of the charts. Robinson continues to be one of Motown's hit makers as the lyricist of chart-breaking songs such as Mary Wells's "My Guy," which in 1964 becomes Motown's first number one pop hit. The success of this song is followed by the Temptations' companion song, "My Girl," by Smokey Robinson and Ronnie White, which exceeds the success of its predecessor and becomes Motown's biggest hit. Motown, also in 1964, adds Martha Reeves and the Vandellas "Dancing in the Street," written by Marvin Gaye, to its repertoire of party songs. The next year, 1965, the Watts riots and the subsequent long, hot summers of the 1960s transform "Dancing in the Street" into a song that is now intimately connected with the politics of resistance.[4]

While black music in the United States is moving into the broad public arena of national entertainment, there is still a confluence of social concerns within this musical context as well as a return to the conjunction of music and literature. The violent losses of 1963 influence John Coltrane to compose "Alabama" and prompt Jazz pianist and vocalist Nina Simone (Eunice Waymon) to write and perform the song "Mississippi, God Damn." And in 1966 she collaborates with Langston Hughes on the Blues song "Backlash Blues." Simone records "Backlash Blues" in 1967. Ten years after Langston Hughes records his poetry, including "Commercial Theater" and selections from "Dream Montage," accompanied by Jazz musician Charles Mingus, whose album *A Modern Jazz Symposium of Music and Poetry with Charles Mingus* is released in 1957, music and poetry combine again when a Harlem group called the Last Poets read their poetry accompanied by a drummer at a May 19, 1968, commemoration in New York of the birthday of Malcolm X.

This 1960s confluence of music and poetry is situated in the literary context of the Black Arts Movement. Within this movement, literature, politics, and music operate in and upon the same discursive space. This literary and arts resurgence among African American writers, artists, and musicians results in poetry, drama, and fiction by Sonia Sanchez, Amiri Baraka, Henry Dumas, Haki Madhubuti, Ed Bullins, Nikki Giovanni, and Gwendolyn Brooks, among others. Most of these writers situate their art within an intertextual context that acknowledges art's political, social, and cultural connective threads. The political and resistant position located in Spiritual-Gospel, Blues, and Jazz is extended in the 1960s and 1970s in recordings by the Last Poets and by Black Arts Movement writers, some of whom present their poems accompanied by music. This politicized position continues in the music of African American musicians from the 1970s, such as Curtis Mayfield on *Young Mods' Forgotten Story* (1969), his album with the Impressions, and on a number of his subsequent solo albums from the early 1970s; on Marvin Gaye's *What's Going On* (1971); and on Gil Scott Heron's *From South Carolina to South Africa* (1975). In the 1980s, music, spoken word, and politics converge again in some types of rap music.

In 1967 Aretha Franklin covers "Respect," a song written and already recorded by Otis Redding. Franklin's voice and phrasing transform Redding's song about establishing one's status in relationships into a celebration of women's rights in their relationships. Franklin's soulful rendition of "Respect" continues in the tradition of her blueswomen predecessors and is followed by the soulful declarations of Laura Lee's "Women's Love Rights" (1971), "Love and Liberty" (1971), and similarly female-focused songs by Betty Wright and others, perhaps even including, in a less triumphant vein, Esther Phillips's pungently acrid "Home Is Where the Hatred Is" (1972). Before the decade ends, James Brown, in 1968, records a song that will become, for African Americans, the anthem of the 1960s era: "Black Is Beautiful: Say It Loud, I'm Black and I'm Proud." The following year, Motown releases another successful, although apolitical, song with the Jackson Five's "I Want You Back."

The 1960s also find Spiritual-Gospel music expanding its sound with the 1960 release of "Halleluja, It's Done," which Shirley Caesar sings in her signature black sermonic style, while politics and Spiritual music conjoin in various freedom songs that civil rights protesters sing as they resist the ingrained social policy of racial exclusion in the United States. And in 1968 James Cleveland establishes the Gospel Music

Workshop of America (GMWA), which takes Charles Albert Tindley's as well as Thomas A. Dorsey's vision for gospel music to another level as Cleveland records live, Spirit-filled gospel concerts. He first records a 1971 gospel concert in Dallas, Texas. During these times of change, other inspirational music—with a Spiritual-Gospel basis—moves from a strictly religious context into popular culture. The Staple Singers record songs that respond to the social and political issues of the day, such as the integration of Little Rock's Central High School in 1957 ("Why? [Am I Treated So Bad]")[5] and the 1965 March from Selma to Montgomery, Alabama ("Freedom Highway"), and in 1972 this Blues-based urban gospel group records its uplifting yet popular song "Respect Yourself." In 1969 the Edwin Hawkins Singers' recording of "Oh Happy Day" moves to number three on the popular music charts, topping Smokey Robinson and the Miracles' "Tracks of My Tears," and severs the seven-decades-old separation of the secular and the spiritual in African American music.

The 1960s end with Jimi Hendrix's virtuoso performance of "The Star Spangled Banner" at Woodstock in 1969 and his New Year's Eve and New Year's Day concerts at the Fillmore East in New York City. In Hendrix's rendition of the National Anthem during his Woodstock performance, this complicated guitarist amplifies the bluesman's (see Hendrix's 1967 recording of "Red House" for a sample of his effective Blues styling) electrified jump guitar style—already an inimitable influence on rock music—and conjoins it with the edgy, discordant rock and roll rhythms as a means by which he comments on the socio-political conditions in the United States. This song offers a musical version of the same idea expressed in Gwendolyn Brooks's 1940s postwar poem "The Anniad," which includes the poet's oxymoronic allusion to the flag as "Pretty tatters blue and red." Hendrix fuses rock, soul, and Blues music so effectively that, when he is compelled to record his performance at Bill Graham's Fillmore East on New Year's Day 1970, his Band of Gypsys (Hendrix, Billy Cox, and Buddy Miles) finds a way to win the audience with its rocking soul sound, inculcated with social messages (on "Changes" and "We've Got to Live Together"), propelling Buddy Miles to national prominence. Later Hendrix persists in this vein on "Freedom," recorded later that year. Aretha Franklin and Donny Hathaway continue this political impetus in popular African American music with their 1972 reprise of Nina Simone and Weldon Irvine Jr.'s song "To Be Young, Gifted and Black." Simone records this song in 1970 after she is inspired by Lorraine Hansberry's play with the same title, but the Franklin and

Hathaway version has the greater impact in popular music and among African Americans.

For some musicians during the 1970s, what is old is new again. This is true in the case of Dexter Gordon's "neobop," which reawakened interest in its 1940s and 1950s predecessor, bebop. Similarly, Art Blakey and the Jazz Messengers' hard bop brings innovative new sounds to a waning African American Jazz audience. Jazz continues to take on various shapes in the 1970s, including the solo improvisations and accessible Jazz sounds of the musicians on Creed Taylor's CTI label: flautist Hubert Laws, guitarist George Benson, pianist Herbie Hancock, and trumpeter Freddie Hubbard. Taylor's label specializes in returning Jazz to a public that is moving away from this music. Before establishing his own label, Taylor also produced Grover Washington Jr.'s *Inner City Blues* (1971), on which Washington covers the political tunes "Mercy, Mercy Me (The Ecology)" and "Inner City Blues" from Marvin Gaye's *What's Going On* album and gives them an accessible instrumental Jazz styling. Yet, typical of the times, there still is room for the Modern Jazz Quartet, a group with a performance history dating from 1952. The music of the Modern Jazz Quartet is a fusion of Jazz and classical sounds. As music historian Eileen Southern observes, the 1970s again remind us that "[n]o fine line of distinction exists between blues and jazz singers and those singing rhythm and blues in the early years of the genre" (*Music* 502).

The decade of the seventies is a crucial marker of the ever-present changing same in African American music. In the 1970s Joe Tex (Joe Arrington Jr.) with "Ain't Gonna Bump No More" (1977), following on his 1967 success with "Skinny Legs and All,"[6] and Rufus Thomas with his various jocular as well as dance-titled songs, such as "The Breakdown" (1973), which follows his "Do the Funky Chicken" (1969) dance craze, continue the playful and raucous style in African American music exemplified in earlier times by Peetie Wheatstraw (William Bunch). Gil Scott Heron's "Johannesburg," "The Revolution Will Not Be Televised," "Winter in America," and "The Bottle" all retain a social and political impetus that is consciously situated in much, but not all, of the African American music that predates the 1980s; Heron addresses what appears to be a post-1980s change in African American music in his 1994 song "Message to the Messengers." The late decades in the twentieth century also find civil rights activist Bernice Johnson revivifying general interest in the Spirituals and other African American folk music in 1973 with the all-female a cappella group Sweet Honey in the Rock. This same year Berry Gordy becomes the head of the multimedia (records, publishing, film, and television) corporation Motown Industries. By the end of the 1970s the Sugar Hill Gang brings to a popular, commercial audience an urban mixture of music and poetry in "Rappers Delight"; but entertainment, not politics is the emphasis of this new sound in African American music.

Contemporary African American fiction writers regularly use music as a metaphor in which they locate ideas, emotions, and experiences. Toni Morrison in *Sula*, her novel of friendship and self-awareness, contrasts a Blues philosophy and a Jazz philosophy through her depiction of Nel Wright Greene and Sula Peace. Albert Murray in *Train Whistle Guitar* portrays the making of a twentieth-century male Blues personality. His main character Scooter lives a Blues childhood that shapes his psyche in profound ways and helps him to encounter life as it actually is, not as an ideal. And in *Sent for You Yesterday*, John Edgar Wideman uses Blues and Jazz music to link generations and to illustrate that life, as with music, is part of a process of change.

Morrison, Murray, and Wideman consciously tie music to the worlds they portray in their novels. Wideman and Murray make music central to their fictional environment, and Morrison uses music to support her fictional world. In Wideman's novel, music is the connective that brings his main Blues character into a cultural site from which he had once felt disconnected. For Murray's main character, Scooter, the Blues world in which this character lives protects him and prepares him to leave that protection inculcated in Blues philosophy. Morrison's novel is connected to music through its intertextual position as a cultural object that is situated in an African American cultural context that resonates Blues and Jazz aesthetics and philosophy. This musical and philosophical context produces Morrison's Blues character Nel Wright Greene and this character's compliment as well as her complement, the Jazz character Sula Peace, who finds comparable symmetry in Nel's Blues.

Toni Morrison: *Sula*

Toni Morrison's recuperation of African American folk culture, including music, in literature is the focus of many of the scholarly discussions of her writing. Alan J. Rice observes that Morrison "continually uses black musical forms as conscious similes, metaphors, and structuring devices." Morrison's "Jazz aesthetic," he further notes, "can be traced from her first novel *The Bluest Eye* through *Jazz*." Rice correctly concludes that Morrison "is in fact the inheritor of a tradition of the use of jazz in prose stretching back through Ellison, Hurston, and McKay" ("Finger Snapping" 113–14). Anthony J. Berrett also finds that Morrison uses Jazz frequently in her novels. Berrett, in fact, states that "Morrison wants her fiction to do 'what music used to do'" in African American culture. So Morrison's fiction, "rather than just replace music, . . . absorb[s] many of those qualities which have made music so expressive for black people over the years" (267–68). Both Rice and Berrett accurately assess Morrison's uses of music in her fiction, as there is general recognition, for instance, of the Jazz cadences that she inscribes in the language of as well as the Jazz rhythms that shape the structure of her novel *Jazz*. Some readers also recognize the Blues qualities in her novels and may be attentive to Morrison's nod to the Blues, as she situates the female space in *Beloved* at 124 Bluestone (blues tone/blue stone). Morrison's novel *The Bluest Eye* resonates with the music of the 1950s and 1960s, as the opening words, from the narrator, in Morrison's first novel collect a pithy phrase found in African American group culture that also is collected in the Lee Andrews and the Hearts's recording of "Quiet as It's Kept." Keith Byerman in *Fingering the Jagged Grain* associates Nel with "blues expression" (201) and recognizes Morrison's intertextual relation between music and fiction in *Sula*. Yet Neither Rice nor Berrett addresses Morrison's more subtle uses of music as a metaphor in her novel *Sula* (1973).[7]

Toni Morrison's *Sula* spans forty-six rapidly changing years and focuses on her two main characters, Nel and Sula, who are nine years old when the novel begins in 1919, the year of Red (bloody) Summer, an event that finds black people under siege from white people's resistance to assertions—from black people—of legitimate citizenship. Morrison opens part 1 of her novel with an untitled chapter that establishes a context for subsequent events in the text. The black residents who live in the hills that Morrison mockingly refers to as "up in the Bottom" (5) are at a juncture of displacement and change. In this chapter Morrison, whose botanical imagery permeates her novels, metaphorically describes the residents who live up in the Bottom as "nightshade and blackberry patches . . . [torn] from their roots" (3). She elaborates this metaphor through the events she depicts in *Sula*.

Over the course of the novel Morrison shows that the economic base in the valley and hill community of Medallion, Ohio, changes from farming to industry. When farming is the main means of support in the region, the black residents live in the "hilly land, where planting was back breaking" (5). When, however, "hot dusty progress" replaces farming, the black residents in the hills move down into the valley, and the white residents who live in the valley move up into the "lovely" Bottom. Through word play on the term "Bottom" and through incidents Morrison presents in the novel, she represents paradox in the lives of the black residents in Medallion. The conditions of their lives are shifting yet consistent. Whether they live on the barely arable land in the rural hills or in the burgeoning urban valley—whether they are subsisting "up in the Bottom" or surviving down in the valley—it does not matter; they are still at the bottom. The "bottom," or "black bottom," is a term that, in the early decades of the twentieth century, refers to neighborhoods where black people live, particularly in the South. The black bottom also is a dance that was familiarized in song by Ma Rainey and Jelly Roll Morton (Ferdinand Joseph La Menthe; one of the earliest important Jazz composers) at the early part of the twentieth century. Rainey records the song "Ma Rainey's Black Bottom" in 1927 and Morton records "Black Bottom Stomp" in 1926.[8] In 1913, prior to Rainey's and Morton's songs, Robert Nathaniel Dett publishes his Spirituals-based piano suite *In the Bottoms*, and in 1922 William Grant Still writes his chamber orchestra piece *Black Bottom*.

Morrison also establishes that the physical displacement and change in the people of Medallion parallels a change in the psyches of the people in her novel. They must adjust psychologically to new ways of living that are an inevitable result of change in their physical environment. Morrison illustrates these changes and the impact they have on the black residents of Medallion through her portrayal of Nel Wright as a Blues character who holds tightly to previously established patterns in life, even though her true disposition is adventurous and self-directed. And through her depiction of Sula Peace as a Jazz character who makes her own rules and breaks all of the established ones, Morrison illustrates change.

Nel and Sula are reared in a Blues environment up in the Bottom. Morrison exemplifies the Blues lives of people in the Bottom through her description of "a dark woman in a flowered dress doing a bit of cakewalk, a bit of black bottom" to harmonica music. Morrison further evinces Blues as the informing philosophy among the black residents of Medallion through her description of the misperceptions that a white valley resident has about the music and the woman dancing in the yellow dress: "The black people watching her would laugh and rub their knees, and it would be easy for the valley man to hear the laughter and not notice the adult pain that rested somewhere under the eyelids, somewhere under their headrags, somewhere in the palm of the hand, somewhere behind the frayed lapels, somewhere in the sinews curve. . . . [T]he pain would escape him even though the laughter was part of the pain" (4). The black residents in Medallion inscribe multiple levels of meanings in their music, some of which may seem contradictory; but in these multiple and contradictory meanings, the music expresses the disjuncture that also is part of their lives. Thus, the laughter and pain that occupy the same space in the music also resound in the complex lives of the Blues People in Morrison's novel.

Morrison depicts the woman's Blues dancing as a vivid and singular expression of group feelings. Through the movements of her body, she enacts the pain of their existence and displays how laughter stands face-to-face with pain and quells it. The other residents form a foundation of similar feelings, and they support her singular expression through their laughter and musical accompaniment that also commingle with the pain in their supporting voices. The other residents do not join the dance because they see in it their own pain and laughter, yet they do not condemn the dance because they understand it. The white resident from the valley, however, only hears the laughter and mistakes it for childish joy, devoid of adult concerns and complexities, when, in fact, those adult issues are in the laughter, shaping its Blues tone.

Through this contrast Morrison substantiates how dominant society's analyses misread the signs that elucidate the lives of the people in the Bottom. So as the dominant sign systems and marginal sign systems—which overlap and contrast—meet through encroaching modernism in Medallion, the impact they have in the lives of Morrison's black characters is dramatic, particularly for Nel and Sula. Morrison further supports her elucidation of Blues as the informing philosophy in the Bottom through numerous passages in *Sula* that evince Blues philosophy. Morrison, to take a case study from the novel, illustrates this philosophy through her narrator's explanation of the view that the people in the Bottom have about evil. For them, "precautions must naturally be taken to protect themselves from [evil]. But they let it run its course, fulfill itself, and never invented ways either to alter it, to annihilate it or prevent its happening again. So also were they with people. . . . The purpose of evil was to survive it and they determined . . . to survive floods, white people, tuberculosis, famine and ignorance. They knew anger but not despair." In their book *Toni Morrison*, Wilfred Samuels and Clenora

Hudson-Weems engage the question of Sula as an evil character. Their discussion illustrates the complexity of Morrison's conception of evil as she presents it in *Sula* and as she addresses evil in connection with her title character. These scholars view Sula as a "scapegoat" and a "pariah" to the residents of the Bottom (7, 33). Both scapegoats and pariahs often attain this status unjustly, as is aptly illustrated in Shirley Jackson's chilling short story "The Lottery" and in Toni Morrison's painfully honest short novel *The Bluest Eye*. Most often these surrogate sufferers are chosen as concrete replacements, as substitutes or supplements for the collective body. They assuage communal fear of impending danger as well as of its own implication in the forbidden. The scapegoat or pariah substitute allows a community to shift its burden and palliate its sense of guilt or fear. Surrogate sufferers function as postmodern simulacra, empty containers, a dangerous supplement, designed to hold the community's burdens.[9]

Perhaps for some readers of this novel, Morrison's positioning of Sula as a pariah or scapegoat among the residents of the Bottom makes this character an incarnation of evil.[10] I read this passage as Morrison's demonstration of the error in this position, which is held among the black people in the Bottom. Morrison "does not assess this age-old concern [good and evil] in strictly religious, particularly Christian, terms. In Morrison's discourse evil is not a sin against God, per se. Conceptually, it is inverted to become a sin against One's self; it is One's failure to act existentially." And, as Odette Martin further explains, Sula represents "an explicit criticism of Black values and patterns of behavior. . . . She is neither evil nor a fixed unchanging Absolute . . . ; she represents potential" (41).[11]

Sula is the character in Medallion's Bottom community who enters chaos and survives; for this reason, she possesses a similar quality as that which Ralph Ellison's Trueblood has. This quality strikes awe in Ellison's Mr. Norton during his encounter with Trueblood in *Invisible Man*.[12] The ability to move through chaos is evident in Sula as well and is unacknowledged yet secretly admired by some, and covertly respected among others in the Bottom, as Sula well knows. They will love her when all of their hidden desires become manifest and they can no longer shift their own deviations from societal rules onto Sula, whose transgressions by no means match theirs: "Oh, they'll love me all right. It will take time, but they'll love me. . . . After all the old women have lain with the teen-agers; . . . when Lindbergh sleeps with Bessie Smith . . . then there'll be a little love left for me," Sula asserts (145–46).

Morrison selects these among other transgressions as a means by which she discloses the complexity of desire and race. Interestingly, her allusion to Charles Lindbergh and Bessie Smith reminds readers of Lindbergh's opposition, in the late 1930s, to the United States' participation in the war effort and of his visits to Nazi Germany (145–46). Morrison's allusion also suggests the lindy hop dance craze, inspired by Charles Lindbergh's 1927 flight to Paris. The connection between Lindbergh and Bessie Smith raises the additional historical specter of the white male desire for the black female body and the connection between such desires and the making of the Blues that Bessie Smith sings. Ralph Ellison in the Prologue to *Invisible Man* makes a similar connection between the making of the Spirituals and the white male desire for the black female body. In this novel, Sula does not allow social criticism of her to diminish her recognition of the hidden transgressions that permeate her society, including the transgressions of the people who live in the Bottom. Shortly after Sula's death, her predictions about the people in the Bottom are evident: "A falling away, a dislocation was taking place. Hard on the heels of the general relief that Sula's death brought[,] a restless irritability took hold" (153).

Morrison moves her emphasis from community concerns and toward the shaping of a distinct personality, as she investigates, through her characters, resistance to the preset rules located in the dominant discourse as well as similarly limiting rules in Medallion (Samuels and Hudson-Weems 7). By doing this, Morrison both critiques the limitations on personality found among Blues residents in the Bottom and moves Sula into a Jazz space that allows this character to interrogate this Blues foundation while simultaneously bringing to that Blues space, without fear of destruction, a new shaping of female personality. In Morrison's definition of evil in *Sula*, moreover, she does not include her character Sula. Sula is among the life's events, including people, natural disasters, diseases, and racialized discourses that the residents in the Bottom do not try to "alter" or "annihilate." They survive them, just as they survive "evil days" such as "the time when the sky was black for two hours with clouds and clouds of pigeons." The "plague of robins" that accompanies Sula's 1937 return is an "oppressive oddity" for Medallion, yet Sula greets the dead birds and their "pearly shit" as though they are a "trivial phenomenon" on her path. In the midst of the Depression and impending war, as well as President Franklin Roosevelt's second phase of his New Deal, there is a generalized recognition of the need to brace for uncertainty; this need seems outside Sula's purview (89–90). She lives in the shifting moments that her life brings her.

Nel is Morrison's Blues character, and Sula is her Jazz character. Through her characterizations of Nel and Sula, I find Morrison's most extensive use of Blues and Jazz philosophy in *Sula;* at the same time Morrison elucidates the intimate and intricate connection between Jazz and Blues. With the exception of the Deweys and Shadrack, Morrison presents the other residents in the Bottom as Blues characters who retain a strong connection to the group foundation yet represent singular perspectives on life.

Shadrack and the Deweys, Morrison's Jazz riffs in the novel, fill an open space that allows for difference. Morrison again points out the Blues philosophy of the residents in the Bottom through their ability to accept Shadrack as a variation from their basic foundation: "Once the people understand the boundaries and nature of his madness, they could fit him, so to speak, into the scheme of things" (15). Shadrack, for example, lives just outside the main residential area in the Bottom. He is a shattered veteran of the first war for democratic rights who, through his madness, realizes that the life he has experienced and that he perceives among those in the Bottom would seem desperate enough for some people to commit suicide, but among the people in the Bottom, suicide is unthinkable—"it was beneath them" (90). Shadrack, a character who suggests his biblical counterpart in terms of his ability to survive the fire and turmoil to which he has been subjected, breaks the cultural code among the black people in Medallion and decides to announce a day to reject the established system of rules, a day when unthinkable thoughts can be expressed and perhaps enacted: National Suicide Day. No one in the Bottom takes seriously Shadrack's pronouncement of a day for suicide, but they allow him his yearly parade. More important than the name of the infamous day is its purpose: Shadrack wants to control fear by making a place for it (14). This idea is riffed throughout the novel as Morrison, in a fashion similar to that in Ralph Ellison's depiction of black veterans in *Invisible Man,* occasionally introduces Shadrack into her novel to resound a message of resistance.

Shadrack's enigmatic encounter with Sula, for example, demonstrates Morrison's use of the shattered veteran as a voice that riffs visionary possibilities through her novel. When Sula accidentally kills Chicken Little (60–61), she believes Shadrack may have seen her. Shortly afterward Shadrack and Sula encounter each other at his shack. His statement to Sula, Morrison makes clear, is singularly his (156). Shadrack's statement is the single word "Always" (63). This one word takes on polysemous qualities as it recalls Josephine Baker's rendition of the Irving Berlin tune by that name. Both Baker and Sula are women who defy the prevailing racial and gender narratives. Shadrack's statement also is as confounding as an oblique parable, and—as is the case with parables—each person's interpretation takes its own shape and encodes its own possibility. Sula, on her death bed eighteen years after she encounters Shadrack, internalizes Shadrack's comment to her (157), but she has forgotten the source from which she gained it. Sula's understanding of Shadrack's enigmatic message is that "Always" means that death is "a sleep of waters always" (149), a return to something akin to a universal womb. For her, he affirms that there is no burning hell or spiritual torment in death. Sula, then, must account for her actions within her own mind; there is no retributive accounting after death. Morrison further illustrates that Shadrack has a completely contrasting understanding of his message to Sula. Shadrack remembers that "he had said 'always' so she would not have to be afraid of the change. He had said 'always' to convince her, assure her, of permanency"—in their friendship, or perhaps of some sort of unchanging life without end. Shadrack's interpretation, of course, is naïve, so when he sees Sula's dead body at the funeral home, he realizes that life is not forever; thus, people need not make a day to opt out of it. Sula's death in October 1940 illustrates Shadrack's error as he realizes that Sula would never visit him again (157–58).

Through Shadrack, Sula—unwittingly—is exposed to a perspective about afterlife that contraposes the dominant ideas about life and death found among the residents in the Bottom. Because Sula brings her own interpretation to Shadrack's statement, she gives it personal meaning and is not distracted by Shadrack's confused and befuddled interpretation. Morrison depicts Shadrack as a radical rupture from the group, yet he is not persecuted or disciplined into conformity since in the Bottom "aberrations were as much a part of nature as grace" (118). The people in the Bottom know that "Shadrack . . . [is] crazy but that did not mean that he didn't have any sense, or even more important, that he had no power." In the same way that Sula has internalized Shadrack's "knowledge," the other people who live in the Bottom have "absorbed . . . into their thoughts [his] annual solitary parade" (14–15), which is designed to allow people to confront the things that they fear most.

With Shadrack's last Suicide Day parade, Morrison sets in motion her final riff on the idea of the possibilities of transformation in life that can arise when fear is engaged instead of avoided. This last parade, Shadrack's first to include other people who live in the Bottom, is a "curious disorder" and a "headless display" (160). The few residents of the Bottom who join Shadrack's parade comprise a Jazz expression of collective improvisation on Shadrack's Blues-inspired yet Jazz-like contemplation of chaos. With their fear removed, Morrison illustrates how the people who join Shadrack's parade remember their "teeth unrepaired, the coal credit cut off, the chest pains unattended, the school shoes unbought," so they openly resist. Each participant in Shadrack's parade brings his or her own concerns, his or her own distinct voice to this parade. Morrison, then, employs a Jazz philosophy in her depiction of the last Suicide Day parade. Morrison situates this instance of resistance in 1941, the early part of a decade that is filled with African American responses to and resistance against overt practices of racial exclusion in both the North and the South, including exclusion from the armed forces in this same year that the United States joined the Allied forces. In the midst of this second important war, Shadrack remembers 1919; and perhaps he fears an imminent repetition of Red (bloody) Summer (161).

The participants in Shadrack's parade destroy the tunnel that has become a means of economic growth for everyone in Medallion except the black residents. They "smash the bricks they would never fire in yawning kilns, split the sacks of lime stone they had not mixed or even been allowed to haul. . . . Old and young, women and children, lame and hearty, they killed, as best they could, the tunnel they were forbidden to build" (161). The directionless behavior of the residents in this uprising results in many deaths, but as with Shadrack's confounded message to Sula, his parade allows townspeople to confront their fears and enact conditions of both loss and growth. Their actions are improvised, a Jazz response to the moment, but the impact is lasting because it erodes the fear that impedes the growth of the people who live up in the Bottom. Sula recognizes Shadrack's impact on her life eighteen years after their first encounter. The people who live up in the Bottom realize the forward movement of Shadrack's inadvertent influence on their lives twenty years later. By 1965, Morrison's narrator observes that things seem so much better (161, 163).

Morrison's other Jazz riff in *Sula* is the Deweys (37–38). She not only employs them as a riff throughout the novel but also depicts them as Jazz characters. The deweys, Eva's collection of wayward youth, are everywhere; they seem idle; they are not socialized within the community, yet they are not exiled. Morrison establishes that "the deweys would never grow. They had been forty-eight inches tall for years now, and while their size was unusual it was not unheard of. . . . [T]hey remained boys in mind. Mischievous, cunning, private and completely unhousebroken . . ." (84). Morrison illustrates the deweys' Jazz style in her description of them: "Stouthearted, surly, and wholly unpredictable; the deweys remained a mystery not only during all of their lives in Medallion but after as well" (39); thus, the deweys remain uncontained and loosely connected to ties that would support the Blues-based philosophy in Medallion. Morrison's characterization of the deweys, as well as of Shadrack, points to the implications of Jazz as radical free subjectivity. Their freedom is potentially liberating, but their lack of direction and discipline is potentially destructive.[13]

Morrison also uses specific references to music in *Sula*, but they are few. Tar Baby, a boarder in Eva's house, "wants a place to die privately, but not quite alone." He sings, in a beautiful hill voice, the Spiritual-Gospel song "In the Sweet By-and-By." Death does not come soon for Tar Baby, so he begins living on music and little else (69) as well as attending prayer meetings where he sings "Abide with Me" (94) until Shadrack's last parade, when he is killed. Morrison also makes specific reference to singing and songs when the Junior Choir sings "Nearer My God to Thee" and "Precious Memories" at Chicken's funeral (64) and when she mentions the Bert Williams record "Save a Little Dram for Me" on the occasion of Jude Greene and Nel Wright's wedding (79). Sula's encounter with her grandmother after the younger woman returns from college in Tennessee is another instance of Morrison's specific references to music. Sula blasphemes against God and speaks against the authority of her grandmother when she accuses the older woman of killing her own son, Plum. Eva's response to the impudent words of her granddaughter is to sing "Amazing Grace" (93). And four years later, following Sula's funeral, black people from Medallion arrive at Sula's grave to sing "Shall We Gather at the River" (150, 173).

Many of Morrison's few specific references to songs are Spiritual-Gospel songs, and her characters sing these songs at funerals; or Tar Baby, who wants a funeral, sings them. Morrison, then, associates the Spiritual-Gospel songs in *Sula* with the transformation and change that she depicts throughout the novel. Her connection between this music and death suggests the fading away of an older era and an older form of expression. The only Spiritual-Gospel reference that Morrison does not associate with death is sung by Eva, who is a Blues character. Morrison's confrontation between Eva and Sula still enacts a conflict of old and new. Eva, as well as her song—"Amazing Grace"—represents an older era and that era's philosophy, as well as its music. Through Eva, Morrison demonstrates that these older Spiritual-Gospel ideas are strong, yet they are being challenged. This idea is exemplified when Sula puts Eva in a home for people who have lost control of either physical or mental faculties, or both; and by extension Eva's music and ideas also are pushed to the margin of life in Medallion. There is nothing wrong with Eva, and Nel disagrees with Sula's actions and observes that Eva is "odd, but she got sense" (100). After Sula locks Eva away, the older woman persists and lives past ninety years of age. Morrison demonstrates, then, that the change that Sula represents is not able to destroy the older Spiritual-Gospel philosophy, but change does disrupt the old pattern of life. Over time Eva's situation, and thus the older philosophy that she represents, improves among the residents up in the Bottom, but she no longer has a prominent place in their community. She is moved to a better nursing home and is nearly forgotten.

In addition to the Spiritual-Gospel songs, Morrison's only other specific song reference is associated with Nel's marriage to Jude, a tenor in the church quartet. Morrison indicates early in the novel that weddings metaphorically point to impending death (78). She repeats this image through her description of Jude's ideas about his marriage to Nel. Jude thinks that the "two of them together would make one Jude," resulting in the extinction of Nel as a distinct person (83). Morrison represents Nel's wedding as death to the free spirit of the bride, and the song "Save a Little Dram for Me" represents Nel's unacknowledged cry from her soul. Morrison's other references to music are more general. After, for instance, Sula's love interest Ajax leaves, she finds a melody in her head that makes her comment, "[T]here aren't any more new songs and I have sung all the songs there are." She tries to improvise one but is unsuccessful (137). As Sula attempts to make more music that is unique and finds that she cannot, Morrison elucidates the idea that newness has been exhausted. Sula has lived every experience in life that was there for her.

Another instance of Morrison's use of music to express ideas in *Sula* is associated with Shadrack's last Suicide Day parade. Most of the townspeople refuse to attend, even though they understand the "Spirit's touch which made them [the participants] dance . . . understood whole families bending their backs in a field while singing as from one throat" (160), but they do not understand the new music of Shadrack's parade. For most of the town the parade music—Shadrack's ringing of a cowbell—is cacophonous and represents directionless movement. Interestingly, Shadrack's parade is situated in a historical period when bebop is on the musical horizon; it will be a new sound that reworks everything in its musical environment, including Blues. Bebop is not completely unique when it arrives on the scene, but it is an unnervingly different sound for many.

Morrison's Nel and Sula clearly exemplify Blues and Jazz characters. Through Nel Wright, Morrison depicts a potential Jazz character who does not become one because the spirit of adventure and freedom that Jazz represents is rubbed "down to a dull glow" under the conditions that limit Jazz development in the Wright household. Samuels and Hudson-Weems point out that Morrison makes metaphorical connections between her two central characters and the houses in which they lived as a child (1). Nel's home is "oppressive[ly] neat" (29), and her parents are "stern and undemonstrative" (83). As Morrison's Blues character, Nel attempts to break away from the dispiriting influences of her home. At ten years of age, she pulls away from her parents' ideas about who she is and tries to establish a place for her own influence in her life. She says, "I'm me. I'm not their daughter. I'm not Nel. I'm me. . . . Each time she said the word *me* there was a gathering in her like power, like joy, like fear" (28). In this passage Morrison depicts Nel's potential for expressing innovative personal style or Jazz, which is forced into repression by Nel's fear of the consequences for resistance. Certainly, Nel knows that she is biologically the daughter of her parents; thus, her youthful declaration is not expressed as a means of breaking that connection but as a means of breaking the limited and limiting definition they have of her as their daughter, as Nel. She wants to free her imagination that her parents have driven underground (18), and she wants to find a definition of herself that she can shape instead of being completely shaped by the preset ideas of her parents. Nel's eventual marriage and her life in Medallion end this possibility for her. She becomes a part of the fabric of Blues life up in the Bottom.

Sula, in contrast to Nel, lives in a house that exemplifies choices. There are in this house three separate stairways leading to the second floor, rooms with three doors, or rooms that only open onto the porch as well as rooms that were accessible only from another bedroom (30). The environment in Sula's house is "wooly"; she receives no discipline (29). Through the youthful Sula, Morrison depicts the growth of a developing

Jazz personality that is positioned in a Blues philosophy that shapes both Sula and Nel. Unlike Nel, Sula, as Morrison's Jazz character, successfully begins making herself at a very young age. Sula's most wrenching experience, of the many unusual and terrifying situations that she sees in her grandmother's house (her uncle killed by her grandmother; her mother burned to death; the torpor of Tar Baby) is her overhearing her mother, Hannah, say, ". . . I love Sula. I just don't like her" (57). These words cause Sula to retreat upstairs in her grandmother's house and set her on the path of an "experimental life" (118). The acrid parts of her character result from the painful realities of life that she experiences and sees in her home. Morrison, then, contrasts the stark and excessive order in Nel's house and the cluttered and loose organization of Sula's home life; the firm discipline of Nel's parents and the wild freedom in Sula's house; and the emotional aloofness of Nel's parents with Sula's most wrenching youthful experience. Through this contrast, Morrison demonstrates how the dispositions of her two characters are shaped from both internal and external influences. Nel and Sula both have adventurous personalities that grow differently because they have been nurtured differently.

Despite the differences that Morrison creates between Nel and Sula, she indicates that the girls share a similar disposition. Nel and Sula speak with one voice. For Nel, a conversation with Sula seems to be a conversation with herself (95). They "had difficulty distinguishing one's thoughts from the other's" (83). Sula, for instance, saw Nel as "the closest thing to both an other and a self" (119). And Eva, Sula's grandmother, tells Nel that the two women are the same. "You. Sula. What's the difference. . . . Just alike. Both of you" (168–69). Sula and Nel determine early in their lives that they will make something else of themselves besides another version of womanhood that life in Medallion offers. Sula persists; Nel eventually conforms. Morrison's delineation of Sula's distinct personality and her free home life illustrate Sula's increased potential as a character who could reject being firmly entrenched in a group. Sula, for instance, "could hardly be counted on to sustain any emotion for more than three minutes" (53). Her stride is "fluid" (95). And she does not fit any mould, so whatever form she takes is not set, does not congeal. She is always open to the possibility of change.

Morrison firmly joins Sula to Jazz philosophy through this character's attitude about permanency and change. Morrison depicts Sula's ideas through Nel's thoughts, suggesting that Nel has lost this part of herself as a result of her conformity to received rules and ideas. Nel, while in her grief over losing her husband Jude because of his sexual encounter with her best friend Sula, remembers Sula's ideas about the tortures of hell. Sula believes that the "real hell of Hell is that it is forever." For Sula, "doing anything forever and ever was hell." Nel disagrees: "Hell ain't things lasting forever. Hell is change" (107–8). Thus Morrison's Blues character seeks a type of permanency on which she can depend and to which she can be connected. But Sula believes there is no real permanency; she has an attitude of "elusiveness and indifference to established patterns of behavior" (127). Sula seems to have pieces of experience that she returns to, retains fragments of, but there is nothing to which she wants to make a permanent connection, not Medallion, not Jude, not her family. Thus Sula, as with the birthmark on her eye, potentially represents "a stemmed rose" (52), beautiful and fragile; a copperhead or a rattlesnake (103–4), dangerous and hidden; a "tadpole" (156), a sign that she is privy to concealed knowledge; or "Hannah's ashes marking her from the beginning" (114), the potential for evil. Sula also does not worry that others may interpret her in any way they choose. Sula "was distinctly different. Eva's arrogance and Hannah's self-indulgence merged in her and, with a twist that was all her own imagination, she lived out her days exploring her own thoughts and emotions, giving them full reign, feeling no obligation to please anybody unless their pleasure pleased her. . . . She had no center, no speck around which to grow. . . . For that reason she felt no compulsion to verify herself—be consistent with herself" (118–19). She lives a moment-to-moment Jazz life.

Jazz as an improvisation on a Blues fragment is a way to change an old idea without destroying it. Morrison does this in her portrayal of Sula, a character who mirrors fragments of experience from Eva, her grandmother. Eva cuts off her leg for the survival of her family (31, 34–35); Sula cuts off the tip of her finger to protect Nel (54–55). Eva burns Plum in his bed to avoid watching him die slowly (47–48); Sula watches Hannah burn "because she was interested" (78). Eva matched wits with men and she "loved maleness, . . . but she did not participate in the act of love" (41); Sula "stirred a man's mind, but not his body" (104), but if she is intimate with men, she "discards them without any excuse that the men could swallow" (115). Thus, Morrison makes Eva Peace the prototype for Sula. As with Jazz and Blues, Sula—Jazz—develops from the context that Eva—Blues—has situated for her, but Sula does not replicate her predecessor. Sula breaks the rules within which Eva and others in Medallion operate. Morrison's Blues character Eva takes actions throughout the novel that exemplify a radically singular response to the adversity in her life, but she continues to operate within an established Blues pattern. Sula, however, refuses to be contained and moves beyond the established pattern of life in Medallion. As a Jazz character, Sula's responses to life often differentiate her from others and emphasize her position outside of the typical life in Medallion.

Eva, however, tries to bring Sula into the group philosophy. "You need to have some babies. It'll settle you," she tells Sula. From Eva's perspective, women "got no business floatin' around without no man." Sula boldly rejects Eva's advice, which would anchor the younger woman in Medallion's group philosophy. "I don't want to make somebody else, I want to make myself," she says (92). Morrison's Jazz character, clearly, rejects having the responsibility for any life except her own; she also rejects having any authority in control of her life, except herself. Sula rejects not only a male authority in her life but also the authority of her grandmother by rudely telling her not to speak about Sula's decision not to be committed to a man. Later Sula also rejects the authority of God. Morrison takes Sula's Jazz independence to its limit, in terms of the attitudes of the people in the Bottom, when Sula goes beyond being insolent with her grandmother and questions the efficacy of God. Eva tells Sula that by disrespecting her grandmother, God will punish her. Sula replies, "Which God? The one watched you burn Plum?" (92–93). Sula's attitude appalls Eva, who immediately condemns her granddaughter to hell fire. But Sula is intractable. She persists in her rejection of conformity. She tells Eva, "Whatever's burning in me is mine! . . . And I'll split this town in two and everything in it before I'll let you put it out" (93). Sula's struggle with her grandmother for selfhood echoes Nel's youthful fight to retain her "me," a fight that Nel loses.

Morrison's portrayal of Sula's response to the pain she causes Nel by having sex with Jude evinces Sula's free Jazz personality. Angela Davis, in *Blues Legacies*, discusses blueswomen as critical of the larger discourse on female sexuality, yet my attribution of Sula's sexual freedom to a Jazz instead of Blues is consistent with Davis's assessment.[14] Davis's blueswomen, while sexually liberated, recognize that social boundaries such as marriage change one's sexual availability. Sula, however, has no concept of possessing someone in an intimate relationship and is surprised that Nel has become "one of *them*. . . . One of the spiders [that is] more terrified of the free fall than the snake's breath below. . . . If they were touched by the snake's breath, however fatal, they were merely victims and knew how to behave in that role (just as Nel knew how to behave as the wronged wife). But the free fall, oh no, that required—demanded—invention. . . . Now Nel belonged to the town and all of its ways, . . . and a flick of their tongues would drive her back into her little dry corner . . ." (120). Morrison conveys in this passage Sula's disappointment that Nel has accepted the safe, established lifestyle of the town. Yet Morrison affirms Sula's Jazz philosophy[15] through this character's analysis of falling into a pit of snakes. Sula releases herself to the "free fall" and is unhappy because Nel has surrendered to the bite of the snakes instead of inventing a means of avoiding them.

Nel no longer understands Sula's behavior, but out of love, obligation, and a sense of correctness she visits Sula just before her Jazz philosophy friend dies in 1940. Sula attempts to bring Nel out of her "dry corner" and back into the free fall of life, so she reminds her of the way they used to be when they were younger. As the two women attempt to negotiate the rough terrain over which their lives have come, Sula tells Nel that her "mind," not love, is what caused her to do what she did with Jude (143–44). This attitude confounds Nel. Sula persists in returning to the old words that used to comprise the lyrics of their "duet" (97). She tells Nel, "I got my mind. And what goes on in it. Which is to say, I got me" (143). Nel has forgotten her earlier attempts to have herself, but Sula has not (28). So as Sula lies dying, she shows Nel the difference between their lives through an analysis of the way they will die. Nel and the other Blues women up in the Bottom, from Sula's perspective, are "dying like a stump"; their lives have been cut down, stunted, trimmed back and left to rot over time without having really lived. As for herself, Sula is "going down like one of those redwoods. I sure did live in this world" (143). For Sula, life has consisted in spreading her branches, dropping and replacing leaves, shooting up and out and experiencing the lushness of life. From her perspective, dying after living such a life seems an appropriate transition. So she asks Nel, "How do you know . . . who was good. How do you know it was you. . . . Maybe it wasn't you. Maybe it was me" (146). When set against the dominant cultural imperatives for women, the typical female Blues character has apparent freedoms that appear to move her away from "the prevailing representations of womanhood" that Angela Davis examines (13). The Hannahs and Evas, for instance, are comfortably situated among Blues People. Sula, though, stretches this Blues discourse to its breaking point and does not survive the novel. Morrison's strategy in this novel, it seems, is to ask why the Sulas are not an option as well, among Blues People.

Nel takes twenty-five years following Sula's death to realize what she has lost by rejecting her own innovative Jazz style. This recognition becomes clear to Nel when, after a confrontation with Eva at the home for the elderly (164), she thinks about Sula's funeral. Sula is buried without much grief among the black residents of Medallion. Nel is the only black person who attends the funeral; a few other black people loiter around the edge of the "colored part of the Beechnut Cemetery" at the burial (150, 173). Thus, Morrison illustrates a fragmenting of Blues philosophy among the black people in Medallion. They are fragmented into many pieces that no longer form a common foundation.

Morrison elucidates this idea of fragmentation when rain interrupts this small group of black people who come after Sula's funeral and sing "Shall We Gather at the River." Perhaps the rain is Sula's answer (173), a way to wreak revenge on Medallion; instead of using water as the traditional cleansing force, Morrison makes the rain a message from Sula that directs the people toward their own minds and discourages them from relying too heavily on "gathering" with others and drowning en masse. Morrison's narrator observes that the people who sing at Sula's grave are "quite unaware of the bleak promise of their song" (150). Through Nel's emotional memories of Sula's death, Morrison illustrates Nel's true ideas about Spiritual-Gospel external authority and about Blues philosophy's investment in group ideas that encourages conformity to a set shaping of concepts, even if those concepts are widely encompassing. Nel now is able to understand what she has truly lost in the anonymity of the group. She has lost the Sula in herself, the freedom to be herself. Nel has lost her *"me"* (28).

Albert Murray: *Train Whistle Guitar*

Albert Murray permeates his novel *Train Whistle Guitar* (1974) with Blues aesthetics. This novel is a Bildungsroman of sorts, which depicts how the Blues life of the central character, Scooter, is made. Scooter not only matures over the course of this novel but also is inculcated with a Blues philosophy that strengthens his personal constitution and allows him to absorb the disappointments and difficulties of Blues life without becoming devastated. Murray reclaims Blues and examines its persistence in people who are reared in Blues environments while living in contemporary times. He further demonstrates that Blues is a powerful resource for people who live in an unpredictable world. For Murray, the Blues has an intertextual relation with the dominant culture. This means, of course, that the Blues contains traces of cultural elements from the dominant society. More important, though, Murray asserts that the Blues is omni-American; that is, the Blues informs the dominant culture in significant ways which allow us to refer to the United States as a Blues culture (*Omni* 13–22; *Blue Devils* 11–17, 143–221).[16] Yet Murray, in *Train Whistle Guitar* and his book *Stomping the Blues*, still situates the Blues among African Americans, who are the largest cultural influence on this music.

Train Whistle Guitar is set in 1940s Gasoline Point, Alabama, at the crossroads of a briarpatch and modernity (3). Murray's briarpatch[17] image is a complex black intracultural space that evinces Blues aesthetics and philosophy thick with possibility for the people in Gasoline Point, yet it is still thorny, wild, and prickly. The residents in Gasoline Point have made a wild briarpatch into a place where life moves along in relative comfort, as life goes. Murray employs popular songs from the 1930s and 1940s, such as "The Hut-Sut Song (A Swedish Serenade)," to indicate the historical context of his novel. This song, popularized by Sammy Kay and His Orchestra, celebrates postwar victory.

Murray's young protagonist Scooter, who calls himself Jack the Rabbit, says he is an inhabitant of the briarpatch along with his best friend Little Buddy. As inhabitants of the untamed region of their town, Scooter and Little Buddy learn to survive the thorns, unpredictable underbrush, and wildlife in the briarpatch. Thus, they learn to negotiate difficult territory and to respond with determination. Murray's characterization of Scooter and Little Buddy also illustrates the multivalence of Blues communities. Murray establishes that a Blues philosophy surrounds Scooter and Little Buddy, and his use of repetition, his use of words that denote addition, and his lack of punctuation, which would indicate breaks and transitions, all point to Blues aesthetics. This writing style exemplifies Murray's employment of Blues music techniques such as repetition and discontinuity to inform his Blues writing style.

Even though Scooter and Little Buddy are inseparable as little boys, their lives take very different shapes, as do Toni Morrison's Jazz and Blues characters Sula Peace and Nel Wright, who were childhood friends living in a similar socio-political environment forty years earlier. Little Buddy is a more freely moving Blues character than Scooter, who is more rooted in group connections than his friend. Little Buddy exemplifies the qualities of a loosely connected contemporary bluesman or jazzman. Scooter playfully describes him as a "rapscallion" (168), and in terms of school, Little Buddy "was never going to be any more of a schoolboy than he was absolutely forced to be" (38). Music is the thing that keeps his interest because he believes that he has "the inside claim on Luzana Cholly and Stagolee" (182), a claim he does not really want to share with Scooter. Murray also shows Little Buddy's propensity for freedom through this character's description of himself: "Me my name is Jack the rabbit because my home is also in the also and also of the briarpatch because that is also where I was also bred and also born. . . . My home is also nowhere and also anywhere and also everywhere." Hence, Little Buddy is part of and absorbed in a Blues life that connects him to the briarpatch because he was born there in its wildness and unpredictability, and he does not break from it; yet Murray suggests that Little Buddy's disposition does not situate him firmly in any discourse within or outside his local briarpatch; he has the potential to free himself from Gasoline Point and to experience any place he chooses. Scooter, in contrast, even though he too lives in the briarpatch (4), retains a closer connection to the customs of the people in his hometown. Murray associates Scooter with baseball (34), Mother Goose, and the old stories of enslaved ancestors (56, 75). But Scooter is "as smart as [he is] . . . devilish" (161), and as early as elementary school, Scooter "already also was even then" a schoolboy (38). Scooter does not demonstrate, as Little Buddy does, a propensity to remain free and unconnected, even though he exhibits a sense of adventure.

Despite these contrasts in their personal lives, Scooter and Little Buddy are exposed to a great number of similar experiences that contribute to their Blues lives. Murray points out that they "had been as profoundly conditioned by the twelve-string guitar insinuations of Luzana Cholly and the honky-tonk piano of Stagolee Dupas (fils) as by anything you had ever heard or ever overheard in church at school by the fireside or from any other listening post." Thus, the influences in the homes of the boys as well as in the neighborhood in which they live make a significant impact on their lives. This outside Blues influence teaches the boys that life is "engaging and frequently enraging mysteries and riddling ambiguities which encompass all possibilities. . . . But [they] . . . also knew something else: no matter how accurate your . . . data . . . the application of flesh-and-blood behavior must always leave something to chance and circumstance" (106–7).

Through his portrayal of Blues musicians such as Luzana Cholly, Stagolee Dupas, and Claiborne Williams, Murray illuminates the environment that helps shape the lives of Scooter and Little Buddy. Murray also juxtaposes Gasoline Point's local bluesman and a well-known name in folk Blues to illustrate the proliferation of Blues as well as its resistance to monological ideologies of fixed authority. Luzana Cholly is a "twelve-string guitar player second to none, including Leadbelly." Scooter is unable to remember if there was a time when he had not heard Luzana playing his Blues guitar (8). Luzana's life is one of chance, Blues, and riding the rails, all of which will remain his life's activities. The only time he has had any regulation in his life was during his military service and during his various incarcerations. The traveling guitar man, then, lives a Jazz life that has romantic appeal to Scooter and Little Buddy because Luzana seems disconnected from family and from the need for any family members in his life (14). Through the Jazz style and Blues philosophy of Luzana Cholly, Murray discloses the Blues influences on his main character, Scooter. These influences cause Scooter to want the freedom that he perceives in the life and music of Luzana, but Murray demonstrates that Scooter does not understand the price of Luzana's freedom.

Stagolee Dupas (fils) is another Blues force that affects the lives of Scooter and Little Buddy. Stagolee is a "low-down dirty blues" piano player whom Scooter and Little Buddy believe is to "honed steel and patent leather what old Luzana Cholly was to blue steel and rawhide" (98–99). Thus, Stagolee Kid has taken the music of Luzana Cholly to another stage in its development by making the old music respond to the new times. Murray even uses their instruments to suggest change. Luzana's guitar is always with him; he takes his musical instrument with him, as he lives an itinerant life. There is nothing to interfere with his music and his freedom. Stagolee Kid, though, has to find a piano to play wherever he goes. While he may travel, he depends on finding a piano among the people he meets on the road, and in some ways he is tied to their expectations of him and his expectations of them. They expect good-time music, and he expects that because they want this music, they will have an instrument for him. A group connection, thus a Blues philosophy, is more firmly established for Stagolee. Murray, however, elucidates Jazz style for Luzana, who can choose to play anywhere and anytime he decides to express himself musically.

Murray points out, though, that both Stagolee and Luzana are masters of innovative and imaginative wit. Stagolee Kid's innovation is exhibited through his additions to the ballad about "the original Bad Man Stagolee," a heroic character from African American folklore. In vernacular terms he is a "bad" character, or outlaw trickster, whose exploits gain respect and veneration from people because he defeats the machinations of oppressive power. Stagolee Kid "used to start adding some of his own new verses, he would keep on going until he had verses for every key on the piano" (99). Luzana Cholly also is innovative and imaginative. He would "make up new ballads right on the spot just to tell . . . [Scooter and Little Buddy] stories" (10). Murray, then, elucidates aspects of Jazz and Blues characterization and philosophy in these two Blues musicians and reveals that regular contact between Scooter and Little Buddy and Luzana Cholly and Stagolee Kid mirrors the musical philosophy through which the boys will shape themselves.

Murray adds New Orleans' jazzy bluesman Claiborne Williams to Scooter's Blues repertoire. Williams plays "his kind of blues" (131) piano at Joe Lockett's-in-the-Bottom. Scooter and Little Buddy do not have the personal contact with Williams that they have with Old Luze and Stagolee. The boys, in fact, observe Claiborne Williams playing by watching from a tree outside the window at Lockett's, a jook joint that they are not allowed to enter. While the visiting Williams is the featured musician, Stagolee is also in the club. Murray uses the encounter between these two Blues pianists as examples of respect and camaraderie for Scooter and Little Buddy. Both men are well respected in the town, and they respect each other as well. Williams's flamboyant style and Stagolee Kid's lively gut-bucket style complement the evening instead of creating conflict. Scooter and Little Buddy believe "a knock-down-drag-out-contest between them would have been something to witness all right. . . . But [Scooter doesn't] believe . . . any music they might have made while frankly trying to out do each other would have been as good as what you always heard when they used to play as if they were members of the same band." Through Scooter's placement of Claiborne Williams among the other Blues influences in his life, Murray further represents an environment of almost idealistic cohesiveness among the musicians. Scooter says, "And besides, although by that time we had come to think almost as much of Stagolee as we did of Luzana Cholly . . . we also liked Claiborne Williams too much to want to take sides against him" (132–33). Murray, then, presents the Blues musicians as exemplars of the possibilities for cooperation available to Scooter and Little Buddy as they encounter other young men.

Another way that Murray depicts Scooter's musically rich environment is through specific references to songs and musicians. These references are too numerous to present here, but a few examples will establish more firmly the influence of African American music, as well as popular music, on the people in Gasoline Point. Through Murray's use of specific references to music, Scooter's recreational and love life resound Blues aesthetics and illustrate how Blues aesthetics might be located in popular music. Murray introduces three song titles that riff throughout the novel, titles that help emphasize the idea with which each song is associated. Murray first presents these song titles at a baseball game where the band plays "Sundown," a song that Murray later refers to by the title of Walter Donaldson's tune "At Sundown." This tune is found in a number of pop and swing repertoires: Tommy Dorsey, Benny Goodman, Oscar Peterson. The Canadian Oscar Peterson records "At Sundown" in Canada during the 1940s before his United States' debut in 1949. Somehow, though, Murray's allusion also carries a resonance of the bluesman Son House's "Sundown." Murray also riffs another Walter Donaldson tune, "Little White Lies," a rendition by Don Byas, perhaps, or maybe Tommy Dorsey. Cole Porter's "Precious Little Thing Called Love" is another Jazz riff in this novel (34). These songs form a basic musical line that Murray worries throughout his narrative. During Stagolee's practice session, for instance, these titles are repeated and changed when Murray adds a Benny Goodman favorite, "Dream a Little Dream of Me" by Gus Kahn and Isham Jones (124). Stagolee's connection to these songs, including the popular tunes, situates them in Blues aesthetics. These are songs that Scooter has made his own. Murray demonstrates how popular versions of these songs have little to do with the Gasoline Point versions that have been shaped by the innovation of Stagolee Kid, and by Scooter's memories.

Murray continues to worry the song titles from the baseball game through his portrayal of Scooter's youthful love interests. Scooter associates Elva Lois Showers, the girl who strings him along, with the song "Precious Little Thing Called Love" (151). Murray's young Blues character remembers being rejected by Johnnie Mae Lewis, who "danced off with Sonny Kemble . . . to 'Little White Lies' of all the rain sad and honeysuckle melodies." And it is Olivet Dixon, an older boy, and "At Sun-down" that remind Scooter of his inexperience (156). Murray's repeated uses of these song titles resound his earlier reference to them at the baseball game and reveal the omni-American aspects of the people of Gasoline Point as well as the importance of lessons learned through the experiences of youthful love. Scooter's first real sexual encounter, however, is with Deljean McCray. Murray does not use the springtime, little-boy-fun, popular baseball music to represent Scooter's memories of Deljean. Scooter says, "[T]he song I remember when I remember her snapping her fingers and rolling her stomach and snatching her big hips and pouting her lips and winking and rolling her eyes at the same time is 'How Come You Do Me Like You Do,'" a tune Louis Armstrong first performed in 1924. She also used to sing "Ja-Da," which calls to mind Oscar Peterson as well as guitarist Eddie Condon and His All Stars. Scooter associates Deljean with more deeply Blues philosophical music than the music he associates with baseball games and childhood fun. Their encounter affects his life in a more profound way than his encounters with the other girls; Murray evinces, then, a mature Blues theme when he adds "How Come You Do Me Like You Do" and "Ja-Da" to the other song titles (160), and in this way he illustrates the depth of the impact Deljean has in Scooter's life.

Murray also employs specific references to Spiritual-Gospel songs in *Train Whistle Guitar*. People in Gasoline Point strongly assert the twentieth-century perspective on religious and secular music; for them, there are clear and distinct differences between Blues and Spiritual-Gospel, and thus, the two types of music should be separated. But, of course, Murray shows that this is not completely true. Gasoline Point church members maintain that Stagolee plays "low-down dirty blues even when it was not." Their assessment results from Stagolee's style of playing, which "was liable to barrelhouse you right out into the black alley in the simple process of vamping the chords to 'Nearer My God to Thee.'" Murray further discloses that some church members are not "as hard set against blues music when it came to Luzana Cholly. . . . Because on occasion even Mama and Uncle Jerome used to forget." Murray evinces a connection between older—very likely less-commercialized—Blues of Luzana Cholly and the people in Gasoline Point who hold deep religious convictions, because Luzana represents the older down-home Blues. His music expresses a life philosophy that returns the "church folk" to their own ideas before they were reinterpreted in institutionalized religion and commercial music (98–99).

In much of the novel, Murray associates men with the Blues and Jazz he portrays. He brings women into the music of Gasoline Point through a Monday morning ritual that adds to his literary uses of both Spiritual-Gospel and Blues music. Murray establishes as much musical variety among the women as he depicts among the men of Gasoline Point. He elucidates Spiritual-Gospel philosophy through Scooter's mother Melba. She, "unlike Miss Sister Lucinda Wiggins was never one to make even the slightest display of her religious devotion in public." As a result of Miss Melba's reserved religious expression, she fills her house with humming on Monday mornings: "and what she would be humming was most likely a prayer meeting hymn or an Amen Corner moan." Miss Sister Lucinda Wiggins, however, "used to wake up sometimes with so much leftover Sunday spirit and Holy Ghost that she had to tell the whole world about it" as she washed her clothes in the smoking washpot outside. Miss Libby Lee Tyler would often join her; "the two of them would begin singing and humming back and forth at each other and before long somebody else would join in." Murray establishes that this music is connected to the Blues music that permeates the novel and moulds Scooter's life when Scooter says, "Nothing makes me remember Miss Sister Lucinda Wiggins and Miss Libby Lee Tyler . . . so much as when two trumpet players began trading blues choruses" (94–96).

Monday morning singing among the women also occasionally includes Blues. Miss Honey Houston is likely to be the person whose Blues song is heard on Monday mornings. Miss Houston "always used to begin with the same opening verse: Going to see Madame Ruth / Going to see Madame Catherine . . . (Got a world full of trouble / And Sweet daddy so doggone mean)." The various Blues songs to which Miss Houston adds her traveling phrase probably are not heard until she is having difficulty in her relationship with a man. With these lines Murray suggests that Miss Houston sings her man-troubles to the world. If it is not Miss Houston's singing that Scooter hears, it is, sometimes, Miss Eula Bacote playing Blues records on her Victrola. Scooter remembers Miss Bacote "above everybody else when [he] . . . remember[s] somebody who used to wake up on Monday morning and let the whole neighborhood know that she had had another bad case of the blues, no matter what all the preachers and church folks in the state of Alabama said." Miss Bacote always begins by playing Bessie Smith's latest Blues recording. She also listens to Ma Rainey, Mamie Smith, Trixie Smith, and Ida Cox and purchases the latest Jelly Roll Morton, King Oliver, and Louis Armstrong recordings (101–2).

Through Murray's depiction of music and women in Gasoline Point, he forges a firm connection between Blues and Spiritual-Gospel aesthetics and philosophy, as all of the female singers have a similar mode and context—Monday mornings—for their music. Murray's use of Monday morning as the women's Blues and Spiritual-Gospel moment not only suggests the leftover spiritual energy from Sunday services that Murray mentions but also suggests T-Bone Walker's Blues tune "Stormy Monday Blues," recorded in 1947, in which Walker asserts that Tuesday is not necessarily better than Monday. Murray makes most of his specific references to music through the women in his novel. The men in his novel, in contrast, are situated in an itinerant lifestyle that is based in Blues philosophy, a lifestyle that women rarely engage in and often suffer from, as the bluesmen in their lives may at any moment decide that they have a mind to ramble.[18] Scooter, however, gains his own ideas about music and life among Gasoline Point's bluesmen.

Murray imbues *Train Whistle Guitar* with African American music. He even uses it to shape the technique and form he employs throughout the novel. Repetition and expansion, for example, are salient features of Blues music. Murray's uses of repetition are numerous. He repeats words within a sentence—"my home is also in the also and the also" (4)—and he uses a technique that involves his introduction and later expansion of an idea or character. This technique is exemplified in his portrayal of Luzana Cholly and Stagolee Dupas, as well as Charlene Wingate and other characters. Murray also employs another form of repetition, Jazz riffs, which resound an idea or image throughout the novel. His most pervasive use of riffing is in his repetitions of the name, or some version of the name, of Miss Lexine Metcalf, who is Scooter's favorite teacher. Her name resounds the idea that Scooter enjoys and finds pleasure in learning and that he is expected to become educated. Murray also makes substantial references to the word "blue" in his novel. The word blue then becomes a Jazz worrying repetition throughout *Train Whistle Guitar*: "blue steel" (7), "smoke-blue," "Philamayork-skyline-blue," "sporty blue limp walk (which told the whole world that you were ready for something because at worst you had only been ever so slightly strained and bruised by all the terrible situations you had been through)" (15), "blue horizon mist" (3), "the color of freedom was blue" (67), "Blue-back Webster," "blue devils" (97), "boy blue expectations" (111), and so on. Murray's many and varied uses—his worrying—of the word blue resound the idea that Gasoline Point, Alabama, is a Blues community and its aesthetic and philosophy contribute to shaping Scooter's character.

Another type of Jazz riff that Murray uses is very subtle yet illuminating. Often in the course of representing the speech of one of his characters, Murray uses phrases or titles from songs without indicating that a song is being represented. With these verbal riffs, Murray connects his character to music through the song that each character quotes and at the same time resounds the song and/or a version of its philosophy in his novel. Scooter's mother, for instance, is associated with Spiritual-Gospel when she begins her week acknowledging God's "infinite and amazing grace" (94). Miss Sister Lucinda Wiggins begins her Monday mornings telling "the whole wide world" (96) about God. These phrases resound the hymns "He's Got the Whole World in His Hands" and "Amazing Grace." During one of the times that people get together at Scooter's house, his Uncle Jerome explains a recent epidemic as a warning from God that he has destroyed the earth once and "He could do it again although He had promised that it would be the fire next time" (59); this statement suggests James Baldwin's book-length essay *The Fire Next Time* as well as the traditional Spiritual-Gospel song to which Baldwin's essay refers. In another instance, Murray again uses Uncle Jerome to riff a song title in the novel as he talks about the Civil War: "[A]nd gentlemen, sir, *before I'd be a slave, I'll be buried in my grave*. . . . [And] . . . he would also say that freedom was a road through wilderness . . . (so *don't let nobody turn you round*)" (67). Murray's use of Spiritual-Gospel references to the Spirituals "Oh Freedom" and "Don't Let Nobody Turn You Around" illustrate how songs such as these are established guideposts to life's problems; they function in a similar way as the Yoruba proverb, which is a storehouse of philosophical knowledge about life. Through these riffs from Spiritual-Gospel music Murray indicates that the adults in *Train Whistle Guitar* who are not Blues musicians but are important in Scooter's life evince a Spiritual-Gospel philosophy.

Murray also limns the idea that the voice is a supreme instrument in Blues music. *Train Whistle Guitar* is Murray's literary representation of a Blues voice; his novel is a Blues instrument that uses the various expressive techniques of Blues music to speak about—to voice—Blues life, aesthetics, and philosophy. He writes this idea into the title of his novel, which refers to the Blues guitarist's ability to replicate on his instrument sounds that he hears, particularly train whistles and human voices. Both train whistles and the human voice, moreover, recall to mind freedom trains. Thus, Murray resounds the idea of freedom on the Underground Railroad, where voice whistles were used to signal escapes; and he resounds the idea of the freedom of hopping railroad trains that signify their approach and departure by the sound of a whistle.

Luzana Cholly, for instance, "was forever turning guitar strings into train whistles which were not only the once-upon-a-time voices of story tellers but of all the voices saying what was being said in the stories as well" (15). And Stagolee Dupas uses his voice to hum "all the instrument fills, riffs and solo takeoff[s] . . . as if he were a one man band" (123). With his portrayal of these two bluesmen, Murray exemplifies a Blues voice as a musical instrument as well as a musical instrument, Blues guitar, that replicates the voice. Through examples of Jazz riffs and worrying repetitions and examples of Jazz voice-instrument imitation and Blues instrument-voice imitation, Murray discloses how Blues and Jazz musicians reveal the art in repetition and how Blues musicians make the technique of repetition through imitation and revision a premier form of musical expression. Murray, then, employs Blues repetition as he revises—in the form of the novel—and imitates the practice of Blues musicians and writes a Blues novel.

Situated in all of the music we find in *Train Whistle Guitar* is Murray's story of Scooter's growth into maturity. He uses both a Spiritual-Gospel–influenced incident and a Blues-influenced incident to mark crucial points of growth in Scooter's life. Murray's Blues-influenced incident occurs in the novel when Scooter and Little Buddy take a premature step toward independence and decide to hop a train, meet up with Luzana Cholly, and travel the country (28). Murray illustrates Scooter's firm ties to a larger group through this character's constant thoughts about home and his questions about how long he and Little Buddy will be gone. Little Buddy, who is more disposed to a Jazz life free of connections, does not know when they will go home, and he does not care. Scooter, conversely, does care, and he "suddenly remember[s] . . . the barbershop and them [the men] talking about baseball and boxing and women and politics . . . and [hearing] old King Oliver's band play 'Sugarfoot Stomp' on the Victrola in Papa Gumbo's cookstop next door." Scooter now is unsure that he wants to hop the train. He wants to and he doesn't want to. Scooter also is not sure that Little Buddy's nonchalance is real, but Scooter's own unexpressed feelings are clear: "I was thinking about Mama and Papa and Uncle Jerome and Miss Tee . . . and I couldn't keep myself from hoping it was all a dream." Murray, in this passage, anchors Scooter firmly in literary Blues, as this character is tied to an established pattern in life and is not really inclined to break from it. When the train comes, though, Scooter and Little Buddy hop it, even though Scooter has secretly changed his mind (21–25).

Twelve miles into their train adventure, the two boys meet Luzana, who threatens to beat them but returns them to Gasoline Point instead. Luzana shows Scooter and Little Buddy that they are not yet ready to choose to live a rambling life like his when, on their return to Gasoline Point, he picks them up and puts them on the train instead of allowing them to hop it. Murray illustrates some of the harsh realities of Luzana's Jazz life as this character reveals to Scooter and Little Buddy that his life consists of more than just wandering the country and singing his music. There are things in Old Luze's past that make his present life possible; and those are not necessarily things into which he wants to encourage Scooter and Little Buddy. Luzana's desire for Scooter and Little Buddy to experience the world in a different way than he has recalls to mind Nanny's desires for Janie in Zora Neale Hurston's *Their Eyes Were Watching God*. At this point, the old bluesman brings reality into the boys' romantic notions about his experiences that inform his Blues music and his Jazz life. Old Luze tells the boys that his itinerant life is more than "just a notion." Scooter learns, "fresh from the getting place," about the hardships and adversities in being on the road, and he also learns about the hope in Blues life as well. That hope, Luzana tells Scooter, has something to do with him, and with change, and with education. Luzana makes clear that Scooter and Buddy understand that they should take their Blues cultural experiences and combine them with the various other experiences that the world has to offer him (27–30). Through Luzana's talk with Little Buddy and Scooter, Murray comments on the new possibilities that a Blues philosophy offers the two boys (107).

Murray, then, elucidates the idea that the boys must make their own Blues tunes, not because Luzana Cholly's are obsolete but because Blues is a constantly "changing same" (Baraka, *Black Music* 180). Murray's Jazz character Luzana Cholly carefully directs Scooter and Little Buddy back into the protection of the town because he recognizes that they are not ready to decide on a Jazz life that fragments them from their homes and that they do not understand that whichever life they choose, Blues or Jazz, will have to be shaped by a new set of experiences, different from the drifting, train-riding life that he leads. Luzana prepares them to make and accept change.

Murray depicts Gasoline Point as a Blues environment that has a profound impact on Scooter's life; Scooter's Blues experiences in his hometown prepare him to live successfully in the larger world. Murray illustrates the empowering influence of the Blues environment in Gasoline Point when Scooter inadvertently finds out that his Aunt Tee, not Miss Melba, is his birth mother. When Scooter overhears the adults discussing him, Murray surrounds his young Blues character Scooter with a Spiritual-Gospel environment. Murray establishes this environment at Scooter's house following Ike Meadows's funeral. Murray conveys the idea that Scooter is in a Spiritual-Gospel environment because residents of Gasoline Point are telling about their experiences of being born again and singing songs such as "Get Right With God"; and as Scooter falls asleep in Miss Melba's lap the people are singing "The Blood Done Sign My Name" (171). The last song in this passage establishes a connection between Aunt Tee and Scooter that explains her interest in him and his interest in school (Aunt Tee attended college but never finished): they share blood. Aunt Tee's blood, then, signs her name on him no matter who rears him. Even though this novel is set in a predominately Blues community, Murray surrounds Scooter with Spiritual-Gospel philosophy in the adults in his home, which suggests that perhaps Scooter's mind has not yet developed the resources from which he can draw solutions to potentially devastating situations. In the absence of his parents—who are not aware that he has gained an important piece of mature knowledge—as a source for solutions, Scooter is left in the hands of God, the final resource for solutions to which his Spiritual-Gospel parents turn.

Murray also establishes throughout the novel that Scooter does not live only in the world of his parents; he lives among the Blues People of Gasoline point as well. The impact of this Blues community on Scooter is significant. Scooter, then, has the basic elements of a Blues philosophy, so he is not crushed to find that all is not as it seems in the world. Murray's worldlier Little Buddy now concedes that Scooter's naïveté is eliminated. Now that he knows the truth about Aunt Tee, it is as "good as giving [Scooter] the inside claim on old Luzana and old Stagolee . . . and all that. Because . . . [Scooter is] welcome to Old Lady Metcalf and all that old school stuff. But shoot man. . . . Not that," which is the inside story on life (182). Well, Scooter now does have "the inside story," which allows him to join Little Buddy in a more fully matured Blues philosophical approach to the world.

John Edgar Wideman: *Sent for You Yesterday*

John Edgar Wideman infuses music throughout his novel *Sent for You Yesterday* (1983). Beginning with his title, which is taken from the title of a 1938 Jazz tune by Count Basie with Jimmy Rushing on vocals, Wideman writes music into the lives of his characters and their Homewood neighborhood. *Sent for You Yesterday* is Wideman's third novel about the Homewood area of Pittsburgh, Pennsylvania, where he was reared. Wideman depicts Homewood as an urban Blues neighborhood in which most of the residents are loosely linked to one another, even though they do not interact as a group. They are brought together by similar economic and social conditions that limit their access to life outside Homewood or outside similar neighborhoods. Thus, Wideman uses literary Blues to illustrate a neighborhood that is becoming increasingly detached from group ties and group ideas. Wideman depicts three generations of the French family living in Homewood, and he illustrates increasing alienation among his characters as each generation moves farther outside its small neighborhood. Wideman also employs music as a metaphor to illustrate the development of each generation.

To emphasize the importance of music to the ideas that Wideman depicts in *Sent for You Yesterday*, he employs a substantial number of specific references to music and a number of riffed fragments from music. Wideman's literary uses of music include specific references to songs such as "You Are My Sunshine," which John French sings to Freeda to comfort her when she is afraid (24), and "How Long Blues," which Lucy hums (196); riffs on "Didn't He Ramble" (115), "In the Sweet By-and-By," "Down by the Riverside" (139), "Falling Rain Blues" (192), and Ma Rainey's "C. C. Rider" (44); a guitar named Corrine that Freeda French's Uncle Bill Campbell plays; childhood ditties such as "Ride a Little Pony" (52); and various musicians' names, such as Billy Eckstine (175), Sarah Vaughan, Dinah Washington, Ella Fitzgerald, Billie Holiday (200), and Duke Ellington (203). Wideman immerses readers in Spiritual-Gospel, Blues, and Jazz philosophies that support his portrayal of characters as well as his theme. Wideman's Jazz theme conveys the idea that there is a space in Blues aesthetics for distinct Jazz voices to extend and reshape themselves—a self that includes Blues fragments—instead of operating from a group foundation of similarity. And he illustrates this idea through his story and his delineation of literary Spiritual-Gospel, Blues, and Jazz characters.

Through his characterization of his Spiritual-Gospel character Freeda French, whom he describes as having a neck "the smooth ivory color of piano keys" (82), Wideman illustrates qualities of literary Blues that fill the streets of Homewood and make it a Blues neighborhood. Freeda, the almost-white-looking grandmother of the novel's narrator, remembers that when she was a child Homewood was a quiet neighborhood until it became a haven for black migrants from the South. In her study of African American migration narratives, *"Who Set You Flowin'?"* Farah Jasmine Griffin explains that changes in social and political forces encourage south-to-north migration among black people in the 1940s, which was a period of intense change; this decade marks a third wave of such movement among African American people.[19] Wideman's Freeda resents this influx of southern black people but is unable to avoid their influence on her life. To Freeda, they were a "black tide" that transformed Homewood forever." They brought their music with them: "The music was everywhere. . . . And worst of all, that low down, down home stuff had crawled inside her. Messed with the way she walked and talked and thought about things. In the streets, in her house, in the church. The music everywhere now, even in her head . . ." (41–44). Wideman's image of the Blues permeating Freeda's body and her thoughts establishes Blues as an intertextual influence on the lives of people in Homewood. It affects them even when they actively reject it.

Freeda is a Spiritual-Gospel character who is married to a Blues character, John French. Wideman establishes that Freeda is strengthened both by her secure home with John and by her faith, yet she questions the reality of life that is promised in the hymn "Farther Along," which offers that in time we will understand the answer to life's questions. Freeda wonders if there will be a "bright day, a clear singing day farther along when the dead ones, the lost ones, the ones hurt and suffering beyond tears . . . would be all right." Wideman also depicts Freeda's Spiritual-Gospel musical philosophy through his characterization of her as someone who seeks external answers, that is, someone who seeks comfort through calling on the power of God to provide solutions. While Freeda's position in Spiritual-Gospel seems tenuous at times,

Wideman makes it clear that "[s]ometimes the songs helped. If you loved God and loved your man and loved your children you were safe. The music would say that much to her" (33).

As a Spiritual-Gospel character, Freeda consoles herself with the idea that the "music could soothe her, quiet her, and she'd see her worst fears were nothing more than a child's cry in the darkness." She also finds in the songs that she sings in church "a vast emptiness, a desert of bones ... moaning oceans of tears.... But she held on to her God, and held on to her family and swore to herself she would cling as long as there was breath in her body." Through Wideman's connection of Freeda to Spiritual-Gospel and the ideas that collect around it, he discloses Freeda's Spiritual-Gospel philosophy. Wideman further emphasizes his use of a Spiritual-Gospel philosophy to portray Freeda when the narrator describes Freeda's thoughts in Spiritual-Gospel song phrases. Wideman does not use a specific song title, nor does Freeda or the narrator sing the song. Instead, Wideman incorporates phrases from Spiritual-Gospel songs into his text as a subtle Jazz riff that associates Freeda with Spiritual-Gospel philosophy. Freeda thinks about the hymns she sings at the Homewood AME Zion Church, and she visualizes a garden where she is alone with God: "A garden in the music where she could *come to Him alone*, where the *dew was still on the roses*. And the voice she'd hear as *she tarried there*, that voice was in the music too" (32–33). By using phrases from C. Austin Miles's "In the Garden" as a verbal riff in Freeda's speech, Wideman affirms Freeda's Spiritual-Gospel philosophical principles.

Through his portrayal of John and Freeda French, Wideman illustrates a Blues philosophy as it exists among the residents of Homewood. Despite his portrayal of Freeda as a Spiritual-Gospel character, she lives in a Blues home, as her husband John is a Blues character, and the French family members are deeply embedded in the Blues philosophy of their Homewood neighborhood. Even though the Frenches recognize that they live under adverse conditions, they will not deviate far from established group behavior. Wideman demonstrates John French's Blues philosophy when he "finds" a Victrola and brings the music that Freeda despises into her house. "So the music wasn't only in the streets it was prowling inside her own house now.... *Shaking peaches from trees* and *moving on down the highway* and lonesome train whistles blowing and hollering like a mountain jack and *See, see rider, gal, See what you have done*"

(43–44). Through Wideman's riff on these phrases and motifs from Blues songs, including Ma Rainey's "C.C. Rider,"[20] he depicts the Blues aesthetics of Homewood that has come into the French home.

Wideman further emphasizes French's Blues philosophy through the experiences that are part of his daily life. Anaydee's memories of her niece's, Freeda's, husband singing on the corner of Hamilton and Homewood with Albert Wilkes—the Jazz pianist—and their other friends show French's early exposure to the ideas—expressed through the music—that help him survive the hardships he faces in life (51). Now, as an adult, French is the best man to call to hang wallpaper. Even the white employers know that he is the best, so they all want him for their primary jobs (67). Despite the quality of his work, French still leaves home every morning and stands on the corner of Frankstown and Homewood wondering if he will be picked for work. French, though, will not break from this pattern of life because he is committed to his wife and to his children. Thus, he is connected to an established foundation where he devises his singular solutions to the impediments he encounters in life.

French's Blues life is a part of him that he accepts, even when Wilkes questions his sincerity. Wilkes challenges French: "You like it out here just like I do. Acting a fool. Running wild come and go as you please. How come you a family man? . . . You gon answer me this morning . . . , where ain't nothing but sweet light and you and me and the truth if it's in you" (64). Wilkes's questions cause French to think about his daughter Lizabeth, the narrator's mother, as well as about his wife Freeda. French tells Wilkes that they are his reason for being a family man. In Albert Wilkes's Jazz music, however, French recognizes himself. French perceives himself in Wilkes's Blues fragments, which resound French's own Blues life and inform Wilkes's Jazz aesthetics and philosophy. He also recognizes himself in an undertone in Wilkes's Jazz elaborations from the Blues. Thus, when Wilkes is situated comfortably in his playing, French can find his own "face grinning back at [him] like a mirror" (68). Wideman's John French, then, establishes that Wilkes's Blues-Jazz playing reflects back on and moves away from Blues. Hence, French perceives Wilkes's as well as his own Blues in the music Wilkes plays, but he also perceives in this music the Jazz that shapes his own unexpressed style. French's refusal to locate himself in Jazz philosophy recalls Nel Wright Greene in Toni Morrison's *Sula*. While Nel's refusal of Jazz results from her repression of it, French's refusal results from his choice to live a settled Blues life, while knowing of his Jazz desires.

On the morning Wilkes returns to Homewood, French walks away from the humiliation of working for "the man." Through French's actions, Wideman exemplifies this character's undertones of Jazz that are reflected in Wilkes's music. As French leaves, he says, "Tell em [his prospective employer] I'm gone. Tell em I got business. Tell em don't need no corn and lasses . . ." (71). John French, however, will not break away from the established pattern for long. He is different from his good friend Albert Wilkes, but on this morning he reaches a breaking point and resists the conditions of his life. Yet John's Blues ties to his family preclude his breaking from the established pattern of his life for any extended period of time.

Albert Wilkes is a free subject, a free actor, in Homewood. He is exiled from Homewood for killing, in self-defense, a police officer with whom he has a dispute about a woman (51). Wilkes, one of Wideman's Jazz characters, is differentiated from others in Homewood because no one "could tell Albert Wilkes nothing." He is "bold enough to traipse up to Thomas Boulevard in the middle of the day and knock on the front door of that white woman and bold enough to stay as long as he wants" (64). Wilkes's behavior, as befits his Jazz personality, violates all of the tacit social policies that define and limit his position in society.

Wideman clearly contrasts John French's Blues life with Albert Wilkes's Jazz life when French thinks it would not "be so bad if he [Wilkes] used the back door and creep around at night like anybody with good sense. No. Not Albert Wilkes. Albert gon play it like he plays that piano. It's him. Couldn't be nobody else but him you hear him play once and nobody else get on them keys sound like Albert" (65). Albert's life, then, is like his music. It is all his own, made from his particular shaping of the materials of his life, with no permanent attachments to any group. Wideman's characterization of Wilkes demonstrates that Blues philosophy creates a space for Jazz resistance. The residents of Homewood, for instance, try to protect Wilkes when he returns. They understand the adverse conditions that create him. Thus, John French responds when "piano playing" Albert Wilkes seeks him for advice about how he can find a way to stay in Homewood (25).

Through his portrayals of Albert Wilkes and John French, Wideman evinces how Blues and Jazz characters find points of correspondence that allow their coexistence. He illustrates this coexistence when Wilkes returns to Homewood dressed in clothes that make him invisible because they are so conspicuous. Wilkes says, "Folks see that big hat and see the long coat and don't think about somebody trying to hide. They think well here's one more fool trying to show off so they ignore whoever is in the hat and coat. . . . Like I was invisible" (78). Here Wideman rewrites Ralph Ellison's Jazz character Rinehart as well as Ellison's concept of invisibility. Wilkes's big black hat and long gray duster coat is analogous to Rinehart's dark glasses and big hat. John French wants to find a way to keep Wilkes in Homewood, so he advises him "lay low in your invisibility clothes." While Wilkes's life-style is not the one French chooses, he believes there is a place in Homewood for Wilkes: "How they gon chase you out your own briarpatch? How we gon let em? No way, my man." John French situates Wilkes within the intellectual space of the untamed briarpatch, with its uncontrollable treasures such as Blues and Jazz and its coded knowledge about moving through a chaotic world. Through this encounter between Wilkes and French, Wideman makes clear the idea that Jazz and Blues are not mutually exclusive, that Blues philosophy clears a space for the chameleon-like changes of Jazz, and that Blues philosophy does not reject in principle the change, resistance, and options that Jazz represents, even though a Blues character would not enact Jazz philosophy. The dominant society finds Albert Wilkes threatening because "what counted wasn't murdering puppets in uniforms so much as it was the ones who pulled their strings. The ones who ran Homewood without ever setting foot in Homewood" (79–80). Here John French intimates to readers the circumstances of Wilkes's death.

Wideman depicts his second generation of Blues and Jazz characters in the "middle people" (198) in Homewood—John French's son Carl and Carl's friend, Brother Tate. Brother Tate lives with the Tates, who also have taken in Albert Wilkes and half of the other displaced people in Homewood (39). Carl, similar to his father, remains close to the established pattern of life among the people in Homewood; he is, then, the next generation Blues character. He fights in the war in the 1940s, goes to art school, continues his relationship with Lucy, Brother's sister, and lives like many others in Homewood.

Brother Tate, conversely, is part of yet separate from the pattern of life in Homewood—very much like Albert Wilkes. Brother, a Jazz character, is "a man who could be whatever he wanted to be, [because he] . . . picked the way he wanted to live and how he wanted to die" (199). Wideman depicts Brother as music embodied in flesh. He is an albino; he has "no color which said there's a black man or a white man in front of you" (15). His blackness is "crouched in the shadow of the uveal tract [and gives him] a way of being unseen" (135). As with music, Brother's appearance defies racial categories. Brother Tate does not talk, yet "his silence wasn't really silence. Brother made noise all the time. Drumming his fingertips on the edge of the kitchen table, . . . cracking his knuckles, patting his feet, boogeying outrageously in the middle of the floor you'd hear the silent music making him wiggle his narrow hips. . . . [H]e'd flip his lower lip like it was the string of a bass fiddle. He'd hum and grunt and groan, and Brother could scat sing and impersonate all the instruments in a band. Brother would make all that music, all that noise, but he never said a word" (16).

Wideman's description of Brother Tate evinces the expressive qualities in musical sounds. Through all of the abstract qualities in music, it ultimately reaches something very intimate in people; as Wideman's music embodied in flesh, Brother does not need to talk to communicate. Wideman makes Brother the music that fills the spaces between Albert Wilkes's absences: "Somebody had named the notes, but nobody had named the silences between the notes. The emptiness, the space waiting for him that night seven years ago. Nobody ever would name it because it was emptiness and silence and the notes they named, the notes he played were just a way of tipping across it, of pretending you knew where you were" (55).

Brother was six or seven when Wilkes left Homewood (91), yet he remembers Wilkes playing "honky-tonk and gut bucket and low down dirty blues" (163). Brother's incessant sounds fill a Jazz space that is opened by Wilkes's seven-year absence and at the same time Brother's sounds suggest the name of the silence—Wilkes, Jazz, resistance, change—while never naming it. With the death of Wilkes, Wideman again leaves a seven-year absence between Wilkes's playing and the sounds of his piano in Homewood.

Wilkes's Jazz aesthetic remains in Homewood, through the sounds of Brother, even after the police kill Wilkes while he is playing piano at the Tates' house (102). Wilkes's music, also, is revived in Brother Tate after Brother spends a substantial number of hours observing Wilkes before sitting down at the piano to play seven years after Wilkes's death. Brother's playing was so much like Wilkes's that "it wasn't strange at all that somebody got happy and shouted, *Play, Albert. Play Albert Wilkes. Albert's home again*, because good piano playing and Albert Wilkes were just about the same word in Homewood" (89).

Wideman employs a Jazz riff on 1940s bebop to affirm Brother's link to Jazz: "Nobody cared that Brother hadn't ever played a note before

Thursday because what they heard Saturday was so fine. . . . Brother was three times seven the first night he played the piano at the Elks Club. . . . Nineteen forty-one . . . it was round about midnight" (89–90). With a phrase culled from the title of a Thelonious Monk composition, "'Round Midnight," Wideman evinces Brother's Jazz aesthetic by resounding the bebop of his era and by suggesting that Brother's music extends and elaborates Wilkes's honky-tonk, gut-bucket, bluesy Jazz (163). Jazz in Homewood, then, continues in Brother Tate. Through Brother—an albino whose parents and name are unknown—Wideman retains Jazz at the margin of Homewood—even while Wilkes is exiled and even after his murder. As with Wilkes, Brother, too, is a free agent. Brother has "[n]o name. No color. No nothing if you think about it, . . . no words, no father" (27, 28). He has only his music and Carl. Through his characterization of Brother Tate and Albert Wilkes, Wideman establishes a musical link of continuation and change across generations, affirmed in the novel's epigraph: "Past lives live in us, through us. Each of us harbors the spirit of people who walked the earth before we did, and those spirits depend on us for continuing existence . . ."

Wideman's central character, Doot, is the narrator in *Sent for You Yesterday*, and he represents the third generation of music in Homewood. Readers learn very little about him, though, except as his family members' lives become a part of his own life. Since many of the events in Wideman's novel take place before Doot is born, these events are told from the narrator's memories of stories he heard in his home and around Homewood. Wideman's narrator is the nephew or grandchild of most of the characters in the novel, yet he is named only as a sound, a disconnected tone moving through the music that pervades the lives of the people in Homewood. Doot is a free-floating riff that seems to be both part of and not part of the story he tells.

Throughout the novel Wideman depicts Doot as a voice that is alienated from Homewood and its music. But eight years after Brother's death on the railroad tracks, Doot is placed "inside the weave of voices" (93). He becomes part of the music of Brother Tate and Albert Wilkes. Doot is written into the song of Homewood through the stories of his Uncle Carl and Lucy, Carl's companion and Brother Tate's sister. Through the stories of Carl and Lucy, Wideman also explicates the meaning of his title, which refers to Doot. Wideman's narrator has not believed that he is part of the Blues-Jazz life of Homewood. He does not play the music and he has no memory of hearing Brother play, since Brother stopped playing in 1946 when Doot was about five years old (17, 93). He also does not feel he is a part of the life with which Brother's and Wilkes's music is connected. When Doot tells of Wilkes's return, he reminds readers, "I am not born yet" (17). He is tied to this major event in Homewood only through what others say; and Wideman's portrayal of Doot suggests that this character erroneously believes that his distance from the events he narrates severs his ties to Wilkes, to Wilkes's music, and to Jazz.

Another factor contributing to Doot's alienation is his fragmented connection to the house on Cassina Way. Doot's mother Lizabeth and his Uncle Carl are reared in the house on Cassina Way. Brother is a constant visitor there. Albert Wilkes visits there too, but Doot lives on Cassina Way only one or two years as an infant and toddler. And, he believes, the only stories that he has to tell about Homewood are not filled with music that speaks to triumph. His stories tell of murdering junkies, suffocating death, and shame (22–23). There is no surviving music in any of Doot's stories, and he is unable to link himself to the music of Brother Tate and Albert Wilkes, even though he remembers Brother Tate, who named him "Doot. Doot" (16). Wideman's narrator says, "If I missed Brother playing between '41 and '46 then I missed him forever, because . . . Brother stopped playing the piano just as suddenly as he stopped talking. . . . One day in one of the stories I'm sure someone will tell me, I did hear Brother play. . . . One day I'll be in the Tate's living room listening. I'll hear Brother. I'll hear Albert Wilkes" (93). Doot wants to know if there is a story that says he heard Brother playing in the Tates' living room, just as there are stories that say Brother heard Wilkes playing. Doot tries to find a way to attach himself to Homewood's musical continuum, but he is unsuccessful on his own.

Through Lucy, Wideman joins Doot and Blues-Jazz sounds. Lucy connects Doot to the music in a way that exemplifies Doot's own era. Doot does not hear Brother play the piano. Doot's connection to the music that lives on Homewood's streets and in the lives of the Homewood people comes through Lucy's story about how Doot heard the music on a modern Victrola. Lucy tells Doot that he danced with her to the Jazz piano of Count Basie with Jimmy Rushing singing "Sent for You Yesterday" (202). Lucy's words confirm what Carl tells Doot earlier that day, but Carl's version of Doot's link to the music focuses on his nephew's attempt to dance alone. Doot, Carl says, "[w]anted to do [his] own thing. . . . [Lucy] got . . . [Doot] moving but she had to turn you loose" (119). Carl's story elucidates Wideman's portrayal of Doot as a distinct and differentiated voice among many other voices. Doot, as a Jazz character, responds to the fragments of his experiences but is not permanently linked to any foundation of similarity.

Doot's dance with Lucy illustrates his connection to the music in Homewood, but he wants that tie to be separate, personal, his own. He is situated in an even more distant connection to his Blues fragments than Wideman's other Jazz characters, Brother Tate and Albert Wilkes. Doot, then, does not see himself and his music as part of the fabric of Homewood. He believes he is completely disconnected from Homewood's earlier Jazz and Blues lives. Until Lucy tells Doot that they danced to the tune "Sent for You Yesterday," recorded in 1938, he does not perceive that there is a space for his voice in the stories of Carl and Lucy, nor his tune in the music of Wilkes and Brother. Through Wideman's specific reference to "Sent for You Yesterday," he establishes that there is a place for Doot among the music in Homewood. It has been there for eight years, but Doot has not recognized it as his.

Wideman elucidates Doot's place among the Homewood Blues-Jazz residents by introducing Doot's music into the "weave" of the music of Wilkes and Brother (93). After Doot learns that the Jazz sounds of Basie and Rushing, through which Wilkes and Brother also are heard, moved him to dance when he was younger, Lucy turns on the radio. The music on the radio is "[n]ot jazz and not blues . . . but it's Black music. Not fast and not slow, a little of both." The music is Smokey Robinson's soulful Motown hit from 1969, "Tracks of My Tears."[21] Doot's music evokes the spirit of Brother Tate, who "appears in the doorway, . . . grinning." This music also calls forth the spirit of Albert Wilkes, who goes "for the piano bench." Wideman confers Wilkes's and Brother's approval on Doot's expansion and reshaping of Blues and Jazz with the new sounds of rhythm and blues and soul. Here Wideman also elucidates Doot's limited understanding of the expansiveness of the music that lives in him and through him. Wideman's title, then, refers to Doot's eight-year absence from the weave of the music. Brother Tate is dead eight years, and Rushing's words "Sent for You Yesterday" voice Brother's exasperated statement to Doot. Brother has been calling Doot to become part of the musical continuum, but Doot does not believe there is a place for him. Now Wideman's narrator is present in the way expressed by Basie and Rushing. Even though Doot's musical predecessors sent for him yesterday, yet he only arrives today, Doot, at last, has found his way into the music (207). Wideman, then, writes another generation into the musical weave of Homewood, and by extension into African American music.

five

JAZZ ME BLUES
Reading Music in James Baldwin's "Sonny's Blues"

During the early part of the twentieth century, Langston Hughes, Claude McKay, Sterling Brown, and James Weldon Johnson made conscious efforts to combine literature and music and to discuss the effects of music on the literary production of African American writers. Later, writers such as Ralph Ellison, James Baldwin, Albert Murray, and Amiri Baraka add to this discussion concerning the importance of the relationship between music and their writing and the relationship between music and African American literature in general. More recent inquiry into this issue has expanded the discourse on music in African American literature. In her book *Give Birth to Brightness*, Sherley Anne Williams discusses all types of black music as well as black musicians as a unitary entity that is part of a community tradition that has moved into literature. Robert O'Meally examines Blues and Spiritual-Gospel music as crucial retainers of social codes that Ralph Ellison's narrator in the music-infused novel *Invisible Man* must learn to recognize. In *Blues, Ideology, and Afro-American Literature*, Houston Baker situates his well-known "vernacular theory" of music in African American literature within an "economics of slavery" (3, 26). William J.

Harris and Nathaniel Mackey both examine Jazz in African American literature. Mackey, in his book *Discrepant Engagement: Dissonance, Cross-Culturality, and Experimental Writing*, presents an intriguing study of Jazz as cross-cultural "dissonance" and "noise." For Mackey, music is the ground of contention through which social issues are worked and through which cultures intersect (24). William J. Harris discusses music in the poetry of Amiri Baraka, situating Baraka's poetry within a Jazz form of expression that is in binary opposition to Western capitalist culture. Within Harris's context, Jazz in literature is a form of "creative destruction" (16–18). For these writers and scholars many of the issues and concepts that inform black music in the United States also inform African American literature.

Black writers, during and since the Harlem Renaissance, have moved a life philosophy found in Blues and Jazz into literature. James Baldwin, though, was reared in a strongly religious Harlem family. In the titles of his books he uses Spiritual-Gospel allusions, philosophy, and aesthetics more consistently, perhaps, than any other major African American writer: *Go Tell It on the Mountain; The Fire Next Time; One Day, When I Was Lost; Just Above My Head; The Amen Corner.* As a result of Baldwin's musical inclusiveness, resulting in his use of important references to Spiritual-Gospel, his short story "Sonny's Blues" provides a rare and concise exemplar of the literary uses of Spiritual-Gospel, Blues, and Jazz music in fictional texts that have been shaped by African American experiences.

Baldwin's title character, Sonny, and his nameless narrator, Sonny's brother, traverse the complexities of life and music simultaneously in an effort to understand each other as well as the world in which they live. Baldwin's combination of critical issues, characters, and literary uses of music illustrates how music operates in some African American fiction and in "Sonny's Blues" through a complex of intertextual relations that point to the ways in which music has become a metaphor that collects important life concepts and ideas as the music moves into literature.

In my interrogation of these life concepts and ideas as they operate in African American fiction, I hope I have presented another way of reading music in narratives that have retained a persistent intertextual connection to the oral forms of signification found in Spiritual-Gospel and Blues. I also want to expand ideas concerning the well-established concept of music as a site where historical as well as social-political-cultural experiences of black life are located. In, for instance, Jazz—as a type of music that has developed among black people in the United States yet has become dispersed more widely than its predecessors—there still are traces of the forms of signification that link it to both Spiritual-Gospel and Blues, and, in certain forms, to African American literature. I already have presented definitions of Spiritual-Gospel, Blues, and Jazz as critical categories for reading music in fiction by African American writers. In this concluding chapter, I want to demonstrate one writer's use of Spiritual-Gospel, Blues, and Jazz as they operate together in one fictional text. James Baldwin's classic short story "Sonny's Blues" incorporates all three literary uses of music. In my reading of this story, I refocus scholarly attention on the complex operations of culture, history, and politics as shaping influences in the music and in this music-infused story.

Among the scholars who discuss Baldwin's uses of Blues in this story is John M. Reilly. Reilly, however, does not address Baldwin's literary uses of Jazz. My definition of literary Blues is consistent with many aspects of Reilly's general view of the music, yet in contrast to my approach to Baldwin's story, Reilly establishes a hierarchy between the narrator and Sonny. This hierarchy privileges Sonny's antibourgeois attitude but does not recognize his Blues qualities as well as the importance of those Blues qualities to Sonny's Jazz ambitions. In Reilly's reading of "Sonny's Blues," he presents a contracted discussion of Baldwin's portrayal of Sonny as a character who, along with his brother, grows in understanding throughout the story. In, for instance, the same way that Sonny helps the narrator understand Jazz music and Jazz life, the oldest character in the story, Creole, helps Sonny understand the Blues qualities in the music that he, Sonny, wants to use to give expression to his life. Reilly also situates his discussion of the story in terms of a black-white binary opposition, which positions the narrator as a conformist to the "white ways" half of this opposition and Sonny on the black Blues culture side. I read "Sonny's Blues" as a story that interrogates the problematical issues related to intragroup—in contrast to a black-white binary—concerns with the complexities of identity and as a story that makes reference to a larger shared concern with racialized social policies in the United States.

In terms of Baldwin's uses of music, the critical focus here departs from Richard Albert's position on Baldwin's use of Ethel Waters, whom Albert views as an inauthentic blueswoman, on Louis Armstrong as a sycophant, and from his views on the character Creole as implicated in group and cultural perfidy. This approach also turns away from Reilly's oppositional hierarchy of proletariat versus bourgeois ideology as well as from Harris's duel/dualism and Darryl Hattenhauer's ingenuous take on the black/not black theme. I turn toward an understanding of the informing concepts of an African American cultural space that Baldwin mines.

"Sonny's Blues" was first published in the *Partisan Review* in 1957. Music is a pervasive informing metaphor in this short story, as Baldwin permeates his fictional environment with musical images and ideas. He demonstrates his emphasis on musical metaphors through his title as well as through his description early in the story of the "[o]ne boy [who] was whistling a tune, at once very complicated and very simple, it seemed to be pouring out of him as though he were a bird, and it sounded very cool and moving through all that harsh, bright air, only just holding its own through all those other sounds" (88). As Richard Albert observes, this boy prepares readers for Baldwin's introduction of the new bebop sound, as he compares the boy's whistling to a bird and points to the disjunction and dissonance between the music and the environment in which it is situated (180). In addition, Baldwin's description of the jukebox in the bar, which "was blasting away with something black and bouncy," further prepares readers to probe the importance of music within this story (90). These musical qualities also are evident in Baldwin's characterization of Sonny and the narrator and in the combinative qualities of Creole. Throughout this complex narrative Baldwin incorporates a number of Stephen Henderson's musical "poetic references": "[a]llusion to song titles," "quotations from songs," and "language from Jazz life." Baldwin also depicts with striking efficacy Spiritual-Gospel, Blues, and Jazz characters as well as a Blues theme in this story, which accumulates in one narrative important aspects of African American literary uses of music described in earlier chapters.

Baldwin's narrator, unlike the younger brother Sonny, follows a path of little resistance in his attempt to find a place of comfort for himself in the face of societal oppression. He joins the military, attends college, marries, and avoids trouble. Sonny, in contradistinction, joins the military and finds that his brother's path in life is not for him. Sonny is unable to move in the direction of the dominant society, and he is unable to make modified success there his triumph, as his older brother does. When Sonny considers the restrictions that society places on him, his approach is not to find a space for himself that resembles what he is denied. Rather, he resists by rejecting those things that are valued by the dominant society and that he must struggle twice as hard to get and maintain. In other words, everything that his brother represents Sonny rejects, including the Blues.

Sonny's penchant for Jazz is representative of his full-scale rejection of what he views as his brother's acceptance of the oppression against which Sonny blindly rebels. Through Creole, Sonny learns that there is something in his brother, and in the Blues, that also is in him, and in Jazz. The narrator also learns the same lesson. The narrator comes to realize his connection to Sonny's Jazz because he recognizes his Blues life within Sonny's music: "It was beautiful because it wasn't hurried and it was no longer a lament. I seemed to hear with what burning he had made it his, with what burning we had yet to make it ours, how we could cease lamenting. Freedom lurked around us and I understood, at last, that he could help us to be free if we would listen, that he would never be free until we did" (122). At the end of the story the voices of the brothers are brought together in the song "Am I Blue." In this way the distinctions between the brothers are collapsed as Baldwin emphasizes their Blues similarities, which branch from a Jazz site that includes Blues traces.

"Sonny's Blues" opens with the nameless narrator, a Blues character, meditating on his current disappointment; he has not been able to care for his brother, which he promises his mother he will do. As the narrator considers his own personal failure, he also recognizes that his feeling of oppression and captivity is part of life in a modern, urban, racialized environment where people are "trapped in the darkness which roared outside" (86). The narrator, a former military man who is now an algebra teacher, has personally triumphed beyond his troubles in life. But this is not enough for him. Before the narrator's mother dies, she leaves Sonny in his care. Sonny, unfortunately, ends up in jail for being involved in drugs. Part of the narrator's earthly triumph is to help his brother, Sonny, understand that he needs a personal response to difficulty that can be successful instead of self-destructive. Yet in the faces of his algebra students, Baldwin's narrator recognizes Sonny's attitude toward the hostile society in which they live. He understands that "their heads bumped abruptly against the low ceiling of their actual possibilities" (87) because in those students' voices, in their childhood laughter, he hears the Blues-making disappointments imposed on them by racialized social policies that are deliberately and violently resistant to social justice.

Baldwin's narrator realizes that he, his brother, and his students live in a country that reluctantly mandates equal education for them in the Brown I and II decisions in 1954 and 1955. Within months of the Supreme Court's final decision to desegregate public schools "with all deliberate speed," Emmett Till—fourteen years old—is murdered. His murderers are acquitted, and they later make a venomous and public confession for which they are paid handsomely, as their account of this murder is published in *Look* magazine. The narrator's students live in a world that attempts to limit them, yet they, as did Emmett Till, seem likely to answer yes when asked whether they are as good as white people. The narrator recognizes that his students, as well as Sonny, while embroiled in "rage," do not discern or refuse to accept the narrator's Blues philosophy. These Blues philosophical principles provide them with a means by which they can navigate, in singular ways, the racial terrain that is imposed on their lives. Sonny's brother, however, implicitly acknowledges that Sonny's new music and his own music connect in crucial ways, as the narrator observes that his students' voices allow him to hear his brother and himself (87–88).

Baldwin's narrator recognizes his Blues connection to Sonny and his students, yet he fails to acknowledge, until later, the viability of Sonny's own musical/philosophical alternative. For Sonny's older brother, success means triumph in the same way that he, the narrator, finds it. Sonny, though, would rather die first. When Sonny rejects his brother's counsel, Baldwin connects the narrator to the Blues by having the narrator whistle a Blues tune that was popularized by Ethel Waters: "You going to need me, baby, one of these cold, rainy days" (109). Through this Blues tune Baldwin makes a connection between Jazz and Blues. Sonny's Jazz will need the narrator's Blues in order to thrive. While the narrator painfully realizes this, he does not recognize that he, too, needs to hear Sonny's Jazz. The narrator is rather smug in his approach to Sonny when he is in his younger brother's apartment in Greenwich Village. For the older brother, Sonny's life is chaotic and strange, and Sonny seems disconnected from his actual family/community as he makes what the narrator perceives as new familial connections among diverse Jazz people in the bohemian environment of the Village.

Sonny, throughout most of the story, is blocked within his misunderstanding of Blues, yet he is unable to avoid the Blues he rejects. He encounters Blues-making disappointments daily. For Baldwin's developing Jazz character, however, there is no way that he can move away from Blues to make a Jazz statement about his current life because he will not acknowledge his own Blues experiences. He wants to call them something else—Jazz. Baldwin illustrates Sonny's Blues experiences through his narrator's memories of Sonny when the younger brother was about the age of the narrator's algebra students. Baldwin's narrator remembers that Sonny "had been bright and open." His potential for success, however, is "trapped in the darkness" of his society, which has no place for

Sonny or for boys like Sonny who reject the notion that they should occupy an inferior place in society. Sonny's life, like the narrator's students' lives, is one in which, unfortunately, he perhaps finds that drugs "did more for them than algebra could" (88). Thus, Baldwin demonstrates that Sonny's dashed hopes link him to the Blues—at least as a fragment in his life, if not as a site to which he establishes a group connection. The narrator observes that some "escape the trap, most don't" (95). And his brother Sonny is on the verge of not escaping. Sonny becomes involved in drugs and spends time in jail, but these attitudes do not alter Sonny's perspective on his brother's Blues life. From Sonny's limited viewpoint, his brother's apparent silence and seeming acquiescence are demeaning. Yet in order for Sonny to convey the Jazz qualities he desires, he must recognize its numerous intertexts, Blues being one of its most bountiful connections.

Neither of the brothers recognizes that Jazz has no limit to the variety of voices that it can make its own. When Sonny's brother whistles the Ethel Waters tune outside the apartment where his brother cannot hear him, he demonstrates his own blindness and distance in his relations with Sonny. He, too, cannot recognize how Blues is a part of Sonny's Jazz life. The narrator erroneously sees his singular solution as *the* Blues solution instead of as one among many Blues solutions. At one point in the story Sonny and his brother are discussing suffering, and they agree that everyone suffers. While the narrator suggests that one perhaps should just endure it, since suffering is part of life, Sonny insists, "*Everybody* tries not to [suffer]. You're just hung up on the *way* some people try—it's not *your* way!" (119) Through this exchange Baldwin again demonstrates the contrasting life philosophies—which can be explained through music—of the brothers. Sonny moves toward differing and different solutions, while his brother finds one solution that works and settles on it.

When Sonny finally does need his brother again, there is a wide emotional gulf of contrasting responses to experiences between them. Sonny's drug experiences and his rejection of social values such as work and education provide no context from which he can speak with his brother. Baldwin's narrator does not understand that Sonny cannot fight within as his brother does; Sonny rebels by standing outside that which oppresses him. Sonny's stance is another approach to the potentially spirit-crushing society in which both men live. Through Baldwin's use of music as a metaphor that represents the lives of his two characters, he limns the chasm that separates Sonny and his brother. The narrator rejects Sonny's "goodtime" music, Jazz; and Sonny does not value "that old-time, down home crap," which Sonny associates with musicians such as Louis Armstrong (103). The musical sound and social commentary of Charlie Parker have more appeal for this aspiring Jazz musician than the sound and image of Louis Armstrong. Again, Sonny misses the connection between Armstrong and Parker; thus he does not see the connection between Jazz and Blues, himself and his brother.

His characterization of Sonny makes clear Baldwin's critique of Sonny's attitude. Baldwin's Sonny seems to respond to the Armstrong who sang Andy Razaf and Fats Waller's "What Did I Do to Be So Black and Blue." This song troubles many who perceive it as an expression of self-contempt. Combined with Armstrong's performance style, which includes exaggerated—and for some, minstrel-like—facial expressions, Razaf's cuttingly ironic lyrics and Waller's music ostensibly beg for the humanity of black people by use of an old variation, at least dating to the nineteenth century, on the good-bad/black-white binary that suggests that black people can be white inside. Another reading of this tune would demonstrate, however, a dramatic use of irony by Armstrong, Waller, and Razaf, especially if the seeming minstrel effect of Armstrong's facial expression is contrasted with the signifying effect of the words in the song. Rather than focusing on the black-white color imagery, one might focus on the black-blue color imagery to discern how the words to this jazzy Blues tune are a subtle social critique. The up-tempo, rhythmic music, which is in contrast with the lyrics, expresses these musicians' real ideas on the potentialities one can find even while black and blue.

In Armstrong's rendition of "Black and Blue" there is triumph and indomitability, which augment Razaf and Waller's ironic lyrics and music. Armstrong acquired a large white audience after his music became more commercial during the swing era, so this song has more to say to that white audience than to black people or to Armstrong himself. Even Razaf's writing of "Black and Blue," which was a last-minute addition to the Broadway version of the musical revue *Connie's Hot Chocolates*, is embroiled in the lyricist's canny attempt to critique the racial environment that, in 1929, permeated New York's music and theater scene. The more convincing argument in Armstrong's favor, however, is his earlier musical work, which is within the general tradition of Blues music. His repertoire includes well-crafted tunes based in a traditional Blues idea of an internalized sense of joy in one's self, despite limitations. Blues tunes that Armstrong recorded in 1925 as part of the Hot Five group illustrate this side of Armstrong's music: "(Yes!) I'm in the Barrel" and "Gut Bucket

Blues." Yet Sonny does not seem to acknowledge this part of Armstrong's musical repertoire when he dismisses Armstrong as a musician and disparages Armstrong's use of the signifying practice that is an intertext of Jazz music and that beboppers such as Charlie Parker, John Coltrane, or Miles Davis use in resistant transformations—such as playing with their backs to the audience—during their performances.

Baldwin's critique of Sonny's misunderstanding of Jazz is even deeper if Sonny is aware of Armstrong's earlier music, and if it is that music to which Sonny refers. Either way, Baldwin demonstrates that Sonny must evince a more comprehensive conception of Jazz aesthetics. Sonny needs to understand not only the significance of Blues to Jazz but also the signifying in Blues as well as in Jazz.[1] Pancho Savery positions Sonny's perspective on Louis Armstrong within Jazz, but the words that Baldwin puts in Sonny's mouth, I believe, challenge this view. Despite our current understanding of Armstrong, Sonny's perspective is that Armstrong represents the old and the blue, a notion that, I argue, Baldwin's story rightly critiques.

Much of the music of Sonny's musical master, Charlie Parker, in contrast to Sonny's assessment, is Blues-based. Parker's music extends and expands other music in his environment, including Blues, popular music, Broadway theater music, and concert hall music. One cannot speak with clarity about Charlie Parker's music without acknowledging the aforementioned musical influences, which were at the core of his innovations and improvisations. Parker and the musicians in his bands rework George and Ira Gershwin's "I Got Rhythm"[2] on a variety of tunes: "Moose the Mooche," "Max Is Making Wax," "Bird's Nest," and "Dexterity." Parker's version of "Embraceable You" is his own interpretation of this Gershwin tune, and Gershwin's "'S Wonderful" is the informing tune in "Stupendous." Sonny, more important, does not recognize that numerous tunes performed by Charlie Parker and his musicians are informed by Blues. One can begin with "Cool Blues," "Dark Shadows," "Carvin the Bird," "Bongo Bop," and "Bird Feathers," all of which are based in basic twelve-bar Blues music. Then there is "The Hymn," which is based in the Blues tune "Wichita Blues." In "Sonny's Blues," Baldwin positions his title character so that he can come to understand that Parker musically expands Armstrong; he does not annihilate him.

Sonny, as yet, has not developed his Jazz aesthetic. As the title of Baldwin's story states, he takes readers through Sonny's Blues as this character tries to emerge into Blues' newest extension, Jazz. Despite Sonny's rejection of Blues, his behavior demonstrates that his life is influenced by shared—not just individual—disappointments, imposed on him by racial categorization, and that he employs sheer strength of will to live through and in that disappointment. What Sonny fails to understand is the way that Jazz allows him to hear many voices at once, including the Blues fragments that he denies in his own life and that shape much of Jazz.

Sonny rejects the past while, conversely, his brother is comfortable in the Blues world of yesterday's pain and today's hard-won comfort, the maintenance of which becomes a daily triumph. Both men, nevertheless, are pulled toward Spiritual-Gospel music. The mother in this story represents Spiritual-Gospel philosophy; her life is a constant prayer for survival on earth and a final reward of heavenly triumph. Her life's work has been guided by God. Mama's Spiritual-Gospel viewpoint is first introduced when she is mentioned in Sonny's letter to his brother after his niece Gracie dies: "I wish I could be like Mama and say the Lord's will be done, but I don't know it seems to me that trouble is the one thing that never does get stopped and I don't know what good it does to blame it on the Lord" (93). The mother's Spiritual-Gospel philosophy is reinforced as she engages in her last conversation with the narrator and through her choice of song in moments of contemplation: "She was humming an old church song, 'Lord you brought me from a long ways off'" (97–101). Baldwin's use of Spiritual-Gospel, as represented in the mother, also recurs as a musical riff that appears later in the story and resounds her earlier appearances in the story. At the same time, the last references to her subtly indicate the ties that both men have with each other. As a trace in Blues, which both men represent, and in Jazz, to which Sonny aspires, is Spiritual-Gospel aesthetic.

Baldwin masterfully returns the mother's Spiritual-Gospel aesthetic through the revival singers, and her presence through a musical riff reinforces the idea that at bottom there are fragments of similarity between her two very different sons. As the narrator watches the "old-fashioned revival meeting" on the street outside his window, he observes Sonny in the crowd listening to the people sing, "Tis the old ship of Zion. . . . [I]t has rescued many a thousand." Sonny's walk reminds his brother of "Harlem hipsters, only . . . [Sonny has] imposed on this his own half-beat" (110–12). Here, Baldwin's narrator realizes that his error has been in failing to see his brother as a distinct personality; instead, he has viewed him as undifferentiated chaos that is situated in and resists against the racialized discourse of the United States.

In a similar fashion as the narrator's earlier use of the Blues tune from Ethel Waters's repertoire, this Spiritual song is a message to Sonny. He is being told that he is missing vital pieces in his Jazz music and in himself if there is nothing for him in the older music. The subtlety of the Spiritual's message reaches Sonny far more poignantly than the smug attitude that his brother demonstrates earlier in the story at Sonny's apartment in Greenwich Village. Sonny also is able to connect to the love of his mother through the Spiritual tune. Shortly after this, both men watch from the window and listen to the revivalist sing "If I Could Hear My Mother Pray Again!" Sonny and his brother have been unable to find a common musical or personal ground between them, yet the music of their mother provides this seemingly comfortable neutral ground. The revivalists depart the street singing a song that denotes the mother's wish for both of her sons: "God Be with You Till We Meet Again."

In this passage, the narrator receives a message through his mother's Spirituals; the music suggests to him that his responsibility to Sonny is not to make him over but to see in Sonny their differences as well as their similarities. The Blues philosophy of the older brother and Sonny's desire for Jazz aesthetics and philosophy have been concatenated by the Spiritual-Gospel music of the mother who, as Spiritual-Gospel did for Blues and Jazz, gave birth to both of them. The appreciation both men have for the music of their mother has created some closure in the gulf that separates them. Sonny is now able to invite his brother to hear him play Jazz at "a joint in the village," and his brother is able to accept (112–13).

At the club, Baldwin introduces Creole, a character reminiscent of Jazz musician Charles Mingus, whose Blues-influenced Jazz music continuously resounds the Blues basis of Jazz. Both Baldwin's character Creole and jazzman Mingus play upright bass and revel in the Blues qualities of their music. Creole is a Jazz character, and, as his name suggests, he is a mixture; he contains many musical and cultural parts. He is, among other things, a character with all of the musical parts of the past as well as his own unique Jazz style. Creole is older than Sonny and the narrator, who is seven years older than his brother. His strong, distinctive voice among the many other distinct voices in the club is evident: "He had a big voice . . . , [and when he spoke] heads in the darkness turned" (118). These qualities situate Baldwin's Jazz character in a position to expose the confluence of Blues and Jazz that escape Sonny's and the narrator's notice.

Creole immediately begins the subtle process of showing Sonny the space for himself and his brother within the full range of Sonny's own music. Sonny's brother is warmly welcomed, and Creole stresses the importance of the brother's presence. Soon the band begins to play. As Creole musically attempts to get Sonny to realize that Jazz is Blues and gospel as well as new expression, he restrains the other band members and begins a musical call-and-response "dialogue" with the young musician. As Sonny struggles along, it is clear that he is still missing something in his music. Creole realizes that he must bring Sonny into the depths of himself, which will bring him into an understanding of what Jazz really is. So "without an instant's warning, Creole started into something, it was almost sardonic, it was 'Am I Blue.'" At this point Sonny's playing expands. Previously, "[h]e and the piano stammered, started one way, got scared, stopped, started another way, panicked, marked time, started again." But on hearing "Am I Blue," "Sonny was part of the family again. . . . Then Creole stepped forward to remind them that what they were playing was the blues" (120–21). Earlier in the story Baldwin portrays the narrator's Blues philosophy through a tune with which Ethel Waters is associated; and he makes the tie between the brothers and the connection between their musical philosophies even more perceptible through "Am I Blue," another Waters favorite, which she performed in 1929 in the film *On with the Show*.[3] Yet an "almost sardonic" Billie Holiday version enjoys much success during the time period in which Baldwin's story is situated.

Baldwin's character Creole, or the music for which he is a metaphor—Jazz, is the catalyst that Sonny and his brother need to come together as men who are both different and similar. Sonny also needs Blues in order to speak fully through his voice as a Jazz musician. Creole shows them that they are both alike and different, in ways that are similar to the repetitions and revisions in Blues and Jazz music. Sonny has to realize that he cannot reject the "down-home" without rejecting a part of himself. Creole demonstrates that Jazz is not created ex nihilo. Jazz is "keeping it [Blues] new." After Sonny accepts Blues, Creole "stepped back, very slowly, filling the air with immense suggestion that *Sonny speak for himself*" (121; emphasis added). Sonny now has created for himself a space within Jazz, a confident Jazz expression of innovative personal style.

In "Sonny's Blues," Baldwin figures Spiritual-Gospel, Blues, and Jazz through his fictional characters. At the center of this story are Blues characters, while a Blues philosophy shapes the critical issues in this story.

Jazz, in this story and in many others, is an emerging viewpoint for which a space of acceptance is opened. While it is clear that in the beginning Sonny is lost in a musical void, his brother—though more mature because he understands his Blues experiences and recognizes that the solutions are "all within"—has found a comfortable yet narrow space for his life. Both brothers have to expand their perceptions. The narrator has to accept, even if he cannot express, Jazz. Baldwin demonstrates his narrator's former fears about Jazz and the qualities that it suggests when at the club Sonny's brother recognizes a "circle of light" that he perceives as having the potential to consume the Jazz musicians "in flames." In the end, however, the narrator no longer fears the closeness to chaos[4] that Jazz brings Sonny, so the narrator says that Sonny "could help us to be free if we would listen." And, for his part, Sonny has to engage the old music before he can locate himself in Jazz. He has to step into the deep water of Blues without drowning (115–22).

Jazz characters in African American fiction frequently are marginalized, but their inclusion in fiction as well as in drama (Lyons in August Wilson's *Fences* and Nelson in Alice Childress's *Wedding Band*.) makes an important statement about the way that African American fiction creates a space for nonconformity, a space that repeats the musical practice of black people and reinscribes African American history as well as experiential narratives.[5] Creole, as Jazz in "Sonny's Blues," is Baldwin's way to make familial and musical connections as well as political, social, and cultural alterations in the landscape of the United States. In many African American fictional texts, black writers employ Jazz in ways that move away from an emphasis on similarity, which is the quality that Creole uses to bring Sonny and his brother together. Instead, many black writers focus on a Jazz aesthetic of difference, while recognizing intertextual traces from predecessors as well as from the contemporary cultural milieu, as is the case in the collective improvisational style of bebop.

Baldwin's conclusion in "Sonny's Blues" suggests a personal triumph for the narrator as well as for Sonny. According to Williams, "Sonny's brother begins to understand not so much Sonny, as himself" (149). Triumph for both results from personal strength of character. The narrator requires a high level of internal strength to attain his personal accomplishments, and his brother Sonny successfully struggles to maintain the strength to remain outside the dominant society without destroying himself. The reconciliation of Sonny and the narrator demonstrates a Blues process of singular voices finding a way to live within the context of a shared problem.

In "Sonny's Blues," Baldwin represents the lives of his characters through the three major forms of music that have prevailed as influences among African American musicians in the twentieth century. In so doing, he has shown the propinquity of the experiences in African American music to both the social real and life as depicted in many of the narratives by black writers.

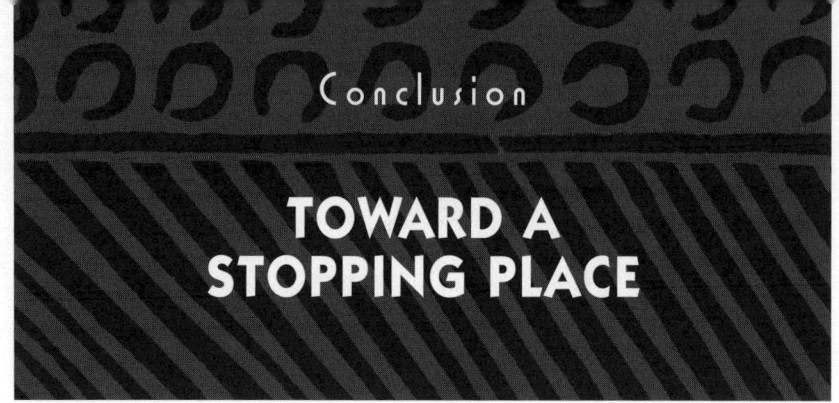

Conclusion

TOWARD A STOPPING PLACE

Stating that the convergence of the social real and art operate in African American fiction is almost a commonplace. It is even almost glib to say that a number of African American fictional texts draw from the cultural well of music. What I have endeavored to demonstrate in the preceding pages is how this convergence occurs not only in its most obvious way, as specific references to music and musicians, but in its sometimes nuanced and at other times quite pronounced social, aesthetic, and philosophical intersections with history, society, and politics. What I found was that there was far more cultural activity of this sort—intersections of fiction and music—than the contemporary scholarship has addressed. In fact, among writers of the twentieth century, for the most part only Toni Morrison, Ralph Ellison, and James Baldwin have gained sustained criticism on their uses of music in their fiction. Yet even with these writers, much of this scholarship, as I see it, addresses clear cases of specific references to music. The writers mentioned above as well as other African American writers also use the stories found in music as sites for elaboration and change, as this music clearly—as I endeavored to have demonstrated—collects valuable social ideas, concepts, and ideals. I hope that somehow I have shown when and where this intersection occurs in the literature I discuss in this book.

One may argue that in this study there is a thin description of musical and social history. This thin description of history may inadvertently appear to make history the background of literary studies and subordinate to the thick descriptions of the fictional narratives. In fact, my approach emphasizes the historical positioning, that is, the historicity of the literary texts that I read, yet this approach does not diminish the textuality of history. This means that I acknowledge the ways in which history is determined by multiple discourses (body of rules) that allow me to position history within my readings of the literary texts and to suggest how history, at the same time, also operates outside of the fictional narratives. My intention, then, was to point to the convergence of poetics, society, and politics. History is in my readings of the literary texts just as it is in the literature, yet history precedes my readings in this study only as a reminder of some of the historical locations out of which the production of the literary texts operate and to which the literary texts themselves often do not speak directly. I also take the approach that I do in the preceding pages as a result of our contemporary position within a culture in which a commodified consumerism proliferates and in the process effaces a sense of historicity.

African American music continues to expand and reshape itself as an intracultural discourse and as an intertextual site for the production of cultural knowledge. In the contemporary music scene of the twentieth century fin de siècle, many of the musical innovations of previous decades have become established traditions, and Amiri Baraka's concept of the changing same in African American music is now an internalized and established discursive formation among African American musicians. This era finds Blues, Jazz, and Spiritual-Gospel persisting yet changing. There are generational extensions in the music found in the Blues of Big Bill Morganfield, son of Muddy Waters; in the New Orleans Jazz music family of Branford, Wynton, and Delfayo Marsalis, sons of Ellis Marsalis; in T. S. Monk, son of Thelonious Monk; and in Ravi Coltrane, son of John Coltrane. There also are new names keeping African American music alive: Cassandra Wilson, Lynn White, Keb Mo, India.Arie, Yolanda Adams, Donnie McClurkin, and Kirk Franklin, among others. The contemporary music business and popular cultural forms in the United States thrive on music influenced by Blues, Jazz, and Spiritual-Gospel sounds.

In the political and social sphere, church bombings were resurrected in the 1990s, and a black man suffered a contemporary lynching in Jasper, Texas, after he was chained to the back of a truck and dragged several miles to his death by avowed white supremacists. The media descriptions of this lynching sound uncannily similar to a fictional lynching in Walter White's 1924 novel *The Fire in the Flint* (236–37). The movie and film industries find the celluloid portrayals of black people in films by Julie Dash, Spike Lee, John Singleton, and a growing number of others. In literature, Blues- and Jazz-influenced poetry and fiction proliferate in books written by Bebe Moore Campbell, Gloria Naylor, Clarence Major, Michael Harper, Yusef Komunyakaa, and many others. There also is a proliferation of literature that is likely shaping a new voice among black writers in the United States. These writers, as with their predecessors, may situate their literary voices within a social-political-cultural tune that speaks of a new way for their day.

APPENDIX
Allusions and References to Musicians and Music in the Narratives

Sport of the Gods (1902)[1]

Quicksand (1928)
Lines from and references to:
   "Swing Low, Sweet Chariot," traditional
   New World Symphony, 1893, Antonín Dvořák
   "Showers of Blessings," E. Condor
   "We'll Understand It Better By and By," 1905, Charles Albert Tindley
   Antonín Dvořák (1841–1904)

The Blacker the Berry . . .: A Novel of Negro Life (1929)
Lines from and references to:
   "St. Louis Blues," 1914, William Christopher Handy
   "Blue Skies," 1927, Irving Berlin
   "Muddy Water (A Mississippi Moan)," 1927, often attr. to Bessie Smith
   "Jelly"[2]
   "Bye, Bye, Blackbird," 1926, Mort Dixon and Ray Henderson
   "Charmin' Betsy," 1929, Henry Thomas[3]

Their Eyes Were Watching God (1937)
Lines from and references to:
   "This Little Light of Mine," traditional
   "Walk in the Light," traditional
   "Sometimes I Feel Like a Motherless Child," traditional
   "Down Hearted Blues," 1922, Alberta Hunter and Lovie Austin
   "Going Away Blues," 1928, Lottie Kimbrough[4]
   "Safe in the Arms of Jesus," F. J. Van Alstyne
   "Ring the Bells of Heaven," William O. Cushing

The Street (1946)
Lines from and references to:
"Swing It Sister," 1932, Harold Adamson and Burton Lane
"Darlin'," 1945, Lucky (Lucius) Millinder and Frances Kraft Reckling
"Night and Day," 1932, Cole Porter (1891–1964)
"Rock, Raleigh Rock"[5]

Invisible Man (1952)
Lines from and references to:
"What Did I Do to Be So Black and Blue," 1929, Andy Razaf,
    Harry Brooks, and Thomas "Fats" Waller
"A Mighty Fortress Is Our God," 1529, Martin Luther
New World Symphony, 1893, Antonín Dvořák
"Swing Low, Sweet Chariot," traditional
"Dry Southern Blues," 1926, Blind Lemon Jefferson[6]
Symphony no. 5, 1808, Ludwig van Beethoven
"The Holy City," Stephen Adams and Frederick E. Weatherly
"My Old Cabin Home," 1908, W. H. Drumeller
"Back Water Blues," 1927, Bessie Smith
"St. Louis Blues," 1914, William Christopher Handy[7]
"Bread of Heaven," 1875, William D. Maclagan[8]
"Lead Me to a Rock that Is Higher Than I," traditional[9]
"Hiding in Thee," William O. Cushing and Ira D. Sankey
"Go Down, Moses," traditional
"Boogie Woogie Blues," 1936, Albert Ammons
"John Brown's Body," traditional
"Media Luz," 1925, Carlos Cesar Lenzi and Edgardo Donato
"Many a Thousand Gone," traditional
"Jelly, Jelly, Jelly," usually attr. to Billy Eckstine and Earl Hines
"Old Ship of Zion," usually attr. to Thomas A. Dorsey[10]
"Old Man River," 1927, Oscar Hammerstein II and Jerome Kern
"Joe Louis Blues," 1934, Earl McIntyre
"Buddy Bolden's Blues," Jelly Roll Morton
"Stealin' Stealin,'" 1928, often attr. to Memphis Jug Band[11]
Ludwig van Beethoven (1770–1827)
Daniel Louis "Satchmo" Armstrong (1898/1900–1971)
Antonín Dvořák (1841–1904)
Peter Wheatstraw (William Bunch) (1905–1941)

Sula (1973)
Lines from and references to:
"In the Sweet By-and-By," 1868, Sanford Filmore Bennett and
    Joseph P. Webster
"Abide with Me," Henry F. Lyte and William H. Monk
"Nearer My God to Thee," Sarah F. Adams and Lowell Mason
"Precious Memories," traditional

"Save a Little Dram for Me," Egbert "Bert" Williams
"Shall We Gather at the River (Beautiful River)," 1865, Robert Lowry
"Amazing Grace," 1779, John Newton
Egbert "Bert" Williams (1875–1922)
Bessie Smith (1894–1937)

Train Whistle Guitar (1974)
Lines from and references to:
  "Sugarfoot Stomp (Dipper Mouth Blues)," 1926, Joseph "King" Oliver
    and Louis Armstrong
  "Sundown," usually attr. to Son House
  "At Sundown," 1927, Walter Donaldson
  "Little White Lies," 1930, Walter Donaldson
  "Precious Little Thing Called Love," Cole Porter
  "Oh Freedom," traditional
  "Ain't Going to Let Nobody Turn Me Around," traditional
  "Amazing Grace," 1779, John Newton
  "Nearer My God to Thee," Sarah F. Adams and Lowell Mason
  "St. Louis Blues," 1914, William Christopher Handy[12]
  "Ain't She Sweet," 1927, Milton Ager and Jack Yellen
  "He's Got the Whole World in His Hands," traditional
  "Three Little Words," 1930, Bert Kalmar and Harry Ruby[13]
  "Lilac Time," 1928, L. Wolfe Gilbert and Nathaniel Shilkret
  "My Blue Heaven," 1927, George Whiting and Walter Donaldson
  "Dream a Little Dream of Me," 1930, Gus Kahn and Wilbur Schwandt
  "I'll See You in My Dreams," 1924, Gus Kahn and Isham Jones
  "Kansas City Stomp," 1923, Jelly Roll Morton
  "How Come You Do Me Like You Do," 1924, Gene Austin and Roy Bergere
  "Ja-Da," 1918, Bob Carleton, Nan Lynn, and Ken Lane
  "Squeeze Me," 1925, Clarence Williams and Thomas "Fats" Waller
  "Leaning on the Everlasting Arms," Elisha Albright Hoffman and
    Anthony Johnson Showalter
  "Get Right with God," traditional
  "No Hiding Place," traditional
  "The Blood Done Sign My Name," traditional, often attr. to
    Huddie Ledbetter
Huddie Ledbetter (Leadbelly) (1889–1949)
King Oliver's Creole Jazz Band
Bessie Smith (1894–1937)
Ma Rainey (1886–1939)
Mamie Smith (1883–1946)
Trixie Smith (1896–1967)
Ida Cox (1896–1967)
Ferdinand Joseph La Menthe (Jelly Roll Morton) (1891–1941)
Jelly Roll Morton and the Red Hot Peppers
Daniel Louis "Satchmo" Armstrong (1898/1900–1971)

Sent for You Yesterday (1983)
Lines from and references to:
    "Sent for You Yesterday and Here You Come Today," 1938, Count Basie
        and Eddie Durham
    "You Are My Sunshine," 1930, Jimmie Davis and Charles Mitchell
    "Farther Along," 1937, J. R. Baxter and W. B. Stevens
    "In the Garden," 1912, C. Austin Miles
    "Peach Tree Blues," traditional/often attr. to James Yank Rachell[14]
    "Lay Down My Burdens (Down by the Riverside)," traditional
    "Lonesome Train," Eddie "Cleanhead" Vinson[15]
    "C. C. Rider," 1924, traditional/usually attr. to Ma Rainey
    "'Round Midnight," 1947, Thelonious Monk[16]
    "Didn't He Ramble," often attr. to Al Hirt[17]
    "In the Sweet By-and-By," 1868, Sanford Filmore Bennett and
        Joseph P. Webster
    "Down by the Riverside (Ain't Going to Study War No More)," traditional
    "Falling Rain Blues," 1925, Lonnie Johnson[18]
    "The How Long Blues (When the Evening Train's Been Gone)," 1928,
        Leroy Carr and Scrapper Blackwell
    "The Hut-Sut Song (A Swedish Serenade)," 1941, Leo V. Killion,
        Ted Michael, and Jack Owens
    "God Bless America," 1938, Irving Berlin
    "America the Beautiful," 1913, Katherine Lee Bates
    "Tracks of My Tears," 1965, William "Smokey" Robinson
    William "Count" Basie (1904–1984)
    Jimmy Rushing (1903–1972)
    William Clarence "Billy" Eckstine (1914–1993)
    Sarah "Sissy" Vaughan (1924–1990)
    Dinah Washington (1924–1963)
    Ella Fitzgerald (1918–1996)
    Billie "Lady Day" Holiday (1915–1959)
    Lester "Prez" Young (1909–1959)
    Edward Kennedy "Duke" Ellington (1899–1974)
    William "Smokey" Robinson (1940–)

"Sonny's Blues" (1957)
Lines from and references to:
    "Old Ship of Zion," usually attr. to Thomas A. Dorsey (see note 10)
    "If I Could Hear My Mother Pray Again," James Rowe and
        James W. Vaughn
    "The Lord Has Brought Me a Mighty Long Way," traditional
    "God Be with You Till We Meet Again," Thomas A. Dorsey and
        Artelia W. Hutchins[19]
    "Am I Blue," 1929, Grant Clarke and Harry Askt
    Daniel Louis "Satchmo" Armstrong (1898/1900–1971)
    Charlie "Bird" Parker (1920–1955)

NOTES

Introduction

The subtitle of the introduction is taken from the song "We'll Understand It Better By and By," written by Charles Albert Tindley in 1905.

1. Throughout this study I use the terms "blueswomen" and "bluesmen" to refer to actual musicians or to characters who are musicians in the literary texts. I do not use this term to refer to people who are situated within a Blues-making environment yet are not musicians.
2. See Eileen Southern (*Music* 93) along with Donald Petesch (88, 244–45) for an extensive discussion of the role of minstrelsy in black music in the nineteenth century.
3. See the following writers on the influence of philosophical concepts, epic, and narrative qualities in African American art and literature: Lovell (114); Titon (27); Murray, *Omni* (146); Ellison, *Shadow* (78–79, 94); Baldwin, "Many Thousands" (24, 36).
4. Donald Petesch points out that "[s]ocial history from the Civil War into the modern period . . . [was] preoccupied with first restoring, then retaining the old relations under the new 'freedom.' Central to this restoration . . . [was] the assertion of difference between whites and blacks, a difference earlier presumed under slavery but now formulated into laws and given vivid form through the arts" (21–28, 79).
5. See Noel Ignatiev's *How the Irish Became White* and his "Immigrants and Whites." See also David Roediger's *The Wages of Whiteness: Race and the Making of the American Working Class* and George Lipsitz's *The Possessive Investment in Whiteness: How White People Profit from Identity Politics.*
6. See Willard Gatewood's *Aristocrats of Color: The Black Elite, 1880–1920* on the lives of free men and women of color in the United States.
7. See Charles T. Davis's discussion of ancient Greco-Roman culture, which he describes as "neither exclusively white nor black" (315–16).

8. Richard Allen's collection, published in 1801, of Spiritual songs and hymns preceded Douglass's narrative. Allen compiled songs that were popular among black Methodists at the time, some of which were hymns by Isaac Watts, Charles Wesley, John Newton, Alexander Pope, and others, including original songs by black song makers. Allen, however, does not present an extended discussion of the songs. The table of contents of Allen's hymnal is in Southern's *Readings in Black American Music*.
9. The importance of improvisation is taken up by Ortiz Walton (54–57) as well as by Ralph Ellison in "The Charlie Christian Story," reprinted in Ellison's *Shadow and Act* (234), and Amiri Baraka in "African Slaves" (28).
10. In 1925, William Stanley Braithwaite in "The Negro in American Literature" connected this literature to a response to hypocrisy in the United States just as Douglass found a similar response in the music he heard (171). Robert Stepto confirms the paradoxical lived experiences of enslaved black people in his discussion of the contradiction in the idea of the traveling pass, which allowed black people to "travel while in bondage" (xiii).
11. Margaret Dickie and Thomas Travisano's view of modernism as a moment in cultural history that allowed female writers to insert their voices into a fracturing cultural space can be similarly applied to African American writers (10). And in W. Lawrence Hogue's terms, "[A]s the different experiences of women and racial and sexual . . . [groups] emerge into the cultural and sociopolitical spheres, high modernism, which is modelled historically and primarily on white middle class male experiences, is eroded, thereby opening the way for other forms of literary modernism to emerge" (105). Also consider Linda Hutcheon's argument that "the ex-centrics' agenda only partially overlap and do not coincide with that of the postmodern" (69). For a discussion of African Americans' relations to postmodernism, see Wahneema Lubiano's essay "Shuckin' Off the African American 'Native Other.'"
12. Amritjit Singh also uses the term "paradox" to discuss Du Boisian double-consciousness (5).
13. Donald Petesch refers to the literary use of the contradiction of being absent while present as "a complex literary strategy" (9, 76).
14. I use the term "text" in its broad poststructural sense as an intersecting of sign-systems operating as process, thus freed from fixity. See Julia Kristeva's *Revolution in Poetic Language* and Roland Barthes's "Theory of the Text."
15. See Ralph Ellison's "Richard Wright's Blues" and James Baldwin's "Many Thousands Gone" for discussions of the importance of music in African American fiction.
16. See also James Baldwin's *Go Tell It on the Mountain*, *The Fire Next Time*, and *If Beale Street Could Talk*. Contemporary writer E. Lynn Harris is

similarly allusive, especially making reference to Spiritual-Gospel music and vernacular culture, with titles such as *Just as I am*, *And This Too Shall Pass*, and *Abide with Me*.

17. At the 2000 Harlem Book Fair, writer Omar Tyree lamented the fact that his publisher changed the title of his 1997 book from his preference, "Burned Out," to the musically allusive (from the Aretha Franklin tune) *A Do Right Man*. His complaint raises the question of the contemporary uses of music by African American writers: Is it a mass marketing tool by book publishers or cultural selection by the writers?

18. J. Saunders Redding notes that this story is "so detached and objective that the writer's race could not have been detected" by readers of the magazine (231).

19. When Chesnutt includes this story in his collection *The Conjure Woman*, he gives the white northerner the name John in later stories, but this character remains nameless in the first story in this collection, "The Goophered Grapevine."

20. See Donald Bogle's discussion of Bert Williams and the use of burnt cork on the faces of black minstrel performers in his *Toms, Coons, Mulattoes, Mammies, and Bucks: An Interpretive History of Black in American Film*.

21. I agree with Darwin Turner's view of Toomer's *Cane* as an early and artistically well executed literary text on "Southern Black peasant life." I take a different position, however, on the perceptivity of Toomer's narrator (xx, xxii).

22. Robert Jones's insights on Toomer as a writer in the plantation tradition contributed to my discussion (xiv–xviii).

23. William Stanley Braithwaite maintains that "[s]o objective is . . . [Toomer's *Cane*] that we feel that it is a mere accident that birth or association has thrown him into contact with the life he has written about. He would write just as well, just as poignantly, just as transmutingly about the peasants of Russia, or the peasants of Ireland, had experience brought him in touch with their existence" (181).

24. Hughes's *Tambourines to Glory* is a short novel constructed quickly and for financial gain from his gospel play of the same name. Many refer to *Not Without Laughter* as Hughes's only novel, as it is a longer narrative that is consistent with traditional definitions of the novel.

25. Richard Wright, interestingly, emphasizes Spiritual-Gospel music in his writing. See Wright's *Uncle Tom's Children* (1940). In this collection of stories Wright frequently uses Spiritual-Gospel music as well as the black sermonic tradition to suggest a strength and beauty that are found in the midst of difficulty. Wright, as did Dunbar, rejects Jazz and Jazz-influenced music as somehow inauthentic. See Kinnamon and Fabre's *Conversations with Richard Wright* for this writer's comments on Jazz.

26. Throughout this study, I use Amiri Baraka's appellation, "Blues People," to designate literary characters who have internalized the philosophical concepts and ideas that are situated in Blues music and that shape Blues communities. They are Blues-influenced yet are not Blues musicians. In his book *Blues People*, Baraka describe Blues People as possessing "some of the most complex and complicated ideas about the world imaginable" (7).
27. See Ellison's essay "Richard Wright's Blues" (78–79).

1. Muddy Waters

"Muddy Waters" is the stage name used by Blues singer McKinley Morganfield, and "Muddy Water" is the name of a song recorded by Bessie Smith in 1927 (*The Complete Recordings, Vol 3*, Columbia/Legacy C2K47474).

1. I employ the capitalized form of the terms "Spiritual," "Spiritual-Gospel," "Blues," and "Jazz" as a way of pointing to their multifarious significations as proper nouns that collect the aesthetic and philosophical aspects of African American life. While I disagree with Kimberly W. Benston's location of Blues within a discourse of the "tragic" and the "guilt," presented in his essay "Tragic Aspects of the Blues," I agree with what he seems to suggest when he refers to Blues with a capital "B" as a distinct entity from Blues as "a genre of song and poetry." I extend this view to the extramusical aspects in African American music and I also include Spiritual, Spiritual-Gospel, and Jazz. I relate this use of these terms to the capitalization of the German word *Dasein*, which suggests nontangible yet actual states that refer to life's experiences. Spiritual, Spiritual-Gospel, Blues, and Jazz, for me, operate in a similar way but are in no way analogous to the German term.
2. See Eileen Southern (86, 165), John Lovell (111–17), and Zora Neale Hurston's essay "Characteristics of Negro Expression" on the complex question of African American Christianity.
3. Wyatt Tee Walker (46) as well as James Weldon Johnson comment on the wide range of themes that exist in Spiritual-Gospel music. Johnson, in his *Book of American Negro Spirituals*, vol. 1, points out that almost all of life's themes, except sex, are covered in the Spirituals (12).
4. For a more detailed discussion of wandering verses, see Eileen Southern (172, 176).
5. Wyatt Tee Walker presents an extensive discussion of this movement in Spiritual music; he also identifies the return of Spirituals to their roots in what he terms "urban spirituals," more commonly referred to as gospel music.
6. Bonds and Hughes became good friends, and a later Bonds's composition titled *Three Dream Portraits* (1959) uses Hughes's poems "Dream Variation,"

"Minstrel Man," and "I, Too." Bonds and Hughes collaborated on *The Ballad of the Brown King*, which had an unsuccessful premier in 1954. Bonds wrote the score and Hughes the libretto for this composition; a performance of this piece eventually aired on CBS's *Christmas USA* in 1960.

7. Over time Spiritual and Blues music have proven to be prodigiously flexible. They have been important in African American culture in general, to classically trained African American composers, as well as to European composers. Dvořák, for instance, was inspired by the Spirituals sung by his talented student, Harry T. Burleigh, and despite Dvořák's misconceptions about Native American music and African American music being "practically identical," his assertion that his Symphony no. 9 in E Minor, op. 95, *From the New World*, was inspired by Native American melodies illustrates the impact that the music he heard in the United States had on his musical ideas. The second movement of this symphony includes his Spiritual-like tune, to which lyrics and the title "Going Home" were later added; the fourth movement seems to transform the plaintive sounds of "Swing Low, Sweet Chariot" into a magisterial piece that strongly recalls Dvořák's classical genius, or perhaps the rhythmic elements of this piece recall the Native American chants to which the composer refers. Jan Swafford in *The Vintage Guide to Classical Music* states that Dvořák's most productive years were the three he spent in the United States "ostensibly imitating its music." Dvořák also wanted to influence the direction of symphonic music in the United States. He "suggested that inspiration for a truly national music might derive from the Negro melodies or Indian chants. . . . The most potent as well as the most beautiful among them . . . are certain of the so-called plantation melodies and slave songs. . . . The music of the people is like a rare and lovely flower growing amidst encroaching weeds. . . . The fact that no one has as yet arisen to make the most of it does not prove that nothing is there" (ellipses in original; see Swafford 308–10).

The musical influence of black people in the United States also had an effect on other European classical composers. After visiting the United States and meeting George Gershwin in 1928, French-born orchestral composer Maurice Ravel considered Jazz "one of the most important musical developments of the century." His violin sonata shows Blues influences, and "jazz ideas . . . also . . . [are] strong in the two piano concertos he wrote" after his visit. Russian composer Igor Stravinsky, who became a United States citizen in 1945, found inspiration in folk material early in his career. His earliest commissioned ballet, *The Firebird (L'Oiseau de feu)*, was based on a Russian fairy tale, and *Petrushka*, the ballet that launched his international career, also was based on Russian folk material. So his fascination with ragtime and Jazz seems a consistent musical interest. The American music that is in debt to formerly enslaved Africans prompted Stravinsky to compose some pieces he called ragtime and to include some ragging syncopations in his 1923–24 Concerto for Piano and Wind Instruments (375, 415, 418).

8. Lawrence Levine in *Black Culture and Black Consciousness* also points to a shift from community to communal consciousness among African American people, and he also situates Blues firmly in modernity (221).

9. Nellie McKay discusses a similar use of "I" in the autobiographical texts of women and in the texts of people in developing nations in her essay on Zora Neale Hurston, "'Crayon Enlargements of Life': Zora Neale Hurston's *Their Eyes Were Watching God* as Autobiography." Albert Murray briefly addresses this issue in *Stomping the Blues*. Henry Louis Gates Jr. in *The Signifying Monkey* makes similar observations, as does John Lovell in *Black Song: The Forge and the Flame*.

10. Albert Murray observes that "with no aid from existentialism [Blues has] . . . always known that there were no clear-cut solutions for the human situation" (*Omni* 167).

11. In his book *Black Music* (180), Amiri Baraka uses this Aristotelian concept to describe the various permutations of black music; his terminology has proved exceedingly useful in the study of African American culture, especially music.

12. Julia Kristeva defines text and textuality similarly as a "translinguistic apparatus which redistributes the order of the language by putting a communicative utterance, aiming to inform directly, in relation with different utterances" (quoted in Barthes 36).

13. See the introduction to Margaret Waller's English translation, *Revolution in Poetic Language* (9).

14. See Greenblatt's "Fiction and Friction" in *Shakespearean Negotiations*; Kristeva's "Intertextuality and Literary Interpretation," in *Kristeva Interviews*, "Breaching the Thetic: Mimesis," in *Revolution in Poetic Language*, and "Word, Dialogue, and Novel," in *Desire in Language*; Roland Barthes "Theory of the Text," in Robert Young's *Untying the Text*; John Frow's "Intertextuality and Ontology," and Louis Montrose's "New Historicisms" and "Texts and Histories."

15. Stephen Henderson (50), Jeff Todd Titon (3–5), and Eileen Southern all point to the variation in the musical structure of Blues. Southern in *The Music of Black America* notes that the three-line stanza is "an apparent throwback to African origins, for the three-line stanza is uncommon in American [outside the Blues] and European repertories" (323–33).

16. I find intriguing Jacques Derrida's discussion of the paradox of singularity or iterability, which "both puts down roots in the unity of a context and

immediately opens this non-saturable context onto a recontextualization. All this is historical through and through." For Derrida, "[a]n absolute, absolutely pure singularity, if there were one, would not even show up, or at least would not be available for reading. To become readable, it has to be *divided*, to *participate* and *belong*." He further states that "the 'best' reading would consist in *giving oneself up to* the most idiomatic aspects of the work while also *taking account* of the historical context, of what is *shared*" (Attridge 63, 68). This perspective, I think, is useful in thinking about both Blues singularity and innovative personal style in Jazz.

17. Ella Fitzgerald's rendition of "A Tisket, a Tasket" (1938) is the most obvious example of the nursery rhyme in Jazz. A similar influence from children's music is found in Blues tunes such as Lee Dorsey's "Waiting for My Ya-Ya" (1961), and a contemporary example of the uses of classical music in Jazz is Cyrus Chestnut's "Für Elise" on his *Charlie Brown Christmas* CD, issued in 2000.
18. I borrow Emily Dickinson's sense of the term "slant" as she uses it in her poem no. 1129, "Tell all the Truth but tell it slant."
19. Henry Louis Gates Jr. in *The Signifying Monkey* points out the importance of riffing as a form of repetition and—in the case of signifying—inversion and the suggestion of "dissemblance." His example is John Coltrane's version of "My Favorite Things," which suggests but radically departs from Julie Andrews's version of the same song. In literature, Gates points to Langston Hughes's 1961 long poem *Ask Your Mama: Twelve Moods for Jazz*. In this poem, Hughes riffs the phrase "Ask your mama," positioning this poem in vernacular tradition and in music. I demonstrate the movement of riffs into fiction by black writers.
20. See Albert Murray's *Stomping the Blues* (196) and *Omni Americans* (56); John Lovell's *Black Song* (5); Richard Wright's "The Literature of the Negro in the United States" (227); and Amiri Baraka's *Black Music* (14).

2. Stormy Blues

"Stormy Blues" is the title of a song written and recorded by Billie Holiday in 1954 (*The Billie Holiday Songbook*, PolyGram 823 246-4).

1. In *The Novels of the Harlem Renaissance*, Amritjit Singh presents a similar discussion of Booker T. Washington's miscalculation of modernity's impact on black lives (7).
2. See Farah Jasmine Griffin's *"Who Set You Flowing?"* for a more detailed discussion of this phenomenon.
3. In her important study of literary lynching, *Exorcising Blackness*, Trudier Harris investigates the uses to which African American writers put

images of lynching; she also makes useful observations on the differences between the ways in which black male and black female writers use such images, observing that black male writers present far more graphic details of the actual lynching than do black females. In Harris's study, she discusses Dunbar's "Lynching of Jube Benson" (85–86). See also Miriam Decosta-Willis's *Memphis Diary of Ida B. Wells* and Walter White's *Rope and Faggot: A Biography of Judge Lynch* as well as White's novel *The Fire in the Flint*, both of which address the issue of lynching and African American responses to it in the early decades of the twentieth century.

4. See Joy James's discussion of anti-lynching campaigns in her *Transcending the Talented Tenth*. James points to the initiation of such campaigns as the diligent efforts of black women beginning in 1892, prior to the 1909 founding of the NAACP.
5. Madame C. J. Walker died just months after donating to the NAACP's anti-lynching campaign.
6. There are numerous other independent black religious groups that were established in the early decades of the twentieth century, including Father Divine's (George Baker's) Peace Mission Kingdoms, established in 1915, and his mission called Heaven, founded in 1933 at 20 West 155th Street in Harlem (Baker did not allow his members to accept public aid during the Depression); George Hurley's Universal Hagar's Spiritual Church, founded in Detroit in 1923; Ali established the Moorish Science Temple as the first mosque in the United States in Newark, New Jersey, in 1913; Micheaux's Church of God was founded in Newport News, Virginia, in 1919; McGuire's African Orthodox Church was founded in 1921; the Ahmadiyya branch of Islam was established in 1921; and the United House of Prayer for All People, established in 1925 by Charles Emmanuel Grace (Marcelino Manuaela de Graca, or "Daddy Grace") in 1934. The most notable civil rights organization, the NAACP, was formed in 1909 after Du Bois's Niagara Movement—established in 1905—joined forces with a biracial coalition. These groups, along with traditional as well as invisible black churches that have a history dating back to the eighteenth and nineteenth centuries, have found ways to contribute to change for African American people.
7. Garvey's impact on the early-twentieth-century African American social and cultural milieu often goes without notice, yet his UNIA has a widespread appeal among working-class African Americans (for a time Garvey's publication *Negro World* greatly exceeded the NAACP's *Crisis* in circulation) that it lacks among the predominately middle-class New Negroes of the same period, pointing to a "class cleavage" among black people in the 1920s. See Walter Kalaidjian's *American Culture Between the Wars* (83). Amritjit Singh expands this discussion of class separation among black

people in the 1920s. Singh furthers his argument on this point concerning class by pointing out that the 1926 exchange between George Schuyler ("The Negro-Art Hokum") and Langston Hughes ("The Negro Artist and the Racial Mountain") in the *Nation* presents another example of a class divide among African Americans (12).

8. My information about the Southern Negro Youth Congress was obtained from Esther Cooper Jackson, James Jackson, and Dorothy Burnham, all of whom spoke at the 1999 National Endowment for the Humanities Summer Institute on the "Civil Rights Movement: History and Consequences" at the W. E. B. Du Bois Institute for Afro-American Studies at Harvard University. Dorothy Burnham, an activist in her own right, was on the New York committee on the Scottsboro case; she was the wife of the Louis Burnham, the first executive secretary of the SNYC. James and Esther Jackson were members of this youth organization. Esther Jackson has a book, *Prophets in Their Own Country*, forthcoming from Westview Press. See also Robin D. G. Kelley's *The Hammer and Hoe: Alabama Communists During the Great Depression* (195–231).

9. These insights on the role of Charles Houston in the NAACP were contributed by Patricia Sullivan during the 1999 National Endowment for the Humanities Summer Institute on the "Civil Rights Movement: History and Consequences." Also see Sullivan's *Days of Hope*.

10. This song is regularly referred to as the Black National Anthem (formerly the Negro National Anthem) and is often sung at important gatherings.

11. See Wright's "Jazz and Desire" for his views on Jazz (242).

12. This Blues tune was written as a campaign song in 1909 for Memphis politician Edward Crump's mayoral bid. The popularity of the original song, "Mayor Crump's Blues," encouraged Handy to publish it. He changed the title to "Memphis Blues."

13. See Eileen Southern (*The Music* 304–5, 349) as well as Abbe Niles's introduction to W. C. Handy's *Blues: An Anthology* (35).

14. Fletcher Henderson published music regularly and often used the pseudonym George Brooks.

15. Peetie Wheatstraw (William Bunch) fashions in his Blues music a similar alliance-with-the-devil attitude that is associated with Robert Johnson; this self-fashioning of a trickster/devil persona has a long history in African American folk and Blues traditions.

16. Hazel Carby comments on this issue in her book *Race Men*. She discusses Huddie Ledbetter ("Leadbelly") and critiques the Lomaxes for "invent[ing] their own version of the dangerous, if gifted, black male." My perception of a good deal of the commentary on Robert Johnson is that it contains something of this phenomenon of the deliciously attractive yet dangerous black man in it. His uses of devil images seem, to me,

to have a presence in earlier African American cultural contexts and are not particularly striking or innovative in his music.

17. Carr, however, is well known for his 1928 hit "How Long Blues," which gained even more popularity after Big Joe Turner recorded his version of this Blues classic.
18. William Manuel Johnson also organized, in 1917, the Original Creole Band.
19. See Donald Bogle's *Toms, Coons, Mulattoes, Mammies, and Bucks* for a discussion of black film and "social problem" films in the 1930s and 1940s. See also Phyllis Klotman's essay on Wallace Thurman's stint in Hollywood: "The Black Writer in Hollywood, Circa 1930: The Case of Wallace Thurman."
20. Others, including Cab Calloway, Lionel Hampton, and Dizzy Gillespie, were well known for similarly entertaining stagecraft, which some musicians as well as others found offensive.
21. David Levering Lewis discusses this aspect of the Cotton Club in his *When Harlem Was in Vogue* (105–6, 170–74).
22. William "Big Bill" Lee Conley Broonzy was asked to perform in the 1938 concert as a replacement for Robert Johnson, who had just died.
23. Thadious Davis in her substantial biography of Larsen provides scholars of the Harlem Renaissance with a detailed analysis of Nella Larsen and the issues that shape her writing (6). Davis takes a very different view on Larsen's genealogy than does Charles R. Larson in his biographical essay.
24. Lott critiques what he terms the "revisionist corrective . . . inaugurated by Frederick Douglass"; this "corrective" presents minstrelsy as inauthentic and racist. Lott argues that this view does not recognize the "productive" moments of minstrelsy, which combine with the racist and regressive moments.
25. Dunbar's comments on sadness and on experiencing sadness resonate something of John Keats's sentiments in "Ode on Melancholy." While Dunbar's stance on this sadness is ironic, he does suggest that the people in the Banner Club are involved in feeling this emotion in ways that others may not. The problem seems to be that they have few other options.
26. This is clearly a critique of the attitudes that Larsen likely witnessed during her stays at Tuskegee and Fisk Universities.
27. Deborah McDowell in her article "The 'Nameless . . . Shameless Impulse': Sexuality in Nella Larsen's *Quicksand* and *Passing*," collected in *"The Changing Same,"* perceptively discusses this cabaret passage as a point at which Helga's sexual conflicts are expressed completely. The presence of Dr. Anderson and the descriptions of the Jazz music point to Larsen's continued focus on race and gender in this passage.
28. Perry reads Helga as a character who seeks sexual fulfillment, and as a middle-class black female character such desires are rarely acknowledged

in literature, a point Hazel Carby supports in *Reconstructing Womanhood*. Carby states that Helga is "the first truly sexual black female protagonist in Afro-American fiction" (174). For Perry then this makes Helga "one of the more interesting creations found in the Harlem Renaissance novels" (74). While I believe that Helga wants sexual fulfillment, throughout most of the novel she represses that desire and by the end gains her desire in a quite unfortunate manner. Hence, on this point, Cheryl Wall in *Women of the Harlem Renaissance*, Hortense Thornton in "Sexism as Quagmire," as well as I read Helga substantially differently from Perry and Carby in terms of her expressions of sexual desire.

29. Cheryl Wall suggests that Dvořák's "Going Home" would have been a better musical impetus for Helga's longing for Harlem. Wall also reads the undertones of "Swing Low" within the useful context of appropriation and power. For this scholar, Helga "honors the source." I, however, view Helga's reaction to the music as a response that situates this character within an essentialist position, as Larsen uses the music to connect Helga to her father's heritage, yet the music is outside the father's culture.

30. Although *Quicksand* is not a novel about passing, Larsen uses a number of the conventions from passing novels to develop her story. Helga's return to Harlem is consistent with the treatment of passing in twentieth-century novels by black writers such as Jessie Fauset in *Plum Bun* as well as Larsen in her novel titled *Passing*. African American writers tend to subvert the tragic aspects of their characters' dual heritage and return them to an African American cultural environment. A notable exception among black writers who wrote passing novels is James Weldon Johnson; in his short novel *The Autobiography of an Ex-Colored Man*, Johnson does not have his main character return to an African American cultural environment, although Johnson does subvert the notion that living in a white cultural environment is a full gain for his dual-heritage character. Nineteenth-century white writers such as Mark Twain and George Washington Cable, however, promulgated the notion that their dual-heritage characters are somehow tragic, even if these writers critique the social policies that cause the supposed tragedy for their characters. In the twentieth century, William Faulkner's *Light in August* continues the theme of the unfortunate aspects of dual heritage. Hazel Carby in *Reconstructing Womanhood* discusses the issue of the biracial character in African American fiction as an extension of a literary practice that "enabled the exploration in fiction of relations which were socially proscribed" (171). She disagrees with Barbara Christian's assessment of the role of the biracial character as a strategy for gaining sympathy from white audiences, especially white female audiences (88–90).

31. For Margaret Perry (76) and David Levering Lewis (232), Helga's marriage is unconvincing; Amritjit Singh, however, views Helga's retreat to religion as plausible (101), and Cheryl Wall believes that Larsen presents "a caricature of the religious aspects of the culture" (113).
32. Hazel Carby in *Reconstructing Womanhood* argues that the birth of Helga's last child signals this character's "certain death" (174).
33. For an important critique of traditional perspectives on the Blues, see Ann Ducille's "Blues Notes on Black Sexuality: Sex and the Texts of Jessie Fauset and Nella Larsen." Ducille's critique is especially poignant in its rejection of the "blues as sexual signifier" (423), but she also brings a valuable critical perspective on the question of valorizing the Blues as the "grand signifier of *the* black experience" (420).
34. See Henry Louis Gates Jr.'s *Signifying Monkey* for a full discussion of the uses of signifying in vernacular and literary culture.
35. See Eric Lott's *Love and Theft: Blackface Minstrelsy and the American Working Class*. Lott rejects the notion that minstrelsy imposes negative stereotypes on black people and that its images are always detrimental.

3. These (Blackness of Blackness) Blues

The song "These Blues" was written and recorded by Charles Brown in 1995 (*Charles Brown: These Blues*, Verve 523022).

1. In the 1940s and 1950 writers such as Richard Wright in *Savage Holiday* (1954), Gwendolyn Brooks in *Annie Allen* (1949), Zora Neale Hurston in *Seraph on the Suwanee* (1948), Ann Petry in *Country Place* (1947), and James Baldwin in *Giovanni's Room* (1956) respond to this social policy in the publishing industry. In the 1950s Chester Himes recast his autobiographical novel with white characters and titled it *Cast the First Stone* (1953). Himes's novel has been reissued under the title Himes eventually decided on, and the expurgated parts were restored. Other writers, such as Willard Motley and Frank Yerby, wrote novels with either white central characters or a broad ethnic mix of characters.
2. Robin D. G. Kelley discusses the Double V in his book *Hammer and Hoe*.
3. Petry indicates that Boots may have contrived to gain a 4-F classification in order to avoid military service. Malcolm X, in his *Autobiography of Malcolm X*, also tells how he and others avoided service in the military in the 1940s.
4. Lerone Bennett in *Confrontation: Black and White* addresses this historical moment as a period of naïveté on the part of African Americans (169–70).
5. See Donald Bogle's *Toms, Coons, Mulattoes, Mammies, and Bucks* for a detailed discussion of blacks in film and the "problem film."
6. See Scott De Veaux's *Birth of Bebop* for a fuller discussion of this issue.

7. Marian McPartland's 1980 essay "The Untold Story of the International Sweethearts of Rhythm" provides useful information on this important female Jazz group, which was formed in 1938 at the Piney Woods Country Life School located near Jackson, Mississippi. They performed, with varying personnel, nationally and internationally until 1948.
8. Mexican Americans protested police intimidation in their neighborhoods following false accusations of murder against twenty-three Chicanos in 1942. This emotional climate fueled more outbreaks after a mob of sailors attacked a Chicano in a theater in 1943. For several days following this attack, and in response to the subsequent outbreaks of resistance from Mexican Americans, mobs of sailors, soldiers, and marines as well as some civilians targeted young men in zoot suits and attacked them. These racially motivated attacks point to the racial anxiety of those European Americans who feared the darkening of the demographics in the area.
9. The swing and cool Jazz sounds of Chet Baker, Paul Whiteman, Benny Goodman, Paul Desmond, Miles Davis (whose musical breadth spans bebop through rap), Stan Getz, Gerry Mulligan, Lennie Tristano, Bill Evans, Dave Brubeck comprise just a few of the musicians in this group.
10. Lee Morgan's album *Sidewinder* was released in 1963.
11. Hurston's "muck" is a black cultural space describing southern itinerant life.
12. See Jacques Derrida's discussion of general iterability in "'This Strange Institution Called Literature': An Interview with Jacques Derrida"; this interview is published in Derek Attridge's *Jacques Derrida: Acts of Literature*. Attridge's view on Derrida's concept of iterability is that it is "the necessary repeatability of an item experienced as meaningful, which at the same time can never be repeated exactly since it has no essence that could remain unaffected by the potentially infinite contexts . . . into which it could be grafted" (18). See also Jacques Derrida's *Limited Inc*, especially "Signature Event Context" and "Limited Inc a b c . . ." In the latter piece, sections m and n are especially applicable here.
13. Trudier Harris in her Mercer University Lamar Memorial Lecture, which was published as *The Power of the Porch: The Storyteller's Craft in Zora Neale Hurston, Gloria Naylor, and Randall Kenan*, uses the porch as a metaphor in African American literature. The porch in African American storytelling, as Harris suggests in this book, is a site that reenacts the call-and-response pattern from folk culture. It is a communal space upon which intracultural insider aspects of African American culture are exhibited. See Dolan Hubbard's *Sermon and the African American Literary Imagination* for another view of the porch in Hurston's *Their Eyes Were Watching God*.

14. Lorraine Bethel also addresses the ineffectual status of the pedestal.
15. See Ellease Southerland on the spiritual power and importance of the number nine in Hurston's novels.
16. As Cheryl Wall notes, it is interesting that Janie is the one who initiates the courtship ritual of the battleship.
17. Ralph Ellison presents a riff on this line from Hunter's song in his well-known essay "The World and the Jug" in which he responds to Irving Howe's critique of Ellison's novel in favor of Richard Wright's *Native Son*.
18. Hurston's "mah tongue is in mah friend's mouf" recalls Walt Whitman in "Song of Myself."
19. Robert Stepto argues that Janie's voice never asserts its authority over and in the novel; he further suggests that Hurston was unable to give "Janie her voice outright" (166). While my discussion of this novel does not focus on this issue, I would aver that Janie's dispersed voice—in Phoeby, who will tell others—is a direct critique of the notion of authoritative voices such as Joe Starks's, which tyrannized Janie. Hence, the last thing that Hurston would have Janie do is to become that against which she has struggled to escape. Mary Helen Washington's Position that the novel presents women's exclusion from the power of the word addresses an important aspect of the novel, yet Washington does not acknowledge Hurston's revision of the ways in which that power should be employed. Washington believes that the novel leaves Janie without a voice. Instead, I would say, Janie's voice is potentially everywhere in Eatonville, and perhaps beyond.
20. For further implications on Petry's allusions to Benjamin Franklin and his Junto, including an incisive discussion of Franklin's model of the "self-made man" as one that was "never intended to include women or black men," see Marjorie Pryse's essay "'Pattern against the Sky': Deism and Motherhood in Ann Petry's *The Street*" (118).
21. In an essay titled "Ann Petry's Demythologizing of American Culture and Afro-American Culture," Bernard Bell presents a similar discussion of Lutie's materialist dreams (108–9).
22. See Hilary Holladay on Wright's influence on Petry's novel (63).
23. Murray reminds us that Ellison, in "Richard Wright's Blues," places Wright's autobiographical *Black Boy* in the same category that Murray ascribes to Ellison, thus making Wright's book the "literary equivalent of the blues" (162). Murray, however, says that "Baldwin and Wright seem to have overlooked the rich possibilities available to them in the blues tradition" (166).
24. Robert O'Meally associates this passage in the novel with a familiar African American folktale that tells a similar story and that may allude to a similar broken promise made by President George Washington (82).

25. See my discussion in chapter 4 on the operation of questions of evil within the context of Toni Morrison's novel *Sula*. There I argue that Morrison, in her novel, suggests an intracultural perspective on evil similar to that which Ellison presents.
26. A different view on Trueblood is taken by Houston Baker in his section of *Blues, Ideology and Afro-American Literature*, titled "To Move without Moving: Creativity and Commerce in Ralph Ellison's Trueblood Episode." Baker analyzes Ellison's Trueblood passage as a parodic play on Freud's mythic incest narrative and as a repetition of the Christian myth of the Fall. Hortense Spillers in "'The Permanent Obliquity of an In(pha)llibly Straight': In the Time of the Daughters and the Fathers" also discusses Ellison's Trueblood passage. Spillers addresses the question of incest in African American literature and takes the view that the incest taboo establishes a limitation on the law of the father through a process of momentary restraint, or what Spillers refers to as "a situation of blindness and overcoming" (149). I situate and focus my discussion of Ellison's Trueblood in an intracultural as well as intertextual investigation of music into literature.
27. James Baldwin uses similar imagery in "Sonny's Blues" to illustrate the paradoxical conditions of Blues life. Baldwin's narrator says, "Some escaped the trap, most didn't. Those who got out always left something of themselves behind, as some animals amputate a leg and leave it in the trap." During a cab ride through their old neighborhood, Baldwin's narrator states that he and Sonny "both were seeking that part of ourselves which had been left behind. It's always at the hour of trouble and confrontation that the missing member aches" (95).
28. James Baldwin also uses the Spiritual "Old Ship of Zion" in reference to his mature Spiritual-Gospel female character in "Sonny's Blues."
29. I take a different position than O'Meally does on this encounter between Invisible Man and Wheatstraw. O'Meally says that Ellison's narrator connects with the Blues in Wheatstraw's song (88). I, however, see Ellison's narrator as continuing to stand outside that to which he needs to make a connection.
30. In *God Sends Sunday*, a short novel by Arna Bontemps, published in 1931, he reproduces lines from this Blues song. After Lil Augie realizes that Florence Dessau is unavailable to him because she is being kept by a white man who also is Augie's boss, Augie goes home and sings this song while playing his accordion: "If you don't b'lieve I love you / Look whut a fool I been / If you don't b'lieve I'm sinkin' / Look whut a hole I'm in. / If you don't b'lieve I'm leavin' / count de days I'm gone" (37).
31. Ellison's Brotherhood sections of *Invisible Man* may reflect his own experiences with leftist organizations as well as his knowledge of his

mother's experiences with Eugene Debs's Democratic Socialist candidate for political office in Oklahoma when Ellison was a youth.

32. Robert O'Meally comments on Ellison's use of this Jazz tune in *Invisible Man* in his article on Ellison's novel (91–92).

33. For Ellison's childhood memories of Rushing, see Ellison's "Remembering Jimmy," which is collected in *Shadow and Act*. Also, Ellison's use of the name Rinehart and his term "Rinehart methods" is interesting because of its possible association with Mary Roberts Rinehart. Rinehart was a detective-story writer who used realism, humor, and unique twists to enliven her tales. She is best known for her story *The Circular Staircase*, which she and Avery Hopwood made into a play entitled *The Bat*. Rinehart's unique twist in this play—the detective who is supposed to solve the crime is actually the criminal—was later imitated in many detective stories. Ellison seems to appropriate this idea in his characterization of Rinehart in *Invisible Man*. He indicates that Rinehartism—false hope—is part of the problem. O'Meally also associates the name Rinehart with Jimmy Rushing's Blues tune. See O'Meally's "*Invisible Man*: Black and Blue" (90). See also Robert E. Fleming's discussion of Rinehart as an outlaw-trickster figure (430). Then there also is the Jazz musician Django Reinhardt, and within the context of Ellison's multiple signifying style, Reinhardt the Belgian Jazz guitarist also may be suggested by Ellison's character.

34. In "Change the Joke and Slip the Yoke," an essay responding to Stanley Hyman, Ellison discusses Rinehart as another version of "his grandfather's cryptic advice" (*Shadow and Act* 57).

35. Ellison explains the grandfather's approach in "Change the Joke and Slip the Yoke" (56). Ellison refers to this approach as "a kind of jiujitsu of the spirit, a denial and rejection through agreement."

4. Dizzy Atmosphere

"Dizzy Atmosphere" is the title of a piece written by John Birks "Dizzy" Gillespie (*Oscar Peterson and Dizzy Gillespie*, Pablo Records PACD-2310-740-2).

1. See Clayborne Carson's *In Struggle: SNCC and the Black Awakening of the 1960s* for a full discussion of SNCC and its association with the Black Panther Party as well as the phrase "Black Power." Carmichael's use of this term results from the influence of Willie Ricks a SNCC colleague of Carmichael's (208–11).
2. The MFDP was established in 1964 in Jackson, Mississippi.
3. Julian Bond's similarly integrated delegation from Georgia failed in its attempt to unseat an all-white delegation from that state in 1964.
4. See Suzanne Smith's *Dancing in the Street: Motown and the Cultural Politics of Detroit*.

5. This song was not recorded until 1963.
6. Syl Johnson repeats Joe Tex's theme and style in his 1968 "I'll Take Those Skinny Legs"
7. Interestingly, Berrett begins his discussion of Morrison's "literary jazz" by focusing on *The Bluest Eye;* he skips *Sula* and moves to *Song of Solomon* and then *Tar Baby.*
8. August Wilson's play about Ma Rainey—*Ma Rainey's Black Bottom*—connects her to the black bottom as both a song and a dance.
9. See Derrida's ". . . That Dangerous Supplement . . ." in Derek Attridge's *Jacques Derrida.*
10. While, for me, the writer of a piece of literature is not necessarily the final arbiter for all that actually occurs in a text, the writer's position must weigh in among others that are available. In a 1976 interview with Robert Stepto, which is published in *Chant of Saints,* Morrison comments on the question of Sula as evil. Morrison says that she wants to complicate the concepts of good and evil. She also points out that Sula "never does anything as bad as her grandmother or her mother did" (218). Morrison also addresses the issue of evil in an interview with Bettye J. Parker in *Sturdy Black Bridges.* Morrison tells Parker that the approach to evil among black people "is what preoccupied" her in *Sula:* "We try to avoid it or defend ourselves against it but we are not surprised at its existence or horrified or outraged" (253). Morrison also tells Parker that she likes both characters—Nel because she gets things done yet gets no recognition, Sula because she lives in the moment. Naana Banyiwa-Horne in "The Scary Face of the Self" recognizes that "Morrison's depiction of . . . [Sula] makes it difficult to dismiss her as purely evil," as too many readers recognize her within themselves. Yet Banyiwa-Horne takes the view that Sula is the "darker side" of Nel, since Sula's "attitude toward life" embodies "amorality" (28, 30–31). Banyiwa-Horne further points out that others in the Bottom desire to engage in similar transgressions, yet they are restrained by their fear of ostracism. Again, Sula's surface-level behavior is not too different from that of Eva and Hannah, but these women are not ostracized. There must be something different about Sula that disturbs this community's comfort level. These, I believe, are the complicating issues that Morrison presents in the novel as I discuss it. Keith Byerman in *Fingering the Jagged Grain* agrees with Banyiwa-Horne as they both take the position that by the standards of the people in the Bottom, Sula is evil (Byerman 199; Banyiwa-Horne 29). Yet Morrison presents a similar critique of unfortunate community attitudes in her short novel *The Bluest Eye.* Sula then is not evil, just as Pecola isn't, as she is situated within the novel's logic. Perhaps, one might argue, the people in the Bottom erroneously believe that Sula is evil, and

Morrison portrays their error in her novel. See also Angela Davis's *Blues Legacies*. In this book she addresses the question of Satan—a representative of evil—as a trickster in African American Blues culture. Davis takes as her example the bluesman Robert Johnson (123, 379). Another bluesman trickster figure is found in Peter Wheastraw/William Bunch, whom Ellison uses in *Invisible Man* as a Blues philosophy guide for his nameless and invisible narrator.

11. My view of evil in Morrison's novel is distinctly different from Martin's view that Morrison's black characters in the Bottom "come to celebrate 'evil' as a good." Again, I believe that Morrison presents evil within the philosophy of her Blues People as a very complicated and subtly nuanced issue. Odette Martin's article takes an intriguing view of Morrison's novel. She argues a number of concerns, including the potential difficulty of Morrison's "attack" on the literature of uplift, which Martin suggests that Morrison views as a *"failure"* of the "rational" (37), and Martin takes Morrison's novel as "an allegory of Black literary history" (37). Martin views the characters in *Sula* as allegories of actual New Negro/Harlem Renaissance persons. In the Deweys, for instance, Martin sees the "three big guns of the New Negro movement" (38). And in Shadrack she sees "historical orgins" of the Harlem Renaissance in 1919.

12. In "The Scary Face of the Self: An Analysis of the Character of Sula in Toni Morrison's *Sula*," Naana Banyiwa-Horne takes a position similar to mine on the connection between readers' as well as Morrison's other characters' responses to Sula and Norton's response to Trueblood in Ellison's *Invisible Man*. We, however, come to very different conclusions about the operations of these elements in both novels.

13. Morrison's use of the Deweys suggests an oblique allusion to bebop musician Miles Davis, though this is hard to determine as there is nothing in the novel to confirm that Morrison's Deweys have a direct connection to Jazz music at all. They only illustrate her use in this novel of literary Jazz philosophy in the Bottom.

14. Davis's position is that post-emancipation blueswomen as well as black people in general valued the ability to control their familial as well as their sexual lives, which had been restricted when they were enslaved. Davis argues that sexuality was one thing that the post–Civil War system of exclusion could not easily control.

15. Angela Davis in her study of Ma Rainey, Bessie Smith, and Billie Holiday describes some of the characteristics that comprise the lives of blueswomen in similar terms that I use to discuss Jazz characters: mobility, liberated sexuality, rejection of bourgeois values. Davis's study presents the behavior of actual Blues singers. In this investigation of a discourse of music-into-literature, Blues and Jazz characters in fiction take their

definition from a Blues or Jazz aesthetic or philosophy as it is collected in the social, historical, and political construction of the music, which includes but is not necessarily based in the lives of the musicians.

16. In *The Blue Devils of Nada*, Murray discusses the impact Blues has had on the United States—as an influence on music, focusing on Ellington, Basie, and Armstrong; as an influence on art, emphasizing Romare Bearden; and as an influence on literature, concentrating on Hemingway. Murray argues that F. Scott Fitzgerald's position as Jazz writer is unwarranted and that Hemingway "qualifies as an honorary Blues musician precisely because he was always writing Blues stories without ever trying to do so. Murray's assessment of Hemingway results from Murray's emphasis on the heroic aspects in the Blues, which Murray discusses in his book *The Hero and the Blues*. Hemingway, in Murray's terms, "came to represent in fiction that fundamental aspect of the contemporary U.S. sensibility that the blues expresses in music" (216). While I find Murray's argument about Hemingway intriguing, I would not talk about Hemingway's writing in the same terms.

17. This perspective on the briarpatch also is addressed by Eleanor Traylor in Frye's "How to Think Black." Robert Stepto's African American "ritual ground" refers to a similar concept, which Stepto defines as a social as well as a cultural space "redefined in some measure by" African Americans (68).

18. See Angela Davis in *Blues Legacies,* Hazel Carby in "It Jus Be's Dat Way Sometime," and Daphne Duval Harrison in *Black Pearls* for other discussions of this issue.

19. Post–Civil War northward migration of black people and postwar migration in the 1920s mark the first two large waves of migration among African Americans.

20. The various spellings for Rainey's song often obliterate the meaning of her phrase "C.C. Rider," which refers to chitlin (or sometimes chicken) circuit, a reference to the meals that were regularly served to itinerant musicians or even preachers who frequently passed through various towns, often leaving disappointed women along the way.

21. In June 1969, this Smokey Robinson song, performed by Smokey Robinson and the Miracles, was number eight on the pop charts; the inspirational "Oh Happy Day," sung by the Edwin Hawkins Singers was number three.

5. Jazz Me Blues

The song "Jazz Me Blues" was first recorded by Lucille Hegamin in 1920 and later recorded by the Count Basie Band (*Jazz Collector Edition: Count Basie*, LaserLight MC 79 704).

1. See Henry Louis Gates Jr.'s important book *The Signifying Monkey* for more on signifying in African American vernacular culture.
2. Of course, the question of who extends or borrows from whom is complicated, as Gershwin's borrowing from black musicians is well known, and his frequent visits uptown as witnessed by Fats Waller and other musicians is well documented. Gershwin's "I Got Rhythm" is a case in point. The melody in this tune repeats musical phrases from William Grant Still's *Afro-American Symphony;* these phrases are ones Still had used regularly on stage and in his improvisations. Additionally, anyone familiar with Gershwin's musical adaptation—*Porgy and Bess*—of the white playwright DuBose Heyward's Broadway play *Porgy* will recognize strains of "Sometimes I Feel Like a Motherless Child" in the Gershwin tune "Summertime." Parker has, perhaps, taken this music back and applied his bebop contemporary Thelonious Monk's clarion call to create music that they can't play—music that can't be mass produced and copied by anyone with a rudimentary knowledge of it. See Samuel A. Floyd's *Black Music in the Harlem Renaissance*.
3. See Donald Bogle's *Toms, Coons, Mulattoes, Mammies, and Bucks* for a discussion of Ethel Waters's early film career (118).
4. Kimberly Benston discusses chaos and Jazz in his enlightening essay "Late Coltrane: A Re-membering of Orpheus."
5. This approach to Jazz characters is found in Toni Morrison's title character Sula, Ralph Ellison's Rinehart in *Invisible Man*, and John Edgar Wideman's Albert Wilkes and Brother Tate in *Sent for You Yesterday*.

Appendix

Tracking down recording and creative attribution data on Spiritual-Gospel and Blues, in particular, and in many ways Jazz as well, is a daunting task, as anyone who has researched this music knows. The appropriation of riffs, communal songs, traveling phrases from Blues, and wandering verses from the Spirituals as personal property is widespread in the history of this music; and, at a certain level, the widespread use (though not ownership), by anyone with the desire, of all of these elements of the music is central to the aesthetic of this music, especially when we consider the close ties to oral roots that we find in Spiritual-Gospel, Blues, and Jazz. By adding "usually attr. to" or "often attr. to" to some titles I have indicated that these titles are traditionally attributed to a particular writer. What I am attempting to point to in these cases is that there is some indication that the song or tune may have been in circulation within the culture prior to the point at which a particular lyricist or composer claimed legal rights or before a performer circulated the song or tune through recording. I have included publication dates for the songs and compositions for which I could locate this information. Although I have attempted to locate the most accurate information available to me, I am sure that somewhere I have gone amiss.

1. Paul Laurence Dunbar's novel was published in 1902, prior to the date of the first published Blues, "Baby Seals Blues," in 1912 and prior to the release of the first recorded Blues, "Crazy Blues," in 1921. The year after Dunbar's novel was published is also the year the first ragtime band, lead by Wilbur Sweatman, was recorded. This means that Dunbar's use of references to ragtime and Blues in his novel most likely draws from the oral culture with which he had some knowledge rather than from recordings. Dunbar quotes at least five Blues songs, yet at the time he published *The Sport of the Gods* he could not have heard them on recordings or purchased the sheet music.
2. Thurman's reference to whipping it to a "jelly" could refer to numerous songs in which this traveling phrase and the ideas it suggests occur.
3. The traveling phrase "a yellow girl rides in an automobile/(limousine)" typically provides a call for the response "a black girl rides on a mule/(in an old hay wagon); she's getting by just the same." This is a traveling phrase or set piece in a number of Blues songs. Henry Thomas's recording in 1929 presents an early version of this traveling phrase, but "Black Gal Swing" by Son Bonds (a.k.a. Sleepy John Estes), recorded in 1941, powerfully demonstrates the sense of this Blues phrase.
4. Charlie Campbell recorded "Going Away Blues" in 1937, the same year Hurston's novel was published.
5. In *The Street* Ann Petry refers to this as a swing tune. I have been unable to locate this tune in any source with which I am familiar.
6. The traveling phrase "she had feet like a monkey" or some version of it is found in a number of Blues songs, including this one by Jefferson.
7. Ellison's reference to "St. Louis Mammy" is perhaps his satiric variation on Handy's "St. Louis Blues."
8. Ellison's "bread and wine" refers, of course, to a popular Christian motif found in a number of hymns, including Helen E. Fromm's "Trial of the Cross (This Do in Remembrance of Me)," which was published in 1953, just after the publication of Ellison's novel.
9. Ellison uses this theme from the traditional Spiritual, which John Wesley Work III collected in his book *American Negro Songs*. This idea is repeated in William G. Fischer and E. Johnson's similarly titled hymn "The Rock that Is Higher Than I," and in William Cushings and Ira D. Sankey's hymn "Hiding in Thee."
10. According to Eileen Southern in *Readings in Black American Music*, Thomas Wentworth Higginson made a written record of the songs he heard sung by the black soldiers in the Union army during the Civil

War; Higginson published these songs first in 1867, then in 1870. Higginson collected three different versions of "The Old Ship of Zion."
11. Ellison's use of the traveling phrase "if I don't think I'm sinking, look what hole I'm in" was very likely familiar to him from Kokomo Arnold's "Head Cuttin' Blues," which was recorded in 1937, or maybe from Louise Johnson's "All Night Blues," which was recorded in 1930. But the Memphis Jug Band's 1928 version appears to be the earliest instance of this phrase on a recording.
12. Murray's reference to visiting Madame Ruth may be his variation on a theme from Handy's "St. Louis Blues."
13. This song is in the Amos and Andy movie *Check and Double Check* (1930), Freeman Gosden's (Amos as well as Kingfish on the radio production) and Charles Correll's (Andy on the radio production) notorious blackface film. Correll and Gosden gathered an all-black cast for the television series, which ran from 1951 to 1966.
14. There are so many Blues tunes that use the "shaking peaches from trees" traveling phrase that I find it difficult to assign any one of them to Wideman's riff.
15. There are a plethora of train Blues, especially lonesome train Blues. Vinson's version seems the most powerful for the situation in *Sent for You Yesterday*.
16. Thelonious Monk's tune "Round About Midnight" was recorded by two Jazz musicians before Monk recorded the tune in 1947. Cootie Williams recorded "Round About Midnight" in 1944, and Dizzy Gillespie recorded this tune in 1946.
17. The numerous rambling Blues that use the traveling phrase "didn't he ramble" make it difficult to select one tune for this riff. Other possibilities include Robert Johnson's "Ramblin' on My Mind" or Alberta Hunter's "I've Got a Mind to Ramble."
18. The traveling phrase "blues falling down like rain/hail/showers of rain" is repeated in many Blues songs, most notably in Robert Johnson's "Hell Hound on My Trail" (1937).
19. There is a version of this song in the *Gospel Pearls*, which is attributed to Jeremiah E. Rankin and William G. Tomer; the Dorsey and Hutchins version is in *Songs of Zion*.

WORKS CITED AND CONSULTED

Works Cited

Albert, Richard N. "The Jazz-Blues Motif in James Baldwin's 'Sonny's Blues.'" *College Literature* 11 (1984): 178–85.

Armstrong, Louis. "Black and Blue." *Jazz Collector Edition*. MC 79 700, 1967.

Attridge, Derek, ed. *Jacques Derrida: Acts of Literature*. New York: Routledge, 1992.

Baker, Houston A., Jr. *Blues, Ideology, and Afro-American Literature: A Vernacular Theory*. Chicago: U of Chicago P, 1984.

———. *Modernism and the Harlem Renaissance*. Chicago: U of Chicago P, 1987.

Bakhtin, Mikhail. *The Dialogic Imagination*. Austin: U of Texas P, 1981.

Baldwin, James. "Many Thousands Gone." *Notes of a Native Son*. 1955. Boston: Beacon, 1984. 24–45.

———. "Sonny's Blues." *Going to Meet the Man*. New York: Laurel, 1965. 86–122.

Banyiwa-Horne, Naana. "The Scary Face of the Self: An Analysis of the Character of Sula in Toni Morrison's *Sula*." *Sage* 2.1 (1985): 28–31.

Baraka, Amiri [Leroi Jones]. "African Slaves/American Slaves: Their Music." 1963. *The LeRoi Jones/Amiri Baraka Reader*. Ed. William J. Harris. New York: Thunder's Mouth, 1991. 21–33.

———. *Black Music*. New York: Quill, 1967.

———. *Blues People / . . . /: Negro Music in White America*. 1963. New York: Morrow, 1980.

Barthes, Roland. "Theory of the Text." *Untying the Text: A Post-Structuralist Reader*. Ed. Robert Young. Boston: Routledge, 1981.

Bell, Bernard. "Ann Petry's Demythologizing of American Culture and Afro-American Culture." *Conjuring: Black Women, Fiction, and Literary Tradition*.

Ed. Marjorie Pryse and Hortense J. Spillers. Bloomington: Indiana UP, 1985. 105–15.

Bennett, Lerone. *Confrontation: Black and White.* 1965. Baltimore: Penguin, 1966.

Benston, Kimberly W. "Tragic Aspects of the Blues." *Phylon* 36 (1975): 164–76.

Berrett, Anthony J. "Toni Morrison's Literary Jazz." *CLAJ* 32 (1989): 267–83.

Bethel, Lorraine. "'This Infinity of Conscious Pain': Zora Neale Hurston and the Black Female Literary Tradition." *All the Women Are White, All the Blacks Are Men, but Some of Us Are Brave.* Ed. Gloria T. Hull et al. Old Westbury, NY: Feminist Press, 1982.

Bluestein, Gene. "The Blues as Literary Theme." *Massachusetts Review* 8 (1967): 596–617.

Bogle, Donald. *Toms, Coons, Mulattoes, Mammies, and Bucks: An Interpretive History of Blacks in American Film.* New expanded ed. New York: Continuum, 1993.

Bontemps, Arna. *God Sends Sunday.* New York: AMS, 1931.

Braithwaite, Deborah Willis. *Van Der Zee: Photographer, 1886–1983.* New York: Harry N. Abrams, 1993.

Braithwaite, William Stanley. "The Negro in American Literature." *Black Expression: Essays by and about Black Americans in the Creative Arts.* Ed. Addison Gayle Jr. New York: Weybright and Talley, 1969. 169–81.

Byerman, Keith E. *Fingering the Jagged Grain: Tradition and Form in Recent Black Fiction.* Athens: U of Georgia P, 1985.

Carby, Hazel. "It Jus Be's Dat Way Sometime: The Sexual Politics of Women's Blues." *Feminisms: An Anthology of Literary Theory and Criticism.* Ed. Robyn Warhol and Diane Price Herndl. New Brunswick, NJ: Rutgers UP, 1991. 746–758.

———. *Race Men.* Cambridge, MA: Harvard UP, 1998.

———. *Reconstructing Womanhood.* New York: Oxford UP, 1987.

Carson, Clayborne. *In Struggle: SNCC and the Black Awakening of the 1960s.* 1981. Cambridge, MA: Harvard UP, 1995.

Chesnutt, Charles W. "The Goophered Grapevine." *The Conjure Woman.* Ann Arbor: U of Michigan P, 1969. 1–35.

Christian, Barbara. "Trajectories of Self-Definition: Placing Contemporary Afro-American Fiction." *Conjuring: Black Women, Fiction, and Literary Tradition.* Ed. Marjorie Pryse and Hortense J. Spillers. Bloomington: Indiana UP, 1985. 233–48.

Crawford, Richard, and Jeffrey Magee, comps. *Jazz Standards on Record, 1900–1942: A Core Repertory.* Chicago: CBMR, 1992.

Cullen, Countee. "Yet Do I Marvel." *The Norton Anthology of African American Literature.* Ed. Henry Louis Gates Jr. and Nellie Y. McKay. New York: Norton, 1997. 1305.

Dahl, Linda. *Stormy Weather: The Music and Lives of a Century of Jazzwomen.* 1984. New York: Limelight, 1996.

Davis, Angela Y. *Blues Legacies and Black Feminism: Gertrude "Ma" Rainey, Bessie Smith, and Billie Holiday.* New York: Pantheon, 1998.

Davis, Charles T. *Black Is the Color of the Cosmos: Essays on Afro-American Literature and Culture, 1942–1981.* New York: Garland, 1982. Ed. Henry Louis Gates Jr. Washington, DC: Howard UP, 1989.

Davis, Thadious M. *Nella Larsen: Novelist of the Harlem Renaissance, a Woman's Life Unveiled.* Baton Rouge: Louisiana State UP, 1994.

DeCosta-Willis, Miriam, ed. *The Memphis Diary of Ida B. Wells.* Boston: Beacon, 1995.

Derrida, Jacques. *Limited Inc.* Evanston: Northwestern UP, 1988.

De Veaux, Scott. *The Birth of Bebop: A Social and Musical History.* Berkeley: U of California P, 1997.

Dickie, Margaret, and Thomas Travisano, eds. *Gendered Modernisms: American Women Poets and Their Readers.* Philadelphia: U of Pennsylvania P, 1996.

Dickinson, Emily. "Tell all the Truth but tell it slant." *The Complete Poems of Emily Dickinson.* Ed. Thomas H. Johnson. Boston: Little, Brown, 1960.

Douglass, Frederick. *Narrative of the Life of Frederick Douglass An American Slave: Written by Himself.* 1845. New York: Signet-NAL, 1968.

Du Bois, W. E. B. *The Souls of Black Folk.* 1903. Introd. John Edgar Wideman. 1990. Notes. Nathan Huggins. New York: Vintage-Random, 1990.

Ducille, Ann. "Blues Notes on Black Sexuality: Sex and the Text of Jessie Fauset and Nella Larsen." *Journal of the History of Sexuality* 3 (1993): 418–44.

Dunbar, Paul Laurence. *The Complete Poems of Paul Laurence Dunbar.* 1896. New York: Dodd, 1913.

———. *The Sport of the Gods.* Miami: Mnemosyne, 1969.

Ellison, Ralph. *Invisible Man.* New York: Vintage-Random, 1952.

———. *Shadow and Act.* New York: Random, 1953.

Fleming, Robert E. "Ellison's Black Archetypes: The Founder, Bledsoe, Ras, and Rinehart." *CLAJ* 32 (1988/89): 426–32.

———. *Willard Motley.* Boston: Twayne, 1978.

Floyd, Samuel A., Jr., ed. *Black Music in the Harlem Renaissance: A Collection of Essays.* Knoxville: U of Tennessee P, 1990.

Fordham, John. *Jazz: History, Instruments, Musicians, Recordings.* New York: Dorling Kindersley, 1993.

Foucault, Michel. *The Archaeology of Knowledge* and "The Discourse on Language." 1969. 1971. New York: Pantheon, 1972.

Franklin, Benjamin. *The Autobiography of Benjamin Franklin.* Boston: Bedford, 1993.

Frow, John. "Intertextuality and Ontology." *Intertextuality: Theories and Practices.* Ed. Michael Worton and Judith Still. Manchester, Eng.: Manchester UP, 1990. 45–55.

Gates, Henry Louis, Jr. *The Signifying Monkey: A Theory of African-American Literary Criticism.* New York: Oxford UP, 1988.

———. "*Their Eyes Were Watching God:* Hurston and the Speakerly Text." *Zora Neale Hurston: Critical Perspectives Past and Present.* Ed. Henry Louis Gates Jr. and K. A. Appiah. New York: Amistad, 1993. 154–203.

Gatewood, Willard B. *Aristocrats of Color: The Black Elite, 1880–1920.* Bloomington: Indiana UP, 1990.

Green, Mildred Denby. *Black Women Composers: A Genesis.* Boston: Twayne, 1983.

Greenblatt, Stephen. *Shakespearean Negotiations.* Berkeley: U of California P, 1988.

Griffin, Farah Jasmine. *"Who Set You Flowing?": The African American Migration Narrative.* New York: Oxford UP, 1995.

Harris, Trudier. *Exorcising Blackness: Historical and Literary Lynching and Burning Rituals.* Bloomington: Indiana UP, 1984.

———. *The Power of the Porch: The Storyteller's Craft in Zora Neale Hurston, Gloria Naylor, and Randall Kenan.* Athens: U of Georgia P, 1996.

Harris, William J. *The Poetry and Poetics of Amiri Baraka: The Jazz Aesthetic.* Columbia: U of Missouri P, 1985.

Harrison, Daphne Duval. *Black Pearls: Blues Queens of the 1920s.* New Brunswick, NJ: Rutgers UP, 1988.

Hattenhauer, Darryl. "Verbal and Musical Rhetoric in James Baldwin's 'Sonny's Blues.'" *Estudos Anglo-Americanos* 9–11 (1985): 1–7.

Henderson, Stephen. *Understanding the New Black Poetry: Black Speech and Black Music as Poetic References.* New York: Morrow, 1973.

Hogue, W. Lawrence. *Race, Modernity, Postmodernity.* Albany: State U of New York P, 1996.

Holladay, Hilary. *Ann Petry.* New York: Twayne, 1996.

Hubbard, Dolan. *The Sermon and the African American Literary Imagination.* Columbia: U of Missouri P, 1994.

Huggins, Nathan Irvin. *Harlem Renaissance.* London: Oxford UP, 1971.

Hughes, Langston. *Fine Clothes to the Jew.* New York: Knopf, 1927.

———. "Jazz as Communication." *The Langston Hughes Reader.* New York: George Braziller, 1958. 492–94.

———. "Songs Called the Blues." 1940. *The Langston Hughes Reader.* New York: George Braziller, 1958. 159–61.

Hurston, Zora Neale. "Characteristics of Negro Expression." 1934. *The Sanctified Church.* Berkeley: Turtle Island, 1981. 49–68.

———. "Spirituals and Neo-Spirituals." *The Sanctified Church.* Berkeley: Turtle Island, 1981. 79–84.

———. *Their Eyes Were Watching God.* New York: Lippincott, 1937. Foreword. Sherley Anne Williams. Urbana: Illiniois–U of Illinois P, 1978.

Hutcheon, Linda. *A Poetics of Postmodernism: History, Theory, Fiction.* New York: Routledge, 1988.

Ignatiev, Noel. *How the Irish Became White.* New York: Routledge, 1995.

———. "Immigrants and Whites." *Race Traitor.* Ed. Noel Ignatiev and John Garvey. New York: Routledge, 1996. 15–23.

James, Joy. *Transcending the Talented Tenth: Black Leaders and American Intellectuals.* New York: Routledge, 1997.

Johnson, Hannibal B. *Black Wall Street: From Riot to Renaissance in Tulsa's Historic Greenwood District.* Austin, TX: Eakin, 1998.

Johnson, James Weldon. Preface. *God's Trombones: Seven Negro Sermons in Verse.* 1927. New York: Penguin, 1976. 1–11.

Johnson, James Weldon, and J. Rosamond Johnson, eds. *The Books of American Negro Spirituals: Two Volumes in One.* 1925 and 1926. New York: Da Capo, 1977.

Jones, Robert B. Introduction. *The Collected Poems of Jean Toomer.* Ed. Robert B. Jones and Margery Toomer Latimer. Chapel Hill: U of North Carolina P, 1988. ix–xxxiv.

Kalaidjian, Walter. *American Culture Between the Wars: Revising Modernism and Postmodern Critique.* New York: Columbia UP, 1993.

Kelley, Robin D. G. *Hammer and Hoe: Alabama Communists During the Great Depression.* Chapel Hill: U of North Carolina P, 1990.

Kent, George. "Ralph Ellison and Afro-American Folk and Cultural Tradition." *Ralph Ellison: A Collection of Critical Essays.* Ed. John Hersey. Englewood Cliffs, NJ: Prentice-Hall, 1974.

Klotman, Phyllis. "The Black Writer in Hollywood, Circa 1930: The Case of Wallace Thurman." *Black American Cinema.* Ed. Manthia Diawara. New York: Routledge, 1993. 80–92.

Kristeva, Julia. *Desire in Language: A Semiotic Approach to Literature and Art.* Ed. Leon S Roudiez. Trans. Thomas Gora and Alice Jardine. New York: Columbia UP, 1980.

———. Interview. "Intertextuality and Literary Interpretation." *Julia Kristeva Interviews.* Ed. Ross Mitchell Guberman. New York: Columbia UP, 1996. 188–203.

———. *Revolution in Poetic Language.* Trans. Margaret Waller. New York: Columbia UP, 1984.

Larsen, Nella. *Quicksand* and *Passing.* 1928 and 1929. Ed. and Introd. Deborah E. McDowell. New Brunswick, NJ: Rutgers UP, 1986.

Leab, Daniel. "'All Colored'—But Not Much Different: Films Made for Negro Ghetto Audiences, 1913–28." *Phylon* 36 (1975): 321–39.

Levine, Lawrence W. *Black Culture and Black Consciousness: Afro-American Folk Thought from Slavery to Freedom.* London: Oxford UP, 1977.

Lewis, David Levering. *When Harlem Was in Vogue.* 1979. New York: Oxford UP, 1981.

Lipsitz, George. *The Possessive Investment in Whiteness: How White People Profit from Identity Politics.* Philadelphia: Temple UP, 1998.

Locke, Alain, ed. *The New Negro.* 1925. Preface. Robert Hayden. New York: Atheneum, 1968.

Logan, Rayford W. *The Betrayal of the Negro: From Rutherford B. Hayes to Woodrow Wilson.* Rev. ed. London: Collier-Macmillan, 1965.

Lott, Eric. *Love and Theft: Blackface Minstrelsy and the American Working Class.* New York: Oxford UP, 1993.

Lovell, John, Jr. *Black Song: The Forge and the Flame.* 1972. New York: Paragon, 1986.

Mackey, Nathaniel. *Discrepant Engagement: Dissonance, Cross-Culturality, and Experimental Writing.* New York: Cambridge UP, 1993.

Margolick, David. *Strange Fruit: Billie Holiday, Café Society, and an Early Cry for Civil Rights.* Philadelphia: Running, 2000.

Marley, Bob. "Redemption Song." *Legend: The Best of Bob Marley and the Wailers.* Island Records, 90169-4, 1980.

Martin, Odette C. "Sula." *First World* 1.4 (1977): 35–44.

Martin, Waldo E., Jr., ed. *Brown v. Board of Education: A Brief History with Documents.* Boston: Bedford/St. Martin's, 1998.

McDowell, Deborah. *"The Changing Same": Black Women's Literature, Criticism, and Theory.* Bloomington: Indiana UP, 1995.

———, ed. *Quicksand* and *Passing.* New Brunswick, NJ: Rutgers UP, 1986.

McKay, Nellie Y. "'Crayon Enlargements of Life': Zora Neale Hurston's *Their Eyes Were Watching God* as Autobiography." *New Essays on* Their Eyes Were Watching God. Ed. Michael Awkward. New York: Cambridge UP, 1990.

McPartland, Marian. "The Untold Story of the International Sweethearts of Rhythm." 1996. *Reading Jazz: A Gathering of Autobiography, Reportage, and Criticism from 1919 to Now.* Ed. Robert Gottlieb. New York: Vintage, 1999. 638–51.

Miller, James. A. "Janie's Blues." *A Rainbow 'Round Her Shoulder.* Ed. Ruth Sheffey. Baltimore: Morgan State UP, 1982. 59–67.

Montrose, Louis. "New Historicisms." *Redrawing the Boundaries.* Ed. Stephen Greenblatt and Giles Gunn. New York: MLA, 1992. 392–418.

———. "Texts and Histories." Prologue. *The Purpose of Playing: Shakespeare and the Cultural Politics of the Elizabethan Theatre.* Chicago: U of Chicago P, 1996.

Morrison, Toni. *Playing in the Dark: Whiteness and the Literary Imagination.* Cambridge, MA: Harvard UP, 1992.

———. *Sula.* New York: NAL, 1973.

Murray, Albert. *The Blue Devils of Nada.* New York: Pantheon, 1996.

———. *The Omni Americans: Black Experience and American Culture.* New York: Da Capo, 1970.

———. *Stomping the Blues.* New York: McGraw-Hill, 1976.

———. *Train Whistle Guitar.* 1974. Boston: Northeastern UP, 1989.

Neal, Larry. "Ellison's Zoot Suit." *Ralph Ellison: A Collection of Critical Essays.* Ed. John Hersey. Englewood Cliffs, NJ: Prentice-Hall, 1974. 58–79.

Nietzsche, Friedrich. *The Genealogy of Morals.* 1887. Garden City, NY: Doubleday, 1956.

Niles, Abbe. "The Story of the Blues." *Blues: An Anthology.* 1926. Ed. W. C. Handy. New York: Da Capo, 1990. 12–45.

O'Meally, Robert, "*Invisible Man:* Black and Blue." *The Craft of Ralph Ellison.* Ed. Robert O'Meally. Cambridge, MA: Harvard UP, 1982. 78–104.

Parker, Bettye J. "Complexity: Toni Morrison's Women—An Interview Essay." *Sturdy Black Bridges: Visions of Black Women in Literature.* Ed. Roseann P. Bell et al. Garden City, NY: Anchor, 1979. 251–57.

Perry, Margaret. *Silence to the Drums: A Survey of the Literature of the Harlem Renaissance.* Westport, CT: Greenwood, 1976.

Petesch, Donald A. *A Spy in the Enemy's Country: The Emergence of Modern Black Literature.* Iowa City: U of Iowa P, 1989.

Petry, Ann. "In Darkness and Confusion." *Black Voices.* Ed. Abraham Chapman. New York: NAL, 1968.

———. *The Street.* 1946. Boston: Beacon, 1985.

Pryse, Marjorie. "'Pattern against the Sky': Deism and Motherhood in Ann Petry's *The Street.*" *Conjuring: Black Women, Fiction, and Literary Tradition.* Ed. Marjorie Pryse and Hortense J. Spillers. Bloomington: Indiana UP, 1985. 116–31.

Redding, J. Saunders. "American Negro Literature." *Black Expression: Essays by and about Black Americans in the Creative Arts.* Ed. Addison Gayle Jr. New York: Weybright and Talley, 1969. 229–39.

Reilly, John M. "'Sonny's Blues': James Baldwin's Image of Black Community." *Negro American Literature Forum* 4 (1970): 56–60.

Rice, Alan J. "Finger Snapping to Train Dancing and Back Again: The Development of Jazz Style in African American Prose." *Yearbook of English Studies* 24 (1994):105–16.

Roediger, David. *The Wages of Whiteness: Race and the Making of the American Working Class.* New York: Verso, 1991.

Russell, Michele. "Slave Codes and Liner Notes." *All the Women Are White, All the Blacks Are Men, but Some of Us Are Brave: Black Women's Studies.* Ed. Gloria T. Hull et al. Old Westbury, NY: Feminist Press, 1982. 129–40.

Samuels, Wilfred D., and Clenora Hudson-Weems. *Toni Morrison.* Boston: Twayne, 1990.

Savery, Pancho. "Baldwin, Bebop, and 'Sonny's Blues.'" *Understanding Others: Cultural and Cross Cultural Studies and the Teaching of Literature.* Ed. Joseph Trimmer and Tilly Warnock. Urbana: NCTE, 1992. 165–76.

Simawe, Saadi A., ed. *Black Orpheus: Music in African American Fiction, from the Harlem Renaissance to Toni Morrison.* New York: Garland, 2000.

Singh, Amritjit. *The Novels of the Harlem Renaissance: Twelve Black Writers, 1923–1933.* University Park: Pennsylvania State UP, 1976.

Smith, Suzanne. *Dancing in the Street: Motown and the Cultural Politics of Detroit.* Cambridge, MA: Harvard UP, 2000.

Southerland, Ellease. "The Influence of Voodoo on the Fiction of Zora Neale Hurston." *Sturdy Black Bridges: Visions of Black Women in Literature.* Ed. Roseann P. Bell et al. Garden City, NY: Anchor, 1979. 172–83.

Southern, Eileen. *The Music of Black Americans: A History.* New York: Norton, 1983.

———, ed. *Readings in Black American Music.* 2d ed. New York: Norton, 1983.

Spencer, Jon Michael. *Black Hymnody: A Hymnological History of the African American Church.* Knoxville: U of Tennessee P, 1992.

———. *The New Negroes and Their Music: The Success of the Harlem Renaissance.* Knoxville: U of Tennessee P, 1997.

Spillers, Hortense J. "'The Permanent Obliquity of an In(pha)llibly Straight': In the Time of the Daughters and the Fathers." *Changing Our Own Words.* Ed. Cheryl A. Wall. New Brunswick: Rutgers UP, 1989. 127–49.

Stepto, Robert. *From Behind the Veil: A Study of Afro-American Narrative.* Urbana: U of Chicago P, 1979.

———. "'Intimate Things in Place': A Conversation with Toni Morrison." *Chant of Saints.* Ed. Michael S. Harper and Robert B. Stepto. Urbana: U of Illinois P, 1979. 213–29.

Sullivan, Patricia. *Days of Hope: Race and Democracy in the New Deal Era.* Chapel Hill: U of North Carolina P, 1996.

Swafford, Jan. *The Vintage Guide to Classical Music.* New York: Vintage, 1993.

Tanner, Tony. "The Music of Invisibility." *Ralph Ellison: A Collection of Critical Essays.* Ed. John Hersey. Englewood Cliffs, NJ: Prentice-Hall, 1974. 80–94.

Thornton, Hortense. "Sexism as Quagmire: Nella Larsen's *Quicksand*." *CLAJ* 16 (1973): 285–301.

Thurman, Wallace. *The Blacker the Berry . . . : A Novel of Negro Life.* 1929. New York: Collier, 1970.

Titon, Jeff Todd, ed. *Downhome Blues Lyrics: An Anthology from the Post–World War II Era*. 1981. 2d ed. Urbana: U of Illinois P, 1990.

Toomer, Jean. *Cane*. 1923. Introd. Darwin T. Turner. New York: Liveright, 1975.

Turner, Darwin. Introduction. *Cane*. 1923. New York: Liveright, 1975.

TuSmith, Bonnie. *Conversations with John Edgar Wideman*. Jackson: UP of Mississippi, 1998.

Walker, Alice. Foreword. *Zora Neale Hurston: A Literary Biography*. 1977. By Robert E. Hemenway. Urbana: U of Illinois P, 1980. xi–xx.

Walker, Wyatt Tee. *"Somebody's Calling My Name": Black Sacred Music and Social Change*. Valley Forge, Pa.: Judson, 1979.

Wall, Cheryl A. *Women of the Harlem Renaissance*. Bloomington: Indiana UP, 1995.

Walton, Ortiz. "Comparative Analysis of the African and the Western Aesthetics." *The Black Aesthetic*. Ed. Addison Gayle Jr. Garden City, NY: Anchor, 1972. 154–64.

———. *Music: Black, White, and Blue: A Sociological Survey of the Use and Misuse of Afro-American Music*. New York: Morrow, 1972.

White, Walter F. *The Fire in the Flint*. 1924. New York: Negro Universities P, 1969.

———. *Rope and Faggot: A Biography of Judge Lynch*. 1928. New York: Arno, 1969.

Wideman, John Edgar. *Sent for You Yesterday*. 1983. New York: Vintage, 1988.

Williams, Sherley Anne. *Give Birth to Brightness: A Thematic Study in Neo-Black Literature*. New York: Dial, 1972.

Worton, Michael, and Jiudith Still, eds. *Intertextuality: Theories and Practices*. Manchester, Eng.: Manchester UP, 1990.

Wright, Richard. "Jazz and Desire." Interview. *Conversations with Richard Wright*. Ed. Keneth Kinnamon and Michel Fabre. Jackson: UP of Mississippi, 1993. 242–43.

———. "The Literature of the Negro in the United States." *Black Expression: Essays by and about Black Americans in the Creative Arts*. Ed. Addison Gayle Jr. New York: Weybright and Talley, 1969. 198–229.

Works Consulted

Adorno, Theodor W. "On Jazz." 1936. Trans. Jamie Owen Daniel. *Discourse* 12 (1989–90): 45–69.

———. "Perennial Fashion—Jazz." 1953. *Prism*. Eds. Samuel Weber and Shierry Weber. Cambridge, MA: MIT UP, 1983. 119.

Afolabi-Ojo, G. J. *Yoruba Culture*. N.p.: U of Ife and U of London P, 1966.

Alakija, Oluwole. "Is the African Musical?" *Negro Anthology*. Ed. Nancy Cunard. London: Wishart, 1934.

Albert, Richard N. "A Bibliography of Jazz Fiction." *Bulletin of Bibliography* 46 (1989): 129–39.

———, ed. *From Blues to Bop: A Collection of Jazz Fiction*. Baton Rouge: Louisiana State UP, 1990.

Allen, Richard. *A Collection of Spiritual Songs and Hymns Selected from Various Authors*. Philadelphia: Ormrod, 1801.

Awkward, Michael. *Inspiriting Influences*. New York: Columbia UP, 1989.

Baker, Houston A., Jr. *Afro-American Poetics: Revisions of Harlem and the Black Aesthetic*. Madison: U of Wisconsin P, 1988.

———. *Singers of Daybreak: Studies in Black American Literature*. Washington, DC: Howard UP, 1974.

Baldwin, James. "Everybody's Protest Novel." *Notes of a Native Son*. 1955. Boston: Beacon, 1983.

Bascom, Lionel C. *A Renaissance in Harlem: Lost Voices of an American Community*. New York: Bard, 1999.

Bearden, Romare, and Harry Henderson. *A History of African-American Artists: From 1792 to the Present*. New York: Pantheon, 1993.

Bell, Bernard. *The Folk Roots of Contemporary Afro-American Poetry*. Detroit: Broadside, 1974.

Bell, Roseann P., et al., eds. *Sturdy Black Bridges: Visions of Black Women in Literature*. Garden City, NY: Anchor, 1979.

Bennett, Lerone, Jr. *Before the Mayflower: A History of the Negro in America, 1616–1964*. 1962. Rev. ed. Baltimore: Penguin, 1966.

Benston, Kimberly W. "Late Coltrane: A Re-membering of Orpheus." *Chant of Saints*. Ed. Michael S. Harper and Robert B. Stepto. Urbana: U of Illinois P, 1979. 413–24.

———. *Speaking for You: The Vision of Ralph Ellison*. Washington, DC: Howard UP, 1987.

———. "Tragic Aspects of the Blues." *Phylon* 36.2 (1975): 169–81.

Berliner, Paul F. *Thinking in Jazz: The Infinite Art of Improvisation*. Chicago: U of Chicago P, 1993.

Bigsby, C. W. "The Flight of Words: The Paradox of Ralph Ellison." *The Second Black Renaissance: Essays in Black Literature*. Ed. C. W. Bigsby. Westport, CT: Greenwood, 1980.

The Black Press: Soldiers Without Swords. Prod. Stanley Nelson. Videocassette. California Newsreel, 1998.

Blake, Susan L. "Black Folklore in the Works of Ralph Ellison." *PMLA* 94 (1979): 21–35.

Boggs, Grace Lee. *Living for Change: An Autobiography*. Minneapolis: U of Minnesota P, 1998.

Breton, Marcela. *Hot and Cool Jazz Short Stories*. New York: Plume, 1990.

Brown, Sterling A. "The Blues." *Phylon* 13 (1952): 286–92.

———. *The Collected Poems of Sterling A. Brown.* Ed. Michael S. Harper. New York: Harper, 1980.

———. "Negro Folk Expression: Spirituals, Seculars, Ballads and Work Songs." *Phylon* 14 (1953): n.p.

———. "Spirituals, Blues, and Jazz: The Negro in the Lively Arts." *Tricolor* 3 (1945): 62–70.

Bontemps, Arna. "Rock, Church, Rock." *Common Ground* 3 (1942): n.p.

Borneman, Ernest. *An Anthropologist Looks at Jazz.* New York: Jazz Music Books, 1946.

———. "The Roots of Jazz." *Jazz.* Ed. Nat Hentoff and Albert J. McCarthy. New York: Rinehart, 1959. 3–20.

Bradley, David. "Black and American in 1982." *Esquire* May 1982: 60.

Brewer, J. Mason. *American Negro Folklore.* Chicago: Quadrangle Books, 1968.

Bryant, Clora, et al. *Central Avenue Sounds: Jazz in Los Angeles. 1998.* Berkeley: U of California P, 1999.

Buermeyer, Lawrence. "The Negro Spirituals and American Art." *Opportunity* 4 (1926): n.p.

Busby, Mark. *Ralph Ellison.* Boston: Twayne, 1991.

Byerman, Keith E. "Words and Music: Narrative Ambiguity in 'Sonny's Blues.'" *Studies in Short Fiction* 19 (1982): 367–72.

Campbell, James. *Talking at the Gates: A Life of James Baldwin.* New York: Viking, 1991.

Cataliotti, Robert. *The Music in African American Fiction.* New York: Garland, 1995.

Charters, Samuel. *The Bluesmen.* New York: Oak Publications, 1967.

———. *The Poetry of Blues.* New York: Avon, 1970.

———. *The Root of the Blues: An African Search.* New York: Perigree Books, 1981.

Chotzinoff, Samuel. "Jazz: A Brief History." *Vanity Fair* June 1923: n.p.

Cuney-Hare, Maud. *Negro Musicians and Their Music.* Washington, DC: Associated Publishers, 1936.

Cunningham, Virginia. *Paul Laurence Dunbar and His Song.* New York: Dodd, Mead, 1947.

Dance, Stanley. *Jazz Era: The 'Forties.* London: MacGibbon and Kee, 1961.

Davin, Tom. "Conversation with James P. Johnson." *Jazz Review* June 1959: 14–17; July 1959: 10–13.

Derrida, Jacques. *Of Grammatology.* 1967. Trans. Gayatri Chakravorty Spivak. Baltimore: Johns Hopkins UP, 1976.

Dett, R. N. *The Dett Collection of Negro Spirituals.* Chicago: Hall and McCreary, 1936.

De Veaux, Scott. *The Birth of Bebop: A Social and Musical History.* Berkeley: U of California P, 1997.

Diawara, Manthia. *Black Cinema*. New York: Routledge, 1993.
Domini, John. "A Conversation with Ishmael Reed." *American Poetry Review* 7.1 (1978): 33.
Dvořák, Antonín. "Music in America." *Harper's News Monthly* 1895: n.p.
Early, Gerald. *One Nation Under a Groove: Motown and American Culture*. Hopewell, NJ: Ecco, 1995.
Epstein, Dana. "Black Spirituals: The Emergence into Public Knowledge." *Black Music Research Journal* 10 (1990): 58–64.
Esman, A. H. "Jazz: A Study in Cultural Conflict." *American Imago* 8 (1951): 219–26.
Essien-Udom, E. U. *Black Nationalism: The Search for an Identity*. 1962. Chicago: U of Chicago P, 1995.
Europe, James Reese. "Negro's Place in Music." *New York Evening Post* 13 March 1914: n.p.
Fabre, Michel. *The Unfinished Quest of Richard Wright*. New York: William Morrow, 1973.
Feinstein, Sascha, and Yusef Komunyakaa, eds. *The Jazz Poetry Anthology*. Bloomington: Indiana UP, 1991.
Fiedler, Leslie. *Love and Death in the American Novel*. New York: Stein and Day, 1975.
Finkelstein, Sol. *Jazz: A People's Music*. New York: Citadel, 1948.
Fischer, Russell G. "Invisible Man as History." *CLAJ* 17 (1974): 338–67.
Forman, James. *The Making of Black Revolutionaries*. 1972. Illustrated ed. Seattle: U of Washington P, 1997.
Foucault, Michel. *Discipline and Punish: The Birth of the Prison*. Trans. Alan Sheridan. New York: Vintage, 1979.
Fraden, Rena. *Blueprints for a Black Federal Theatre, 1935–1939*. New York: Cambridge UP, 1996.
Frazier, E. Franklin. *Black Bourgeoisie*. New York: Collier, 1957.
———. *The Negro Church in America*. New York: Shocken Books, 1963.
Frye, Charles, et al. "How to Think Black: A Symposium on Toni Cade Bambara's *The Salt Eaters*." *Contributions in Black Studies: A Journal of African and Afro-American Studies* 6 (1983–84): 33–48.
Gabbin, Joanne V. *Sterling Brown: Building the Black Aesthetic Tradition*. Charlottesville: UP of Virginia, 1994.
Garon, Paul. *Blues and the Poetic Spirit*. 1975. Preface. Franklin Rosemont. New York: Da Capo, 1979.
Gates, Henry Louis, Jr. *Black Literature and Theory*. New York: Methuen, 1984.
Gayle, Addison Jr., ed. *The Black Aesthetic*. 1971. Garden City, NY: Anchor-Doubleday, 1972.
———, ed. *Black Expression: Essays by and about Black Americans in the Creative Arts*. New York: Weybright and Talley, 1969.

Gilroy, Paul. "Sounds Authentic: Black Music, Ethnicity, and the Challenge of a Changing Game." *Black Music Research Journal* 11 (1991): 111–35.

Gospel Pearls. Ed. and comp. Music Committee of the Sunday School Publishing Board, National Baptist Convention. Nashville: Sunday School Publishing Board, National Baptist Convention, USA, n.d.

Grant, Joanne. *Ella Baker: Freedom Bound.* New York: John Wiley, 1998.

Green, J. Ronald. *Straight Lick: The Cinema of Oscar Micheaux.* Bloomington: Indiana UP, 2000.

Gruver, Rod. "The Blues as Dramatic Monologues." *JEMF Quarterly* 6 (1970): 28–31.

———. "The Blues as Secular Religion." *Down Beat Music Annual '70.* Chicago: Maher, 1970. 24–29.

Guralnick, Peter. *Sweet Soul Music: Rhythm and Blues and the Southern Dream of Freedom.* Boston: Little Brown, 1986.

Handy, W. C., ed. *Blues: An Anthology.* 1926. New York: Da Capo, 1990.

Harlem Renaissance: Art of Black America. New York: Harry N. Abrams, 1987.

Harley, Sharon. *The Timetables of African-American History: A Chronology of the Most Important People and Events in African-American History.* New York: Simon and Schuster, 1995.

Harris, Norman. *Connecting Times: The Sixties in Afro-American Fiction.* Jackson: U of Mississippi P, 1988.

Harris, Trudier. *Black Women in the Fiction of James Baldwin.* Knoxville: U of Tennessee P, 1985.

Harrison, Max. "Charlie Parker" *Jazz.* Ed. Nat Hentoff and Albert J. McCarthy. New York: Rinehart, 1959. 277–86.

Harvey, David. *The Condition of Postmodernity: An Enquiry into the Origins of Cultural Change.* Cambridge, MA.: Basil Blackwell, 1989.

Heilbut, Anthony. "'If I Fail, You Tell the World I Tried': Reverend W. Herbert Brewster on Records." *Black Music Research Journal* (1986): 119–26.

Hemenway, Robert E. *Zora Neale Hurston: A Literary Biography.* 1977. Urbana: U of Illinois P, 1980.

Henderson, Stephen. "Cliché, Monotony, and Touchstone: Folksong Composition and the New Black Poetry." *Black Southern Voices.* Ed. John Oliver Killens and Jerry W. Ward Jr. New York: Meridian, 1992. 529–49.

Hentoff, Nat, and Albert J. McCarthy, eds. *Jazz.* New York: Pinehart, 1959.

Hentoff, Nat, and Nat Shapiro. *Hear Me Talkin' to Ya: The Story of Jazz by the Men Who Made It.* New York: Dover, 1966.

Higginbotham, Evelyn Brooks. "Rethinking Vernacular Culture: Black Religion and Race Records in the 1920s and 1930s." *The House that Race Built.* Ed. Wahneema Lubiano. New York: Pantheon, 1997. 157–77.

Higginson, Thomas Wentworth. "Negro Spirituals." *Atlantic Monthly* 19 (1867): n.p.

Holladay, Hilary. *Ann Petry*. New York: Twayne, 1996.
Holloway, Joseph E, ed. *Africanisms in American Culture*. Bloomington: Indiana UP, 1990.
Horowitz, Floyd R. "The Enigma of Ellison's Intellectual Man." *CLAJ* 7 (1963): 126–31.
———. "Ralph Ellison's Modern Version of Brer Bear and Brer Rabbit in *Invisible Man*." *Mid Continent American Studies Journal* 4.2 (1963): 21–27.
Howe, Irving. *Decline of the New*. New York: Horizon, 1970.
Hughes, Langston. *Selected Poems*. 1959. New York: Vintage-Random, 1974.
Hull, Gloria T., et al., eds. *All the Women Are White, All the Blacks Are Men, but Some of Us Are Brave*. Old Westbury, NY: Feminist Press, 1982.
Ivy, James W. "Ann Petry Talks About First Novel." *Sturdy Black Bridges: Visions of Black Women in Literature*. Ed. Roseann P. Bell et al. Garden City, NY: Anchor, 1979. 197–200.
Jackson, George Pullen. *White and Negro Spirituals*. New York: J. J. Agustin, 1939.
Jemie, Onwuchekwa. "Jazz, Jive, and Jam." *Langston Hughes*. Ed. Harold Bloom. New York: Chelsea House, 1989.
Jensen, David. *Spreading Rhythm Around: Black Popular Songwriters*. New York: Simon, 1998.
Jerde, Curtis D. "Black Music in New Orleans: A Historical Overview." *Black Music Research Journal* 10 (1990): 18–24.
Jimoh, A. Yemisi. "African American Literature: The African Continuum—Folklore, Myths, and Legends." *Western Journal of Black Studies* 13 (1989): 36–44.
Johnson, Charles S. "Jazz, Poetry and Blues." *Carolina Magazine* 58 (1928): 16–20.
Johnson, James Weldon. *The Book of American Negro Poetry*. 1922. Rev. ed. New York: Harcourt, 1931. 3–48.
Johnson, Maria V. "'The World in a Jug and the Stopper in [Her] Hand': *Their Eyes Were Watching God* as Blues Performance." *AAR* 32 (1998): 401–14.
Jones, Gayl. *Liberating Voices*. Cambridge, MA: Harvard UP, 1991.
Keepnews, Peter. *Legends of Jazz*. Columbia House Music Collection Legends of Jazz Series. Terre Haute, IN.: Columbia House, 1990–.
Keil, Charles. *Urban Blues*. Chicago: U of Chicago P, 1962.
Kennington, Donald. "Bibliography of Jazz and Literature." *The Literature of Jazz*. Chicago: ALA, 1971. 104–10.
———. *The Literature of Jazz: A Critical Guide*. Chicago: ALA, 1970.
Kinnamon, Keneth, ed. *James Baldwin: A Collection of Critical Essays*. Englewood Cliffs, NJ: Prentice-Hall, 1974.
Kinnamon, Keneth, and Michel Fabre, eds. *Conversations with Richard Wright*. Jackson: U of Mississippi P, 1993.

Klein, Marcus. "Ralph Ellison." *After Alienation*. New York: World, 1964.

Klotman, Phillis R. "Langston Hughes's Jess B. Semple and the Blues." *Phylon* 36 (1975): 68–77.

Kornweibel, Theodore, Jr. *"Seeing Red": Federal Campaigns Against Black Militancy, 1919–1925*. Bloomington: Indiana UP, 1998.

Kostelantz, Richard. "The Politics of Ellison's Booker: *Invisible Man* as Symbolic History." *Chicago Review* 19.2 (1967): 5–26.

Larson, Charles R. *An Intimation of Things Distant: The Collected Fiction of Nella Larsen*. New York: Anchor, 1992.

Leonard, Neil. *Jazz and the White Americans*. Chicago: U of Chicago P, 1962.

Levin, Harry. "What Was Modernism?" *Refractions*. New York: Oxford, 1966.

Lincoln, C. Eric. *Black Muslims in America*. 3d ed. Lawrenceville, NJ: Africa World, 1994.

——. *Race, Religion, and the Continuing American Dilemma*. 1986. New York: Hill & Wang, 1999.

Lindbergh, Charles. "Appeal for Isolation: Let Us Look at Our Own Defense." *Vital Speeches of the Day* 5 (1939): 751–52.

——. "Aviation, Geography, and Race." *Readers Guide* 35 (1939): 64–67.

Locke, Alain. "The Negro Spirituals." *The New Negro*. 1925. Ed. Alain Locke. New York: Atheneum, 1986. 199–213.

Lubiano, Wahneema, ed. *The House that Race Built: Black Americans, U.S. Terrain*. New York: Pantheon, 1997.

——. "Shuckin' Off the African American 'Native Other': What's Po-Mo Got to Do with It?" *Cultural Critique* 18 (1992): 149–86.

Maultsby, Portia K. "Africanisms in African-American Music." *Africanisms in American Culture*. Bloomington: Indiana UP, 1990.

Marvin, Thomas G. "Children of Legba: Musicians at the Crossroads in Ralph Ellison's *Invisible Man*." *American Literature* 68 (1996): 587–608.

McCarthy, Albert J. "The Re-Emergence of Traditional Jazz." *Jazz*. Ed. Nat Hentoff and Albert J. McCarthy. New York: Rinehart, 1959. 305–24.

McNeil, Genna Rae. *Charles Hamilton Houston and the Struggle for Civil Rights*. Philadelphia: U of Pennsylvania P, 1985.

Midnight Ramble: The Story of the Black Film Industry. Prod. Pamela Thomas and Bestor Cram, Shanachie Production. Videocassette. PBS, 1994.

Moi, Toril, ed. *The Kristeva Reader*. New York: Columbia UP, 1986.

Moses, Wilson Jeremiah, ed. *Classical Black Nationalism: From the American Revolution to Marcus Garvey*. New York: New York UP, 1996.

Murray, Albert. *The Hero and the Blues*. Columbia: U of Missouri P, 1973.

Nadel, Alan. *Invisible Criticism: Ralph Ellison and the American Canon*. Iowa City: U of Iowa P, 1988.

Neal, Mark Anthony. *What the Music Said: Black Popular Music and Public Culture*. New York: Routledge, 1999.

Oliphant, Dave, ed. *The Bebop Revolution in Words and Music*. Austin: Harry Ransom Humanities Research Center, 1994.

O'Meally, Robert, ed. *New Essays on* Invisible Man. New York: Cambridge UP, 1988.

Ostendorf, Berndt. "Ralph Ellison: Anthropology, Modernism, and Jazz." *New Essays on* Invisible Man. New York: Cambridge UP, 1988. 95–121.

Oyewole, Abiodun, and Umar Bin Hassan. *On a Mission: Selected Poems and a History of the Last Poets*. New York: Holt, 1996.

Pratt, Louis H. *James Baldwin*. Boston: Twayne, 1978.

Quarles, Benjamin. *The Negro in the Making of America*. 1964. 3d ed. New York: Simon, 1996.

Rabinowitz, Peter. "Whiting the Wrongs of History: The Resurrection of Scott Joplin." *Black Music Research Journal* 11 (1991): 157–75.

Regon, Bernice Johnson. "Let the Church Sing 'Freedom.'" *Black Music Research Journal* (1986): 104–18.

Revell, Peter. *Paul Laurence Dunbar*. Boston: Twayne, 1979.

Rice, Alan J. "Jazzing It Up a Storm: The Execution and Meaning of Toni Morrison's Jazzy Prose Style." *Journal of American Studies* 28 (1994): 423–32.

Rose, Tricia. *Black Noise: Rap Music and Black Culture in Contemporary America*. Hanover, NH: Wesleyan UP, 1994.

Sanders, Mark A. *Afro-Modernist Aesthetics and the Poetry of Sterling A. Brown*. Athens: U of Georgia P, 1999.

Saunders, James Robert. *The Wayward Preacher in the Literature of African American Women*. Jefferson, N.C.: McFarland, 1995.

Savage, Barbara Dianne. *Broadcasting Freedom: Radio, War, and the Politics of Race, 1938–1948*. Chapel Hill: U of North Carolina P, 1999.

Sherard, Tracey. "Sonny's Bebop: Baldwin's 'Blues Text' as Intracultural Critique." *AAR* 32 (1998): 691–705.

Shih, Hsio Wen. "The Spread of Jazz and the Big Bands." *Jazz*. Ed. Nat Hentoff and Albert J. McCarthy. New York: Rinehart, 1959. 173–87.

Singer, Barry. *Black and Blue: The Life and Lyrics of Andy Razaf*. New York: Macmillan, 1992.

Skerrett, Joseph, Jr. "The Wright Interpretation: Ralph Ellison and the Anxiety of Influence." *Speaking for You: The Vision of Ralph Ellison*. Ed. Kimberly W. Benston. Washington, DC: Howard UP, 1987. 217–30.

Songs of Zion. 1921. Supplemental Worship Resource 12. Nashville: Parthenon, 1981.

Spellman, A. B. *Four Lives in the Bebop Business*. New York: Schocken Books, 1966.

Spencer, Jon Michael. *Black Hymnody: A Hymnological History of the African-American Church*. Knoxville: U of Tennessee P, 1992.

———. *The New Negroes and Their Music: The Success of the Harlem Renaissance.* Knoxville: U of Tennessee P, 1997.
Standley, Fred L., and Louis H. Pratt. *Conversations with James Baldwin.* Jackson: U of Mississippi P, 1989.
Sundquist, Eric J., ed. *Cultural Contexts for Ralph Ellison's* Invisible Man. Boston: Bedford, 1995.
———. *To Wake the Nations: Race in the Making of American Literature.* Cambridge, MA: Harvard UP, 1993.
Taft, Michael. *Blues Lyric Poetry: A Concordance.* 3 vols. New York: Garland, 1984.
Tate, Claudia. "Notes on the Invisible Women in Ralph Ellison's *Invisible Man.*" *Speaking for You: The Vision of Ralph Ellison.* Ed. Kimberly W. Benston. Washington, DC: Howard UP, 1987. 163–72.
Taylor, Art. *Notes and Tones: Musician-to-Musician Interviews.* New York: Da Capo, 1993.
Thomas, Hugh. *The Slave Trade: The Story of the Atlantic Slave Trade, 1440–1870.* New York: Simon and Schuster, 1997.
Tracy, Steven. *Langston Hughes and the Blues.* Urbana: U of Illinois P, 1988.
Walker, Margaret. *Richard Wright: Daemonic Genius.* New York: Amistad, 1988.
Wall, Cheryl, ed. *Changing Our Own Words: Essays on Criticism, Theory, and Writing by Black Women.* New Brunswick, NJ: Routledge UP, 1989.
Wallace, Michele. *Invisibility Blues: From Pop to Theory.* London: Verso, 1990.
Walton, Ortiz. *Music Black, White, and Blue: A Sociological Survey of the Use and Misuse of Afro-American Music.* New York: William Morrow, 1972.
Ward, Brian. *Just My Soul Responding: Rhythm and Blues, Black Consciousness, and Race Relations.* Berkeley: U of California P, 1998.
Wardlow, Gayle Dean. *Chasin' That Devil Music: Searching for the Blues.* San Francisco: Miller Freeman, 1998.
Weatherby, W. J. *James Baldwin: Artist on Fire.* 1989. New York: Dell, 1990.
Werner, Craig. *A Change Is Gonna Come: Music, Race, and the Soul of America.* New York: 1999.
———. *Playing the Changes: From Afro-Modernism to the Jazz Impulse.* Urbana: U of Illinois P, 1994.
Williams, Martin. "Bebop and After: A Report." *Jazz.* Ed. Nat Hentoff and Albert J. McCarthy. New York: Rinehart, 1959. 289–301.
Willis, Susan. *Specifying: Black Women Writing the American Experience.* Madison: U of Wisconsin P, 1987.
Willis-Braithwaite, Deborah, ed. *Van Der Zee, Photographer: 1886–1983.* New York: Harry Abrams, 1993.
Woodward, C. Vann. *The Strange Career of Jim Crow.* 1955. New York: Oxford, 1974.

Work, John W., comp. *American Negro Songs: A Comprehensive Collection of 230 Folk Songs, Religious and Secular.* New York: Howell, Soskin, 1940.

Wright, Richard. "Blueprint for Negro Writing." *Within the Circle: An Anthology of African American Literary Criticism from the Harlem Renaissance to the Present.* Ed. Angelyn Mitchell. Durham, NC: Duke UP, 1994. 97–106.

———. Foreword. *The Meaning of the Blues/(Blues Fell This Morning).* By Paul Oliver. New York: Collier, 1960.

Young, Al. "Statement on Aesthetics, Poetics, Kinetics." 1972. *New Black Voices.* Ed. Abraham Chapman. New York: NAL, 1972. 553–54.

A SELECTED LIST OF BIOGRAPHIES AND AUTOBIOGRAPHIES OF MUSICIANS

Armstrong, Louis. *Louis Armstrong in His Own Words: Selected Writings.* Ed. Thomas Brothers. 1999.
Albertson, Chris. *Bessie.* 1972.
Basie, William. *Straight Ahead.* 1981.
———, as told to Albert Murray. *Good Morning Blues: The Autobiography of Count Basie.* 1985.
Bechet, Sidney. *Treat It Gentle: An Autobiography.* 1978.
Bergreen, Laurence. *Louis Armstrong: An Extravagant Life.* 1997.
Boujut, Michel. *Louis Armstrong.* 1998.
Broonzy, William Lee Conley, with Yannick Bruynoghe. *Big Bill's Blues.* 1955.
Brothers, Thomas, ed. *Louis Armstrong in His Own Words.* 1999.
Caesar, Shirley. *The Lady, the Melody, and the Word: An Autobiography.* 1998.
Carr, Ian. *Miles: The Definitive Biography.* 1982.
Catalano, Nick. *Clifford Brown: The Life and Art of the Legendary Trumpeter.* 2000.
Chambers, Jack. *Milestones: The Music and Times of Miles Davis.* 1998.
Chilton, John. *Billie's Blues: The Billie Holiday Story, 1933–1959.* 1975.
———. *Let the Good Times Roll: The Story of Louis Jordan and His Music.* 1995.
———. *Sidney Bechet: The Wizard of Jazz.* 1996.
Cole, Bill. *John Coltrane.* 1976.
———. *Miles Davis: The Early Years.* 1974.
Coltrane, John. *John Coltrane Speaks.* 1981.
Dance, Stanley. *The World of Count Basie.* 1980.
———. *The World of Duke Ellington.* 1981.
Davis, Miles, with Quincy Troup. *Miles: The Autobiography.* 1989.

Dixon, Willie, with Don Snowden. *I Am the Blues.* 1989.
Ellington, Edward Kennedy. *Music Is My Mistress.* 1973.
Feinstein, Elaine. *Bessie Smith: Empress of the Blues.* 1985.
Franklin, Aretha, with David Ritz. *Aretha: From These Roots.* 1999.
Giddins, Gary. *Satchmo.* 1988.
Gillespie, Dizzy, with Al Fraser. *To Be, or Not . . . to Bop: Memoirs.* 1979.
Gourse, Leslie. *The Ella Fitzgerald Companion: Seven Decades of Commentary.* 1998.
———. *Sassy: The Life of Sarah Vaughan.* 1993.
Hadju, David. *Lush Life: A Biography of Billy Strayhorn.* 1996.
Handy, D. Antoinette. *Jazz Man's Journey: A Biography of Ellis Louis Marsalis Jr.* Lanham, Md.: Scarecrow, 1999.
Harris, Michael. *The Rise of Gospel Blues: The Music of Thomas Andrew Dorsey.* 1992.
Hasse, John Edward. *Beyond Category: The Life and Genius of Duke Ellington.* 1993.
Havens, Richie. *They Can't Hide Us Anymore.* 1999.
Holiday, Billie, with William Duffy. *Lady Sings the Blues.* 1956.
Horricks, Raymond. *Profiles in Jazz: From Sidney Bechet to John Coltrane.* 1991.
King, B. B., with David Ritz. *Blues All Around Me: The Autobiography of B. B. King.* 1996.
Lieb, Sandra. *Mother of the Blues: A Study of Ma Rainey.* 1981.
Litweiler, John. *Ornette Coleman: A Harmolodic Life.* 1992.
Lomax, Alan. *Mister Jelly Roll.* 1950.
Mingus, Charles. *Beneath the Underdog: His Words as Composed by Mingus.* Ed. Nel King. 1971.
Nicholson, Stuart. *Billie Holiday.* 1995.
———. *Ella Fitzgerald: A Biography of the First Lady of Jazz.* 1995.
———. *Reminiscing in Tempo: A Portrait of Duke Ellington.* 1999.
Nisenson, Eric. *'Round About Midnight: A Portrait of Miles Davis.* 1982. Updated ed. 1996.
Oliver, Paul. *Bessie Smith.* 1960.
O'Meally, Robert. *Lady Day: The Many Faces of Billy Holiday.* 1991.
Porter, Lewis. *John Coltrane: His Life and Music.* 1998.
Priestly, Brian. *Mingus: A Critical Biography.* 1983.
Reisner, R. G. *Bird: The Legend of Charlie Parker.* 1962.
Russell, Ross. *Bird Lives: The High Life and Hard Times of Charlie (Yardbird) Parker.* 1973.
Santoro, Gene. *Myself When I Am Real: The Life and Music of Charles Mingus.* 2000.
Shipton, Alyn. *Groovin' High: The Life of Dizzy Gillespie.* 1999.
Simone, Nina. *I Put a Spell on You.* 1992.

Spellman, A. B. *Four Lives in the Bebop Business*. 1985.
Still, William Grant. *William Grant Still: A Study in Contradictions*. Ed. Catherine Parsons Smith. 2000.
Szwed, John F. *Space Is the Place: The Lives and Times of Sun Ra*. 1998.
Thomas, J. C. *Chasin' the Trane: The Music and Mystique of John Coltrane*. 1975.
Troupe, Quincy. *Miles and Me*. 2000.
Waters, Ethel, with Charles Samuels. *His Eye Is on the Sparrow*. 1950.
White, John. *Billie Holiday: Her Life and Times*. 1987.
Wilson, Peter Niklas. *Ornette Coleman: His Life and Music*. 1999.
Woideck, Carl. *Charlie Parker: His Music and Life*. 1996.
Wolff, Daniel, et al. *You Send Me: The Life and Times of Sam Cooke*. 1995.

INDEX

General Index

absent while present. *See* paradox
Adams, Yolanda, 217
aesthetics, 3, 4, 5, 11, 25–26, 28, 29, 31–32, 38, 55, 72, 107, 114, 216, 242n; Blues, 3, 29, 31–32, 84, 88, 102, 103, 104, 107, 113, 124, 131, 148; definition of, 3, 31–32; estrangement from, 3–4; Jazz, 3, 28, 29, 31–32, 36, 70, 102, 112, 146, 149; Spiritual-Gospel, 3, 31–32, 36, 72
Africa and African, 1, 2, 6, 7, 13, 22, 23, 25, 32, 66, 71, 88, 140; oral cultures, 1
African Orthodox Church. *See* McGuire, George Alexander
Agyeman, Jaramogi Abebe. *See* Cleage, Albert
Ahmadiyya (Islam), 43, 230n
Albert, Richard, 204, 205
Aldrich, Thomas Bailey, 13
Ali, Muhammad (Cassius Clay), 157
Ali, Noble Drew (Timothy Drew), 43, 230n; Moorish Science Temple, 43, 230n
alienation, 6, 8, 15, 191, 198
Allan, Lewis, 50
Allen, Richard, 224n
Alston, Charles, 46, 47, 95
American Federation of Musicians' strike, 98
Ammons, Albert, 24, 220
Amos and Andy, 52, 244n; *Check and Double Check* (film), 52, 244n
Andrews, Julie, 229n

Andrews, Lee and the Hearts, 163
Anti-lynching League. *See* Barnett, Ida B. Wells
Apex Club, 53
Apollo Theater, 53, 99
arhoolie, 49
Arkansas Race Riot, The, 44
Armstrong, Louis (Satchmo), 2, 5, 17, 50, 52, 87, 96, 131–34 passim, 147, 184, 185, 204, 209, 210, 220, 221, 222; Hot Five, 5, 50, 209; Hot Seven, 5, 50
Arnold, Kokomo, 244n
asunrara, 1
Atlantic Monthly, 8, 13, 14
Attaway, William, 91; *Blood on the Forge*, 91
Austin, Lovie, 219

Baker, Chet, 235n
Baker, Ella, 155
Baker, George (Father Divine), 230n
Baker, Houston, 13, 21, 56, 103, 109, 130, 202, 237n; *Blues Ideology and Afro-American Literature*, 21, 103, 202, 237n; mastery of form, 13; *Modernism and the Harlem Renaissance*, 113; vernacular theory, 56
Baker, Josephine, 169
Bakhtin, Mikhail, 31; dialogism, 11
Baldwin, James, 12, 21, 39, 103, 187, 202–15, 216, 224n, 234n, 236n, 237n; *The Amen Corner*, 223; *The Fire Next Time*, 187, 224n; *Giovanni's Room*, 234n; *Go Tell It on the Mountain*, 224n; *If Beal*

Baldwin, James *(continued)*
  Street Could Talk, 224n; "Many Thousands Gone," 21, 223n, 224n; "Sonny's Blues," 12, 21, 39, 202–15, 222, 224n, 237n
Ballard, Florence, 158
Ballard, Hank, 157
Bambara, Toni Cade, 12,
Band of Gypsys. *See* Hendrix, Jimi
Baraka, Amiri (LeRoy Jones), 39, 159, 202, 203, 217, 224n, 226n, 228n, 229n; on changing same, 29, 161, 189, 217
bards, 1
Barnett, Charlie (Mad Mab), 53
Barnett, Ida B. Wells, 42, 43, 44; Anti-Lynching League, 42; *Arkansas Race Riot*, 44; Negro Fellowship League, 42
Barthes, Roland, 31, 224n, 228n
Basie, William (Count), 5, 49, 53, 54, 96, 97, 147, 148, 191, 199, 200, 201, 241, 222
Basin Street (New Orleans), 53
Beal Street (Memphis), 53
Beavers, Louise, 51
bebop, 5, 96–99 passim, 160, 173, 210, 214, 240; flatted fifths (bebop sounds), 38
Bechet, Sidney, 54
Beethoven, Ludwig van, 220
Bennett, Lerone, 234n
Benson, George, 161, 242
Benston, Kimberly, 226
Berlin, Irving, 169, 219, 222
Berrett, Anthony J., 163, 239n
Bethel, Lorraine, 104, 236n
big bands, 5
Biggers, John, 95; *Jubilee Ghana Harvest Festival*, 95
Bill of Rights, 6
Birdland, 99
Birth of a Nation (film). *See* Griffith, D. W.
Birth of a Race Photoplay Corporation, 51; *Birth of a Race* (film), 51

Black Arts Movement, 159
black bottom, 32; as dance, 53, 164; definition of, 164; Jelly Roll Morton and, 164; Ma Rainey and, 164; as neighborhood, 20, 32, 163–73 passim,182, 239n, 240; Robert Nathaniel Dett and, 164; William Grant Still and, 164
Black Cabinet, 45
Black Jews. *See* Commandment Keepers of the Living God
Black/Negro National Anthem ("Lift Every Voice and Sing"), 46, 231n
Black Panther Party, 156, 238n
Black sermonic tradition, 46, 132, 156, 159, 225n
Black Swan Records, 47
Black Swan, The. *See* Greenfield, Elizabeth Taylor
Blacker the Berry, The. See Thurman, Wallace
Blackstone Theater (Chicago), 51
Blackwell, Scrapper, 222
Blakey, Art, 100, 161; and Jazz Messengers, 100, 101, 161
Bland, Bobby Blue, 157
bloody/red summer (1919), 43, 93, 163, 170
Blues, 23–24, 26, 28, 29, 36, 103–16, 117, 120, 128, 131, 137, 143–47 passim, 157–90 passim, 195, 196, 199, 200, 202–18 passim, 241–44n; aesthetics, 3, 29, 31–32, 38, 84, 88, 103, 104, 107, 113, 124, 131, 139, 162, 179, 183, 186, 187, 191, 194, 240n; blue notes (Flatted thirds and sevenths), 38; capitalization of, 226; characters, 34–35, 56–90 passim, 107, 116–18 passim, 123, 124, 129, 130, 131, 132, 137, 138, 142, 145, 148, 162, 164, 168, 170, 173, 175, 179, 180, 183–85 passim, 190–96 passim, 205, 240n; classic, 48; classical music and, 24, 227n; community in, 26–27, 105, 116, 179, 186–87, 190; definition of, 23–24, 26, 28,

33, 34, 55, 130; down home, 48, 49, 100; Ellison's definition of, 130–31; literary/metaphor in fiction, 33, 36, 37, 56, 189; modernity in, 146–47; philosophy of, 3, 20, 24, 26, 28, 33, 35, 36, 60, 61, 66, 81, 84, 88, 89, 90, 102, 103, 105, 106, 109–16 passim, 127, 129, 130, 131, 133, 142, 143, 144, 146, 147, 148, 151, 152, 154, 162, 164, 165, 168, 171, 174, 178, 179, 181, 186, 187, 189, 190, 191, 193–96 passim, 207, 212, 213, 215, 240n; singularity in, 26–30 passim, 32, 34, 102, 105, 113, 115, 117, 119, 124, 125, 129, 137, 138, 142, 147, 151, 154, 165, 168, 176, 194, 208, 229n; themes in literature, 34–35, 54, 55, 78–90 passim; traveling phrases in, 23, 78, 112, 145, 185, 205, 242–44n; triumph in, 35, 61, 63, 69, 73, 199, 205–11 passim; womanist, 55, 73, 104
Blues People, 19, 27, 37, 53, 61, 62, 89, 104–6 passim, 109–11 passim, 114, 116, 119, 127, 144, 165, 177, 190, 226n, 240n; definition of, 26–27
bluesmen, 103, 112, 126, 142, 160, 180–83 passim, 186, 188, 189, 223n, 240n; definition of, 180, 223n
blueswomen, 1, 77, 109, 114, 159, 176, 204, 240n; definition of, 77
Bogle, Donald, 51, 52, 225n, 232n, 234n, 242
Bolden, Charles (Buddy), 147
Boley, Okla., 102
Bonds, Margaret T., 24, 226–27; *Ballad of the Brown King* (with Langston Hughes), 227; and Langston Hughes's poetry, 227; *Three Dream Portraits*, 226
Bradford, Perry, 47
Braithwaite, William Stanley, 224, 225
Brewster, Herbert, 99, 146

briarpatch, 111, 179, 180, 196; defined, 179, 196
Brooks, Gwendolyn, 101, 159, 160, 234n; "The Anniad," 160; *Annie Allen*, 101, 234n
Broonzy, William Lee Conley (Big Bill), 48, 49, 53, 54, 100, 232n
Brown, Charles, 234n
Brown, James, 101, 159
Brown, Sterling, 12, 202; "Ma Rainey," 12; "Memphis Blues," 12; "Strong Men," 12
Brown v. Topeka Board of Education, 94, 206
Browning, Elizabeth Barrett, 8
Brubeck, Dave, 235n
Bullins, Ed, 159
Bunch, William. *See* Wheatstraw, Peter
Burleigh, Harry T., 24, 227n
Burnett, Chester Arther (Howlin' Wolf), 100
Burnham, Dorothy, 231
Byas, Don, 97, 183,
Byerman, Keith, 163, 239n
Byron, Gordon George Noel, 8

Cabin in the Sky (film), 94
Cable, George Washington, 233n
Caesar, Shirley, 159
Calloway, Cab, 87, 232n
Campbell, Bebe Moore, 12, 13, 18, 218; *Singing in the Comeback Choir*, 13; *Your Blues Ain't Like Mine*, 12
Campbell, Charlie, 243n
Carby, Hazel, 21, 55, 67, 77, 231n, 233n, 234n, 241n
Carmichael, Stokley, 156, 238n
Carnegie Hall, 53–54, 97
Carr, Leroy, 49, 222, 232n
Catlett, Elizabeth, 95
Central Avenue (Los Angeles), 53, 97, 98
Central High School (Little Rock), 95, 160
changing same. *See* Baraka, Amiri
Charleston (dance), 53

Chaucer, Geoffrey, 17
Cherry Blossom club (Kansas City), 50, 53
Chesnutt, Charles, 2, 13, 18, 51, 225n; *Conjure Woman*, 225n; "The Goophered Grapevine," 13–14, 225n; *The House Behind the Cedars*, 51; mask of whiteness, 13
Chestnutt, Cyrus, 229
Childress, Alice, 214
Christian, Charlie, 54, 98
Church of God (Micheaux), 43, 230
church burnings and bombings, 156, 217
Civil Rights Act (1964), 156
Civil Rights Movement, 155, 156, 159
Civil War, 1, 2, 6, 9, 223n, 243–44n
Clansmen, The. *See* Dixon, Thomas
Clark Monroe's Uptown House, 98
Clarke, Kenny (Klook/Klook-Mop), 97, 98
classical music, 24, 25, 29, 32, 72, 95, 139, 157, 161, 227n
Cleage, Albert (Jaramogi Abebe Agyeman), 93
Cleveland, James, 159
close reading, 4
Club Alabam (Los Angeles), 53, 98
Coleman, Ornette, 5, 32, 149, 157
Collins, Addie Mae, 156
Coltrane, John, 5, 32, 149, 157, 158, 210, 217, 229n; free-form Jazz, 5
Coltrane, Ravi, 217
Commandment Keepers of the Living God (Black Jews; Beth B'nai Abraham Synagogue), 44
Commission on Civil Rights, 93
Condon, Eddie (and His All Stars), 184
Congress of Racial Equality, 93, 156
connective social narratives/energies, 2, 6, 12, 19, 22, 31, 39
Constitution of the United States of America, 6
Cook, Will Marion, 24

Cotton Club, 49, 50, 52, 83, 232n; closes, 98; in Los Angeles (Frank Sebastian's), 97, 98; in New York, 49, 50, 97, 98, 100
Cox, Billy, 160
Cox, Ida, 48, 185, 221
Crisis, 230n
CTI Records. *See* Taylor, Creed (CTI Records)
Cullen, Countee, 42, 66; "The Dark Tower," 42; "Yet Do I Marvel," 66
cultural historicism, 38, 39

Dark Tower (literary salon). *See* A'Lelia Walker
Dash, Julie, 218
Davenport, Charlie (Cow-Cow), 24
Davis, Angela, 45, 63, 77, 109, 114, 176, 177, 240n, 241n; *Blues Legacies*, 63, 114
Davis, Miles Dewey, III, 5, 32, 210, 235n, 240n
Davis, Sallye, 45
Davis, Thadious, 55, 78, 232
Democratic National Convention, 156, 238
Depression, The, 44, 53, 123
Derrida, Jacques, 228n, 229n, 235n, 239n
Desmond, Paul, 235n
Dett, Robert Nathaniel, 17, 24, 164
diachronic. *See* intertextuality
dialect, 17, 62; and James Weldon Johnson, 62; and Paul Laurence Dunbar, 17
dialogism. *See* Bakhtin, Mikhail
Dickinson, Emily, 229n
discourse, 31, 32; definition of, 31; as discursive formation, 31, 33, 56; dominant, 32; and Michel Foucault, 31; music-literary, 30, 31, 33, 37, 39, 40, 56, 63, 240n; racial, 3, 81, 84
dissemination, 30
Divine, Father. *See* Baker, George

Dixon, Thomas, Jr., 51; *The Clansmen*, 51; *The Leopard's Spots*, 51; *The Traitor*, 51
Dodds, Johnny, 17
Donaldson, Walter, 183, 221
Dorsey, Lee, 229n
Dorsey, Thomas A (Georgia/Barrelhouse Tom), 48, 53, 141, 160, 220, 244n
Dorsey, Tommy, 183
double meanings, 11, 23, 138, 143, 152
Double V campaign, 92, 234n
double-consciousness (doubleness), 4, 5, 7, 8, 9, 10, 28, 224n, *see also* Du Bois, W. E. B.
Douglass, Aaron, 46
Douglass, Fredrick, 4–7 passim, 9, 10, 11, 13, 146, 153, 232n; *Liberator*, 224; *Narrative of the Life of Fredrick Douglass; An American Slave, Written by Himself*, 4, 11, 13
Down Beat Room, 98
Du Bois, W. E. B., 4, 6, 7–11 passim, 13, 15, 67, 93, 224n; double-consciousness, 4, 7, 8, 9, 10, 224n; Niagara Movement, 43; Sorrow songs, 7, 8; *The Souls of Black Folk*, 4, 7, 8, 9, 10, 11, 13
Dumas, Henry, 159
Dunbar, Paul Laurence, 2, 11, 12, 13, 18, 19, 41, 42, 46, 51, 54, 55, 56–66 passim, 79, 113, 118, 143, 150, 151, 225n, 232n, 243n; *The Sport of the Gods*, 12, 19, 41, 51, 54, 56–66 passim, 79, 113, 118, 219, 243n; "We Wear the Mask," 150; "When Malindy Sings," 11
Dunham, Katherine, 46
Dvořák, Antonín, 24, 72, 84, 95, 139, 219, 220, 227n

Eckstine, Billy, 96, 191, 220, 222
Ed Small's Paradise. *See* Small's Paradise
Edwin Hawkins Singers, 160, 241n
Elaine, Ark., 44; sharecroppers' union, 44
Ellington, Edward Kennedy (Duke), 5, 18, 49, 50, 52, 83, 92, 96, 99, 191, 222
Ellison, Ralph, 2, 9, 13, 20, 21, 24, 33, 37–38, 46, 61, 76, 79, 92, 101–3 passim, 111, 113, 120, 130–54 passim, 196, 202, 216, 223n, 224n, 226n, 236n, 237n, 242–44n; *Going to the Territory*, 130; invisibility, 19, 120, 131; *Invisible Man*, 2, 20, 38, 61, 79, 92, 101, 102, 111–13, 120, 130–54 passim, 166–68 passim, 202, 220, 237n, 240n; "Richard Wright's Blues," 76, 130, 224n, 226n; *Shadow and Act*, 130, 223n, 224n, 238n; Trueblood passage, 136–37, 139, 237n
Emancipation, 9, 26
epic in African American music, 2, 223n
Europe, James Reese, 47
Evans, Bill, 235n
Evans, Ernest (Chubby Checker), 157
Evers, Medgar, 156
ex-centric. *See* Hutcheon, Linda
Executive Order 8802, 92

Fagan, Eleanor. *See* Holiday, Billie
Fair Employment Practices Committee (FEPC), 92
Faulkner, William, 233n
Fauset, Jesse, 233n, 234n
field hollers, 1
Fili, 1
Filmore East (Bill Graham's), 160
Fisher, Rudolph, 12, 18; "Common Meter," 12
Fisk Jubilee Singers, 1, 47
Fisk University, 67
Fitzgerald, Ella, 50, 97, 191, 222, 229n
forced communalism, 25, 26

Ford, Arnold Josiah, 44
Foucault, Michel, 31; and discourse/discursive formations, 31
fragmentation, 5, 7, 8, 28, 34
Franklin, Aretha, 101, 159, 160–61, 225n
Franklin, Kirk, 217
free and not free. *See* Paradox
free Jazz, 5
free men and women of color, 3, 223n
freedom rides, 93
freedom songs, 101, 159
freedom, trains, 11
From Spirituals to Swing (concerts), 54
Fuller, Meta Vaux Warrick, 46

Gaines v. Canada (Lloyd Gaines), 45
Garner, Erroll, 5
Garvey, Marcus, 43, 44, 46, 230n; *Negro World*, 230n; Universal Negro Improvement Association (UNIA), 43, 46, 230n
Gates, Henry Louis, 21, 111, 228n, 229n, 234n, 242n; *The Signifying Monkey*, 21, 228n, 229n, 234n, 242n
Gaye, Marvin, 159
Gershwin, George, 94, 210, 227n, 242n
Gershwin, Ira, 210
Getz, Stan, 235n
Gillespie, John Birks (Dizzy), 5, 32, 35, 87, 96–99 passim, 232n, 238n, 244n
Giovanni, Nikki, 159
Golden Gate Quartet, 54
Goodman, Benny, 5, 183, 235n
Gordon, Dexter, 161
Gordy, Berry, 101, 158, 161; Hitsville USA, 101; Motown (Industries), 101, 158, 159, 161, 162, 200
gospel music/urban spirituals, 25, 226n
Gospel Music Workshop of America (GMWA), 159–60

Grace, Charles Emmanuel (Daddy Grace), 230n
Granz, Norman, 97
Greenblatt, Stephen, 31, 39, 228n; *Shakespearean Negotiations*, 228n
Greenfield, Elizabeth Taylor (The Black Swan), 47
Greenwood (Tulsa, Okla.), 44
Griffin, Farah Jasmine, 21, 192, 229n; *Who Set You Flowin'?*, 192, 229n
Griffith, D. W., 51; *Birth of a Nation* (film), 51
Grimes, Lloyd (Tiny), 99
griots, 1

Hammond, John, 54; From Spirituals to Swing, 54
Hampton, Lionel, 5, 232n
Hancock, Herbie, 161
Handy, William Christopher (W. C.), 47, 51, 54, 78, 219, 220, 221, 231n, 243n
Hansberry, Lorraine, 101, 160; *A Raisin in the Sun*, 101; *To Be Young, Gifted and Black*, 160
Harlem/New Negro Renaissance, 15, 17, 18, 42, 47, 52, 54, 66, 95, 101, 102, 232n, 233n, 240n
Harper, Michael, 218
Harris, E. Lynn, 12, 224; *Abide with Me*, 225; *And This Too Shall Pass*, 225; *If This World Were Mine*, 12; *Just As I Am*, 225
Harris, Trudier, 235n
Harris, William J., 202–5 passim; creative destruction, 203
Harrison, Daphne Duval, 19, 77, 241n
Hart, Clyde, 99
Hathaway, Donnie, 160–61
Hattenhauer, Darryl, 205
Hawkins, Coleman, 47, 53, 96, 99, 157
Hawthorne, Nathaniel, 58; *The Scarlet Letter*, 58, 65
Hegamin, Lucille, 241n

Henderson, Fletcher, 5, 47, 52, 231n; Brooks, George (pen name), 231n; Novelty Orchestra, 47; Rainbow Orchestra, 52
Henderson, Stephen, 205
Hendrix, Jimi, 160; Band of Gypsys, 160
Heron, Gil Scott, 159, 161
Heyward, Du Bose, 242n
Higginson, Thomas Wentworth, 243–44n
Himes, Chester, 234n
Hines, Earl (Fatha), 96, 99, 220
Hirt, Al, 222
Hogue, W. Lawrence, 224n
Holiday, Billie (Eleanor Fagan), 50, 53, 98, 103, 191, 213, 222, 229n, 240n
Holladay, Hilary, 123–24, 236n
Homesteader, The (film), 50
Hooker, John Lee, 50, 100
Hooray for Love (film), 52
Hopkins, Sam (Lightnin'), 100
Horne, Lena, 94
House, Son (Eddie James Jr.), 183, 221
House Un-American Activities Committee (HUAC), 93
Houston, Charles, 45, 231n
Howard Theater (Washington, D.C.), 53
Howells, William Dean, 62
Howlin' Wolf. *See* Burnett, Chester Arthur
Hubbard, Freddie, 161
Hughes, Langston, 11–12, 13, 17–18, 25, 35, 42, 93, 101, 158, 202, 225n, 227n, 229n, 231n; and classical music, 227n; *Ask Your Mama: Twelve Moods for Jazz*, 12, 229n; "Blues I'm Playing," 12; "Commercial Theater," 158; "Dream Montage," 158; *Fine Clothes to the Jew*, 11–12; "Jazzonia," 11, 13, 225n; "The Negro Artist and the Racial Mountain," 231n; "The Negro Speaks of Rivers," 25; *Not Without Laughter*, 18; *Tambourines to Glory*, 17; "Trumpet Player," 12; *The Weary Blues*, 17, 42
Hunter, Alberta, 34, 47, 48, 55, 77, 112, 219, 244n
Hurley, George (Universal Hagar Spiritual Church), 230
Hurst, Fanny, 51; *Imitation of Life*, 51
Hurston, Zora Neale, 19, 20, 32, 37, 38, 46, 51, 61, 79, 92, 102, 103–16 passim, 117, 143, 163, 189, 226n, 234–35n passim; "Characteristics of Negro Expression," 226; *Seraph on the Suwanee*, 103, 234n; "Spirituals and Neo-Spirituals," 103; *Their Eyes Were Watching God*, 19, 20, 38, 61, 79, 103–16 passim, 123, 189, 219, 235n
Hutcheon, Linda, 224n; ex-centric, 11, 224n

Imitation of Life (film), 51, 94
improvisation, 4, 5, 6, 9, 28, 29, 170, 172, 175, 214, 224n; collective, 5, 6, 30, 102, 170, 214; solo, 5, 161
indentured servants, 3
India.Arie, 217
International Sweethearts of Rhythm, 96
intertextuality, 2, 4, 11, 18, 21, 30–39 passim, 53, 54, 132, 142, 162, 163, 179, 192, 203, 208, 210, 214, 217, 237n; as black musical practice, 11, 32; diachronic, 31, 56; Louis Montrose on, 31; Mikhail Bakhtin on, 31; Stephen Greenblatt on, 31; synchronic, 31, 56
intracultural issues (African American), 4, 11, 12, 15, 19, 32, 55, 80, 217, 237n; briarpatch as, 179; color-consciousness, 55, 78–90 passim; freedom as, 11; resistance as, 11
invisibility, 8, 9, 131, 132, 133, 148, 149, 153, 195, 196
invisible church, 25

Invisible Man. See Ellison, Ralph
Irvine, Weldon, 160

Jack and Jill, 45
Jackson, Charlie (Papa), 48, 53
Jackson, Esther Cooper, 231
Jackson, James, 231
Jackson, Mahalia, 99, 146
Jackson, Shirley, 166; "The Lottery," 166
Jackson Five, 159
Jacobs, Marion Walter (Little Walter), 100
James, Joy, 230n
Jazz, 3, 5, 18, 28–30, 36, 106, 109, 133, 147, 148, 150, 157, 158, 159, 161, 162, 163, 167, 171, 174, 175, 176, 181, 185, 188, 189, 191, 195, 197–200 passim, 203–14 passim, 217, 242n; aesthetics, 3, 29, 31–32, 36, 38, 70, 102, 112, 146, 149, 162, 194, 197, 198, 210, 212, 214, 240n; capitalization of, 226; characters, 36, 68, 85, 87, 88, 102, 105, 112–13, 148, 150, 162, 164, 168, 170, 173, 174, 176, 179, 189, 192, 195, 196, 200, 205, 207, 212, 240n, 242n; classical music and, 24, 32, 164, 157, 161, 227n; definition of, 28, 102; free, 5; improvisation in, 5, 28, 29, 102, 210, 214, 242n; innovative personal style in, 29, 35, 148, 173, 178, 213, 229n; as metaphor in fiction, 32, 33, 35, 36, 131; philosophy, 3, 28, 29, 35, 36, 70, 102, 112, 146, 148, 150, 162, 168, 170, 174, 177, 191, 194, 196 240n; themes, 36, 191
Jazz at the Philharmonic (JATP), 97
jazz people, 88, 89, 207
jazzmen, 1, 112, 180, 212; definition of, 180
Jefferson, Blind Lemon, 48, 49, 220, 243n
Jeffries, Jim,156
Jim Crow, 36, 57, 101

jitterbug, 53
Johnson, Bernice (Reagon), 161
Johnson, Bud, 99
Johnson, Jack, 83, 156
Johnson, James P., 53, 54; *Yamekraw*, 54
Johnson, James Weldon, 17, 46, 202, 226n, 233n; *Autobiography of an Ex-Colored Man*, 226; *Book of American Negro Spirituals*, 226n; *God's Trombones*, 17, 46; "Lift Every Voice and Sing," 46
Johnson, Lonnie, 222
Johnson, Louise, 244n
Johnson, Lyndon Baines, 156
Johnson, Noble, 50; Lincoln Motion Picture Company, 50
Johnson, Robert, 48, 49, 53, 231n, 232n, 240n, 244n
Johnson, Syl, 239n
Johnson, William Manuel (Bill), 50, 232; New Orleans Original Band, 50; Original Creole Band, 232n
Jolson, Al, 52; *Jazz Singer*, 52
Jones, Gayl, 13; *Corregidora*, 13
Jones, Isham, 183, 221
jongleurs, 1
jook joint, 32
Joplin, Scott, 24, 47
Joyce, James, 17
jumping-off piece, 5, 29

Kahn, Gus, 183, 221
Kalaidjian, Walter, 230n
Kay, Sammy (And His Orchestra), 179
Keats, John, 232n
Kelley, Robin D. G., 231n, 234n
Kent, George, 133, 149
Kimbrough, Lottie, 219
King, B. B. (Riley), 157
King, Martin Luther, 156; "I Have a Dream," 156
King Lear. See Shakespeare, William
King of Burlesque (film), 52
Kirk, Andy, 96
Komunyakaa, Yusef, 218

Kristeva, Julia, 31, 224n, 228n; *Revolution du langage poetique*, 31, 224n; on textuality, 224n, 228n

Lafayette Theater (New York), 86, 87
Larsen, Nella, 2, 12, 13, 19, 20, 24, 35, 41, 42, 54, 55, 66–78, 84, 232n, 233n, 234n; *Passing*, 78, 232n, 233n; *Quicksand*, 12, 19, 20, 41, 54, 55, 66–78, 232n, 233n
Last Poets, 158, 159
Lawrence, Jacob, 46, 47, 94–95; Migration of the Negro, 95; "Toussaint L'Overture," 47
Laws, Hubert, 161
Leaks, Sylvester, 12
Ledbetter, Hudie (Leadbelly), 49, 181, 221, 231n
Lee, Laura, 159
Lee, Spike, 218
Lenox Avenue (New York), 53
Levine, Lawrence, 228n
Lewis, David Levering, 83, 232n, 234n
Lewis, Norman, 95
Liberator. *See* Douglass, Fredrick
Lincoln, Abbey, 157
Lincoln Motion Picture Company. *See* Johnson, Noble
Lindbergh, Charles, 167
lindy hop, 53
Liston, Sonny, 157
Locke, Alain, 27, 46; *The New Negro*, 46
Long Hot Summers (1960s), 156
Lott, Eric, 59, 86, 232n, 234n
Louis, Joe, 54, 156
Lowell, James Russell, 89
lynching, 42, 43, 44, 218, 229–30n; in fiction, 42, 229–30n

Mackey, Nathaniel, 203; *Discrepant Engagement*, 203
Madhubute, Haki (Don L. Lee), 159
Major, Clarence, 12, 13, 18, 218; *Dirty Bird Blues*, 13
Malcolm X. *See* Shabazz, Malcolm/Malik

March on Washington (1941), 92
March on Washington (1963), 156
marginalization, 8, 9, 10, 11, 19, 32, 36
Marsalis, Branford, 217
Marsalis, Delfayo, 217
Marsalis, Ellis, 217
Marsalis, Wynton, 217
Matthews, Wentworth Arthur, 44
Maxwell Street (Chicago), 53
Mayfield, Curtis, 159
McCarthy, Joseph, 93
McClurkin, Donnie, 217
McCoy, Lizzie Douglass (Memphis Minnie), 48, 49
McDowell, Deborah, 67, 232n
McGee, Howard, 97
McGuire, George Alexander (African Orthodox Church), 43, 230n
McKay, Claude, 18, 43, 163, 202; "If We Must Die," 43
McKay, Nellie, 228
McNair, Denise, 156
McRae, Carmen, 98
McShann, Jay (Hootie), 96, 98
Melville, Herman, 133
Memphis Jug Band, 220, 244n
Memphis Minnie. *See* McCoy, Lizzie Douglass
Micheaux, Oscar, 50, 51; *Body and Soul*, 51; *The House Behind the Cedars*, 51; *Within Our Gates*, 51
migration, 41, 42, 118, 192, 241n; migration narratives, 41, 118, 192
Miles, Buddy, 160
Miles, C. Austin, 193, 222
Mingus, Charles, 158
minstrelsy, 2, 13, 14, 15, 209, 223n; black minstrels, 2; blackface in, 2, 14, 52; and Eric Lott, 59, 86, 232n, 234n; in fiction, 13; irony in, 14; metonym in, 14; reversal of, 2; Topsy in, 86–87
Minton, Henry, 98; Minton's Playhouse, 98, 99
Mississippi Freedom Democratic Party (MFDP), 156, 238n
mneni, 1

Mo, Keb, 217
Modern Jazz Quartet, 161
modernity, 6, 8, 20, 28, 43, 165, 179, 206, 228n
Monk, T. (son of Thelonious Monk), 217
Monk, Thelonious, 5, 32, 96, 98, 198, 217, 222, 242n, 244n
Montrose, Louis, 31, 38, 39, 228
Moorish Science Temple. See Ali, Noble Drew
Morgan, Lee, 101, 235n
Morganfield, William (Big Bill), 217
Morrison, Toni, 10, 12, 20, 102, 110, 155, 162–78 passim, 179, 194, 216, 237n, 239n, 240n, 242n; *Beloved*, 163; *The Bluest Eye*, 163, 166, 239n; *Jazz*, 12, 162, 163; *Paradise*, 102; *Playing in the Dark*, 10; *Song of Solomon*, 239n; *Sula*, 20, 110, 162–78 passim, 194, 220, 237n, 239n, 240n; *Tar Baby*, 239n
Morton, Jelly Roll (Ferdinand Joseph La Menthe), 17, 94, 147, 164, 185, 220, 221; with New Orleans Rhythm Kings, 17; and the Red Hot Peppers, 221
Motley, Archibald, 46
Motley, Willard, 18, 46, 91–92, 234n; *Knock on Any Door*, 91; *Let No Man Write My Epitaph*, 18, 91, 92; *We Fished All Night*, 91
Motown. See Gordy, Berry
Muddy Waters (McKinley Morganfield), 100, 101, 217, 226n
Mulligan, Gerry, 235n
Murray, Albert, 7, 12, 18, 20, 37, 39, 49, 111, 130, 131, 155, 162, 178–90 passim, 202, 228n, 229n, 236n, 241n, 244n; *Blue Devils of Nada*, 241n; *The Hero and the Blues*, 241n; *Omni Americans*, 7, 223n, 229n; *Stomping the Blues*, 179, 228n, 229n; *Train Whistle Guitar*, 12, 18, 20, 37, 49, 111, 162, 178–90 passim, 221
music in literature, 4, 11, 30, 31

music-into-fiction/music as metaphor in fiction, 5, 18, 21, 27, 30, 31, 33, 34, 37, 39, 55, 75, 131, 135, 162, 191, 224n

Nation, 231n
Nation of Islam, 44
National Association for the Advancement of Colored People (NAACP), 43, 45, 156, 230n
National Council of Negro Women (NCNW), 45
National Negro Congress (NNC), 44, 45
Naylor, Gloria, 218
Nazi, 54
necessary collectivity, 25, 26
Neal, Larry, 130,149; "Ellison's Zoot Suit," 149
Negro Dance Group. See Dunham, Katherine
Negro World. See Garvey, Marcus
New Canaan, 6, 36
New Deal, 45, 52
New Negro, 42, 52; *see also* Harlem/New Negro Renaissance
New Negro, The. See Locke, Alain
New World, 1, 3, 22, 25, 26
Newman, Jerry, 98, 99
Newport Jazz Festival, 101
Newton, John, 156, 221, 224n
Newton, Huey, 156
Niagara Movement. See Du Bois, W. E. B.
Nietzsche, Friedrich, 61
Nigeria, 2, 157
Niles, Abbe, 231n
North American Review, 8

Okeh Records, 47
Olatunji, Michael, 157
Oliver, Joseph (King), 5, 50, 185, 188; Creole Jazz Band, 50, 221
O'Meally, Robert, 131, 134, 137, 139, 145, 149, 202, 236n, 237n 238n
Onyx Club, 96

Opportunity, 42
Ory, Edward (Kid), 5, 50; Sunshine Orchestra, 50

Pace, Harry, 47
Paradise Club (Detroit), 53
paradox, 4, 5, 6, 9, 10, 11, 15, 26, 28, 32, 36, 63, 69, 81, 116, 120, 131, 132, 136, 148, 164, 224n, 228n, 237n; absent while present, 9, 10; free and not free, 6; saying and not saying, 10, 65–66; seen and not seen, 9, 120, 131, 132, 196–97
pariahs, 166; social operation of, 166–67
Parker, Charlie, 5, 32, 35, 96–99 passim, 209, 210, 222
Parks, Rosa, 94
Partisan Review, The, 205
passing, 52, 94, 233n
Pathe Records, 47
Patton, Charley, 48
Pekin Inn, 53
Peterson, Oscar, 97, 183, 184
Petry, Ann, 12, 13, 20, 92, 102, 116–30 passim, 149, 234n, 236n, 243n; *Country Place*, 234n, *In Darkness and Confusion*, 92; *The Narrows*, 118; "Solo on Drums," 13; *The Street*, 12, 20, 92, 102, 116–30 passim, 149, 220, 236n, 243n
Pettiford, Oscar, 96, 99
Phillips, Esther, 159
philosophy, 24, 25–26, 31, 32, 36, 69, 102, 112, 132, 135, 136, 142, 172, 176, 184, 216; Blues, 3, 24, 26, 32, 35, 60, 61, 66, 73, 76, 81, 84, 88, 89, 90, 102, 103, 105, 106, 107, 109–16 passim, 118, 128–33 passim, 142–46 passim, 148; definition of, 24, 102; Jazz, 3, 28, 29, 32, 35, 36, 70, 102, 112, 146, 148, 150; Spiritual-Gospel, 3, 23, 26, 32, 33, 34, 72, 123, 124, 132, 134, 137, 139, 141, 148
Pickett, Wilson (Wicked), 157

Piney Woods Country Life School, 235n
Pinky (film), 94
Pious, Robert Savon, 46
Plantation, the, 2
plantation school of literature, 14, 15, 225n
plantation songs, 1, 4, 7, 9, 227n
Plessy v. Ferguson, 94
Pope, Alexander, 224n
Porter, Cole, 183, 220, 221
postmodern, 166, 224n; simulacra, 166
poststructuralism, 30
privilege, 8, 9
Pryse, Marjorie, 118, 236n

Quality (film). *See* Sumner, Cid Ricketts
Quicksand. See Larsen, Nella

race films, 50, 51
race music, 50, 57, 98; Bebop as, 98
race records, 47, 157
raceless writers, 18, 91, 92
racial discourse. *See* discourse
ragtime, 24, 58, 60, 62, 227n, 228n
Rainbow Orchestra. *See* Henderson, Fletcher
Rainey, Ma (Gertrude Pridgett), 34, 48, 53, 55, 63, 77, 164, 185, 191, 194, 221, 222, 239n, 240n, 241n
Randolph, A. Philip, 92
Ravel, Maurice, 227n
Razaf, Andy, 134, 209, 220
Reconstruction, 9, 13, 24, 57
Redding, J. Saunders, 225
Redding, Otis, 157, 159
Reeves, Martha and the Vandellas, 158
Regal Theater, 53
Reilly, John M., 204
Reinhardt, Django, 238
Reol Productions, 51; *The Sport of the Gods* (film), 51
Rhapsody in Blue (film), 94
rhythm and blues, 157, 158

Rice, Alan J., 162
riff, 37, 38, 79, 103, 112, 113, 125, 126, 151, 153, 154, 168, 169, 170, 183, 186, 187, 188, 191, 194, 197, 198, 211, 242n, 244n; definition of in literature, 37; verbal, 38, 105, 112, 113, 187, 193
Roach, Max, 5, 97, 99, 157
Robertson, Carole, 156
Robeson, Paul, 50–51, 93
Robinson, William (Smokey), 158, 200, 222, 241n
Roosevelt, Franklin D., 45, 92
Rosewood, Fla., 44
Ross, Diana, 158
Royal Theater (Baltimore), 53
Rushing, Jimmy, 53, 54, 142, 148, 191, 199, 200, 201, 222
Russell, Michelle, 109, 130

Sanchez, Sonia, 159
Sanders, Pharaoh, 149
Savage, Augusta, 46
Savoy Ballroom, 52, 53, 98
saying and not saying. *See* paradox
scapegoats, 166; social operations of, 166–67
Schmeling, Max, 54
Schuyler, George, 231
Scott, Hazel, 94
Scottsboro Case, 45, 49, 231
Seale, Bobby, 156
seen and not seen. *See* paradox
Seifert, Charles, 46, 47
Sent for You Yesterday. See Wideman, John Edgar
Seraph on the Suwanee. See Hurston, Zora Neale
Shabazz, Malcolm/Malik, 156, 157, 158, 234n; "The Ballot or Bullet," 156
Shakespeare, William, 57; *King Lear*, 57
Shaw, Artie, 95
shouts (plantation), 1
Shrine of the Black Madonna, 93
signifying, 9, 209, 210

Signifying Monkey, The. See Gates, Henry Louis
Simone, Nina, 158, 160
Singleton, John, 218
sit-ins, 93, 155
Sixteenth Street Baptist Church (Birmingham, Ala.), 156
Small's Paradise (Ed Small's), 52, 83, 84, 86, 87
Smith, Bessie, 34, 47, 48, 51, 55, 63, 103, 104, 109, 130, 145, 167, 185, 219, 220, 221, 226n, 240n
Smith, Clara, 48, 77
Smith, Clarence (Pinetop), 24
Smith, Mamie, 47, 48, 185, 221; and her Jazz Hounds, 47
Smith, Trixie, 47, 48, 185, 221
Smith, Willie (The Lion), 53
Something to Shout About (film), 94
"Sonny's Blues." *See* Baldwin, James
soul music, 101, 158, 160
Souls of Black Folk, The. See Du Bois, W. E. B.
Southern, Eileen, 161, 223n, 224n, 226n, 228n, 231n, 243n
Southern Negro Youth Congress (SNYC), 45, 231
Spiritual-Gospel, 22–23, 24, 26, 27–28, 104–7 passim, 123, 132–42, 148, 159, 171, 172, 178, 184, 185, 187, 188, 190, 193, 202, 204, 211, 212, 213, 217, 218, 242n; aesthetics, 3, 31–32, 38, 186, 203, 211; capitalization of, 226; characters, 34, 65, 107, 148, 192, 193, 205, 237n; classical music and, 72, 227n; definition of, 23, 26, 27–28, 33; as a metaphor in fiction, 33, 37, 131, 135; philosophy, 3, 23, 26, 28, 33–34, 72, 123, 124, 132, 134, 137, 138, 139, 141, 148, 185, 186, 190, 191, 193, 203, 211; theme, 34, 54, 64–66 passim; wandering verses in, 23, 242n
Spivey, Victoria, 48

Sport of the Gods, The. See Dunbar, Paul Laurence
St. Louis Blues (film), 51
Staple Singers, 160
Stepto, Robert, 15, 103, 224n, 236n, 239n, 241n; *Behind the Veil*, 15, 103; immersion ritual, 15, 103
Still, William Grant, 24, 54, 95, 164, 242n
Stormy Weather (film), 94
Stowe, Harriet Beecher, 51; *Uncle Tom's Cabin*, 51
Stravinsky, Igor, 227–28n
Strayhorn, Billy, 5
Street, The. See Petry, Ann
Strivers Row, 42
Student Non-Violent Coordinating Committee (SNCC), 155, 156
Sugar Hill, 42
Sugar Hill Gang, 162
Sula. See Morrison, Toni
Sumner, Cid Ricketts, 94; *Quality*, 94
Supremes, The, 158
Swahili, 1
Sweatman, Wilbur, 47, 243n
Sweet Honey in the Rock, 161
Sweeting, Earl R., 46
Swing, 5, 95, 96
synchronic. *See* intertextuality
Synge, John Millington, 17

Tampa Red. *See* Whittaker, Hudson
Taylor, Creed , 161; CTI Records, 161
Taylor, Johnny, 157
Temptations, The, 158
Tennyson, Alfred, 8, 10
Terry, Sonny, 54
Tex, Joe (Joe Arrington, Jr.), 161
textuality, 30; Kristevan, 224n, 228n
Tharpe, Rosetta, 54
Their Eyes Were Watching God. See Hurston, Zora Neale
Thomas, Leon, 149
Thomas, Rufus, 161
Three Deuces Club, 98

Thurman, Wallace, 2, 12, 13, 18, 19, 32, 42, 52, 54, 55, 59, 61, 78–90 passim, 113, 143, 232n, 243n; *The Blacker the Berry*, 12, 19, 42, 54, 55, 61, 78–90 passim, 113, 219; *High School Girl*, 52; *Tomorrow's Children*, 52
Till, Emmett, 94, 206, 207
Tindley, Charles Albert, 49, 160, 219, 223n
Toomer, Jean, 15–19, 225n; *Cane*, 15–17, 225n
Train Whistle Guitar. See Murray, Albert
traveling phrases. *See* Blues
trickster hero/outlaw trickster, 11, 129, 182, 238n
troubadours, 1
Truman, Harry, 93
Turner, Joe (Big), 54, 232n
Turner, Ike and Tina, 157
Tuskeegee Institute, 43, 93, 135, 232n

Underground Railroad, 25, 188
Universal Negro Improvement Association. *See* Garvey, Marcus

Van Der Zee, James, 46
Vaudeville, 1
Vaughan, Sarah, 96, 99, 191, 222
Vendome, 53
Vinson, Eddie (Cleanhead), 222, 244n
Voting Rights Act (1965), 156

Wagner, Wilhelm Richard, 17
Walker, Aaron Thibeaux (T-Bone), 100, 186
Walker, A'Lelia, 42, 43, 86; Dark Tower (literary salon), 42, 86
Walker, Alice, 103
Walker, George, 47
Walker, Madame C. J. (Sarah Breedlove), 43, 86, 230n
Walker, Wyatt T., 226n

Wall, Cheryl, 74, 104, 108, 113, 122, 233n, 234n, 236n
Wallace, Sippie (Beulah Thomas), 48
Waller, Thomas Wright (Fats), 49, 50, 52, 53, 54, 134, 209, 220, 221, 242n
Wallingford, George, 48, 96
wandering verses. *See* Spiritual–Gospel
Washington, Booker, T., 41, 229n
Washington, Dinah, 191, 222
Washington, Freddi, 51
Washington, Grover, 161
Washington, Mary Helen, 236
Waters, Ethel, 47, 48, 204, 207, 208, 213, 242n
Watts, Isaac, 32, 224n
Weaver, Sylvester, 48
Webb, Chick, 50
Wells, Mary, 158
WERD radio station, 99
Wesley, Charles, 32, 224n
Wesley, Cynthia, 156
Wesley, Valerie Wilson, 12
Wheatstraw, Peter (William Bunch), 61, 100, 142–45 passim, 220, 231n, 237n, 240n
White, Booker T. Washington (Bukka), 100
White, Clarence Cameron, 24
White, Lynn, 217
White, Walter, 43, 218, 230n; *Fire in the Flint*, 218, 230
Whiteman, Paul, 52, 235n
Whitman, Walt, 236
Whittaker, Hudson (Tampa Red), 48
Whittier, John Greenleaf, 8
Wideman, John Edgar, 12, 20, 21, 32, 37, 38, 111, 155, 162, 191–201 passim, 242n; *Sent for You*

Yesterday, 12, 21, 38, 111, 162, 191–201 passim, 222, 244n
Williams, Bert (Egbert), 14, 47, 87, 171, 221, 225n
Williams, Claiborne, 182
Williams, Clarence, 17
Williams, Cootie, 244n
Williams, Joe, 100
Williams, Mary Lou, 96
Williams, Sherley Anne, 12, 202, 214
Williamson, John Lee (Sonny Boy), 48, 100
Wilson, August, 214, 239n; *Fences*, 214; *Ma Rainey's Black Bottom*, 239n
Wilson, Cassandra, 217
Wilson, Mary, 158
Wilson, Teddy, 5
Woodruff, Hale, 47
Work, John Wesley, III, 243n
Works Projects/Progress Administration (WPA), 46
worrying the line, 37, 183, 186, 188; definition in literature, 37
Wright, Betty, 157, 159
Wright, Richard, 12, 39, 44, 46, 225n, 234n, 236n; "Bright and Morning Star," 12; on jazz, 46, 23; *Savage Holiday*, 234n; *Uncle Tom's Children*, 46, 225n

Yamekraw. *See* Johnson, James P.
Yerby, Frank, 234n
Yoruba, 1, 187
Young, Al, 13; "Chicken Hawk's Dream," 13
Young, Lester (Prez), 5, 53, 54, 92, 222

Zoot suit riots, 97, 235n

Music Index

A Love Supreme, 157
"A Mighty Fortress Is Our God," 220
A Modern Jazz Symposium of Music and Poetry with Charles Mingus, 158
"A Night in Tunisia," 35, 98, 99
"A Tisket, A Tasket," 229n
"Abide with Me," 171, 220
Afro American Symphony, 242n
"Ain't Gonna Bump No More," 161
"Ain't Going to Let Nobody Turn Me Around," 221
"Ain't Misbehavin'," 50
"Ain't No Restin' Place," 124
"Ain't She Sweet," 221
"Alabama," 158
"All Night Blues," 244n
"Always," 168–69
"Am I Blue," 206, 213, 222
"Amazing Grace," 171, 172, 187, 221
"America the Beautiful," 222
"At Sundown," 183, 184, 221

"Baby Seals Blues," 47, 243n
"Back Water Blues," 145, 220
"Backlash Blues," 158
"Bebop," 35, 98, 99
"Bird Feathers," 210
"Bird's Nest," 210
Black Bottom, 164
"Black Bottom Stomp," 164
"Black Is Beautiful: Say It Loud I'm Black and I'm Proud," 159
"Black, Brown, Beige," 99
"Black, Brown, White," 100
"Blood Done Signed My Name, The," 190, 221
"Blue n Boogie," 98, 99
"Blue Skies," 219
"Blues," 95
"Bongo Bop," 210
"Boogie Woogie Blues," 142, 220
"Bottle, The," 161
"Bourgeois Blues," 49

"Bread of Heaven," 220
"Breakdown, The," 161
"Broke and Hungry," 49
"Buddy Bolden Blues," 147, 220
"Bumble Bee," 48
"Bye, Bye, Blackbird," 219

"C. C. Rider," 191, 193, 194, 222, 241n
"Carvin' the Bird," 210
"Changes," 160
Charlie Brown Christmas, 229n
"Charmin' Betsy," 219
"Cool Blues," 35, 210
"Counting the Blues," 34
"Crazy Blues," 47, 243n
"Creole Rhapsody," 50

"Dallas," 47
"Dancing in the Street," 158
"Dark Shadows," 210
"Darlin'," 220
"Devil's Son-in-Law," 100
"Dexterity," 210
"Didn't He Ramble," 191, 222
"Dizzy Atmosphere," 98, 99, 238n
"Do the Funky Chicken," 161
"Do Right Woman," 225
"Don't Be Weary Traveler," 17
"Don't Let Nobody Turn You Around," 187
"Down Hearted Blues," 34, 48, 112, 219
"Down Home Blues," 48
"Dream a Little Dream of Me," 183, 221
"Dream of Life," 98
"Dry Southern Blues," 144, 220

"Embraceable You," 210
"Epistrophy," 98
"Ethiopia Saluting Colors," 24

"Falling Rain Blues," 191, 222
"Farther Along," 192, 222
Firebird, The (L'Oiseau de feu), 227n
Free Jazz, 157

"Freedom," 160
"Freedom Highway," 160
"Freedom Now Suite," 157
"Freight Train Blues," 77
From South Carolina to South Africa, 159
From the New World, 24, 72, 84, 139, 219, 220, 227n
"Für Elise," 229n

"Get Right With God," 190, 221
"Go Down Moses," 220
"God Be with You Till We Meet Again," 222
"God Bless America," 222
"Going Away Blues," 113, 219, 243n
"Going Home," 233, 227
"Goodbye Newport Blues," 101
"Groovin High," 99
"Gut Bucket Blues," 209-10

"Hallelujah, It's Done," 159
"He's Got the Whole World in His Hands,"187, 221
"Head Cuttin' Blues," 244n
"Hell Hound on My Trail," 244n
"Hiding in Thee," 220, 243
"High Sheriff of Hell," 100
"Holy City, The" 220
"Home Is Where the Hatred Is," 159
"How Come You Do Me Like You Do?," 184, 221
"How Long Blues," 191, 222, 232n
"Hut-Sut Song, The (A Swedish Serenade)," 179, 222
"Hymn, The," 35, 210

"I Be's Troubled," 27
"I Got Rhythm," 210, 242n
"I Want You Back," 159
"I'll See You in My Dreams," 221
"I'm a Rollin'," 6, 27
"I'm Going Back to My Used to Be," 27
"I'm Going Up to Heaven Anyhow," 27
"(Yes!) I'm in the Barrel," 209

"I've Been Mistreated and I Don't Like It," 27
"I've Got a Mind to Ramble," 34, 77, 244n
"If I Could Hear My Mother Pray Again," 222
In the Bottoms, 164
"In the Garden," 193, 222
"In the Sweet By-and-By," 171, 191, 220, 222
Inner City Blues, 161
"Inner City Blues," 161
"It's Tight Like That," 48–49

"Ja-Da," 184, 221
"Jazz Me Blues," 241n
"Jelly, Jelly, Jelly," 219, 220
"Joe Louis Blues," 220
"Joe Turner," 47
"Johannesburg," 161
"John Brown's Body," 220

"Kansas City Stomp," 221
"Kindhearted Woman Blues," 49
"Koko," 99

"Lawdy, Lawdy Blues," 48
"Lay Down My Burden (Down by the Riverside), 191, 222
"Lead Me to a Rock That Is Higher Than I," 139, 220, 243n
"Leaning on the Everlasting Arms," 221
"Lift Every Voice and Sing (Black/Negro National Anthem)," 46, 231
"Little White Lies," 183, 221
"Lonesome Train," 222
"Lord Has Brought Me a Mighty Long Way, The," 211, 222
"Love and Liberty,"159

"Ma Rainey's Black Bottom," 164
"Mannish, Boy," 52, 100
"Many Thousands Gone," 141, 220
"Maple Leaf Rag," 47
"Max Is Making Wax," 210

"Maxwell Street Blues," 53
"Mayor Crump's Blues." *See* "Memphis Blues"
"Me and the Devil Blues," 49
"Media Luz," 220
"Memphis Blues," 47, 231n
"Mercy, Mercy Me (The Ecology)," 161
"Message to the Messengers," 161
"Mississippi God Damn," 158
"Moaning at Midnight," 100
"Mood Indigo," 18, 92
"Moose the Mooche," 210
"Move on Up a Little Higher," 99, 146
"Muddy Water," 219, 226n
My Black Name," 100
"My Blue Heaven," 221
"My Favorite Things," 229n
"My Girl," 158
"My Guy," 158
"My Lord What a Mourning!," 8
"My Old Cabin Home," 220

"Nearer My God to Thee," 171, 184, 220, 221
"Night and Day," 220
"No Hiding Place," 221
"Nobody Knows the Trouble I've Seen," 6, 27
"Now's the Time," 99

"Off the Wall," 100
"Oh Daddy," 48
"Oh Freedom," 187, 221
"Oh Happy Day," 160, 241n
"Old Man River," 220
"Old Ship of Zion," 141, 211, 220, 222, 237n, 244n
"Ornithology," 35

"Parchman Farm," 100
"Peach Tree Blues," 222
"Penitentiary Blues," 49
Petruska, 227
"Please, Please, Please," 101
"Precious Little Thing Called Love," 183, 221

"Precious Memories," 171, 220
"Prison Bound Blues," 49

"Quiet as It's Kept," 163

"Ramblin' on My Mind," 244n
"Rapper's Delight," 162
"Reckless Blues," 34
"Red House," 160
"Respect," 159
"Respect Yourself," 160
"Revolution Will Not Be Televised, The," 161
"Ride a Little Pony," 191
"Ring the Bells of Heaven," 106, 219
"Rock, Raleigh Rock," 220
"Rolling Stone," 100
"Round Midnight," 98, 198, 222, 244

"S'Wonderful," 210
"Safe in the Arms of Jesus," 106, 219
"Save a Little Dram for Me," 171, 172, 221
"Scottsboro Boys," 49
"Sent for You Yesterday," 199, 200, 222
"Shall We Gather at the River?," 171, 221
"Shop Around," 158
"Showers of Blessings," 219
"Sidewinder," 101, 235
"Skinny Legs and All," 161
"Sometimes I Feel Like a Motherless Child," 6, 219, 242
"Squeeze Me," 221
"St. Louis Blues," 78, 210, 220, 221, 243n, 244n
"Star Spangled Banner, The," 160
"Steal Away," 10
"Stealin', Stealin'," 145, 220
"Stop Breaking Down," 49
"Stormy Blues," 229
"Stormy Monday Blues," 100, 186
"Strange Fruit," 50
"Stupendous," 210
"Sugarfoot Stomp," 188, 221
"Summertime," 242n

"Sundown," 183, 221
"Sweet Georgia Brown," 99
"Swing It Sister," 124, 220
"Swing Low Sweet Chariot," 10, 72, 84, 139, 219, 220, 227n, 233n
"Swing to Bop," 99

"Take My Hand Precious Lord," 49
"T-Bone Blues," 100
"Thank God I am Free at Last," 27
"Three Little Words," 221
"These Blues," 234
"This Little Light of Mine," 105, 219
"To Be Young, Gifted, and Black," 160
"Topsy," 99
"Track of My Tears," 160, 200, 222, 241n
"Traveling Blues," 77, 112
"Trial of the Cross (This Do in Remembrance of Me), 243
"Twist, The," 157

"Waiting for My Ya-Ya," 229

"Walk in the Light," 105, 219
"We Insist," 157
"We'll Understand It Better By and By," 1, 219, 223n
"We've Got to Live Together," 160
"Weary Blues," 17
"Weary Woman Blues," 48
"Well You Needn't," 98
"What Did I Do to Be So Black and Blue?" 134, 209, 220
"What's Going On," 159, 161
"Where Did Our Love Go," 158
"Why? (Am I Treated So Bad)," 160
"Wichita Blues," 210
"Wild Women Don't Wear the Blues," 77
"Winter in America," 161
"Women's Love Rights," 159

"Yardbird Suite," 35
"Yonder Come the Blues," 34
"You Are My Sunshine," 191, 222
Young Mod's Forgotten Story, 159
"Young Woman's Blues," 34

Spiritual, Blues, and Jazz People in African American Fiction was designed and typeset on a Macintosh computer system using QuarkXPress software. The text is set in Jansen Text and the chapter openings are set in ITC Kabel. This book was designed by Cheryl Carrington, typeset by Kimberly Scarbrough, and manufactured by Thomson-Shore, Inc. The paper used in this book is designed for an effective life of at least three hundred years.

MAR 2003